# Freedom in the World

## Political Rights and Civil Liberties
### 1981

## A FREEDOM HOUSE BOOK

Greenwood Press issues the Freedom House series "Studies in Freedom" in addition to the Freedom House yearbook *Freedom in the World*.

*Strategies for the 1980s: Lessons of Cuba, Vietnam, and Afghanistan* by Philip van Slyck. Studies in Freedom, Number 1

# Freedom in the World

## Political Rights and Civil Liberties
## 1981

Raymond D. Gastil

With Essays by

Richard W. Cottam
Michael M. J. Fischer
Teresa Rakowska-Harmstone
Selig S. Harrison
Zalmay Khalilzad

Eden Naby
Richard S. Newell
William L. Richter
Leonard R. Sussman

GREENWOOD PRESS

Westport, Connecticut

Copyright © 1981 by Freedom House, Inc.
Freedom House, 20 West 40th Street, New York, New York 10018

ISBN: 0-313-23177-X

First published in 1981

Greenwood Press
A division of Congressional Information Service, Inc.
88 Post Road West
Westport, Connecticut 06881

Printed in the United States of America

10 9 8 7 6 5 4 3 2 1

# Contents

v

PART IV.   COUNTRY SUMMARIES

# Map

# Tables

# Preface

This is the fourth yearbook of Freedom House.* Each has been centered on the presentation of the Comparative Survey of Freedom. The first, in 1978, emphasized, in addition, basic issues in the definition of political and civil freedoms. The 1979 yearbook reported a conference on the possibilities of freedom in the USSR. The 1980 yearbook included discussion of the international struggle for press freedom and for rights to union organization; special reports on the Zimbabwe elections; and additional articles, particularly on Iran, the USSR, and the theory of freedom.

The views of the yearbooks are inherently controversial. Last year's drew praise and blame from a number of sources, particularly foreign governments (to which country descriptions were distributed). Such dispute is desirable; ultimately the purpose of the yearbooks is to make peoples and their governments care.

This volume includes in addition to the Survey and short country descriptions a new table of peoples without governments and an updating of the UNESCO effort to forge a "new world information order," discussed at length in the 1980 edition.

The bulk of this year's volume reports a conference on supporting freedom in Muslim Central Asia, an area defined as Iran, Afghanistan, Soviet Central Asia, and Pakistan. It is a timely topic, but it is much more. In most of the area the United States made great efforts in the last generation at economic, political, and military development, and yet all our efforts have turned bitter. In portions of the area the fifties and sixties showed great promise for a growth in freedom—and yet by 1980 the

_____

*The 1978, 1979, and 1980 yearbooks are available from Freedom House.

hopes for free evolution seemed bleaker than ever. The conference confronted the fact that in Central Asia, as in so many other regions, Americans must simultaneously oppose the threat of Soviet expansionism and respond to problems of human rights that would exist irrespective of this threat. Study of Central Asia also suggests that we cannot develop effective policy on a bilateral basis. Each country we wish to address is caught in a web of regional and worldwide concerns, and our policies must be developed in terms of this nexus.

In addressing the concerns of freedom the yearbooks illustrate again and again the complexity of the issues. Threats to freedom are many and not easily categorized. They come from the left and right, from authoritarians and totalitarians, from indigenous forces and international conspiracies. Historically America has become the bulwark of the rights of man. But millions of the world's politically aware do not automatically understand that we are more than a powerful status quo power. Our commitment to freedom is one that we must demonstrate to every people and every generation, year after year, through both our words and our actions. It is a commitment shored up by military strength, but not one that can be authenticated by military alliances and military balances alone.

We acknowledge, once again, the contribution made by the Advisory Panel for the Comparative Survey. The panel consists of:

Robert J. Alexander, Professor of Economics, Rutgers University; Richard W. Cottam, Professor of Political Science, University of Pittsburgh; Herbert J. Ellison, Professor of History, University of Washington; Seymour Martin Lipset, Senior Fellow, the Hoover Institution; Lucian Pye, Professor of Political Science, Massachusetts Institute of Technology; Leslie Rubin, lawyer, professor, and African specialist; Giovanni Sartori, the Albert Schweitzer Professor in the Humanities, Columbia University, and Robert Scalapino and Paul Seabury, Professors of Political Science, University of California, Berkeley.

We gratefully acknowledge the support of the foundations whose special grants help make possible the year-round research and analysis of the Survey, as well as the publication of this volume. We particulary express our appreciation to the J. Howard Pew Freedom Trust. We also appreciate support from the Earhart Foundation and the Charles Stewart Mott Foundation. These and all other Freedom House programs continue because of the generous support as well of individual members of the organization, trade unions, corporations, and public foundations which contribute to our general budget. Now, as for forty years past, no government funding is sought or accepted by Freedom House.

We also acknowledge the research and editorial assistance of Jeannette C. Gastil in producing this yearbook.

# PART I

# The Survey in 1980

# The Comparative Survey of Freedom: Nature and Purposes

Freedom has as many meanings as advocates. This does not lessen its importance. It is freedom that makes human life more than the cycle of biological survival that defines life for the rest of nature.

In the Comparative Surveys of Freedom, we take a part of the concept, the area of political and civil rights, and develop a human geography of the comparative extent of this area of freedom.[1] For those of us surrounded by such freedom, the effort may seem little more than academic. But for most of the world, freedom in the political sense is a live and burning issue, and its absence may mean the searing pain of torture or death.

*Political rights* are the rights of people to take a guaranteed role in deciding the political future of their own society. In large states this means voting directly on legislation or, more generally, electing representatives to legislate for the people, and executives to administer the laws decided by such representatives. Political rights are not meaningful without the right of political opponents to organize. *Civil liberties* are, in the first place, the guaranteed immunities of citizens from government interference with the expression of opinion, or with political, religious, business, or labor organization, and immunity from arbitrary imprisonment, torture, or execution. Civil liberties imply the rule of law and the right to defend oneself before a court both from government and other citizens. Civil liberties also include a wide variety of ancillary rights, such as those to freedom in choice of residence, in movement, education, and, more generally, to an arena of privacy to which the individual may retire. However, in this Survey emphasis is placed on those civil liberties that make possible an effective and meaningful expression of political rights.

After placing them on scales for political rights and civil liberties we divide all countries on this same basis into free, partly free, or not free

3

categories. At the beginning of 1981 there were sixty independent nations in the world classified *not free*, fifty-one classified as *free*, and another fifty-one as *partly free*. In population terms this means that roughly forty-three percent of the world was considered not free, thirty-six percent free, and the remaining twenty-one percent fell somewhere in between. To be sure, hundreds of millions classified as free were just marginally so, and almost as many classified as partly free could, with slight shifts of arbitrary category boundaries, have been considered not free. The object of the Surveys, now in their tenth year, is not quantitative. We hope only that the presentation allows a reader to better evaluate the changing systems of the world as daily events bring to his consciousness one or another nation or national leader. There is oppression everywhere, but in different forms and degrees; the first lesson of those who would oppose it is to differentiate among its forms.

## GENUINE SUFFRAGE

Westerners, accustomed to freedom, comfortably imagine that the countries of the world assembled together periodically in the United Nations are governed by leaders who reflect the desires and inclinations of their peoples. Yet, for the majority of nations in the UN that lack fully functioning democratic systems, there is little reason to believe this is the case. No matter how popular a leader or system may be initially, if there is no way to legally oppose or criticize the government, or to organize a competitive movement to oppose its leaders through fair elections, then the interests of rulers and followers inevitably diverge—and rapidly. As Wei Jingsheng, the now imprisoned Chinese dissident, wrote recently:

> What is a true democracy? It means the right of the people to choose their own representatives to work according to their will and in their interests. . . .
> . . . nothing can replace the competitive process of the democratic system. Unless there are at least two candidates in the election, the opinion of the voters and their feelings cannot be tested and measured. Then dictators step forward, sometimes vicious and sometimes showing generosity, but always blind to the true feelings of the people. It can be said that dictators exercise dictatorship, cruelty, and suppression because of this blindness rather than because of their sins. . . . It is certain that in this type of extreme dictatorial nation, the right to vote given to the people by [the] constitution is only an empty word. As to the numerous rights of being elected, or impeachment, supervision, accusation, movement, and choice of employment, all are empty words.
> We cannot be easily persuaded that anyone will automatically serve the interests of others, still less that anyone will serve the interests of others at any cost to himself. . . . Do not blame the leaders for letting power go to their heads and for not sincerely working for the people's welfare. . . . A government and leaders which serve the interests of the electorate can only come about through genuine universal suffrage.[2]

Examples of failure to realize these facts are endless in the Western media, whether of the right or left. The flood of visitors to Mao's China around 1970 assumed that the great leader spoke for the Chinese people. Now, once again, as in the aftermath of de-Stalinization in the USSR, we are learning that the West's academic establishment repeatedly misrepresented both the democracy of Mao's China and its material achievements.[3] Today, a new Chinese government tells us that Mao's policies represented in large part the twisted views of a small "gang" within the communist party. Unfortunately, today's leaders are almost as fearful of open democracy as the "gang" they displaced—and again the new "New China's" leaders are being represented as reflecting the "real views" of the Chinese.

About the same time as Mao "spoke for China," the media represented the Shah as the spokesman for all Iranians, the loved if stern leader of a people faithful for millenia to its kings.[4] In 1978 we learned this was not the case, and for a short moment, at least, an Ayatollah spoke for the majority of Iranians. But without an open society, the Ayatollah's popularity may have long since peaked—we will only learn when and to what degree after another convulsion.

Wei is correct to emphasize the importance of "genuine suffrage," for in too many countries the forms of political democracy have been appropriated without the substance. One-party states use elections to mobilize their people, to force applause and a show of unanimity, even when there is none. Their political exercises have generally offered only one list of approved candidates and of course no discussions of issues or even the possible virtues of abstention from the "elections."

Other forms of controlled elections allow more, but only slightly more, freedom. Iran's new Islamic Republic has held elections, but the direct and indirect pressures to exclude from these elections those who think differently from the Ayatollah have brought Iran close to the one-party model. There is choice, but choice can be very deceptive. In countries such as Iraq, Kenya, and Malawi, elections allowing a choice of individuals, but forbidding any discussion of top leaders or their policies, are held in the name of democracy. As in elections last fall in Tanzania and the Ivory Coast, voters in such elections may throw out fifty percent or more of incumbent legislators. This has some democratic significance. Yet the top leadership uses these exercises to deflect criticism from themselves and to eliminate junior leaders who might pose a future challenge. These elections offer no opportunity for mobilizing criticism in support of new policies or new rulers.

There are two practical reasons why freely elected governments are desirable. First, without them we cannot be sure of the meaning of any international agreement. We can be secure allies of peoples, but no lasting alliance can be based on relations with a particular person. International agreements among democratic peoples have meaning, but agreements among potentates have little validity. As a Middle Eastern writer recently pointed out: "How much importance can one attach to the declarations of Arab summit meetings in which none of the summiteers are directly elected by their people, accountable to a process of internal checks and balances, or institutionally supported by a manifest consensus of the people they lead?"[5]

Secondly, in the long run, democracy is more efficient. Even if we suppose, which we should not, that poor peoples are interested primarily in the supply of basic necessities, they may for this reason prefer democracy. While dictators may be able to mobilize a high percentage of a country's abilities for particular efforts (for example, military production or heavy industry), they are unable to correct the steady accumulation of mistakes that accrue from the blocking of critical communication channels and the growing disaffection of large parts of the population that characterize tyranny. As long as there are free countries and the possibility of escape, dictatorships also suffer a steady hemorrhage of their brightest and best educated.

## THE ILLEGITIMACY OF ELITE DOMINANCE

The most important meaning of political freedom has nothing to do with efficiency. It is simply wrong for small elites to take on the directing of a people irrespective of its desires. Tanzania is a nondemocratic, noncommunist country often praised as being "democratic in intent" by the Western media. However, a recent review based on Dean McHenry's *Tanzania's Ujamaa Villages* describes its most important development program as follows:

> Villagization involved the resettlement of 75 percent of rural Tanzania, most of it in two years. For such a massive, and unpopular and inherently coercive operation, it was well organized and involved relatively little violence against persons. It was even successful in the limited sense that people have stayed in the villages now that they are in them, and the ease of providing health, education, and water services has thereby been greatly improved.
>
> The costs of villagization, however, have been crushing. First, the expense of physically moving people often was high. Second, inevitably there was a temporary disruption of food production. When Tanzania had the ill fortune of a drought coinciding with the villagization operations, its foreign exchange reserves were wiped out in the purchase of food. (At least, the government did not permit famine.) Third, the political costs of such an unpopular policy had negative repercussions throughout the economy. Tanzanian industry had been disrupted in the early '70s by demands for workers' participation in management. I believe that these demands could have been turned to positive ends if a serious effort at reeducating managers in their roles had been undertaken. But in the con-

text of villagization, the government was unable either to expend the effort or to risk losing the support of the elite. It did stop worker takeover bids, but to avoid alienating workers in this time of stress it permitted rampant indiscipline in the factories. The result was a halving of worker productivity in this period, with negative consequences for the economy which must be debited to villagization. (Now that the operations are over, worker discipline and productivity are being restored.) The end product has been a seriously weakened Tanzanian economy, which is not more dependent on Western aid than it ever has been before.

What did villagization gain? It made the provision of village amenities easier; for socialist production it may have provided some long-term gains, but created none in the present. Villagization and the pro-collectivist atmosphere that has surrounded it may well assure that when large-scale, more capital-intensive agriculture is undertaken in Tanzania it will be done cooperatively. Thus the policy may have been a preventative to emerging rural class relations. For the present, however, the number of villages engaged in collective agriculture has actually declined and the wealthier peasants have tended to dominate village leadership. The latter follows from Nyerere's judgment . . . that class antagonisms are insufficiently developed in rural Tanzania for class struggle to be successful. The fall in collective farming has been due to the simple fact that it hasn't paid. McHenry's figures indicate that the returns on collective labor are almost always less than the prevailing rates for agricultural day labor. . . . Given Tanzania's current production technology of human-powered, rainfall agriculture, the returns to scale in large-scale production are much too little to compensate for the costs of organization. Thus when permitted a choice the Tanzanian peasant will naturally opt for work on his own family farm. . . . Ultimately, Tanzania's agricultural technology will move to larger-scale operations, significant returns to scale will emerge, and cooperative production may appear profitable and attractive to the average peasant. But for the moment, family farms are more productive and attractive. . . . One can only conclude that villagization has produced far too few near-term gains for the huge costs incurred.

Why did Nyerere make such a bad policy gamble? It wasn't purely ignorance, for early attempts at collective agricultural production had generally failed in Tanzania. A debate rages on villagization between those who see its failure as a consequence of Nyerere's being too socialist and those who mark it up to his not being socialist enough. . . . I personally suspect that Nyerere thought that the failures were due to a lack of effort which full-scale villagization would overcome, that he was a sufficient socialist to try it, and that he was too good a politician to go the radical extra mile which the Marxists recommend. Whatever the reasons, however, the gamble turned out badly and it will be many years before Tanzania recovers from it.[6]

The reviewer documents the disaster that may result from ideological elites imposing their policies on a poor people, but he never raises the point that Nyerere and his clique simply had no right to carry out such an experiment. Warren Christopher points out again and again, in his excellent review of the Carter human rights policy, that a people undergoing social change can only preserve their dignity, an acknowledg-

ment of their full humanity, in a democratic state.[7] The right to this
dignity undergirds all human rights.

The Survey's interest in political freedom should not imply a
disinterest in other forms of freedom: there is frequent overlap. In particular, if there is political freedom there must be freedom to decide on
economic forms. Certainly a country can have a market economy
without having a free political system, but to say, as the Council on
Hemispheric Affairs did recently, that Argentina's military leaders have
"imposed economic freedom on their nation"[8] is doubly contradictory.
For if a people cannot decide on its economic forms, it has little
economic freedom.

The freedoms of most concern to the Survey are often disparaged as
"bourgeois freedoms." Historically the rise of the bourgeoisie under
capitalism and the rise of constitutional democracy were closely related.
Yet this historical fact is far from confirming the relationship under current conditions. Too often the capitalist entrepreneurial class, once it had
obtained its freedoms, strove to deny these to others, and this denial is
repugnant to the system they had helped bring into being. For this reason
Joseph Schumpeter in his classic discussion of the relation of capitalism
and democracy imagined that ultimately constitutional democracy would
destroy capitalism.[9] The workers would eventually have the votes and
they would demand a socialist economy maximizing their shares.

Clearly Schumpeter's vision was at least half-right—the last century
has shown a steady growth in the size of the electorate and the socialization of the economy. Whether societies accustomed to middle-class life-
styles and disenchanted with socialist experiments will now reverse their
direction is unclear. But what is clear is that democracy increasingly gives
peoples the chance to make a decision for socialist, capitalist, or any
other set of economic arrangements. Where this is not the case it
indicates that the democratic institutions have not yet become effective
enough to prevent those who have special access to social institutions
from imposing particular economic arrangements, whether capitalist or
socialist.

## PARTLY FREE, NOT FREE; AUTHORITARIANISM AND TOTALITARIANISM

In the Survey we have found that the most contentious area of judgment is at the boundary of the "partly free" and "free" designations
(*see* pp. 22, 23 below), and of the (5) and (6) scores on political and civil
liberties that are usually involved.

It is frequently objected in this regard that South Africa, with its
oppression of the black majority, should not be regarded as "partly

free'' as long as many apparently more benign countries such as Yugoslavia, Jordan, or Niger are labeled "not free." Certainly, if discrimination by race were the critical issue of the Survey, South Africa would rank above few if any states. However, the working distinction between "partly free" and "not free" is the distinction between societies in which there is a vocal opposition admitted into the public arena and those in which there is not. In these terms South Africa is distinct from "not free" states. Few would argue that any "not free" countries in Table 1 (below) have the kind of effective opposition represented by white opposition political parties, white critical newspapers, and white private organizations in South Africa. The fact that these are white (17 percent of the population) cannot make them irrelevant. We would also argue that the kind of organized black political and economic action represented by labor unions (presently), intermittent black publications, and, most particularly, Chief Buthelezi's Inkatha organization (with hundreds of thousands of members publicly dedicated to changing the system) is not found to this degree in any "not free" society in the table. Therefore, no matter how demeaning the position of blacks in South Africa, the overall picture is significantly better than in "not free" societies. This is not to argue that many blacks might not prefer a black tyranny. They might. The Survey is not based on the claim that political and civil liberties are at all times the most important values in defining the desirability or even level of justice of a society.

Many aspects of South Africa's treatment of its black citizens are reminiscent of the controls in totalitarian rather than authoritarian society. More generally, many have criticized the Survey for not sufficiently taking into account the nonpolitical controls over the details of life that totalitarian society entails. However, political tyranny and totalitarianism may diverge. Totalitarian controls may in large part be imposed by a democratic society, while a thoroughly oppressive society politically may be largely uninterested in the forms of individual social and economic life—as long as there is no challenge to the system. For this reason Khomeini's Iran is slightly freer in the Survey's terms than the Shah's, although it is more totalitarian.[10] Nevertheless—for those who believe in freedom—totalitarianism, its growth and decline, remains an important issue. A survey of freedom on the libertarian-totalitarian dimension would make a valuable companion to the present effort.

The foregoing examples also suggest, however, that the distinction between authoritarian and totalitarian, espoused in some conservative circles, is not as clear in practice as is often supposed. It is true that the claims of communists, fascists, or for example, Islamic fundamentalists are all-encompassing, with the state to be used as the tool for a general restructuring of life. In theory the authoritarian government is by contrast seen as wanting only to guarantee a stable political system. Both models are oversimplified. On the other hand, after their initial flush of experimentation many totalitarian regimes relapse into simply hanging on to power, preserving enough of the theory to make acceptable their persistent refusal to allow free discussion or free elections. Certainly this is the case in Yugoslavia and Hungary. Neither in the USSR nor China are the totalitarian claims of the legitimating ideology widely respected. Positive conformity is more and more replaced by simply "keeping out of trouble." It is not privatism that leads to arrest in such countries, but suspicion that an individual might threaten to deny the legitimacy of the Party and its current leaders.

On the other side many anticommunist authoritarianisms claim the right to transform their societies. Such systems may attempt to drive out whole segments of the population. Socially objectionable literature and art, and especially pornography, are banned (much as in communist states). School curriculums are rewritten to emphasize a particular set of values. Clothing regulations may be enforced from the Colonels' Greece to Mobutu's Zaire. Radical religions such as Jehovah's Witnesses are frequently banned. Labor organization is restricted. Particular racial groups may be favored, whether on the South African or Malaysian scale. As authoritarian states age, some of these enthusiasms may also wane, but others develop. The corruption of the favored ruling class— military, bureaucratic, party, or traditional—may lead to massive government intervention in the economy for particular favorites as in pre-revolutionary Iran or Nicaragua. There are expropriations of peasant properties; opportunity is denied to those out of favor.

Freedom is the enemy of oppression by whatever name. Where the greater oppression is found in communist states this should be revealed. But when it is not, the current ideological struggle should not be allowed to obscure this fact.

## FREEDOM IN THE 1980S

The struggle to preserve and enhance the area of freedom in the world requires attention on several levels. On the most general strategic level we need to identify the most powerful organized, international threat to freedom. Today this is the communist movement, and particularly that part of it backed by the Soviet Union. Its absorption of countries is hard to reverse, and its commitment to allowing democratic processes and laws to control ideology is minimal. On the second level are found the ideological and pragmatic denials in particular countries of the importance of human freedoms. It is on this level that the Soviet Union and Argentina find common ground in opposing "international meddling." This is the level of primary attention of international human rights organizations such as Amnesty International; it is also the focus of the Comparative Survey. The concentration is immediate rather than systemic. On a third level freedom is challenged in every country by numerous examples of minor oppression, by unwillingness to live up to the law because of financial inducement, criminal organization, prejudice, or simple inefficiency.

With the present shift of emphasis in the U.S. government to the most general, strategic level of the struggle for freedom, it is more than ever necessary to emphasize the importance of all three levels, and their interconnectedness. For free societies to survive, their peoples must believe in the reality of their freedoms. The struggle to realize principles in practices must be unrelenting in every country. For the worldwide struggle for freedom to succeed, people in both unfree and free states must believe that what used to be called the "free world," defined as the world outside the communist orbit, offers a better future than the communist world and its copyists.

The Carter administration was faulted for concentrating on the offenses of noncommunist "friends" while ignoring the human rights violations of communist states. Regardless of the correctness of the charge—and it was greatly overstated—there is an often neglected rationale for emphasis on the oppressions of noncommunist states. The world's opinion leaders do not generally blame the United States if freedoms are denied in communist or Soviet-bloc countries. But whether we like it or not, every freedom that is denied in South Africa, Argentina, Haiti, or similar states is laid at our door. Of course, we do not and cannot influence internal policy in these countries to the degree assumed or alleged. Yet this common expectation requires either that the United States actively distance itself from such regimes, or strive publicly to reduce their internal oppressions, or both. Otherwise their every crime haunts us and haunts the long-range future of free institutions everywhere.

The Survey, then, is a tool to be used for a variety of purposes. It quietly demonstrates the differences between contending systems, but also suggests that we should not imagine the distinctions are as clear and unambiguous as some may like. The Survey helps to orient its readers in the world; it may help to preserve balance in the struggle for that world; and it may in the end play its part in reducing the oppressions it evaluates.

## NOTES

1. The Surveys have been published since January 1973 (covering the status of freedom in 1972). They have appeared annually since then in *Freedom at Issue*, and since 1978 in this annual series *Freedom in the World* as well.

2. Wei Jingsheng, selections from James Seymour, ed., *The Fifth Modernization:*

*China's Human Rights Movement 1978-1979* (Stanfordville, New York: Human Rights Publishing Group, 1980), pp. 52, 229-120, 199-200.

3. *See* Harry Harding, "Reappraising the Cultural Revolution,"*The Wilson Quarterly* (Autumn 1980), pp. 132-141. *See also* the comments on recent scholarship on China by Werner Cohn, "Perspectives on Communist Totalitarianism," *Problems of Communism* XXIX, no. 5 (September-October 1980): 68-73.

4. *See* Barry Rubin, *Paved with Good Intentions: The American Experience and Iran* (New York: Oxford University Press, 1980), pp. 132, 337 ff.

5. Rami Khouri, "Withdraw the Blank Check of 'Democracy'," *The Middle East* (September 1980), p. 17.

6. David K. Leonard, "A Crashing Leap for Tanzanian Socialism," *Africa Today* 27, no. 2 (1980): 52-53.

7. Warren Christopher, "Human Rights and the National Interest," U.S. Department of State Bulletin, August 4, 1980.

8. COHA news release, October 3, 1980.

9. Joseph Schumpeter, *Capitalism, Socialism and Democracy* (New York: Harper and Brothers, 1950).

10. An exiled Iranian's response to the present situation well exemplifies the distinction: "Under the old regime there were severe limits on political freedom, but other areas of life were relatively free, and the country was progressing. Now there are fewer limits politically, but there are more severe limits on thought, on belief, even on what one wears, eats and drinks. Earlier, censorship was used to guard against certain political doctrines; now censorship is used to impose particular religious and moral values." ("The Dilemma of Iranian Intellectuals," *Christian Science Monitor*, August 28, 1980).

# Survey Ratings and Tables for 1980

Nineteen-eighty was a mixed year for freedom. There were both gains and losses, with the losses more numerous. Major advances for freedom occurred in Peru and Poland, with lesser advances recorded for several states. While democracies responded increasingly to the demands of their minority peoples, the self-determination rights of most subnational peoples continued to be denied.

## THE TABULATED RATINGS

The accompanying Table 1 (Independent Nations) and Table 2 (Related Territories) rate each state or territory on seven-point scales for political and civil freedoms, and then provide an overall judgment of each as "free," "partly free," or "not free." In each scale, a rating of (1) is freest and (7) least free. Instead of using absolute standards, standards are comparative—that is, most observers would be likely to judge states rated (1) as freer than those rated (2), and so on. No state, of course, is absolutely free or unfree, but the degree of freedom does make a great deal of difference to the quality of life.[1]

In *political rights*, states rated (1) have a fully competitive electoral process and those elected clearly rule. Most West European democracies belong here. Relatively free states may receive a (2) because, although the electoral process works and the elected rule, there are factors which cause us to lower our rating of the effective equality of the process. These factors may include extreme economic inequality, illiteracy, or intimidating violence. They also include the weakening of effective competition that is implied by the absence of periodic shifts in rule from one group or party to another.

Below this level, political ratings of (3) through (5) represent suc-

13

# Table 1
## Independent Nations:
## Comparative Measures of Freedom

| | Political Rights[1] | Civil Liberties[1] | Status of Freedom[2] | Outlook[3] |
|---|---|---|---|---|
| Afghanistan | 7 | 7 | NF | 0 |
| Albania | 7 | 7 | NF | 0 |
| Algeria | 6 | 6 | NF | 0 |
| Angola | 7 | 7 | NF | 0 |
| Argentina | 6 | 5 | NF | 0 |
| Australia | 1 | 1 | F | 0 |
| Austria | 1 | 1 | F | 0 |
| Bahamas | 1 | 2 | F | 0 |
| Bahrain | 5 | 5• | PF | 0 |
| Bangladesh | 3 | 4• | PF | 0 |
| Barbados | 1 | 1 | F | 0 |
| Belgium | 1 | 1 | F | 0 |
| Benin | 7 | 6 | NF | 0 |
| Bhutan | 5 | 5 | PF | 0 |
| Bolivia | 7 – | 5 – | NF – | 0 |
| Botswana | 2 | 3• | F | 0 |
| Brazil | 4 | 3 | PF | + |
| Bulgaria | 7 | 7 | NF | 0 |
| Burma | 7 | 6 | NF | 0 |
| Burundi | 7 | 6• | NF | 0 |
| Cameroon | 6 | 6 | NF | 0 |
| Canada | 1 | 1 | F | 0 |
| Cape Verde Islands | 6 | 6 | NF | 0 |
| Central African Rep. | 7 | 5 + | NF | + |
| Chad | 7 – | 6 | NF | 0 |
| Chile | 6 | 5 | PF | 0 |
| China (Mainland) | 6 | 6 | NF | 0 |
| China (Taiwan) | 5 | 5 | PF | 0 |
| Colombia | 2 | 3 | F | 0 |
| Comoro Islands | 4 | 5 | PF | 0 |
| Congo | 7 | 6• + | NF | 0 |
| Costa Rica | 1 | 1 | F | 0 |
| Cuba | 6 | 6 | NF | 0 |
| Cyprus | 3 | 3 | PF | 0 |
| Czechoslovakia | 7 | 6 | NF | 0 |

**Notes to the Table**

1. The scales use the numbers 1-7, with 1 comparatively offering the highest level of political or civil rights and 7 the lowest. A plus or minus following a rating indicates an improvement or decline in 1980. A rating marked with a period (•) has been changed since the last Survey due to reevaluation by the author. This does not imply any change in the country.

2. A free state is designated by F, a partly free state by PF, and a not-free state by NF.

3. A positive outlook for freedom is indicated by a plus sign, a negative outlook, by a minus, and relative stability of ratings by a zero. The outlook for freedom is based on the problems the country is facing, the way the government and people are reacting to these problems, and the longer run political traditions of the society. A judgment of outlook may also reflect an imminent change, such as the expected adoption of a meaningful new constitution.

4. Official name of Cambodia.

5. Formerly the Gilbert Islands, territory of the United Kingdom.

6. Formerly territories of the United Kingdom.

7. Formerly the New Hebrides Condominium.

| | Political Rights[1] | Civil Liberties[1] | Status of Freedom[2] | Outlook[3] |
|---|---|---|---|---|
| Denmark | 1 | 1 | F | 0 |
| Djibouti | 3 | 4 | PF | 0 |
| Dominica | 2 | 2 | F | 0 |
| Dominican Republic | 2 | 3 | F | 0 |
| Ecuador | 2 | 2 | F | 0 |
| Egypt | 5 | 5 | PF | 0 |
| El Salvador | 5 | 5 − | PF | + / − |
| Equatorial Guinea | 7 | 6 | NF | 0 |
| Ethiopia | 7 | 7 | NF | 0 |
| Fiji | 2 | 2 | F | 0 |
| Finland | 2 | 2 | F | 0 |
| France | 1 | 2 | F | 0 |
| Gabon | 6 | 6 | NF | 0 |
| Gambia | 2 | 3 − | F | 0 |
| Germany (E) | 7 | 7 − | NF | 0 |
| Germany (W) | 1 | 2 | F | 0 |
| Ghana | 2 + | 3 + | F + | 0 |
| Greece | 1• | 2 | F | 0 |
| Grenada | 6 − | 5 | NF − | 0 |
| Guatemala | 6 − | 6 − | NF − | 0 |
| Guinea | 7 | 7 | NF | 0 |
| Guinea-Bissau | 6 | 6 | NF | 0 |
| Guyana | 5 − | 4 | PF | 0 |
| Haiti | 7 − | 6 − | NF | 0 |
| Honduras | 4 + | 3 | PF | + |
| Hungary | 6 | 5 | NF | 0 |
| Iceland | 1 | 1 | F | 0 |
| India | 2 | 3• − | F | 0 |
| Indonesia | 5 | 5 | PF | 0 |
| Iran | 5 | 5 | PF | − |
| Iraq | 6 + | 7 | NF | 0 |
| Ireland | 1 | 1 | F | 0 |
| Israel | 2 | 2 | F | 0 |
| Italy | 1• + | 2 | F | 0 |
| Ivory Coast | 5 + | 5 | PF | 0 |
| Jamaica | 2 | 3 | F | 0 |
| Japan | 1• + | 1 | F | 0 |
| Jordan | 6 | 6 | NF | 0 |
| Kampuchea[4] | 7 | 7 | NF | 0 |
| Kenya | 5 | 4 | PF | 0 |
| Kiribati[5] | 2 | 2 | F | 0 |
| Korea (N) | 7 | 7 | NF | 0 |
| Korea (S) | 5 − | 6 − | PF | + |
| Kuwait | 6 | 4 | PF | + |
| Laos | 7 | 7 | NF | 0 |
| Lebanon | 4 | 4 | PF | 0 |
| Lesotho | 5 | 5 | PF | 0 |
| Liberia | 6 | 6 − | NF − | + |
| Libya | 6 | 7 − | NF | 0 |
| Luxembourg | 1 | 1 | F | 0 |
| Madagascar | 6 | 6 | NF | 0 |

15

**Table 1** *(continued)*

| | Political Rights[1] | Civil Liberties[1] | Status of Freedom[2] | Outlook[3] |
|---|---|---|---|---|
| Malawi | 6 | 7 | NF | 0 |
| Malaysia | 3 | 4 | PF | 0 |
| Maldives | 5 | 5 | PF | 0 |
| Mali | 7 | 6 | NF | 0 |
| Malta | 2 | 3 | F | 0 |
| Mauritania | 7 | 6 | NF | 0 |
| Mauritius | 3• | 3• | PF | 0 |
| Mexico | 3 | 4 | PF | 0 |
| Mongolia | 7 | 7 | NF | 0 |
| Morocco | 4 | 4 | PF | 0 |
| Mozambique | 7 | 7 | NF | 0 |
| Nauru | 2 | 2 | F | 0 |
| Nepal | 3 + | 4 | PF | + |
| Netherlands | 1 | 1 | F | 0 |
| New Zealand | 1 | 1 | F | 0 |
| Nicaragua | 5 | 5 | PF | – |
| Niger | 7 | 6 | NF | 0 |
| Nigeria | 2 | 3 | F | 0 |
| Norway | 1 | 1 | F | 0 |
| Oman | 6 | 6 | NF | 0 |
| Pakistan | 7• – | 5 | NF | 0 |
| Panama | 4 + | 4 + | PF | + |
| Papua New Guinea | 2 | 2 | F | 0 |
| Paraguay | 5 | 5 | PF | 0 |
| Peru | 2 + | 3 + | F + | + |
| Philippines | 5 | 5 | PF | + |
| Poland | 6 | 4 + | PF | + / – |
| Portugal | 2 | 2 | F | 0 |
| Qatar | 5 | 5 | PF | 0 |
| Romania | 7 | 6 | NF | 0 |
| Rwanda | 6 | 6 | NF | 0 |
| St. Lucia[6] | 2 | 2• + | F | 0 |
| St. Vincent[6] | 2 | 2 | F | 0 |
| Sao Tome and Principe | 6 | 6 | NF | 0 |
| Saudi Arabia | 6 | 6 | NF | 0 |
| Senegal | 4 | 4 | PF | + |
| Seychelles | 6 | 6 | NF | 0 |
| Sierra Leone | 5 | 5 | PF | 0 |
| Singapore | 5 | 5 | PF | 0 |
| Solomon Islands | 2 | 2 | F | 0 |
| Somalia | 7 | 7 | NF | 0 |
| South Africa | 5 | 6 | PF | + |
| Spain | 2 | 3• | F | 0 |
| Sri Lanka | 2 | 3 | F | 0 |
| Sudan | 5 | 5 | PF | + |
| Suriname | 7 – | 5• | NF – | 0 |
| Swaziland | 5 | 5 | PF | 0 |
| Sweden | 1 | 1 | F | 0 |
| Switzerland | 1 | 1 | F | 0 |
| Syria | 5 | 7 – | NF – | 0 |
| Tanzania | 6 | 6 | NF | 0 |

**Table 1** *(continued)*

| | Political Rights[1] | Civil Liberties[1] | Status of Freedom[2] | Outlook[3] |
|---|---|---|---|---|
| Thailand | 3+ | 4 | PF | 0 |
| Togo | 7 | 6•+ | NF | 0 |
| Tonga | 5 | 3 | PF | 0 |
| Transkei | 5 | 6 | PF | 0 |
| Trinidad & Tobago | 2 | 2 | F | 0 |
| Tunisia | 6 | 5 | PF | 0 |
| Turkey | 5− | 5− | PF− | 0 |
| Tuvalu | 2 | 2 | F | 0 |
| Uganda | 4+ | 4+ | PF+ | 0 |
| USSR | 6 | 7− | NF | 0 |
| United Arab Emirates | 5 | 5 | PF | 0 |
| United Kingdom | 1 | 1 | F | 0 |
| United States | 1 | 1 | F | 0 |
| Upper Volta | 6− | 5− | PF− | 0 |
| Uruguay | 5+ | 5+ | PF+ | 0 |
| Vanuatu[7] | 2+ | 3 | F+ | + |
| Venezuela | 1 | 2 | F | 0 |
| Vietnam | 7 | 7 | NF | 0 |
| Western Samoa | 4 | 3− | PF | 0 |
| Yemen (N) | 6 | 5 | NF | 0 |
| Yemen (S) | 6 | 7 | NF | 0 |
| Yugoslavia | 6 | 5 | NF | 0 |
| Zaire | 6 | 6 | NF | 0 |
| Zambia | 5 | 6− | PF | 0 |
| Zimbabwe | 3+ | 4+ | PF | − |

cessively less effective implementation of democratic processes. Mexico, for example, has periodic elections and limited opposition, but for many years its governments have been selected outside the public view by the leaders of factions within the one dominant Mexican party. Governments of states rated (5) sometimes have no effective voting processes at all, but strive for consensus among a variety of groups in society in a way weakly analogous to those of the democracies. States at (6) do not allow competitive electoral processes that would give the people a chance to voice their desire for a new ruling party or for a change in policy. The rulers of states at this level assume that one person or a small group has the right to decide what is best for the nation, and that no one should be allowed to challenge that right. Such rulers do respond, however, to popular desire in some areas, or respect (and therefore are constrained by) belief systems (for example, Islam) that are the property of the society as a whole. At (7) the political despots at the top appear by their actions to feel little constraint from either public opinion or popular tradition.

Turning to the scale for *civil liberties*, in countries rated (1) publications are not closed because of the expression of rational political opinion, especially when the intent of the expression is to affect the legitimate political process. No major media are simply conduits for government

# Table 2
# Related Territories:
# Comparative Measures of Freedom

| | Political Rights[1] | Civil Liberties[1] | Status of Freedom[2] | Outlook[3] |
|---|---|---|---|---|
| **Australia** | | | | |
| Christmas Island (in Indian Ocean) | 4 | 2 | PF | 0 |
| Cocos Islands | 4 | 2 | PF | 0 |
| Norfolk Island | 4 | 2 | PF | 0 |
| **Chile** | | | | |
| Easter Island | 7 | 5 | NF | 0 |
| **Denmark** | | | | |
| Faroe Islands | 2 | 1 | F | 0 |
| Greenland | 2 | 1 | F | 0 |
| **France** | | | | |
| French Guiana | 3 | 2 | PF | 0 |
| French Polynesia | 3 | 2 | PF | 0 |
| Guadeloupe | 3 | 2 | PF | 0 |
| Martinique | 3 | 2 | PF | 0 |
| Mayotte | 2 | 2 | F | 0 |
| Monaco[4] | 4 | 2 | PF | 0 |
| New Caledonia | 3 | 2 | F | 0 |
| Reunion | 3 | 2 | PF | 0 |
| Saint Pierre & Miquelon | 3 | 2 | PF | 0 |
| Wallis and Futuna | 4 | 3 | PF | 0 |
| **Israel** | | | | |
| Occupied Territories | 5 | 4 | PF | 0 |
| **Italy** | | | | |
| San Marino[4] | 2 | 2 | F | 0 |
| **Netherlands** | | | | |
| Neth. Antilles | 2 | 2•− | F | 0 |
| **New Zealand** | | | | |
| Cook Islands | 2+ | 2 | F | 0 |
| Niue | 2 | 2 | F | 0 |
| Tokelau Islands | 4 | 2 | PF | 0 |
| **Portugal** | | | | |
| Azores | 2 | 2 | F | 0 |
| Macao | 3 | 3 | PF | 0 |
| Madeira | 2 | 2 | F | 0 |
| **South Africa** | | | | |
| Bophuthatswana[5] | 6 | 6 | NF | 0 |
| South West Africa (*Namibia*) | 5 | 5 | PF | 0 |
| Venda[5] | 6 | 6 | NF | 0 |
| **Spain** | | | | |
| Canary Islands | 2 | 3• | F | 0 |
| Places of Sovereignty in North Africa | 2 | 3• | F | 0 |

**Notes to the Table**

1. 2., 3. See Notes, Table 1.

4. These states are not listed as independent because all have explicit legal forms of dependence on a particular country (or, in the case of Andorra, countries) in the spheres of foreign affairs, defense, etc.

5. The geography and history of these newly "independent" homelands cause us to consider them dependencies.

6. Formed out of the Trust Territory of the Pacific Islands, these territories are at various stages of evolution toward internal autonomy. "Micronesia" in the table this year refers to the much smaller Federated States of Micronesia.

| | Political Rights[1] | Civil Liberties[1] | Status of Freedom[2] | Outlook[3] |
|---|---|---|---|---|
| **Switzerland** | | | | |
| Liechtenstein[4] | 4 | 1 | PF | 0 |
| **United Kingdom** | | | | |
| Anguilla | 2 | 2 | F | 0 |
| Antigua and Barbuda | 2 | 2 | F | 0 |
| Belize | 1 | 2 | F | 0 |
| Bermuda | 2 | 1 | F | 0 |
| Brit. Virgin Islands | 3 | 2 | PF | 0 |
| Brunei[4] | 6 | 5 | NF | 0 |
| Cayman Islands | 2 | 2 | F | 0 |
| Channel Islands | 2 | 1 | F | 0 |
| Falkland Islands | 2 | 2 | F | 0 |
| Gibraltar | 1 | 2 | F | 0 |
| Hong Kong | 4 | 2 | PF | 0 |
| Isle of Man | 2 | 1 | F | 0 |
| Montserrat | 2 | 2 | F | 0 |
| St. Helena | 2 | 2 | F | 0 |
| St. Kitts and Nevis | 2 | 3 | F | 0 |
| Turks and Caicos | 2• + | 2 | F• + | 0 |
| **United States** | | | | |
| American Samoa | 2 | 2 | F | 0 |
| Belau[6] | 3 + | 2 | PF | + |
| Guam | 3 | 2 | PF | 0 |
| Marshall Islands[6] | 3• | 2 | PF | + |
| Micronesia[6] | 3 | 2 | PF | + |
| Northern Marianas[6] | 2 | 2 | F | 0 |
| Puerto Rico | 2 | 1 | F | 0 |
| Virgin Islands | 2 | 3 | F | 0 |
| **France-Spain Condominium** | | | | |
| Andorra[4] | 4 | 3 | PF | 0 |

propaganda. The courts protect the individual; persons are not imprisoned for their opinions; private rights and desires in education, occupation, religion, residence, and so on, are generally respected; law-abiding persons do not fear for their lives because of their rational political activities. States at this level include most traditional democracies. There are, of course, flaws in the liberties of all of these states, and these flaws are significant when measured against the standards these states set themselves.

Movement down from (2) to (7) represents a steady loss of the civil freedoms we have detailed. Compared to (1), the police and courts of states at (2) have more authoritarian traditions. In some cases they may simply have a less institutionalized or secure set of liberties, such as in Portugal or Greece. Those rated (3) or below may have political prisoners and generally varying forms of censorship. Too often their security services practice torture. States rated (6) almost always have political prisoners; usually the legitimate media are completely under government supervision; there is no right of assembly; and, often, travel,

# Table 3 Ranking of Nations by Political Rights

| Most Free | | | | | | Least Free |
|---|---|---|---|---|---|---|
| 1 | 2 | 3 | 4 | 5 | 6 | 7 |
| Australia | Botswana | Bangladesh | Brazil | Bahrain | Algeria | Afghanistan |
| Austria | Colombia | Cyprus | Comoro Is. | Bhutan | Argentina | Albania |
| Bahamas | Dominica | Djibouti | Honduras | China (Taiwan) | Cameroon | Angola |
| Barbados | Dominican Republic | Malaysia | Lebanon | Egypt | Cape Verde Is. | Benin |
| Belgium | Ecuador | Mauritius | Morocco | El Salvador | Chile | Bolivia |
| Canada | Fiji | Mexico | Panama | Guyana | China (Mainland) | Bulgaria |
| Costa Rica | Finland | Nepal | Senegal | Indonesia | Cuba | Burma |
| Denmark | Gambia | Thailand | Uganda | Iran | Gabon | Burundi |
| France | Ghana | Zimbabwe | Western Samoa | Ivory Coast | Grenada | Central African Republic |
| Germany (W) | India | | | Kenya | Guatemala | Chad |
| Greece | Israel | | | Korea (S) | Guinea-Bissau | Congo |
| Iceland | Jamaica | | | Lesotho | Hungary | Czechoslovakia |
| Ireland | Kiribati | | | Maldives | Iraq | Equatorial Guinea |
| Italy | Malta | | | Nicaragua | Jordan | Ethiopia |
| Japan | Nauru | | | Paraguay | Kuwait | Germany (E) |
| Luxembourg | Nigeria | | | Philippines | Liberia | Guinea |
| Netherlands | Papua New Guinea | | | Qatar | Libya | Haiti |
| New Zealand | Peru | | | Sierra Leone | Madagascar | Kampuchea |
| Norway | Portugal | | | Singapore | Malawi | Korea (N) |
| Sweden | St. Lucia | | | South Africa | Oman | Laos |
| Switzerland | St. Vincent | | | Sudan | Poland | Mali |
| United Kingdom | Solomon Is. | | | Swaziland | Rwanda | Mauritania |
| United States | Spain | | | Syria | Sao Tome & Principe | Mongolia |
| Venezuela | Sri Lanka | | | Tonga | Saudi Arabia | Mozambique |
| | Trinidad & Tobago | | | Transkei | Seychelles | Niger |
| | Tuvalu | | | Turkey | Tanzania | Pakistan |
| | Vanuatu | | | United Arab Emirates | Tunisia | Romania |
| | | | | Uruguay | USSR | Somalia |
| | | | | Zambia | Upper Volta | Suriname |
| | | | | | Yemen (N) | Togo |
| | | | | | Yemen (S) | Vietnam |
| | | | | | Yugoslavia | |
| | | | | | Zaire | |

20

# Table 4  Ranking of Nations by Civil Liberties

| Most Free 1 | 2 | 3 | 4 | 5 | 6 | Least Free 7 |
|---|---|---|---|---|---|---|
| Australia | Bahamas | Botswana | Bangladesh | Argentina | Algeria | Afghanistan |
| Austria | Dominica | Brazil | Djibouti | Bahrain | Benin | Albania |
| Barbados | Ecuador | Colombia | Guyana | Bhutan | Burma | Angola |
| Belgium | Fiji | Cyprus | Kenya | Bolivia | Burundi | Bulgaria |
| Canada | Finland | Dominican Republic | Kuwait | Central African Republic | Cameroon | Ethiopia |
| Costa Rica | France | Gambia | Lebanon | Chile | Cape Verde Is. | Germany (E) |
| Denmark | Germany (W) | Ghana | Malaysia | China (Taiwan) | Chad | Guinea |
| Iceland | Greece | Honduras | Mexico | Comoro Is. | China (Mainland) | Iraq |
| Ireland | Israel | India | Morocco | Egypt | Congo | Kampuchea |
| Japan | Italy | Jamaica | Nepal | El Salvador | Cuba | Korea (N) |
| Luxembourg | Kiribati | Malta | Panama | Grenada | Czechoslovakia | Laos |
| Netherlands | Nauru | Mauritius | Poland | Hungary | Equatorial Guinea | Libya |
| New Zealand | Papua New Guinea | Nigeria | Senegal | Indonesia | Gabon | Malawi |
| Norway | Portugal | Peru | Thailand | Iran | Guatemala | Mongolia |
| Sweden | St. Lucia | Spain | Uganda | Ivory Coast | Guinea-Bissau | Mozambique |
| Switzerland | St. Vincent | Sri Lanka | Zimbabwe | Lesotho | Haiti | Somalia |
| United Kingdom | Solomon Is. | Tonga | | Maldives | Jordan | Syria |
| United States | Trinidad & Tobago | Vanuatu | | Nicaragua | Korea (S) | USSR |
| | Tuvalu | Western Samoa | | Pakistan | Liberia | Vietnam |
| | Venezuela | | | Paraguay | Madagascar | Yemen (S) |
| | | | | Philippines | Mali | |
| | | | | Qatar | Mauritania | |
| | | | | Sierra Leone | Niger | |
| | | | | Singapore | Oman | |
| | | | | Sudan | Romania | |
| | | | | Surinam | Rwanda | |
| | | | | Swaziland | Sao Tome & Principe | |
| | | | | Tunisia | Saudi Arabia | |
| | | | | Turkey | Seychelles | |
| | | | | United Arab Emirates | South Africa | |
| | | | | Upper Volta | Tanzania | |
| | | | | Uruguay | Togo | |
| | | | | Yemen (N) | Transkei | |
| | | | | Yugoslavia | Zaire | |
| | | | | | Zambia | |

residence, and occupation are narrowly restricted. However, at (6) there still may be relative freedom in private conversation, especially in the home; illegal demonstrations do take place; underground literature is published; and so on. At (7) there is pervading fear, little independent expression takes place even in private, almost no public expressions of opposition emerge in the police-state environment, and imprisonment or execution is often swift and sure.

It will be noted that the civil liberties rating in some very violent countries such as Guatemala or El Salvador is not (7), as it is for relatively less violent East Germany, Bulgaria, or Malawi. The 1980 yearbook included a discussion of levels of political terror. This is not included this year. However, since levels of political terror and levels of civil liberty are often confounded by the media, a short discussion is still needed.

Political terror is an attempt by a government or private group to get its way through the use of murder, torture, exile, prevention of departure, police controls, or threats against the family. These weapons are usually directed against the expression of civil liberties. To this extent they surely are a part of the civil liberty "score." Unfortunately, because of their dramatic and newsworthy nature, such denials of civil liberties often become identified in the minds of informed persons with the whole of civil liberties.

In fact political terror is a tool of revolutionary repression of the right or left. When that repression is no longer necessary to achieve the suppression of civil liberties, then political terror is replaced by implacable and well-organized but often less general and newsworthy controls. Of course, there is a certain unfathomable terror in the sealed totalitarian state, yet life can be lived with a normality in these states that is impossible in the more dramatically terrorized. It would be a mistake to dismiss this apparent anomaly as an expression of a Survey bias. For the fact is there was, with all the blood, a much wider range of organized and personal expressions of alternative political opinion and judgment in 1980 in Guatemala and El Salvador than in many other states.

In making the distinction between political terror and civil liberties as a whole we do not imply that the United States should not be urgently concerned with all violations of human rights and perhaps most urgently with those of political terror. Again it must be emphasized that the Survey is not a rating of relative desirability of societies—but of certain explicit freedoms.

A cumulative judgment of "free," "partly free," or "not free" is made on the basis of the foregoing seven-point ratings, and an understanding of how they were derived. Generally, states rated (1) and (2) will be "free"; those at (3), (4), and (5), "partly free"; and those at (6) and (7), "not free." When the ratings for political rights and civil liberties differ, the status of freedom must be decided by rough averag-

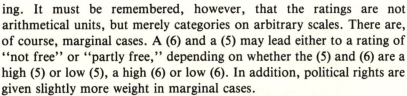

ing. It must be remembered, however, that the ratings are not arithmetical units, but merely categories on arbitrary scales. There are, of course, marginal cases. A (6) and a (5) may lead either to a rating of "not free" or "partly free," depending on whether the (5) and (6) are a high (5) or low (5), a high (6) or low (6). In addition, political rights are given slightly more weight in marginal cases.

The tables also include an entry for "outlook." Since we are not in a position to adequately judge the futures of all the societies under review, this column reports many fewer trends than a more detailed study would discover. Primarily, we include cases where a forthcoming election appears likely to improve the freedoms of a country, or a downward trend is in prospect because a retrogressive process underway at the time of the Survey has not yet actually reached fruition. By the nature of the signals we use, more pluses are likely to appear under "outlook" than minuses.

The reporting period covered by the Survey (January 1 to December 31, 1980) does not correspond with the calendar of short-term events in the countries rated. For this reason the yearly Survey may mask or play down important events that occur during the year.

## Significant Declines in Freedom

Declines in freedom during the year included the final eclipse of the promising but repeatedly thwarted advance toward freedom in *Bolivia*. After this summer's election appeared likely to bring to power a left-of-center government, the military intervened decisively, and apparently with Argentine backing. For the time being the pluralistic spectrum of forces that has made possible democratic hopes in Bolivia has been severely repressed. Those who disagree have been shot, imprisoned, or gone into hiding or exile. The general intervention of Libyan forces in *Chad* further decreased its freedom. In *El Salvador* the level of violence increased during the year on all sides, with a chilling effect on free expression. In *Gambia* two small nonparliamentary parties were banned in the wake of a possible coup attempt. Additional pressures were placed on *East German* writers to stop publication in the West, and for all East Germans to limit contacts with foreigners. Although the revolution's success in *Grenada* initially had a great deal of popular backing, its leaders' continuing unwillingness to open the system to democratic processes and the imprisoning or silencing of opponents reduce the freedom of its people. The already high level of political violence, particularly from the right, rose again in *Guatemala*. Union leaders, peasants, educators, and journalists were among the victims. In this environment fear seems more than ever to be winning out over the formal political and civil rights that persist. The moderate vice-president resigned in protest. Elections in *Guyana* were more than open to serious question—in the control of opposition expression and in the election mechanics

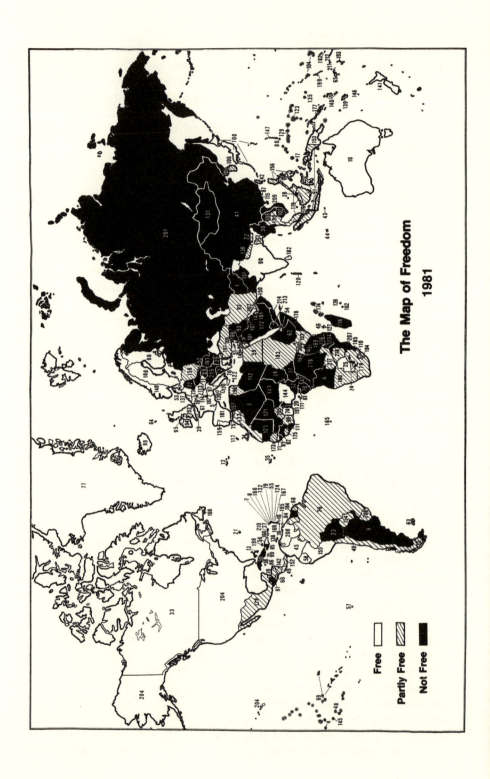

The Map of Freedom
1981

Free
Partly Free
Not Free

## Free Nations

| | |
|---|---|
| 10 | Australia |
| 11 | Austria |
| 13 | Bahamas |
| 16 | Barbados |
| 18 | Belgium |
| 25 | Botswana |
| 33 | Canada |
| 45 | Colombia |
| 49 | Costa Rica |
| 53 | Denmark |
| 55 | Dominica |
| 56 | Dominican Republic |
| 58 | Ecuador |
| 65 | Fiji |
| 66 | Finland |
| 67 | France |
| 71 | Gambia |
| 73 | Germany, West |
| 74 | Ghana |
| 76 | Greece |
| 89 | Iceland |
| 90 | India |
| 94 | Ireland |
| 96 | Israel |
| 97 | Italy |
| 99 | Jamaica |
| 100 | Japan |
| 104 | Kiribati |
| 114 | Luxembourg |
| 122 | Malta |
| 135 | Nauru |
| 137 | Netherlands |
| 141 | New Zealand |
| 144 | Nigeria |
| 148 | Norway |
| 153 | Papua New Guinea |
| 155 | Peru |
| 159 | Portugal |
| 167 | St. Lucia |
| 169 | St. Vincent |
| 177 | Solomon Islands |
| 181 | Spain |
| 182 | Sri Lanka |
| 186 | Sweden |
| 187 | Switzerland |
| 195 | Trinidad & Tobago |
| 199 | Tuvalu |
| 203 | United Kingdom |
| 204 | United States |
| 140 | Vanuatu |
| 208 | Venezuela |

### Related Territories

| | |
|---|---|
| 4 | American Samoa (U.S.) |
| 7 | Anguilla (U.K.) |
| 8 | Antigua and Barbuda (U.K.) |
| 12 | Azores (Port.) |
| 19 | Belize (U.K.) |
| 21 | Bermuda (U.K.) |
| 34 | Canary Islands (Sp.) |
| 36 | Cayman Islands (U.K.) |
| 39 | Channel Islands (U.K.) |
| 48 | Cook Islands (N.Z.) |
| 63 | Falkland Islands (U.K.) |
| 64 | Faroe Islands (Den.) |
| 75 | Gibraltar (U.K.) |
| 77 | Greenland (Den.) |
| 95 | Isle of Man (U.K.) |
| 117 | Madeira (Port.) |
| 127 | Mayotte (Fr.) |
| 132 | Montserrat (U.K.) |
| 138 | Netherlands Antilles (Neth.) |
| 139 | New Caledonia (Fr.) |
| 145 | Niue (N.Z.) |
| 147 | Northern Marianas (U.S.) |
| 157 | Places of Sovereignty in North Africa (Sp.) |
| 160 | Puerto Rico (U.S.) |
| 165 | St. Helena (U.K.) |
| 166 | St. Kitts and Nevis (U.K.) |
| 170 | San Marino (It.) |
| 198 | Turks and Caicos (U.K.) |
| 210 | Virgin Islands (U.S.) |

## Partly Free Nations

| | |
|---|---|
| 14 | Bahrain |
| 15 | Bangladesh |
| 22 | Bhutan |
| 26 | Brazil |
| 40 | Chile |
| 42 | China, Taiwan |
| 46 | Comoro Islands |
| 51 | Cyprus |
| 54 | Djibouti |
| 59 | Egypt |
| 60 | El Salvador |
| 84 | Guyana |
| 86 | Honduras |
| 91 | Indonesia |
| 92 | Iran |
| 98 | Ivory Coast |
| 103 | Kenya |
| 106 | Korea, South |
| 107 | Kuwait |
| 109 | Lebanon |
| 110 | Lesotho |
| 119 | Malaysia |
| 120 | Maldives |
| 126 | Mauritius |
| 128 | Mexico |
| 133 | Morocco |
| 136 | Nepal |
| 142 | Nicaragua |
| 152 | Panama |
| 154 | Paraguay |
| 156 | Philippines |
| 158 | Poland |
| 161 | Qatar |
| 173 | Senegal |
| 175 | Sierra Leone |
| 176 | Singapore |
| 179 | South Africa |
| 183 | Sudan |
| 185 | Swaziland |
| 190 | Thailand |
| 193 | Tonga |
| 194 | Transkei |
| 196 | Tunisia |
| 197 | Turkey |
| 200 | Uganda |
| 202 | United Arab Emirates |
| 205 | Upper Volta |
| 206 | Uruguay |
| 212 | Western Samoa |
| 217 | Zambia |
| 218 | Zimbabwe Rhodesia |

### Related Territories

| | |
|---|---|
| 5 | Andorra (Fr.-Sp.) |
| 17 | Belau (U.S.) |
| 27 | British Virgin Islands (U.K.) |
| 43 | Christmas Island (Aus.) |
| 44 | Cocos Islands (Aus.) |
| 68 | French Guiana (Fr.) |
| 69 | French Polynesia (Fr.) |
| 79 | Guadeloupe (Fr.) |
| 80 | Guam (U.S.) |
| 87 | Hong Kong (U.K.) |
| 113 | Liechtenstein (Switz.) |
| 115 | Macao (Port.) |
| 123 | Marshall Islands (U.S.) |
| 124 | Martinique (Fr.) |
| 129 | Micronesia, Federated States of (U.S.) |
| 130 | Monaco (Fr.) |
| 146 | Norfolk Island (Aus.) |
| 149 | Occupied Territories (Isr.) |
| 162 | Reunion (Fr.) |
| 168 | Saint Pierre & Miquelon (Fr.) |
| 180 | South West Africa— Namibia (S. Afr.) |
| 192 | Tokelau Islands (N.Z.) |
| 211 | Wallis and Futuna (Fr.) |

## Not Free Nations

| | |
|---|---|
| 1 | Afghanistan |
| 2 | Albania |
| 3 | Algeria |
| 6 | Angola |
| 9 | Argentina |
| 20 | Benin |
| 23 | Bolivia |
| 29 | Bulgaria |
| 30 | Burma |
| 31 | Burundi |
| 32 | Cameroon |
| 35 | Cape Verde Islands |
| 37 | Central African Republic |
| 38 | Chad |
| 41 | China, Mainland |
| 47 | Congo |
| 50 | Cuba |
| 52 | Czechoslovakia |
| 61 | Equatorial Guinea |
| 62 | Ethiopia |
| 70 | Gabon |
| 72 | Germany, East |
| 78 | Grenada |
| 81 | Guatemala |
| 82 | Guinea |
| 83 | Guinea-Bissau |
| 85 | Haiti |
| 88 | Hungary |
| 93 | Iraq |
| 101 | Jordan |
| 102 | Kampuchea |
| 105 | Korea, North |
| 108 | Laos |
| 111 | Liberia |
| 112 | Libya |
| 116 | Madagascar |
| 118 | Malawi |
| 121 | Mali |
| 125 | Mauritania |
| 131 | Mongolia |
| 134 | Mozambique |
| 143 | Niger |
| 150 | Oman |
| 151 | Pakistan |
| 163 | Romania |
| 164 | Rwanda |
| 171 | Sao Tome and Principe |
| 172 | Saudi Arabia |
| 174 | Seychelles |
| 178 | Somalia |
| 184 | Suriname |
| 188 | Syria |
| 189 | Tanzania |
| 191 | Togo |
| 201 | USSR |
| 209 | Vietnam |
| 213 | Yemen, North |
| 214 | Yemen, South |
| 215 | Yugoslavia |
| 216 | Zaire |

### Related Territories

| | |
|---|---|
| 24 | Bophuthatswana (S. Afr.) |
| 28 | Brunei (U.K.) |
| 57 | Easter Island (Chile) |
| 207 | Venda (S. Afr.) |

themselves. After a brief opening, political discussion and opposition were again heavily repressed in *Haiti.*

Although the constitution of *South Korea* accepted by a highly controlled referendum in the fall was a formal advance over its predecessor, the scale of the military's arrests, trials, and other suppressions was such as to reduce severely the meaning of the vote and to essentially eliminate the public expression of serious opposition. Censorship was general and even extended to private conversation. (An election in 1981 would only slightly improve this situation.)

The sergeants' revolt in *Liberia* eliminated one type of injustice but seemed likely to institutionalize another more tenacious form. The new regime's initial cruelty has been followed by a reconcentration of power in hands apparently even less willing than their predecessors to accept criticism or submit their system to the challenge of an open ballot. *Libya*'s pursuit of political opponents overseas was combined with even greater fear at home.

In *Suriname* a functioning democratic system was overthrown shortly before an election by another group of sergeants struggling for their own economic interests. Initially, the men with guns maintained a constitutional facade by retaining the president. But he, too, was soon set aside, and the plotters fell to feuding among themselves and suppressing countercoups. The media are under strong pressure. Struggle with opposition elements led to an increase in political imprisonment and execution in *Syria.* The move by *Turkey*'s military to take over government temporarily can be viewed quite differently. Turkey's system faced a major impasse, and violence was continuing at an unacceptable level from both sides. Initially, not acting in a spirit of vengeance, the military's actions were generally popular. They were not seen as acting primarily out of selfish group material interest (as in Suriname) or to punish and suppress challenges to their hegemony (as in South Korea). If they act responsibly, as in the past, they will return the society to democratic forms as soon as possible.

Unfortunately, the year saw an increased suppression of dissent in the *Soviet Union* where dissidents have for the last year and a half suffered under increasing pressure. Today there are very few known dissidents out of jail or not in one or another form of exile, and there is little if any underground publishing activity.

The democratically elected government of *Upper Volta* was overthrown by a military coup in November. In 1979-80 *Western Samoa* saw a newsman expelled and a judge denied reappointment in a manner threatening both judicial and journalistic independence. *Zambia*'s leader took additional repressive steps in extending his control over an already muzzled press. The government increased pressure on local theaters, and further extended control over private economic activity.

## SIGNIFICANT ADVANCES IN FREEDOM

Freedom of expression improved in the *Central African Republic*. In *Ghana* the elected civilian government managed to overcome, at least for the time, the shadow of military intervention that had hung over its beginnings last year. *Honduras* proceeded another step toward return to democratic rule by holding a successful competitive election to the constituent assembly. The opposition party unexpectedly won. Elections in *Iraq* allowed choices, at least among individuals. Elections in *Ivory Coast* allowed for a wide range of choice, although still within the one-party framework. Another constitutional election in *Nepal* went against those desiring a full return to competitive party government. However, the campaign was comparatively fair, and the panchayat system the people approved seemed to be evolving toward a competitive system both in the assembly and the public arena. In spite of some repressions, *Panama* recently witnessed an election with limited but significant opposition, and new papers represented more independent voices. *Peru* returned to full democratic government with a hotly contested presidential election as the culmination of a well-organized process. The media were returned to private control and freedom of expression.

In the context of *Poland*'s emerging pluralist communism, the labor movement's achievement of relative independence and the general liberalization of expression accompanying it marked a significant if always endangered advance. A constitutional change of government under *Thailand*'s latest semi-democratic system gave evidence for more popular control of the government than many imagined. *Ugandan* elections in December in an atmosphere of lethal anarchy were nevertheless accompanied by competitive political activity and an opposition press. In spite of probable interference with the count, the election represented a positive change. In *Uruguay* there was a slight relaxation as parties were able to publicly express opposition to planned constitutional forms. Their message was heard even on the radio. The subsequent ability of the people to reject by referendum the proposed constitution lifts the country provisionally out of the "not free" category. *Vanuatu* (formerly the New Hebrides) managed a difficult transition to freedom, overcoming both the complications of the British-French condominium and a short-lived revolution. Unfortunately, large-scale political imprisonment seemed to go beyond the requirements of the threatened revolt.

*Zimbabwe* was able with outside help to end its exhausting guerrilla war by holding an election that brought the guerrilla leaders to power. However, its gain in freedom was less than might have been expected for several reasons. In political rights the gains were reduced by the fact that blacks had already attained considerable power through 1979 elections, and the 1980 election was accompanied by successful, violent pressure to vote for a particular candidate. In civil rights the country attained a "free" or almost "free" level immediately before and after the voting. However, subsequent events have caused the media, at least, to shift to a supine support of government policy little better than existed in 1979. The relatively independent press was under renewed pressure in November. Progress also occurred in the *Related Territories* of New Zealand, the United Kingdom, and the United States.

## FURTHER COMMENTS ON CHANGES IN FREEDOM

Other alterations in the ratings reflect primarily reevaluations of information or new information that does not apply particularly to changes during the year. *Italy*'s political system now operates with full freedom, and the comparative degree of decentralization through elected municipal and regional assemblies should be fully realized. *Greece*'s political process seems fully democratic. *Japan*'s ruling party has not been replaced, yet recent trends toward democratization in the party and thoroughly open competition within and between the several parties suggest that Japan's is now one of the freer systems in the world. *Malta* was rated down on the basis primarily of evidence from 1977-79 relating to pressures on journalists, doctors, unions, and the opposition. In spite of some increase in torture and terror in *Chile*, its rating was not changed. The referendum held this year was hardly a free process, yet it did allow an opportunity for the system to be publicly questioned, and, in spite of some danger, pluralistic critical opinion continues to be expressed by a number of groups.

In communist *China* the publications of the semi-legal dissident movement of 1978-79 were finally extinguished in 1980. However, the movement lives on; remarkable criticism of the system has emerged in the course of local election campaigns. This augurs well for the future. The right of public demonstration and of expression through wall posters was rescinded, yet there are still reports of an underground literature. In nonpolitical areas, such as economy and religion, China remains much freer than in the past. In the new China totalitarian controls will be less, but its authoritarian organization is apparently not to be questioned.

The situation has been stabilized in *Cyprus*, and the two communal democracies seem to be operating with a fair degree of freedom within their arbitrary limits. *Colombia* continues to represent a highly mixed picture. Particularly in the rural areas, the security services' struggle against guerrilla and other armed bands leads to accusations of torture and arbitrary imprisonment that are in part justified. Nevertheless, as a whole the society is highly pluralistic, and most groups operate with little constraint on a national scene that includes a communist party and labor groups. *India* continued to struggle violently against a variety of anarchical and regional forces. The resulting violence reduces rights. In addition, police violence has been shown in many areas to have reduced rights arbitrarily even in areas of civil peace. *Iran*'s parliamentary elections represented an important if limited freedom, and within narrow limits there was continuing public discussion of alternative policies. *Pakistan*'s president rules autocratically without promised elections, but opposition voices and organizations continue to resist.

The successful election in *Jamaica* in late October 1980 did not change the nation's rating, but after several years of concern over the nation's direction, and a very high level of violence both before and during the election campaign, the successful change of government through election should reassure advocates of free institutions in the Caribbean. *Nicaragua* continues, however, to disappoint the hope for democratic evolution. Political opposition achieved growing legitimacy during the year, only to be repressed at the end.

## ELECTIONS AND REFERENDA

Evidence for political freedom is primarily found in the occurrence and nature of elections or referenda. Therefore, as a supplement to our ratings we have attempted in the accompanying Table 5 to summarize those national elections that occurred in independent countries in 1980. Other elections are included only in the more important cases. The reader should assume that the electoral process appeared comparatively open and competitive unless our remarks suggest otherwise; extremely one-sided outcomes imply an unacceptable electoral process. Voter participation figures are often not comparable, even when available. Many states compel their citizens to vote, in others it is unclear whether participation is a percentage of those registered or of those of voting age.

## RELATION OF POLITICAL-ECONOMIC SYSTEMS TO FREEDOM

The accompanying table of political-economic systems (Table 6) fills two needs. It offers the reader additional information about the countries we have rated. For example, readers with libertarian views may wish to raise the relative ratings of capitalist countries, while those who place more value on redistributive systems may wish to raise the ratings of countries toward the socialist end of the spectrum. The table also makes possible an analysis of the relation between political and economic forms and the freedom ratings of the Survey. Perusal of the table will show that freedom is directly related to the existence of multiparty systems: the further a country is from such systems, the less freedom it is likely to have.

# Table 5
## National Elections and Referenda

| Nation and Date | Type of Election | Percentage Voting | Results and Remarks |
|---|---|---|---|
| **Australia** 10/18/80 | parliamentary | NA (compulsory) | government wins narrowly; court challenges of campaign advertising |
| **Austria** 5/18/80 | presidential | 92 (compulsory) | eighty percent victory |
| 6/23/80 | provincial referendum (Vorarlberg) | 88 | endorse demand for devolution of power |
| **Bolivia** 6/29/80 | parliamentary | NA | fair result, but nullified by subsequent military coup |
| **Cameroon** 4/5/80 | presidential | NA | incumbent unopposed; received 99.99% of vote |
| **Canada** 2/18/80 | parliamentary | NA | liberal victory, change of government |
| 5/20/80 | Quebec referendum | 84 | separatists defeated |
| **Cape Verde Islands** 12/7/80 | parliamentary | 75 | 92.5% support of single list |
| **Chile** 9/11/80 | constitutional plebiscite | 93 (obligatory) | 67% favor proposed constitution; some repression before vote |
| **China (Taiwan)** 12/6/80 | partial parliamentary | 65 | opposition wins some seats; very restricted campaigning |
| **Dominica** 7/21/80 | parliamentary | 80 | opposition party wins |

30

| Country / Date | Type | Turnout | Comments |
|---|---|---|---|
| **Egypt** 5/22/80 | referendum | 87 | 99% approve constitutional proposals; campaign not free. |
| 9/25/80 | consultative council | NA | largely unopposed |
| **France** 9/28/80 | partial Senate | NA | indirect, 42,000 voters |
| **Gabon** 2/80 | parliamentary | NA | "massive support" for single list (results remarkably sketchy) |
| **Germany (West)** 10/5/80 | parliamentary | 89 | government increases margin, especially FDP partner |
| **Guinea** 1/27/80 | parliamentary | 96 | no choice; 99.8% victory |
| **Guyana** 12/18/80 | parliamentary | NA | government wins, opposition receives diminished share; widespread fraud alleged, through campaign repression and more direct means |
| **Honduras** 4/20/80 | constituent assembly | 75 (82) | fair distribution of seats, although some parties excluded; changed government |
| **Hungary** 6/8/80 | general | NA | less than five percent of seats contested; 99% vote for official list; similar results in local elections |
| **Iceland** 6/29/80 | presidential | 90 | woman elected with 34% of vote |
| **India** 1/3-6/80 | parliamentary | 57 | opposition scores convincing victory with 42.7%; other parties split |
| 5/28-31/80 | nine state assemblies | NA | resounding government victories |
| **Iran** 1/25/80 | presidential | ca. 70 | vigorous campaigning, some excluded, Bani Sadr gets over 75% |
| 3/14/80 & 5/9/80 | parliamentary | ca. 50 | some candidates and parties excluded before and after election; irregularities, heterogeneous results favor fundamentalists |

31

**Table 5** *(continued)*

| Nation and Date | Type of Election | Percentage Voting | Results and Remarks |
|---|---|---|---|
| **Iraq** 6/20/80 | parliamentary | NA | contested, but candidates carefully screened; no parliamentary powers |
| **Ivory Coast** 10/13/80 | presidential | 82 | 99.99% for president; no choice |
| 11/9-23/80 | parliamentary | 30 | contested, but all candidates designated by party |
| **Jamaica** 10/30/80 | parliamentary | 76 | 57% won by opposition party in violent campaign |
| **Japan** 6/22/80 | parliamentary | 75 | ruling party regains absolute majorities in relatively high poll |
| **Korea (South)** 10/22/80 | constitutional referendum | 96 | 92% approve in an atmosphere of repression |
| **Morocco** 5/23/80 | referendum | 97 | 99.7% yes; some vocal opposition |
| 5/30/80 | referendum | 91 | 96.7% yes; some vocal opposition |
| **Nepal** 5/2/80 | referendum | 67 | multiparty democracy rejected by modest margin; violent campaign |
| **Nauru** 12/6/80 | parliamentary | NA | contested non-party; prominent MP's defeated. President subsequently reelected |
| **Panama** 9/28/80 | partial parliamentary | 50 | government wins most seats with less than majority; abstaining party manages to keep many away from polls |
| **Peru** 5/18/80 | parliamentary | 62 | free participation by full spectrum of parties |

32

| Country / Date | Type | % | Notes |
|---|---|---|---|
| **Poland** 3/23/80 | parliamentary | 98.9 | pre-selected candidates; some expression of preference possible; abstention is hazardous |
| **Portugal** 10/5/80 | parliamentary | 85 | moderate-conservatives increase majority |
| 12/7/80 | presidential | 84 | incumbent wins with 56% of votes |
| **Romania** 3/9/80 | general | 99.9 | 98.5% vote for government list; some lists rejected locally |
| **Singapore** 12/23/80 | parliamentary | 94 (compulsory) | ruling party wins all seats with 76% of votes; unfair campaigning situation |
| **Solomon Islands** 8/6/80 | parliamentary | 60 | independents maintain position as parties emerge |
| **Spain** March 1980 | regional parliament | ca. 60 | regional parties win pluralities |
| 3/80 | Andalusian referendum | ca. 60 | about 90% favor autonomy; government temporarily slows down process on technicality |
| **Sweden** 3/23/80 | referendum | 74 | majority supports modest nuclear expansion |
| **Switzerland** 3/2/80 | referendums | 34 | rejected further separation of church and state; approve crisis powers for government |
| 11/30/80 | referendum | 42 | approve compulsory crash helmets and seat belts |
| **Tanzania** 10/26/80 | general | 86 | presidents elected unopposed with 93%; each parliamentary seat contested by two selected candidates |
| **Uganda** 12/10/80 | parliamentary | NA | government (military and Tanzanian) party wins narrowly; many irregularities |
| **United States** 11/4/80 | general | 52 | opposition wins presidency and senate |

**Table 5** *(continued)*

| Nation and Date | Type of Election | Percentage Voting | Results and Remarks |
|---|---|---|---|
| **Uruguay** 11/30/80 | constitutional referendum | 80+ | proposed constitution defeated in remarkable outcome; some ineffective repression |
| **Zimbabwe** 2/14/80 & 3/4/80 | parliamentary | 94 | revolutionary party wins overwhelming victory in violent atmosphere; well supervised mechanics |

This could be considered a trivial result, since a publicly competitive political system is one of the criteria of freedom, and political parties are considered evidence for such competition. However, the result is not simply determined by our definitions: we searched for evidence of authentic public competition in countries without competitive parties, and seldom found the search rewarded. Both theoretical and empirical studies indicate the difficulty of effective public political opposition in one-party systems.

The relation between economic systems and freedom is more complicated and, because of our lack of emphasis on economic systems in devising our ratings of freedom, is not predetermined by our methods. Historically, the table suggests that there are three types of societies competing for acceptance in the world. The first, or *traditional* type, is marginal and in retreat, but its adherents have borrowed political and economic bits and pieces from both of the other types. The second and third, the *Euro-American* and *Sino-Soviet* types, are strongest near their points of origin, but have spread by diffusion and active propagation all over the world. The Leninist-socialist style of political organization was exported along with the socialist concept of economic organization, just as constitutional democracy had been exported along with capitalist economic concepts. In this interpretation, the relation of economic systems to freedom found in the table may be an expression of historical chance rather than necessary relationships. Clearly, capitalism does not cause nations to be politically free, nor does socialism cause them to be politically unfree. Still, socialists must be concerned by the empirical relationship between the rating of "not free" and socialism that is found in tables such as this.

In the table, economies are roughly grouped in categories from "capitalist" to "socialist." Labeling economies as capitalist or socialist has a fairly clear significance in the developed world, but it may be doubted that it is very useful to label the mostly poor and largely agrarian societies of the third world in this manner. Raymond Aron, for example, casts doubt on the legitimacy of calling any third world, non-communist society "socialist," regardless of what it may call itself.[2] However, third world states with dual economies, that is, with a modern sector and a preindustrial sector, have economic policies or goals that can be placed along the continuum from socialist to capitalist. A socialist third world state has usually nationalized all of the modern sector—except possibly some foreign investment—and claims central government jurisdiction over the land and its products, with only temporary assignment of land to individuals or cooperatives. The capitalist third world state has a capitalist modern sector and a traditionalist agricultural sector, combined in some cases with new agricultural projects either on

# Table 6

| POLITICAL → | | Multiparty | | Dominant-Party |
|---|---|---|---|---|
| ECONOMIC ↓ | | Centralized | Decentralized | |
| **Capitalist** — Inclusive | | Bahamas F, Barbados F, Colombia[4] F, Costa Rica F, Dominica[4] F, Dominican Republic[4] F, France[3] F, Greece F, Iceland F, Ireland F, Italy[3] F, Japan F, Luxembourg F, Mauritius PF, New Zealand[3] F, Spain F | Australia F, Belgium F, Canada F, Cyprus PF, Germany (W)[3] F, Lebanon PF, Switzerland F, Trinidad & Tobago F, United States F | Malaysia PF |
| **Capitalist** — Noninclusive | | Ecuador F, Fiji[4] F, Gambia[4] F, Guatemala[1] NF, Honduras[1]/[4] PF, Morocco PF, Thailand[1] PF | Botswana F, Papua New Guinea F, Solomon Islands[2] F | Haiti NF, Lesotho PF, Philippines PF, Transkei[5] PF |
| **Capitalist-Statist** — Inclusive | | Ghana F, Jamaica[3] F, Malta F, South Africa PF, Sri Lanka F, Venezuela F | Brazil [1]/[3]/[4] PF | China (Taiwan) PF, Mexico[1] PF, Panama[1]/[3]/[4] PF, Singapore PF |
| **Capitalist-Statist** — Noninclusive | | Bangladesh[1] PF, Peru[4] F, Uganda[3] PF, Zimbabwe[4] PF | India F, Nigeria[3]/[4] F, Vanuatu F | Iran[2]/[4] PF, Indonesia[1]/[4] PF, Paraguay[1]/[3]/[4] PF |
| **Capitalist-Socialist** — Inclusive | | Austria F, Denmark F, Finland F, Guyana PF, Israel F, Netherlands F, Norway F, Portugal[3] F, St. Lucia[3] F, St. Vincent[3] F, Sweden F, United Kingdom[3] F | | Egypt[3]/[4] PF, Grenada[2] NF, Senegal[3]/[4] PF, Syria[1]/[4] NF |
| **Capitalist-Socialist** — Noninclusive | | | | |
| **Socialist** — Inclusive | | | | |
| **Socialist** — Noninclusive | | Notes | | |

## Notes

1. Military dominated; all countries in the nonparty military column are military dominated.

2. Party relationships anomalous.

3. Close decision on capitalist-to-socialist dimension.

4. Close decision on inclusive/noninclusive dimension.

5. Over 50 percent of income from remittances of persons working in South Africa.

# Political-Economic Systems

| One-Party | | | Nonparty | |
|---|---|---|---|---|
| Socialist | Communist | Nationalist | Military[1] | Nonmilitary |
| | | | Chile[3] PF<br>El Salvador[2]/[3] PF<br>Korea (S) PF<br>Suriname NF | Jordan[3]/[4] NF |
| Sierra Leone PF | | Cameroon[3] NF<br>Djibouti PF<br>Gabon NF<br>Ivory Coast[4] PF<br>Kenya PF<br>Malawi NF | Chad NF<br>Liberia NF<br>Niger NF<br>Yemen (N)[3] NF | Bhutan[3] PF<br>Central Afr. Rep. NF<br>Comoro Islands PF<br>Maldives PF<br>Nepal[3] PF<br>Swaziland PF<br>Tonga PF<br>Tuvalu F<br>Western Samoa PF |
| Libya[1]/[2]/[3] NF | | | Argentina NF<br>Turkey[4] PF | Bahrain PF<br>Kuwait PF<br>Nauru F<br>Qatar PF<br>Saudi Arabia NF<br>United Arab Ems. PF |
| | | Zaire[1] NF | Bolivia NF<br>Equatorial<br> Guinea[3] NF<br>Mauritania NF<br>Pakistan[2] NF | Kiribati F<br>Oman NF |
| Seychelles[3] NF<br>Tunisia[4] PF | Poland[3] PF<br>Yugoslavia[3] NF | | Uruguay PF | Nicaragua[2]/[4] PF |
| Burma[1] NF<br>Burundi[1]/[3] NF<br>Congo[1]/[3] NF<br>Somalia[1]/[3] NF<br>Zambia[3] PF | | Madagascar[1]/[3] NF<br>Mali[1] NF<br>Rwanda[1]/[3] NF<br>Sudan[1] PF<br>Togo[1] NF | Upper Volta PF | |
| Algeria[1] NF<br>Sao Tome and<br> Principe[3]/[4] NF | Albania NF<br>Bulgaria NF<br>China (Mainland) NF<br>Cuba NF<br>Czechoslovakia NF<br>Germany (E) NF<br>Hungary NF<br>Kampuchea NF<br>Korea (N) NF<br>Mongolia NF<br>Romania NF<br>USSR NF<br>Vietnam NF | | | |
| Angola NF<br>Benin[1]/[3] NF<br>Cape Verde Is.[3]/[4] NF<br>Guinea NF<br>Guinea-Bissau[1]/[3] NF<br>Iraq[1]/[3]/[4] NF<br>Mozambique NF<br>Tanzania NF<br>Yemen (S) NF | Afghanistan NF<br>Laos NF | | Ethiopia[3] NF | |

family farm or agribusiness models. Third world economies that fall between capitalist and socialist do not have the high taxes of their industrialized equivalents, but they have major nationalized industries (for example, oil) in the modern sector, and their agricultural world may include emphasis on cooperatives or large-scale land reform, as well as more traditional forms.

States with *inclusive capitalist* forms are generally developed states that rely on the operation of the market and on private provision for industrial welfare. Taxes may be high, but they are not confiscatory, while government interference is generally limited to subsidy and regulation. States classified as *noninclusive capitalist*, such as Liberia or Thailand, have not over fifty percent of the population included in a capitalist modern economy, with the remainder of the population still living traditionally. In such states the traditional economy may be individual, communal, or feudal, but the direction of change as development proceeds is capitalistic.

Capitalist states grade over into capitalist-statist or capitalist-socialist nations. *Capitalist-statist* nations are those such as Brazil, Turkey, or Saudi Arabia, that have very large government productive enterprises, either because of an elitist development philosophy or major dependence on a key resource such as oil. Government interferes in the economy in a major way in such states, but not primarily because of egalitarian motives. *Capitalist-socialist* systems, such as those in Israel, the Netherlands, or Sweden, provide social services on a large scale through governmental or other nonprofit institutions, with the result that private control over property is sacrificed to egalitarian purposes. These nations still see capitalism as legitimate, but its legitimacy is accepted grudgingly by many in government. Governments of other states grouped here, such as Egypt or Poland, proclaim themselves to be socialist, but in fact allow rather large portions of the economy to remain in the private domain. Both variants have *noninclusive* versions, such as India or Madagascar.

*Socialist* economies, on the other hand, strive programmatically to place an entire national economy under direct or indirect government control. States such as the USSR or Cuba may allow some modest private productive property, but this is only by exception, and right to such property can be revoked at any time. The leaders of *noninclusive socialist* states have the same goals as the leaders of inclusive socialist states, but their relatively primitive economies or peoples have not yet been effectively included in the socialist system. Such states generally have a small socialized modern economy and a large preindustrial economy in which the organization of production and trade is still largely traditional. It should be understood that the characterizations in the table are impressionistic; the continuum between capitalist and socialist economies is necessarily cut arbitrarily into categories for this presentation.

Political systems range from democratic multiparty to absolutist one-party systems. Theoretically, the most democratic countries should be those with *decentralized multiparty systems*, for here important powers are held by the people at two or more levels of the political system, and dissent is legitimated and mobilized by opposition parties. More common are *centralized multiparty systems* such as France or Japan, in which the central government organizes lower levels of government primarily for reasons of efficiency. *Dominant-party* systems allow the forms of democracy, but structure the political process so that opposition groups do not have a realistic chance of achieving power. Such limitations may be through vote fraud, imprisonment of opposition leaders, or other devices.

The now classical form of *one-party* rule is that in states such as the USSR or Vietnam that proclaim themselves to be *communist*. The slightly larger group of *socialist one-party* states are ruled by elites that use Marxist-Leninist rhetoric, organize ruling parties very much along communist lines, but either do not have the disciplined organization of communist states or have explicitly rejected one or another aspect of communism. A final group of *nationalist one-party* states adopts the political form popularized by the communists (and the fascists in the last generation), but the leaders generally reject the revolutionary ideologies of socialist or communist states and fail to develop the totalitarian controls that characterize these states. There are several borderline states that might be switched between socialist and nationalist categories (for example, Libya). "Socialist" is used here to designate a political rather than economic system. A socialist "vanguard party" established along Marxist-Leninist lines will almost surely develop a socialist economy, but a state with a socialist economy need not be ruled by a vanguard party. It should be pointed out that the totalitarian-libertarian continuum is not directly reflected by the categorization in this table.

Nonparty systems can be democratic, as in the small island of Nauru, but generally they are not. Such systems may be *nonmilitary nonparty* systems ranging from Tonga to Saudi Arabia. Much more important are the many *military nonparty systems*, such as that in Argentina.

## SOVIET AND COMMUNIST THREATS TO FREEDOM

The communist threat to freedom appears in three guises. First, Marxist-Leninist ideology is used in a wide variety of states to legitimize the undermining of the effectiveness of "bourgeois rights" to civil and political liberties. Secondly, the communist model is adopted by many new rulers and revolutionary groups struggling for power. At first this may be merely a way of attracting the money and arms communist nations provide those who use their slogans; later this early label may come to determine policy. Finally, the communist threat is expressed through the relative increase in the actual and perceived power of the Soviet bloc, a bloc whose leaders show remarkably little respect for freedom at home and abroad. It is the increase in the power of this bloc that holds the greatest long-term danger to freedom in the world, a danger that in the minds of many overshadows any short-term gains for freedom that may occur. Recent Soviet gains are not reflected in the Survey because they have occurred primarily in countries already with little or no freedom, such as Kampuchea and Afghanistan.

Whether a country is or is not in the Soviet bloc is open to much dispute. Objective indicators can, however, be found. The Havana conference of Non-Aligned States in 1979 offers evidence for a pessimistic interpretation of Soviet success. Ninety-five countries were willing to attend as full members and several more as observers. Although many of the attendees objected to Cuba's allegiances, they nevertheless met in Havana and elected Castro president of the Non-Aligned Movement. This was in spite of the fact that Cuba and several other members of the Movement (notably Vietnam) were not in any sense non-aligned. The fact that Cuba failed in its attempt to define the Soviet Union as a special friend of the non-aligned world does not affect the significance of Castro's ability to treat the non-aligned movement, and thus most of the world, as a part of the Soviet camp. It was disappointing that opposition to Cuba at the conference was largely marshaled by countries such as Yugoslavia or China, themselves communist. We can only conclude that for the elites of most of the world, democratic and nondemocratic, the old concept that the left can do no wrong is alive and well.

However, under quite different circumstances the votes in the United Nations calling for the immediate withdrawal of the USSR from Afghanistan provides a more reliable indication of the size of the Soviet bloc. The nations voting against the resolution (see *Freedom in the World 1980*, p. 46) can be thought to form the core of the Soviet bloc. Eighteen in January 1980, the list had grown to twenty-two by November (see Table 7.)[3] The four additional states—Madagascar, Sao Tome and Principe, Seychelles, and Syria—were either abstainers or absent in the earlier vote. Syria, at least, is only an addition because of its immediate needs. Two of the list are actually parts of the USSR. A distinction should also be made between those bloc members under proven Soviet control—primarily those that border the USSR—and those that could perhaps break away from the bloc without incurring a massive Soviet intervention. These comments suggest that the "solid core" of the Soviet bloc is less than eighteen states. (Another more economic definition of the "solid core" of Soviet influence is suggested by COMECON's meeting held July 7-19, 1980. It was attended by Bulgaria, Czecho-

# Table 7
# The Roll Call

## United Nations Resolution Reaffirming Demand for Soviet Withdrawal from Afghanistan, November 20, 1980

### In Favor (111)

| | | | |
|---|---|---|---|
| Albania | El Savador | Liberia | Senegal |
| Argentina | Equatorial | Luxembourg | Sierra Leone |
| Australia | Guinea | Malawi | Singapore |
| Austria | Fiji | Malaysia | Solomon |
| Bahamas | France | Maldives | Islands |
| Bahrain | Gabon | Malta | Somalia |
| Bangladesh | Gambia | Mauritania | Spain |
| Barbados | Germany, | Mauritius | Sri Lanka |
| Belgium | West | Mexico | Sudan |
| Botswana | Ghana | Morocco | Suriname |
| Brazil | Greece | Nepal | Swaziland |
| Britain | Guatemala | Netherlands | Sweden |
| Burma | Guinea | New Zealand | Tanzania |
| Burundi | Guyana | Niger | Thailand |
| Cambodia | Haiti | Nigeria | Togo |
| Cameroon | Honduras | Norway | Trinidad & |
| Canada | Iceland | Oman | Tobago |
| Central African | Indonesia | Pakistan | Tunisia |
| Rep. | Iran | Panama | Turkey |
| Chile | Ireland | Papua New | Uganda |
| China | Israel | Guinea | United Arab |
| Colombia | Italy | Paraguay | Emirates |
| Comoros | Ivory Coast | Peru | United States |
| Costa Rica | Jamaica | Philippines | Upper Volta |
| Denmark | Japan | Portugal | Uruguay |
| Djibouti | Jordan | Qatar | Venezuela |
| Dominican | Kenya | Rwanda | Yugoslavia |
| Republic | Kuwait | St. Lucia | Zaire |
| Ecuador | Lebanon | Samoa | Zambia |
| Egypt | Lesotho | Saudi Arabia | |

### Against (22)

| | | | |
|---|---|---|---|
| Afghanistan | Ethiopia | Mongolia | Soviet Union |
| Angola | Germany, East | Mozambique | Syria |
| Bulgaria | Grenada | Poland | Ukraine |
| Byelorussia | Hungary | Sao Tome & | Vietnam |
| Cuba | Laos | Principe | Yemen, South |
| Czechoslovakia | Madagascar | Seychelles | |

### Abstentions (12)

| | | | |
|---|---|---|---|
| Algeria | Congo | Guinea- | Mali |
| Benin | Cyprus | Bissau | Nicaragua |
| Cape Verde | Finland | India | Zimbabwe |
| Chad | | | |

### Absent or Not Voting (9)

| | | | |
|---|---|---|---|
| Bhutan | Iran | St. Vincent | South Africa |
| Bolivia | Libya | & Gren. | Yemen |
| Dominica | Romania | | |

41

slovakia, East Germany, Hungary, Mongolia, Poland, Romania, the Soviet Union, Vietnam, and Cuba on the first level, and also by Afghanistan, Angola, Ethiopia, Laos, Mozambique, South Yemen, and Yugoslavia on the second level.[4])

The nations shown not to be voting in Table 7 represent a variety of ideological viewpoints. Some were simply absent. Others such as Romania no doubt chose to be absent. Such states, together with most of the twelve abstaining states form a group of nations affected in one way or another by the shadow of Soviet power or support, but not yet forced into Moscow's empire. Finland is the now traditional example, but the number of such states in Africa is cause for concern, as is the abstention of India. On the other hand, the willingness of many third world states to condemn the Soviet Union on this resolution indicates their continuing independence.

## SELF-DETERMINATION

A free society allows people individually and collectively to determine their own future. However, in the discussion of freedom, self-determination has come to mean the control by groups over their own collective future. This immediately plunges us into the difficult question of determining the boundaries, spatial or otherwise, of the "group." Surely, as John Stuart Mill pointed out long ago, the most fundamental of individual rights is that of determining with which group to make a political contract. And yet most people ineluctably must live in societies they had no part in choosing. Rejecting the arbitrariness of this situation, new or newly awakened groups demand that political or cultural boundaries be redrawn so that they may achieve a group freedom different from that which history has dealt them.

We have outlined elsewhere the theoretical issues involved in the nationalities question, suggested new terminology, and identified some of the more important ethnic groups striving for enhanced political power or changed affiliations.[5] The tables in these previous studies arranged major subnational peoples alphabetically. In the accompanying table of major peoples with self-determination potential (Table 8) we have reversed that procedure and listed the more important peoples by country. Unlike the previous tables, the present one attempts to include to some extent nonterritorial peoples, such as the American blacks or Hispanics, even though their problems of political self-determination are particularly difficult. This table of major peoples is also generally restricted to relatively large ethnic groups (over one million) that have given some evidence of national consciousness or have come to be treated conventionally as an ethnic unit (for example, American Indians or Vietnamese Montagnards). To be included in the table, an ethnic group must not be politically dominant in a state, nor be a full partner in a binational or tri-national state (such as Belgium or Switzerland). Also partially or entirely excluded are peoples in states that seem to be effectively transethnic, such as Senegal or Papua New Guinea. Rulers of such states are often faced with a plethora of small peoples or nascent nationalities. Where one people emerges as a major issue in such a state (for example, the Ewe of Ghana), this people may be included in the table. In any event, for most countries the ethnic situation is much more complex than the table suggests.

A number of categories in Table 8 raise questions of interpretation. In the table, a low degree of *subnational consciousness* means either that many included in the group do not yet generally identify with the label or others included under the label, or that many in the group take other ethnic or national identities more seriously. For example, a Sard in Italy or an Occitan in France is likely to identify more with Italy and France, respectively, than with the listed subnationality. The *assertion or dissidence* of a subnational people may be in support of more self-determination within the present state *or* in support of the creation of a separate state. Particularly in the case of non-territorial peoples, a desire for separation is unlikely. *Equality of treatment* refers to the extent to which members of the subnational group are treated in the same way as everyone else in the state, or the extent to which the apparent self-determination desires of the people are suppressed or denied by the state.

Table 8 is suggestive rather than definitive. Population figures for ethnic groups are often very imprecise or out-of-date. Definitions of a people are vague enough that the figures are frequently wildly inflated by the group's propagandists and seriously deflated by central governments. Whether a people has political consciousness as a group may be conjectural. In a relatively unfree setting, group identification may be confined to a tiny minority. Often the only binding factor in the prospective national group is opposition to a dominant people, yet it was just such a common opposition by collections of peoples to dominant other peoples that produced many of the nationalities that are recognized today. Italian, Spanish, and Asian Indian nationalisms owe a great deal to such oppositions. In any event, for lack of a better method, collections of minor or primitive peoples are grouped in the table in several cases as subnationalities alongside historically much better known and defined peoples. The Nilotic peoples of the southern Sudan and the Scheduled Tribes of India are two outstanding, if quite different, instances.

The reader will note that there is not a close correlation between how justly or well a people is treated and the strength of its apparent desire for enhanced self-determination. Some of the world's best-treated

# Table 8 Major Peoples with Self-Determination Potential: By Nations

| | Population in Millions with (%) of Total | Subnational Consciousness | Assertion or Dissidence [1] | Equality of Treatment [2] |
|---|---|---|---|---|
| **Afghanistan** | | | | |
| Hazara | 1 (6) | medium | occasional | fair |
| Tajik | 6 (38) | low | slight | good |
| Uzbek | 1.5 (9) | medium | slight | good |
| **Algeria** | | | | |
| Berbers | 4 (21) | medium | cultural | fair |
| **Angola** | | | | |
| Bakongo | 1.5 (22) | medium | occasional | fair |
| Ovimbundu | 2.5 (37) | medium | insurgency | fair |
| **Bangladesh** | | | | |
| Hindus [3] | 17 (19) | high | slight | fair |
| Tribal peoples | 1 (1) | medium | guerrilla war | fair |
| **Bolivia** | | | | |
| Aymara | 1 (19) | low | slight | fair |
| Quechua | 2 (38) | low | slight | fair |
| **Brazil** | | | | |
| Indians | .5 (.4) | high (disunited) | guerrilla war | poor |
| **Bulgaria** | | | | |
| Turks [3] | 1 (11) | medium | slight | poor-fair |
| **Burma** | | | | |
| Karen | 3 (8) | high | insurgency | fair |
| Shan | 2 (6) | high | insurgency | fair |
| Others (Arakanese, Chin, Kachin, Mon, etc.) | 2 (6) | high | insurgency | poor-fair |
| **Burundi** | | | | |
| Hutu [3] | 3.5 (85) | high | occasional | poor |
| **Cameroon** | | | | |
| Bamileke | 2 (24) | medium | occasional | fair |
| Western Region | 1.5 (18) | medium | political | fair |
| **Canada** | | | | |
| French | 6 (25) | high | political | good |
| **India** | | | | |
| Assamese | 11 (1.5) | medium | violent demonstrations | fair-good |
| Bengalis | 53 (8) | medium | none | good |
| Christians [3] | 15[4] (2.2) | high | potential | fair-good |
| Gujeratis | 32 (5) | medium | none | good |
| Kashmiris | 4 (.6) | high | demonstrations (past insurgency) | fair-good |
| Kannada | 28 (4) | medium | none | good |
| Malayalam | 25 (4) | medium | political | good |
| Marathi | 52 (8) | medium | none | good |
| Muslims | 75[4] (11) | high | demonstrations | fair-good |
| Oriyan | 25 (4) | medium | none | good |
| Punjabis | 18 (3) | low | none | good |
| Scheduled castes [3] | 80[4] (12) | medium | demonstrations | fair |
| Scheduled Tribes (Santal, Naga, Mizo, etc.) | 46 (7) | medium-high | passive to insurgency demonstrations | poor-fair |
| Sikhs [3] | 5[4] (.7) | high | political | good |
| Tamil | 48 (7) | medium-high | political | good |
| Telegu | 60 (9) | medium | political | good |
| **Indonesia** | | | | |
| Achenese | 2.5 (1.5) | high | recent guerrilla war | fair |

| Group | Population (millions) (%) | Level | Action | Rating |
|---|---|---|---|---|
| **China (Mainland)** | | | | |
| Chuang | 10 (1) | low | slight | good |
| Hui [3] | 5 (.5) | medium | slight | fair |
| Koreans [3] | 1.5 (.15) | medium | slight | good |
| Miao | 3.5 (.36) | medium | slight | fair |
| Mongols | 2 (.20) | high | potential | poor-fair |
| Tibetans | 3.5 (.36) | high | occasional | fair |
| Uighur | 5.5 (.56) | high | occasional | fair |
| Yi (Lolo) | 4.5 (.46) | medium | none | fair |
| Others | 15 (1.5) | ? | ? | ? |
| **China (Taiwan)** | | | | |
| "Taiwanese" [3] | 15 (85) | medium | agitation | fair |
| **Ecuador** | | | | |
| Indians (Quechua, etc.) | 3 (38) | medium | agitation | fair |
| **Egypt** | | | | |
| Copts [3] | 3-4 (7-10) | high | agitation | fair |
| **Ethiopia** | | | | |
| Eritreans | 2 (6) | high | insurgency | fair |
| Oromo (Galla) | 2-10 (6-30) | medium | guerrilla war | fair |
| Sidamo | 2 (6) | low | guerrilla war | fair |
| Somali | 2 (6) | high | insurgency | fair (?) |
| Tigrinya | 3.5 (11) | medium-high | insurgency | fair |
| **France** | | | | |
| Alsatians | 1 (2) | high | regional agitation | good |
| Basque | .2 (.41) | high | agitation & terror | fair |
| Breton | 1 (2) | high | agitation & terror | fair |
| Corsican | .2 (.37) | high | agitation & terror | fair |
| Occitanian | 2-10 (4-19) | low | none | fair |
| **Ghana** | | | | |
| Ewe | 1.5 (13) | medium | potential | good |
| **Guatemala** | | | | |
| Maya | 3 (43) | low | guerrilla war | poor-fair |
| Batak | 3.5 (2) | medium | agitation (?) | fair |
| Chinese | 3.5 (2) | medium | currently passive | fair |
| Makassarese | 2 (1.5) | low | ? | fair |
| Minahassans | 1 (.7) | medium | ? | good |
| Minangkabau | 6 (4) | medium | ? | good |
| Moluccans (Ambonese) | 1 (.7) | medium | terror (overseas) | fair |
| Papuans | 1 (.7) | medium | guerrilla war | poor-fair |
| Sundanese | 21 (15) | medium | guerrilla war | fair |
| Timorese | 1.5 (1) | low-high | guerrilla war | poor-fair |
| **Iran** | | | | |
| Arabs | .8 (2) | high | guerrilla war | fair |
| Azerbaijani | 7.5 (20) | medium | national partisan | good |
| Kurds | 2 (5) | high | insurgency | fair |
| Baluch | 1 (3) | medium | violent opposition | fair |
| Turkmen | .6 (1.5) | medium | violent opposition? | fair |
| **Iraq** | | | | |
| Kurds | 2 (15) | high | insurgency | poor-fair |
| Shi'ites | 7 (53) | medium | agitation & terror | fair |
| **Israel (including occupied territories)** | | | | |
| Palestinians | 1.5 (30) | high | agitation & terror | fair |
| **Italy** | | | | |
| Sards | 1.5 (3) | low | slight | fair-good |
| **Jordan** | | | | |
| Palestinians [3] | 1 (31) | high | potential | fair |
| **Malaysia** | | | | |
| Chinese [3] | 5 (36) | high | political & guerrilla war | fair |
| East Indian | 1.5 (11) | medium | slight | fair |
| **Mexico** | | | | |
| Indians (Mayan, Nahuatl, etc.) | 5 (7) | low | slight | fair |

# Table 8 (continued)

| | Population in Millions with (%) of Total | Subnational Consciousness | Assertion or Dissidence [1] | Equality of Treatment [2] |
|---|---|---|---|---|
| **Morocco** | | | | |
| Berbers | 6 (29) | low | slight | fair-good |
| Saharaui | .1 (.5) | high | insurgency | fair-good |
| **Mozambique** | | | | |
| Shona (lang.) | 1 (10) | medium | guerrilla war? | good |
| **Nigeria (controversial census)** | | | | |
| Edo | 3 (4) | medium | political | good |
| Ibibio | 3.5 (4) | medium | political | good |
| Ibo | 14 (17) | high | recent insurgency | good |
| Kanuri | 4 (5) | medium | political | good |
| Nupe | 1 (1) | medium | political | good |
| Tiv | 7.5 (10) | medium | political | good |
| Yoruba | 17 (20) | high | political | good |
| **Pakistan** | | | | |
| Ahmadi [3/4] | 1 (1) | high | agitation | poor-fair |
| Baluch | 2.5 (3) | high | recent insurgency | fair |
| Christian [3/4] | 1 (1) | medium | none | fair |
| Hindu | 1 (1) | high | none | fair |
| Pathans | 7 (8) | high | political (armed partisans) | good |
| Sindhi | 10 (12) | medium | political | good |
| **Peru** | | | | |
| Aymara | 1.5 (9) | low | agitation | fair |
| Quechua | 6.5 (37) | low | agitation | fair |
| **Philippines** | | | | |
| Ilocanos | 5 (10) | low | slight | good |
| Muslims | 2 (4) | medium-high | insurgency | fair |
| Pampangans | 1.5 (3) | medium | guerrilla war? | fair |
| Visayans | 14 (29) | low | none | good |

| | Population in Millions with (%) of Total | Subnational Consciousness | Assertion or Dissidence [1] | Equality of Treatment [2] |
|---|---|---|---|---|
| **USSR** | | | | |
| Armenians | 3.5 (1) | high | political | good |
| Azerbaijanis | 5.5 (2) | medium | political | fair-good |
| Bashkir | 1.5 (.6) | low | slight | fair |
| Belorussians | 9.5 (4) | low | slight | fair |
| Estonians | 1 (.4) | high | cultural | fair |
| Georgians | 3.5 (1) | high | political | fair-good |
| Jews [3] | 2 (.75) | medium | emigration | poor-fair |
| Kazakh | 6.5 (2) | medium | slight | fair |
| Kirghiz | 2 (.75) | medium | slight | fair |
| Latvians | 1.5 (.6) | medium | cultural | fair |
| Lithuanians | 3 (1) | high | political & cultural | fair |
| Moldavians | 3 (1) | low | slight | fair |
| Tadzhiks | 3 (1) | low | cultural | fair |
| Tatars (various) | 6 (2) | medium | political | poor |
| Turkmen | 2 (.75) | low | slight | fair |
| Ukrainians | 42 (16) | medium | political & cultural | fair |
| Uzbek | 12.5 (5) | high | cultural | fair-good |
| Polish | 1 (.4) | medium | slight | fair |
| **United Kingdom** | | | | |
| Scots | 5 (9) | medium | political | good |
| Ulster Irish | .5 (.9) | high | political & terror | fair |
| Ulster Scots | 1 (2) | high | political & terror | good |
| **U.S.** | | | | |
| Welsh | 2.5 (5) | medium | cultural | good |
| American Indians | 1 (.5) | high | political | fair-good |
| Blacks [3] | 25 (11) | high (diffuse) | political & cultural & demonstrations | fair-good |
| Puerto Ricans (mainland) [3/4] | 2 (.9) | medium | political | fair-good |
| (island) | 3 (1.5) | medium | political | good |

| | | | | |
|---|---|---|---|---|
| **Romania** | | | | |
| Magyar | 2 (9) | high | cultural | fair |
| **Sierra Leone** | | | | |
| Mende | 1 (29) | medium | political | fair |
| **South Africa** | | | | |
| Asians[3] | 1 (4) | medium | political | poor-fair |
| Blacks (Bantu)[3] | 20 (70) | medium | political & terror | poor |
| Coloureds[3] | 2.5 (9) | high | political | poor-fair |
| **South West Africa** | | | | |
| Blacks | 1 (89) | medium | political & guerrilla war | poor-fair |
| **Spain** | | | | |
| Basque | 1 (3) | high | political | good |
| Catalonians | 6 (16) | high | political | good |
| Galicians | 3 (8) | medium | political & cultural | fair-good |
| **Sri Lanka** | | | | |
| Tamil | 1.5 (11) | high | political & terror | fair-good |
| **Sudan** | | | | |
| Beja | 1.5 (8) | low | mild political | fair-good |
| Southern Blacks (Nilotic peoples) | 5 (27) | medium | political (recent insurgency) | fair-good |
| **Thailand** | | | | |
| Chinese[3] | 5 (11) | medium | none | good |
| Malays | 1 (2) | medium | guerrilla war | fair |
| **Turkey** | | | | |
| Kurds | 3 (7) | medium | terror | poor-fair |
| **Uganda[5]** | | | | |
| Ganda | 2 (15) | high | political & terror | fair |
| Nkole | 1 (7) | low | slight | fair |
| Soga | 1 (7) | low | slight | fair |
| Teso | 1 (7) | low | slight | fair |
| Spanish-speaking | 3/4 10 (5) | medium | political & cultural | fair-good |
| **Vietnam** | | | | |
| Montagnards | 2.5 (5) | medium (diffuse) | guerrilla war | fair |
| **Yugoslavia** | | | | |
| Albanians | 1 (5) | medium | political | fair-good |
| Croats | 5 (22) | high | political | good |
| Macedonians | 1 (5) | medium | political & terror | good |
| Muslims | 2 (9) | medium | slight | good |
| Slovenes | 2 (9) | high | political | good |
| **Zaire[5]** | | | | |
| Bakongo | 3.5 (12) | medium | political | fair |
| Luba-Kasai | 3 (10) | low | occasional insurgency | fair |
| **Zimbabwe** | | | | |
| Ndebele | 1.5 (20) | high | political (armed partisans) | fair-good |

**Notes to the Table**

1. This is in relation to the dominant national people or ruling clique, not foreign occupiers. Often a subnationality claims to have the whole nation's national interest at heart in its dissidence, and credence may be given to this claim.

2. Where conditions of violence do not now permit equal treatment, we judge what the situation would be in peacetime.

3. Nonterritorial. In the case of the Sikhs in India and of South African blacks, only partly nonterritorial.

4. Major overlap with other peoples.

5. Presently no dominant people.

minorities, such as the French of Canada, have been strongest in their
desires for enhanced self-determination. As in other respects, freedom
allows new desires to grow. It is an ever-expanding but at the same time
volatile value to support among nations.

In 1979-80, struggles for group self-determination continued to be
common in every region, but only those few reached world consciousness
that were for one reason or another deemed newsworthy. *Australia* and
*New Zealand* continued to face the challenge of their pre-conquest
peoples. In *Indonesia* the repression of the people of East Timor continued, as did the less publicized occupation of West Irian. The *Philip-
pine* government struggled against several well-established movements,
particularly Muslim separatists in the south and tribal peoples in central
Luzon. *Malaysia* continued to favor the Malays over its large Chinese
minority. It has recently prohibited the establishment of a Chinese
university, and maintains racial quotas for university entrance and a
variety of other positions. In neighboring *Thailand* the small Malay
separatist movement simmered, although Thai policy was hardly
repressive. The ascendancy of the *Vietnamese* people over other ethnic
groups in Indochina intensified during 1979-80 through the occupation
of Cambodia, the continued campaign against the Hmong (Meo) in
Laos, the expulsion of the Chinese, and the suppression of lingering
Montagnard resistance in Vietnam itself.

Mainland *China* improved its treatment of minority peoples in the
period, particularly through increasing reliance on non-Han cadres, the
relaxing of controls on economic activity, and new respect for religious
institutions and beliefs. However, demonstrations in Lhasa suggested
that at least in Tibet a strong desire for enhanced self-determination remained. In *China* (*Taiwan*) the Kuomintang was making another effort
to shift power to the Taiwanese within the party, but demonstrations and
resulting suppressions suggested that there was still a very long way to go.

The well-established subnationalities of *Burma* continued to struggle
for independence, having long since established certain areas of local
autonomy. In *India* the destabilizing struggle of peoples has recently expanded within the democratic context. The Assamese of the Northeast,
together with smaller non-Hindu peoples such as the Nagas, have raised
the intensity of their often violent struggles for self-determination, or at
least enhanced control over their own areas. Their demands are enflamed
by the flood of Bengalis from both Bengal and Bangladesh into their
lands (a flood reflected in *Bangladesh* in the guerrilla struggle of the
peoples of the Chittagong Hills). In a corner of Bengal itself, the
Nepalese demand their own state, a demand fellow Nepalese echo in
nearby Sikkim in struggling for greater self-determination there. Tribal
people in the Indian state of Bihar strive for a state of their own, while
the Indian government must again be concerned with fissiparous tenden-

cies in Kashmir. These are all legitimate demands, yet the response of the Indian government must balance and accommodate these demands with the widely felt need to preserve the stability and integrity of the state. *Sri Lanka*'s problem with its Tamil minority continues amidst accusations of repression.

In *Afghanistan* the major problem of self-determination has shifted from that of the minority peoples against the Pushtu to that of the country as a whole in relation to the USSR. For *Pakistan* the territorial minorities remain dissatisfied within a more than ever repressive society.

The *Soviet Union* remains the largest collection in the world of major peoples denied the right of self-determination. Strict controls make the degree of dissatisfaction, or even of national consciousness, unknowable, but certain peoples—for example, those of the former Baltic republics, the Ukraine, or the Muslim republics—must be presumed to be denied the group self-determination they desire. The commitment of the USSR to the promotion of atheism is an integral part of this denial for these generally religious peoples. It is worth noting, however, that the linguistic self-determination allowed by the USSR is greater than that allowed by the noncommunist states to the south that have restricted or entirely suppressed the use of "non-national" languages in the media or education. New revolutionary regimes in Iran and Afghanistan may or may not improve this situation.

In *Iran*, *Iraq*, and *Turkey* it remains true that the Kurds as well as other tribal peoples are prevented from forging their own political institutions. In 1980 troops battled Kurdish forces in *Iraq* and *Iran*, while in *Turkey* a Marxist party was disbanded largely because it advocated Kurdish language instruction for Kurdish pupils.[6] Similar in intensity to the Kurdish desire for self-determination is that of the Baluch in *Iran*, *Pakistan*, and *Afghanistan*, or the Arabs in southwestern *Iran*. The peoples of *Lebanon* strive more successfully for self-determination within an anarchical context, while the desire for self-rule of the Palestinians of *Israel* and of the occupied territories remains largely repressed. A rather different problem has arisen in those *sheikhdoms* of the Persian Gulf in which indigenous citizens have become greatly outnumbered by immigrants who must live without many of the benefits of their new societies.

Recently the Coptic Christians of *Egypt* have had to contend with considerable repression. On *Cyprus* the Greek-speaking population has received much less than its rightful share in the *de facto* division of the island. *Sudanese* policy toward its southern peoples continues to be marked by a good deal of success and justice. Recent moves to further decentralize the country have enhanced the self-determination of a larger number of territorial peoples in this highly diversified country. *Algeria* continues to fail to meet the aspirations of its increasingly assertive

Berber minority for at least cultural self-determination. The situation in *Morocco*'s recently conquered Western Sahara remains unclear. Shifting tribal populations make the definition of a Saharaui group unclear; the guerrillas may or may not represent the wishes of the majority of Western Sahara's people, a people ethnically almost indistinguishable from Moroccans. Significantly, the proposal of a supervised election has been rejected by both sides.

South of the Sahara the patterns of ethnic oppression are so many and intricate that we can only mention the more significant. *Ethiopia* continues to try to force its many quite different peoples to remain within a unified state. The resulting loss of life and suffering for the Eritreans, Somalis, and others is incalculable. The small Somali tribes of *Kenya* suffer increased pressures because of the conflicting loyalties in which they are trapped. This fall the Kenyan parliament ordered all tribal organizations dissolved. This is understandable in an African state, but reflects scorn for the affiliations of most Kenyans. Ethnic and tribal strains have torn *Chad* apart, and the pieces do not seem to go back together. The south may desire a permanent ethnic division. Like Ethiopia, *Zaire*'s attempt to enforce centralized rule enhances oppression. For the moment, *Nigeria*'s intricate attempt to secure a large measure of local and regional autonomy within a federal structure offers a useful model for other African countries. An active dissident movement in *Cameroon* would like to see a return to a federal solution for at least the English-speaking portion of the country.

In several states authoritarian military rule rests on the recruitment of soldiers or government leaders from particular tribes or areas, with consequent reduction of the self-determination of other peoples. Idi Amin's tribal system in *Uganda* has been destroyed, but what follows is unclear. *De facto* domination by militant tribes continues in *Togo* and *Congo*. More serious is the discriminatory rule in *Burundi* by a minority elite group. Continued guerrilla war in *Angola* is based partly on ethnic differences between rulers and ruled. It is yet another country where the boundaries are really those of colonial empires that were defined with little reference to local aspirations or distinctions. In *Mozambique* an insurgency continues among the Shona-speaking peoples.

South African control in *South West Africa* (Namibia) restricts the self-determination of a variety of black peoples, especially the Ovambo, a significant section of which are engaged in a continuing guerrilla war. More serious is the denial of self-determination to the majority nonwhite population in *South Africa*. Although there have been recent improvements, and moderate nonwhite opposition may now be more openly expressed, the majority remains severely repressed both in its political rights and civil liberties. The inability of South Africa to move further in civil liberties without also surrendering control to the majority is a classic illustration of the close interconnection of political and civil rights.

In Europe the primary denial of self-determination is really that imposed by the Soviet Union on its Eastern European satellites. Within this orbit, *Romania* in turn denies self-determination to its Hungarian minority. *Yugoslavia* certainly grants more self-determination to its constituent peoples than the USSR, but the degree to which its peoples are treated evenhandedly is still determined from the top down rather than by the free choice of the peoples themselves.

In 1978-79 the *United Kingdom* went through the exercise of offering enhanced self-determination to the Welsh and Scots, only to have these peoples fail to muster the votes necessary for ratification. To a degree, especially in Wales, this was due to the previous overwhelming of local populations by centuries of outside dominance. The tragedy of Northern Ireland goes on, with the English caught between the demands of intransigent peoples. *France* faces a number of self-determination movements, both in its few remaining overseas colonies and at home. The Bretons and Corsicans have been especially active. Democracy in *Spain* has shown its willingness to grant the demands of its many ethnic groups. The Basques and Catalonians have been given considerable autonomy, although the former have an extreme fringe that is still far from satisfied. Progress has also been made toward granting similar autonomy to other groups, such as the Galicians and Andalusians. Throughout Europe millions of *Gypsies* (and quasi-Gypsies such as the Tinkers of Ireland) continue to suffer discrimination as a people apart. The movement of workers has exacerbated ethnic relations throughout the continent.

In 1980 *Canada* held a referendum that showed that the majority of Quebeçois are satisfied with the very considerable autonomy they already have. The blacks in the *United States* have largely been incorporated into the political process. The same might be said of Hispanics, except that the continued drift of Spanish-speaking peoples into the United States, both legally and illegally, leaves a large proportion of this highly mobile population inadequately represented in legislatures or defended by legal structures. The degree and means of rectifying this situation in a manner fair to other Americans is debatable. The question of self-determination for *Puerto Rico* has been raised in new forms, both because of international attention and new pressures within the Commonwealth. The people have long enjoyed a high degree of self-determination and rejected independence. The issue of most interest to current voters is the possibility of statehood. Recently, American Indians and Eskimos have continued to receive or anticipate substantial additional compensation for their lands. Most notably, the Sioux were offered a substantial settlement for the Black Hills, and the Penabscots for a section of Maine.

Further south the struggle of the elite to maintain dominance in *Guatemala* has been to a degree the struggle of Mayan peasants against the descendants of Spanish settlers. Small Indian groups in *Brazil, Colombia*, and *Paraguay* continue to suffer under the pressure of advancing settlement, but the Andean Indian peasants in *Ecuador, Peru*, and *Bolivia* have come to play a larger role in their respective societies in recent years.

### CONCLUSION

During 1980 there were many declines in the ability of struggling dissident movements to express opposition opinion—most notably in the Soviet Union, South Korea, Haiti, Libya, East Germany, Syria, Iran, Guatemala, and El Salvador. However, mainland China presented a complex picture of gains and losses that suggested a basis for democratic resurgence. The democratic hopes of Bolivia were crushed; democratic Suriname and not so democratic Liberia succumbed to military coups. Freedom was on the retreat in Seychelles and Zambia. There were partially offsetting gains. Democracy took important forward steps in Ghana, Honduras, Nepal, Thailand, and Vanuatu. Zimbabwe attained full black rule, but its advance in freedom was more tenuous. In Iraq absolutist rule was relaxed by a locally competitive election. The willingness of Uruguay's military to hold a reasonably fair referendum on its authoritarian constitution was unprecedented and encouraging.

Two major gains for the year were in Peru and Poland. This was the year of the Polish worker. It is regrettable that achieving the right of workers to organize their own unions in twentieth-century Europe should have been a great achievement for freedom. Yet in the Eastern European context this was a significant if still embattled gain, one that reverberated through many other sectors of Polish society. Peru held successful general elections, joining Ecuador, Venezuela, and Costa Rica as democratic leaders of Latin America.

The world continued to fail to devise means to respond adequately to the rising tide of struggles of emerging peoples for their own laws and cultures. While significant adjustments to such demands have taken place in recent years in democracies such as the United States, Canada, the United Kingdom, Switzerland, India, and Spain, it remains hardly possible to point to a single example of a state dividing in response to the demand for self-determination. There are hundreds of examples of continued repression of this demand in defense of centralized, and too often inefficient and barbarous governments, and the dominant peoples they represent.

## NOTES

1. For more discussion of methodology *see* R. D. Gastil, *Freedom in the World: Political Rights and Civil Liberties, 1978* (New York: Freedom House and G. K. Hall, 1978), especially pp. 7-30.

2. Raymond Aron, "My Defense of Our Decadent Europe," *Encounter* (September 1977), pp. 7-50, especially p. 33.

3. *New York Times*, November 21, 1980.

4. *Keesing's Contemporary Archives*, November 21, 1980, p. 30588.

5. *See* Raymond D. Gastill, *Freedom in the World, 1978*, pp. 180-215, and the tabular material and discussion of the current situation, pp. 48-60; and also *Freedom in the World: Political Rights and Civil Liberties, 1979* (New York: Freedom House and G. K. Hall, 1979), pp. 45-57. Since these publications, the following works have been found useful: Dov Ronen, *The Quest for Self-Determination* (New Haven: Yale University Press, 1979); Meic Stephens, *Linguistic Minorities in Western Europe* (Llandysul, Wales: Gomer Press, 1976); O. McCagg, Jr. and B. Silver, eds., *Soviet Asian Ethnic Frontiers* (New York: Pergamon, 1979); Raymond Hall, ed., *Ethnic Autonomy—Comparative Dynamics* (New York: Pergamon, 1979); and Georgina Ashworth, ed., *World Minorities* (2 vols.) (Sunbury, U.K.: Minority Rights Group, 1977, 1978).

6. *Keesing's Contemporary Archives*, October 31, 1980, p. 30543.

# PART II

# Press Freedom

# Freedom of the Press: A Personal Account of the Continuing Struggle

## Leonard R. Sussman

R uth, a character in a Tom Stoppard play, says, "I'm with you on the free press. It's the newspapers I can't stand."[1]

Many readers and viewers in free societies would also fight to the death for press freedom, yet yearn for better news coverage. I know of no journalist who insists that news reporting—particularly foreign correspondence—cannot be improved. In the decade-long controversies over the restructuring of the flow of international news, the main issue is no longer whether coverage of the developing countries can be improved (it always can be). The central issue now is whether the news media that operate free of governmental controls should be restricted and assigned political or social objectives.

The history of these controversies was outlined in our 1980 *Freedom in the World.*[2] For most of the past ten years the challenges to the mass news media were differentiated both in origin and intent. The Marxist bloc has wanted the world news services to be re-created in the image of TASS. Many third world governments that control their domestic journalists sought similar shackles for transnational journalism. Two dozen free or partly free developing countries express dissatisfaction with present world-news systems but do not actively seek governmental controls for them. Yet the cacophony at international meetings sounds to independent journalists as though even the moderate pleas for improved coverage are a cloak for ultimate governmental control of worldwide journalism.

The 1980-81 period is a watershed. The biennial general conferences of the United Nations Educational, Scientific and Cultural Organization (UNESCO) have come to be seen as flash points of the controversies. From 1976 at Nairobi through Paris and Belgrade two and four years later, third world expectations rose higher before each month-long debate. A few Western European governments and the United States prepared increasingly before each biennial to meet the challenges. Western strategies included contacting many developing countries in advance of the UNESCO conferences, explaining once again the actual independence of the news media from the Western governments, pleading for moderation in the debate and resolutions, and quietly promising to transfer some communication technology to third world nations.

We shall describe here the outcome of the 1980 UNESCO general conference, after setting that debate in the broader ideological context. For it now appears that the controversies may have come full circle. What began in 1970 as a minor assault by the Soviet Union on the American freedom radios broadcasting into the USSR and Eastern Europe has become a far broader third world challenge. The purely Soviet national aspect has diminished. But the ideological nature of the clash persists. The Marxist definitions of the function of information, including journalism, illuminate and confuse third world perceptions of transnational news reporting. While the Marxist analysis may not be adopted in most third world countries, their perception of journalism as a closely held responsibility and tool of the regime nevertheless threatens freedom in many parts of the world.

We shall describe how the Marxist style of journalism was carried this year into a particular area of the news media controversies—a conference at UNESCO on the "protection of journalists"—and how this, in turn, was indicative of the main thrust of decisions taken last year at UNESCO/Belgrade.


## OBJECTIVITY VS. JOURNALISM WITH IDEOLOGICAL OBJECTIVES

The years of news media controversies come down to the question: What is the primary function of journalism? Put differently, what is the political or philosophical basis of the state in which a particular journalistic style originates? For the nature of journalism in any society meshes with the social and political structure. That truism is repeatedly demonstrated. Protagonists of government-controlled journalism act most of the time as though a single philosophy—theirs—must ultimately prevail. And built into the argumentation for government-directed news flow is an evangelical sense of purpose, almost eschatological in its finality. Free-flow advocates are seldom as ardent. Rarely do they project the positive values of press freedom. They speak defensively. They have no sophisticated campaign designed to enlarge the company of free journalists and free societies.[3]

Free-flow advocates speaking as representatives of democratic governments must emphasize the gap between journalism and the state in their nations. That tends to ensure a bland recitation, one not widely believed in any event by listeners from countries whose regimes dominate their news media as a matter of course. The press defenders of objectivity in journalism are faced with inevitable examples of the imperfectibility of their own systems. Financial, political, cultural, psychological and other influences doubtless affect foreign and domestic news coverage. It is difficult to describe the contrapuntal influences, the alternative media, the counterculture, and the considerable diversity that provide the choices for readers, listeners and viewers in, say, American society. These choices are the safety valves of independent news media systems. Nothing like them exists outside the twenty-five percent of countries that have both a free press and free broadcast services (see Table 9 below).

It is useful, then, to examine four "primers" recently published by the Soviet bloc for training not only their journalists but others from the developing countries. The paperback volumes, between sixty and ninety pages each, have been published by the International Organization of Journalists (IOJ), a Soviet front headquartered in Prague. The authors are Czech, Russian, and Bulgarian.[4]

Early in the series, the Dean of the Faculty of Journalism of Charles University, Prague, discusses what he calls the "attributes of journalism." He finds the most fundamental distinction between the two journalistic systems that he sees as components of opposite political systems.

He asserts that, "Journalism in an abstract form does not exist. It is always concrete, linked with a certain social class whose interests it more or less precisely expresses, defends, and espouses." Journalism, says the author, "cannot be 'independent' of society. . . . It cannot be 'uncommitted' to topical social problems, because it would lose its purpose and cease to be journalism at all." "Faithfulness to facts," he adds, "requires that topical problems should be presented precisely in terms of concrete evidence"—no quarrel there with the free-flow advocate's goal of objectivity. But then the author adds that the "facts" should be presented "with a party bias [to provide] the 'ardent evidence of the facts themselves,' and not in a detached objectivistic way." (The Party, in other words, is to decide the proper selection and interpretation of the "facts" so that the journalist can prepare an "ardent" report. Nothing is left to the journalist's objectivity and the reader's detachment.)

Journalism is described as an "expressly ideological" phenomenon. It "socially orients the public, formulates and expresses its different social opinions, attitudes and deeds, its world outlook, gives an idea of the manifold contemporary phenomena, processes and tendencies in all complexity, of the laws determining the function and development of economic, socio-political, intellectual and ideological life of society—all from respective class positions."

# Table 9
# News Media Control by Countries

| | Generally Free[1] | Partly Free[1] | Generally Not Free[1] | Gov't News Agency[2] | Civil Liberties[3] |
|---|---|---|---|---|---|
| Afghanistan | | | PB | X | 7 |
| Albania | | | PB | X | 7 |
| Algeria | | | PB | X | 6 |
| Angola | | | PB | X | 7 |
| Argentina | | P | B | X | 5 |
| Australia | PB | | | X | 1 |
| Austria | PB | | | X | 1 |
| Bahamas | P | B | | | 2 |
| Bahrain | | | PB | X | 5 |
| Bangladesh | P | B | | X | 4 |
| Barbados | P | B | | X | 1 |
| Belgium | PB | | | X | 1 |
| Benin | | | PB | X | 6 |
| Bhutan | | | PB | | 5 |
| Bolivia | | P | B | X | 5 |
| Botswana | P | B | | | 2 |
| Brazil | P | B | | X | 3 |
| Bulgaria | | | PB | X | 7 |
| Burma | | | PB | X | 6 |
| Burundi | | | PB | X | 6 |
| Cameroon | | | PB | X | 6 |
| Canada | PB | | | | 1 |
| Cape Verde Islands | | | PB | | 6 |
| Central African Rep. | | PB | | | 5 |
| Chad | | | PB | X | 6 |
| Chile | | PB | | X | 5 |
| China (Mainland) | | | PB | X | 6 |
| China (Taiwan) | | PB | | | 5 |
| Colombia | PB | | | X | 3 |
| Congo | | | PB | X | 6 |
| Costa Rica | PB | | | | 1 |
| Cuba | | | PB | X | 6 |
| Cyprus | P | B | | X | 3 |
| Czechoslovakia | | | PB | X | 6 |
| Denmark | PB | | | X | 1 |
| Dominica | PB | | | | 2 |
| Dominican Rep. | P | B? | | | 3 |
| Ecuador | PB | | | X | 2 |

**Notes to the Table**

1. P designates print media; B designates broadcast (radio and TV) media. Print media refers primarily to domestic newspapers and news magazines. Countries in which the media are too little developed or for which there is insufficient information to include in this table are: Comoro Islands, Djibouti, Kiribati, Rwanda, Solomon Islands, Tuvalu, Vanuatu, and Western Samoa.

2. X designates the presence of a government news agency, with or without the availability of private news services also.

3. See Table 1, pp. 14-17.

| | Generally Free[1] | Partly Free[1] | Generally Not Free[1] | Gov't News Agency[2] | Civil Liberties[3] |
|---|---|---|---|---|---|
| Egypt | | P | B | X | 5 |
| El Salvador | | PB | | | 5 |
| Equatorial Guinea | | | PB | | 6 |
| Ethiopia | | | PB | X | 7 |
| Fiji | PB | | | | 2 |
| Finland | P | B | | X | 2 |
| France | P | B | | X | 2 |
| Gabon | | | PB | X | 6 |
| Gambia | PB | | | | 3 |
| Germany (E) | | | PB | X | 7 |
| Germany (W) | PB | | | X | 2 |
| Ghana | | PB | | X | 3 |
| Greece | PB? | | | X | 2 |
| Grenada | | | PB | | 5 |
| Guatemala | | PB | | X | 5 |
| Guinea | | | PB | | 7 |
| Guinea-Bissau | | | PB | | 6 |
| Guyana | | PB | | X | 4 |
| Haiti | | | PB | | 6 |
| Honduras | PB | | | | 3 |
| Hungary | | | PB | X | 5 |
| Iceland | PB | | | | 1 |
| India | P | B | | X | 3 |
| Indonesia | | P | B | X | 5 |
| Iran | | PB | | X | 5 |
| Iraq | | | PB | X | 7 |
| Ireland | PB | | | | 1 |
| Israel | PB | | | | 2 |
| Italy | PB | | | X | 2 |
| Ivory Coast | | P | B | X | 5 |
| Jamaica | P | | B | | 3 |
| Japan | PB | | | X | 1 |
| Jordan | | | PB | X | 6 |
| Kampuchea | | | PB | X | 7 |
| Kenya | | P | B | X | 4 |
| Korea (N) | | | PB | X | 7 |
| Korea (S) | | | PB | X | 6 |
| Kuwait | | P | B | X | 4 |
| Laos | | | PB | X | 7 |
| Lebanon | | PB | | X | 4 |
| Lesotho | | PB | | | 5 |
| Liberia | | | PB | | 6 |
| Libya | | | PB | X | 7 |
| Luxembourg | PB | | | | 1 |
| Madagascar | | | PB | X | 6 |
| Malawi | | | PB | X | 7 |
| Malaysia | | P | B | X | 4 |
| Maldives | | P | B | | 5 |
| Mali | | | PB | X | 6 |
| Malta | | PB? | | X | 3 |
| Mauritania | | | PB | X | 6 |
| Mauritius | PB | | | | 3 |

**Table 9** *(continued)*

| | Generally Free[1] | Partly Free[1] | Generally Not Free[1] | Gov't News Agency[2] | Civil Liberties[3] |
|---|---|---|---|---|---|
| Mexico | | PB | | X | 4 |
| Mongolia | | | PB | X | 7 |
| Morocco | | P | B? | X | 4 |
| Mozambique | | | PB | X | 7 |
| Nauru | PB | | | | 2 |
| Nepal | | P | B | X | 4 |
| Netherlands | PB | | | X | 1 |
| New Zealand | PB | | | X | 1 |
| Nicaragua | P | B | | | 5 |
| Niger | | | PB | | 6 |
| Nigeria | P | B | | X | 3 |
| Norway | PB | | | X | 1 |
| Oman | | | PB | | 6 |
| Pakistan | | | PB | X | 5 |
| Panama | P | B | | X | 4 |
| Papua New Guinea | PB | | | | 2 |
| Paraguay | | PB | | | 5 |
| Peru | PB | | | X | 3 |
| Philippines | | P | B | X | 5 |
| Poland | | P | B | X | 4 |
| Portugal | PB | | | X | 2 |
| Qatar | | | PB | X | 5 |
| Romania | | | PB | X | 6 |
| St. Lucia | PB | | | | 2 |
| St. Vincent | P | B? | | | 2 |
| Sao Tome & Principe | | | PB | | 6 |
| Saudi Arabia | | | PB | X | 6 |
| Senegal | | PB | | X | 4 |
| Seychelles | | | PB | | 6 |
| Sierra Leone | | | PB | | 5 |
| Singapore | | | PB | | 5 |
| Somalia | | | PB | X | 7 |
| South Africa | | P | B | | 6 |
| Spain | PB | | | X | 3 |
| Sri Lanka | P?B? | | | X | 3 |
| Sudan | | | PB | X | 5 |
| Suriname | | | PB | | 5 |
| Swaziland | | | PB | | 5 |
| Sweden | PB | | | X | 1 |
| Switzerland | PB | | | X | 1 |
| Syria | | | PB | X | 7 |
| Tanzania | | | PB | X | 6 |
| Thailand | | P | B | X | 4 |
| Togo | | | PB | X | 6 |
| Tonga | | | PB | | 3 |
| Transkei | | | PB | | 5 |
| Trinidad &Tobago | PB | | | | 2 |
| Tunisia | | P | B | X | 5 |
| Turkey | | P | B | X | 5 |

**Table 9** *(continued)*

| | Generally Free[1] | Partly Free[1] | Generally Not Free[1] | Gov't News Agency[2] | Civil Liberties[3] |
|---|---|---|---|---|---|
| Uganda | | PB | | X | 4 |
| USSR | | | PB | X | 7 |
| United Arab Emirates | | P | B | X | 5 |
| United Kingdom | PB | | | X | 1 |
| United States | PB | | | | 1 |
| Upper Volta | | PB | | X | 5 |
| Uruguay | | PB | | | 5 |
| Venezuela | PB | | | X | 2 |
| Vietnam | | | PB | X | 7 |
| Yemen (N) | | | PB | X | 5 |
| Yemen (S) | | | PB | X | 7 |
| Yugoslavia | | | PB | X | 5 |
| Zaire | | | PB | X | 6 |
| Zambia | | P | B | X | 6 |
| Zimbabwe Rhodesia | | P | B | | 4 |

## Table Summary

| | Countries (general rating) | | Print Media | | Broadcast Media | |
|---|---|---|---|---|---|---|
| | No. | % | No. | % | No. | % |
| Free | 51 | 31.5 | 52 | 34 | 37 | 24 |
| Partly free | 51 | 31.5 | 37 | 24 | 31 | 20 |
| Not free | 60 | 37 | 65 | 42 | 86 | 56 |
| | 162 | 100 | 154[1] | 100 | 154[1] | 100 |

This table suggests that governments in three-fouths of the world have a significant or dominant voice in determining what does or does not appear in the media. The definition of media control does not include regulation such as that practiced by the FCC; government control means control over newspaper or broadcast *content*. In some countries particular media (often broadcasting) may be government financed and indirectly government-managed like BBC, but still be regarded as largely free of government control of content.

In only one-fourth of the nations are both the print and broadcast media generally free; the press is free in one-third. Newspapers tend to be freer than radio or TV. The press is partly free in twenty-four percent, not free in forty-two percent; broadcasting in partly free in twenty percent, not free in fifty-six percent of the nations.

Nearly a half-century ago there were thirty-nine national news services in twenty-eight countries. Seventy percent of these were at least nominally independent of government (Robert Desmond, *The Press and World Affairs*, Appleton-Century, 1937). Today there are 105. The number of government-operated news services has increased rapidly in the past five years in consequence of recommendations made by UNESCO. Sixty-eight percent of the nations have a government news agency: eighty-one percent of the not free, sixty-eight percent of the partly free, and fifty-seven percent of the free countries. Of nations with the lowest civil liberties rating (7), ninety-five percent operate government news agencies. National news agencies often use the world news services of the transnational Western media or TASS. They may then decide what world news may be distributed inside the country. Some national news agencies assign themselves the sole right to secure domestic news for distribution inside or outside the country.

All of this, of course, requires the most centralized control of all media by the state apparatus. The author, as expected, ignores the diverse ownership and competitiveness of "bourgeois journalism." He says all independent media are under "state monopoly capitalism"—a definition that fits Fascist Spain and several third world states today but hardly the developed West.

The author attempts a distinction: "*here* we are, of course, mainly concerned with journalism as an ideological and political institution, and in capitalism also as a profit-making enterprise." Both systems serve ideologies, he says, only one seeks to make money at it. For us, the difference remains: "Capitalist" journalism strives for (though does not always achieve) nonideological, nonpolitically committed reportage. "Socialist" journalism, by its own definition, cannot so strive. The former regards pluralism as an advantage in a mature society; the latter does not risk presenting its people with diverse reports or views. Perhaps Lenin, cited by one primer's author, put it best: Soviet power, he said, must "transfer the press from an organ that predominantly announces political news into an important organ of the economic education of the masses . . . an instrument (of state policy)."

### DEMOCRACY AND "RESPONSIVE DEMOCRACY"

Orwellian transference of terms is especially apparent in the news media debates at UNESCO. While in Belgrade for the 1980 general conference I visited the writer Milovan Djilas.[5] Crossing the river from the conference area to the Djilas's residence my wife and I felt we had visited two Belgrades—the unreal, where UNESCO delegates from mostly authoritarian nations debated the "democratization of information"; the real, the closely watched home of Djilas. He had fought beside Tito, had served as Vice-President of Yugoslavia, and was imprisoned for nine years after criticizing communist tyranny. He is still attacked by state journalists and made a pariah who few but informers will visit. He is, he says, "a nonperson."

The personages at the other Belgrade spoke endlessly of governments' "balancing" the world's news flow, and freeing developing countries from Western news "monopolies" that serve the military-industrial complex.

After pleading for press freedom at the conference where the third world and its communist supporters were calling for a "new world information order," I walked to Mr. Djilas's apartment. The city's grayness contrasted with the colorful conference center, its acres of comfortable discussion space and advanced systems for processing words. That talk factory transformed the *good* words (freedom, democracy, free flow of information) into their opposites (*guided* freedom, *responsive* democracy, *balanced* flow). In Mr. Djilas's apartment one sees the consequence: Perversion of the language of liberty leads to the loss of physical freedom.

At the conference the Yugoslav delegate said that news "must be put to the service of men and women." State intervention thus is needed, the

Algerian elaborated, but denied that it meant a loss of freedom. Only the state by affecting the "intent and nature" of information can balance news reports, declared the East German, while the Tanzanian said his country's press mobilized the people for economic development. Vietnam, restricting "useless and harmful" information, expects journalists to protect the "sovereign rights" of the countries. Cuba called the "First Amendment argument" used by the United States press "arrogant nonsense."

Mr. Djilas bears witness to such distortions. He is oppressed, though he would not replace the communist structure of his country forcibly; rather, he wants Yugoslavia to evolve into a freer society. He has written about the foibles and failures of Stalin and Tito, but his words are banned inside Yugoslavia. His books published abroad are confiscated at the border.

Until dissent from official views is printed and spoken, there can be no free flow of ideas in Yugoslavia. For such speech, more than 200 people were jailed last year, Mr. Djilas says. Ninety percent of the 600 political prisoners are punished for "verbal crimes." Speaking to two or three persons can lead to a 12-year term; often one listener turns informer. Thus, few risk speaking to Mr. Djilas.

Years ago, he was propaganda minister. He sought an open society, personal freedom, and pluralism. He opposed censorship and advocated broader coverage of foreign news. The press still reports Hollywood gossip but only Western political views that do not undercut a Yugoslav position. Three foreign correspondents were recently detained and expelled. Like other authoritarian governments, Yugoslavia's buys Western press reports, selects news deemed suitable for the public, and passes the rest only to the elite. The people receive mainly "good" news about politically friendly states and "bad" news about the unfriendly. "We must wait until an Idi Amin goes before we learn the truth," says Mr. Djilas.

UNESCO is creating a program to transfer communications technology to developing countries. Certainly the democratic West should help politically free third-world nations and those moving toward broader freedoms. They need better domestic communciations and improved coverage of development news for audiences everywhere. Yet, the Soviet delegate said, "technology is not neutral—it always brings a certain ideology." Clearly, the Soviet Union so conceives its technology transfers. A new program should not move ideology with technology.

The depersonalization of a Djilas could occur in many countries that plead for better communications. Their governments guide, harass, censor, jail, expel, and occasionally kill journalists.

Stefania Djilas, his wife, showed me a wall displaying precious reminders: a memorial to Mr. Djilas's family killed in World War II, some photos, and a plaque presented to him in New York in 1968. That was the Freedom Award. I had not seen it since Freedom House presented it twelve years earlier. The plaque read: "Heroic leader and rebel—his reason and conscience turned him against tyranny." In these twelve years, Djilas has earned the award many times over. He could easily have crossed the river into that other Belgrade and mouthed the "democratic" litany of the authoritarian elites.

## "Protection"—What's It Worth?

In the 1930s gangs often intimidated an entire industry. The "fix" began when the swaggering hit men called on a defenseless storekeeper. He was advised that crime in the neighborhood was increasing, and his shop needed "insurance." That gang, of course, would maintain the peace—if paid off. If not, a firebomb—or worse—would shatter the building. The racket was called "protection."

That is, of course, not quite analogous to the "protection of journalists" offered increasingly through UNESCO. Yet there are some similarities. News reporters are being urged to accept protection when away from their homelands. Yet most journalists killed or severely injured on assignment are victims of governmental or counter-governmental terror or violence. As with gangland protection, the journalistic victim is asked to participate in his own victimization. He is told by governments that he will be protected if he pays a certain price: He must demonstrate "responsibility" by reporting in ways that serve predetermined objectives set down by government. The price is high. It amounts to the loss of professional integrity and journalistic freedom.

The protection of journalists is not a new concern. Only recently has its honorable history been co-opted, as have other noble objectives, by those who would exploit legitimate complaints about journalistic performance or physical threats to journalists. The disappearance of war correspondents in Korea and Vietnam in the fifties and sixties, and under conditions of civil conflict in Africa and Latin America in the seventies, motivated several journalist organizations to consider some form of protection.

The Geneva Convention of 1949 provides that journalists working in areas of armed conflict shall be regarded by the combatants as civilians and protected as such as long as they do not take any action to alter their civilian status. The General Assembly of the United Nations adopted a resolution in 1970 "to give the highest priority" to the protection of journalists. The UN Human Rights Commission in 1971 offered a preliminary draft of an international convention. It would have provided a "safety card" and a safety committee that would issue the card to persons duly accredited as journalists. The safety committee could withhold a card from an applicant "without giving reasons." The card, in effect, would become a license to work as a journalist: withholding it, for whatever reason, would deprive a person of livelihood and perhaps alter news reporting. In subsequent sessions of the UN increasingly complex provisions were added to drafts to define a "journalist," control the licensing, and establish supervisory procedures for policing the protective mechanism. One draft article would have required the journalist to carry a card stipulating that the bearer shall not "interfere in the domestic affairs of the receiving state." Any article filled by a foreign correspondent can be locally interpreted as "interference" and used to invalidate the protection procedure, expedite the writer's expulsion, or worse.

Pressure for a formal international convention on protection of journalists inevitably drew together three formidable proponents: 1. communication specialists in the UNESCO secretariat, 2. delegations at UNESCO representing press-control states, and 3. Sean MacBride, the former Irish political leader who headed the International Commission of Jurists and later UNESCO's International Commission for the Study of Communication Problems (the MacBride Commission).

Throughout the two-year life of his commission MacBride repeatedly tried to persuade his fifteen colleagues to include in their report a recommendation for some protection for journalists. The comission not only rejected MacBride's pleas but said in recommendation Number 50:

> The professional independence and integrity of all those involved in the collection and dissemination of news, information and views to the public should be safeguarded. However, the Commission does not propose special privileges to protect journalists in the performance of their duties, although journalism is often a dangerous profession. Far from constituting a special category, journalists are citizens of their respective countries, entitled to the same range of human rights as other citizens. One exception is provided in the Additional Protocol to the Geneva Conventions of 12 August 1949, which applies only to journalists on perilous missions, such as in areas of armed conflict. To propose additional measures would invite the dangers entailed in a licensing system since it would require somebody to stipulate who should be entitled to claim such protection. Journalists will be fully protected only when everyone's human rights are guaranteed.[6]

To this, MacBride appended a footnote:

> I consider this paragraph quite inadequate to deal with what is a serious position. Because of the importance of the role of journalists and others who provide or control the flow of news to the media, I urge that they should be granted a special status and protection. I also urge that provi-

sions should be made to enable a journalist to appeal against a refusal of reasonable facilities. My views on these issues are embodied in a paper entitled *The Protection of Journalists* (CIC Document No. 90) which I submitted to the Commission; I refer in particular to paragraphs 1-17 and 335-53 of this paper.

MacBride's personal paper, together with the one-sentence recommendation Number 51 of the MacBride Commission, ran counter to the view expressed in the preceding paragraph. Number 51 urged the convening of "round tables" to "propose additional appropriate measures" on journalists' protection. So MacBride perservered, as he told this writer he would. "Some day," he said in 1978, "there will be international provision for the protection of journalists. It must come."

To bring that day closer, UNESCO arranged a consultative meeting in Paris, February 16-17, 1981. It asked Pierre Gaborit, professor of political science at the University of Paris-Nord, to prepare the only background paper for the meeting. The paper proposed the establishment of an international commission and periodic international conferences for the protection of journalists. UNESCO initially invited to this consultation representatives of nine nongovernmental groups mainly from the Soviet bloc and activist third world associations. Upon the insistence of the U.S. Department of State, invitations were extended just days before the meeting to four Western press representatives. The views of the nine initial participants, not the four later arrivals, were clearly reflected in the Gaborit paper.

Gaborit outlined the three areas of controversy: 1. the role of states, 2. the definition of a journalist, and 3. "the existence of 'duties' to be observed if not by individual journalists at least by the journalistic profession as a whole."

The definition of a journalist must be both "unambiguous and flexible," Gaborit said. Unambiguous in order to secure state protection, yet flexible to accommodate changing experience. He avoids reopening the debate on the duties of journalists that dominated earlier discussions at UNESCO and elsewhere. Yet this is the heart of the matter. Proponents of UNESCO-style protection generally insist on a *quid pro quo*: physical protection must be accompanied by the fulfillment of journalistic "responsibility." A series of Soviet-sponsored resolutions since 1970 has endeavored to describe the "uses" of the mass news media, and the social and political objectives journalists are to be expected to fulfill. Gaborit preferred to mention this requirement only briefly. He doubted, however, that it would be possible to "claim protection for journalists or even to ask states to facilitate their working conditions" if there was a risk they would use journalism "as a pretext for committing acts" of espionage or "illicit propaganda." Virtually any report found displeasing to a Ministry of Information in an oppressive state can be dubbed "illicit propaganda." And, of course, it is mainly in oppressive states that a journalist would need protection.

Gaborit moved on to the accompanying stipulation: creation of a code of journalistic ethics that would provide the standard for determining whether a journalist is fulfilling his "deontological responsibilities" under the "protection" scheme (using UNESCO language—deontology is the field of ethics dealing with duty, moral obligation, and "right" action). Also linked in Gaborit's outline are "the right-of-correction and the rights of journalists on dangerous missions." In other words, governments will demand the right to "correct" a correspondent's report in return for the protection granted him. Gaborit believes this may be necessary because states may fear that journalists will abuse the privilege of protection and "mount campaigns of propaganda and denigration against them with impunity" and also "that their sovereignty will be infringed."

Gaborit describes in detail the composition and functions of the proposed international commisson for the protection of journalists. The nine member-associations would be heavily weighted in favor of the Soviet bloc and several closely allied third world groups. The commission would issue identification cards, publish annual reports of working conditions of journalists inside and outside their own countries, and study the "ethical rules and regulations governing the journalistic profession so as to facilitate a convergence of views in these matters."

It soon became clear at the Paris meeting in February that there would be no convergence of views of the East-bloc and Western representatives.

Dana Bullen of the World Press Freedom Committee (WPFC) termed the protection proposal "a bad idea—and it should be abandoned entirely." As a journalist for twenty-two years, he said, correspondents working for him were expelled, jailed and killed by assassins while reporting overseas. But the proposals, he said, "would *not* protect journalists" and cannot be implemented "without diminishing freedom of the press." He added, "a card in a reporter's pocket will not save him from a sniper or a mob" and "an emblem on a reporter's arm may draw bullets just as easily as not." Newsmen who are expelled or jailed, he said, "are *not* expelled or jailed because nobody knows they are reporters," but "*because* they are reporters." The freedom of journalists, he added, "is not protected by schemes to regulate them." He concluded, "The real question is whether regulation and control of journalists is what UNESCO wants. If not, it is deceiving itself. This is what such proposals would bring about."

Countering what was called the "Gang of Four" statement was the proposed communique of the Nine. It supported the main thrust of

Gaborit's paper and went beyond it. This draft would have the meeting protest "abuses" of "commercial secrecy" and "political, racial, religious, and other types of discrimination." (The determination of such alleged abuses would entail direct control of journalists.)

The Four countered with a brief draft declaration that "(e)stablishment of an international body that would designate who is a journalist and implement other standards and regulations should be rejected as a potentially improper restraint on freedom of the press." The chairman then proposed a compromise communique that noted that "differences emerged during discussions," but called for "further discussions." The Four opposed that, and compromise efforts failed. UNESCO issued a press release that described the opposing points of view, but a shorter telex of the release sent to news agencies did not include the position of the Four.

This meeting was particularly significant because it was the first time in the history of news media controversies that distinctly different points of view emerged which were not compromised in a consensual statement. Instead, the sharply divergent views stand for the record.[7]

## THE UNESCO WATERSHED

*Freedom in the World 1980* detailed the reasons why that year would be important for international communciations: The UNESCO general conference in Belgrade would dispose of the MacBride Commission's controversial report to the Director-General of UNESCO, approve "normative" programs for the next three years, and formalize a program to transfer communication technology to the developing countries.

What, then, happened at Belgrade?

In the first two of three major arenas, attempts to alter the *content* of the news media predominated. The arenas: disposition of the 312-page, two-year study of the International Commission on Communication Problems (the MacBride report); funding of scores of "normative" programs; and creation of the International Program for Communication Development (IPDC).

1. *The MacBride Commission* sent the UNESCO Director-General eighty-two recommendations. These included a strong condemnation of censorship, and pleas for the free access by journalists to official and unofficial news; expansion of rural news media; reductions in international news-transmission tariffs; cheaper forms of paper-manufacturing; reduction of the commercialization and ownership-concentration of communication; raising of the professional standards of journalists; and measures to "foster the setting up of a new world information and communication order (NWICO)."

This "order" had been defined in proposals to the MacBride Commission that would impose stringent controls over the news media by governmental and intergovernmental agencies. The resolution approved by consensus at Belgrade went beyond urging the Director-General to disseminate the MacBride report. The resolution invited him to continue studies "which did not receive sufficient attention" from the commission "or which deserve attention." This suggests concentration now on a series of twelve "issues requiring further study" listed at the end of the MacBride report. These were issues which the commission in two years either rejected, could not agree upon, or never considered. They include some of the most controversial issues that divide a pluralist world—issues that can never be compromised by those who hold stringently to the independence of journalism from government. These include examinations of international laws to govern the "new order" of information, a journalists' code of ethics, the negative aspects of advertising and the need for an international code, the "juridical aspects" of international news reporting, "protection" of journalists, and a possible tax on transnational corporations to finance third world communications.

The resolution also calls for the defining of a "new international information and communication order," and mandates an international meeting of experts for that purpose. The resolution further provides some advance definitions of a new "order." These would include "elimination of imbalances and inequalities," and the "negative effects of certain monopolies, public or private, and excessive concentrations"; the "right of each nation to inform the world public about its interests," and the "right of the public" to "participate actively in the communication process."

A delegate of the United Kingdom described the resolution's definition of a NWICO as "equivocal, insufficient, and inadequate." He asked, "How can we pretend to lay down guiding considerations which omit such fundamental principles as the right to freedom of thought, opinion, and expression; the free circulation of information and ideas; the freedom of movement; freedom from censorship and arbitrary government control; and access to all sources of information, unofficial as well as official?"

He concluded, "If UNESCO really is ready to reach out to more than just the governments or bureaucrats in the member states, it can no longer proceed on the basis of ill-defined or obscure or tendentious language. It must set aside barren ideological debate and concentrate on practical measures to help the people who need it."

The Venezuelan resolution proposing "a declaration to establish a new information order" also passed (51 in favor, 6 against, and 26 abstentions). The resolution calls for studies of the characteristics of an

NWICO declaration and "the possibility and desirability of its adoption" at the next general conference.

The continuation of ideological debates during the next three years was also assured by the approval of the 1981-83 budget of $625.4 million. This pays for UNESCO's year-round . . .

2. *Studies, conferences, and related programs.* These are the "normative" or standard-setting projects. They provide the research, staff, and events to probe the ideas and procedures for changing the domestic and international news and information systems. These programs cannot legislate change. They can provide—in UNESCO's words—a normative function through:

a. Studies of the impact of advertising on news media.

b. Study of the concentration of "transnational" corporations and their effects on news transmission.

c. Study of news and program exchange by satellite.

d. Program to improve the communications media of "liberation movements" such as the PLO.

e. Ten seminars to study how the "opinions of one nation" are reflected in the media of others.

f. Studies on ways the press portrays development problems.

g. Investigation of principles and procedures of the right of reply and rectification.

h. Investigation of the tie between the concepts of freedom and responsibility, with implications for the preparation of a code of journalistic ethics.

i. Linkage between the "responsibility" of journalists and the protection of journalists in their work.

j. Study of the "democratization of the management of the media."

k. Training of researchers in communication—a key to influencing the content of communications.

The U.S. delegation futilely urged the conference to withhold consideration of the normative communication programs until after the creation of the International Program for Communication Development (IPDC). The American delegate explained that the independent media may not be told by the U.S. government to perform certain tasks or not perform others—no matter how noble the stated objective. The government can neither enforce "responsibility" of journalists or be a party to such enforcement by an intergovernmental body. UNESCO's examination of advertising content and the right of correction would provide further interference by governments in the editorial freedom of journalists. The proposal to examine the protection of journalists, presumably linked to their demonstrated "responsibility," raises anew the creation of a governmentally set code of performance tied in turn to the licensing of journalists.

3. *The IPDC* was approved. The thirty-five-government council will begin to function in 1981. The program is committed solely to technology assistance.

The ideological debates over a "new order" could become increasingly heated and sterile. Such debates at Belgrade tested the stamina as well as the ingenuity of the few supporters of press independence. Indeed, on two occasions, after lengthy negotiating sessions ended, the carefully worded compromise statements were reported to the general conference in forms different from what had been understood by the Western negotiators. Apparently, alteration by the UNESCO secretariat had revised compromises patiently fashioned at the negotiating tables. As one consequence, the resolution passed by the conference defining the "new world information and communication order" does *not* include the commitment to the "free flow of information, of ideas and persons." A commitment made in Paris in April 1980 regarding the organization of the IPDC was similarly altered when the program's statutes were formulated at Belgrade.

A few days after the Belgrade conference ended, UNESCO Director-General M'Bow met in New York with a dozen journalists from major news media. He assured them that UNESCO had no intention of supporting censorship, harming the free press, converting the IPDC into an ideology-transfer mechanism, or even starting all the "normative" programs sanctioned at Belgrade. He left unanswered the question of whether funds would be found to convene the media-analysis conferences proposed in the Soviet and Venezuelan resolutions approved by the general conference. His subordinates created further uncertainty after the very meeting called to reassure American journalists. Although a transcription was promised this author seven times over the next two months, it was finally said to have "disappeared." Apparently M'Bow's remarks were too conciliatory to be made potentially available to the third world.

## UNESCO: FEARS AND IMBALANCE IN REPORTING

Third world complaints about Western press coverage have been repeatedly expressed. Too little is reported of the serious economic and social developments in two-thirds of the countries. Even if daily reports cannot be carried for many places, longer-term "process" stories could be given wider attention. (We have described such valid objections to present coverage in *Freedom in the World 1980*.)

After Belgrade UNESCO took an unprecedented step. It complained to the National News Council in New York that American press coverage of the Belgrade conference had been "disgraceful." The complaint specified:

> During the course of the six weeks of the General Conference, the delegates worked in six major commissions and many sub-groups to produce more than 400 resolutions pertaining to a three year budget of $625,000,000. Among the delegates were leading world authorities in a variety of fields. A survey of 302 press clippings received by Unesco on the Belgrade conference during September and October revealed none (0) on any topic out of Belgrade other than the communications issue and four other controversy-related subjects: the challenge to Israeli credentials by some Arab states, the speech by Yassir Arafat, the denunciation of the Soviet Union by a defecting Afghanistani delegate, and the re-election of the Unesco's Director-General, Amadou-Mahtar M'Bow.
>
> To maintain that the American press presented a balanced, thorough coverage of this meeting is a charade. With scores of renowned experts available and programs of direct and intense interest to millions and millions of people, the world's most sophisticated and advanced news media centered on one topic and a handful of non-program-related events.

In response the National News Council, a voluntary organization with journalistic credentials, undertook a study of the complaint. The staff examined 448 newsclippings and 206 editorials in U.S. newspapers (eighty percent were from the Associated Press and United Press International). Several spot news developments (an attack on the USSR by an Afghan defector, a speech by Yassir Arafat, and a resolution condemning Israel for its policy on Jerusalem) represented forty percent of the coverage. All the rest of the news stories and all the editorials concerned news media issues raised at Belgrade. "Not one story emanating from the six-week conference dealt with any of the reports, speeches or resolutions on UNESCO's basic activities in combating illiteracy, developing alternate energy sources, protecting historic monuments, broadening educational programs for scientists and engineers, sponsoring basic research in food production and ocean sciences, and scores of other fields," the Council reported.

"Without exception," said the report, "the editorials expressed apprehension about UNESCO's involvement" in the worldwide flow of information. Twenty-seven papers suggested that the United States withdraw from UNESCO if it persisted in moves deemed destructive of press freedom. There was little presentation of non-Western viewpoints in the media issues, the Council's report said. The approval at Belgrade of the IPDC "went almost unreported."

The Council quoted the response of Stanley Swinton, director of the AP's world news services, to the UNESCO complaint:

> Was all of UNESCO covered at Belgrade? No, but that gets to the fragility of all coverage. When you ask UNESCO people for specific documents on all the things of importance they say we should be covering, you don't get them. UNESCO is so preoccupied with the matter of communications policy that nothing else is distributed. In fact, if it were not for the controversy on the "new communication order," nobody from the press would be there at all. It's like safe landings at an airport, a non-story.

According to the Report, H. L. Stevenson, editor-in-chief of UPI, ascribed the imputed one-sidedness in Western news reporting of UNESCO to the gatekeepers system—the need of newspaper editors to choose from thousands of stories that come in daily from all over the world. "We can crank out stories of all sorts," says Stevenson, "and much to our amazement see them never get printed. That includes major enterprise stories. We get frustrated about that. I will see an editor much later and ask about a story that was ignored. 'Oh, yeah,' comes the answer. 'I thought it was interesting but I just didn't have the space for it.' "

The National News Council concluded:

> The imbalance that characterized most of the Belgrade news coverage in this country provided an inadequate foundation for independent judgment by Americans of the correctness of the editorial positions their newspapers were taking on the UNESCO communications issue. Equally troublesome, this imbalance set a poor example for third world journalists and other skeptics on what they should find admirable as a model of press freedom and immunity from governmental control in Western journalistic practice.

The report also pointed out that this author had criticized U.S. press coverage while viewing UNESCO's "entire concept with deep reserve." The Council noted that in addressing the plenary of the general conference that I had included "many expressions of approval for projects involving technical assistance to third world journalists." But the Council noted that the press account of my remarks[8] had only mentioned "warnings to UNESCO to shun any moves toward licensing or monitoring journalists." I was quoted, "Every word in the published account [of my speech] was absolutely accurate, but it was unbalanced in its total effect."

In fact, U.S. press coverage of UNESCO/Belgrade was unbalanced because many reports emphasized the dire potentialities of press control as though they had already materialized. Votes taken or a consensus reached were faithfully reported. But *all* of these actions were directed toward further studies and meetings over the next three years. These actions unquestionably target the free press for future governmental restrictions or, at least, repressive standards however enforced. This is undeniably a threat—but too often the reports and certainly the headlines gave the impression doomsday had already arrived. Neither public understanding nor an effective defense of press freedom is helped by exaggerating the present state of the challenge.

For five years I have described this challenge and defended the world-news services. I believe they have been earnestly meeting some of the valid complaints made by moderate third world critics. But the world services can only propose; print and broadcast gatekeepers dispose.

They dispose of most foreign news, particularly of that from the third world. The world-news services follow that lead. But then most third world editors do precisely the same: they spike most news from distant third world places. Changing the criteria of news is a long-term struggle for those who want to read or hear more about the important "soft" news from the third or first worlds. Scientific and cultural developments at Belgrade simply were not covered. As Swinton pointed out, UNESCO is not blameless. It does little to help the Western media find newsworthy material outside the communications field. On their own, most journalists do not sufficiently pursue the soft story at UNESCO.

But this criticism does not validate *most* of the attacks on the Western media made by and through UNESCO. The secretariat and the majority voting do indeed want to use governmental power and UNESCO's "norms" to change drastically the standard of international journalism. They would divert the free flow of information into channels that fulfill governmental objectives, and that would clearly harness the flow.

That did not materialize at Belgrade, though some promoters of further "studies" and conferences clearly have that objective. Nothing done at Belgrade assures the fulfillment of that objective, though it is a bit nearer realization because of steps taken there.

The defenders of press freedom must therefore remain alert. But because they are also the prime carriers of the news about their own fate, they become—not by choice—parties to the controversy. That added burden requires impeccable balancing of the story.

Usually, the immediate action is complex, based on years of contention and—yes—dangerous implications for the future. If the report covers only the immediate action and jumps rapidly to the threats, the story is likely to be unbalanced. It is difficult for a reporter to describe the latest action in only 500 words. Such restriction of space and time can distort the story. And even granting that conflict is a principal ingredient of news, it is essential to provide detail other than conflict.

There were indeed good and bad guys at Belgrade. But there were some not-so-bad guys too—many from the third world. They were large-ly ignored in the coverage, as they are mainly ignored by UNESCO and its secretariat. They are the moderates whose limited criticism of Western journalism is exploited by both the Soviet bloc and third world hardliners. The moderates deserve our understanding, help and most of all, fair coverage of the controversies. The cause of press freedom is best served by "complexifying" rather than oversimplifying the intricate news media issues.

Full, year-round coverage of the issues is needed, not only occasional stories when the conflict heats up. The world-news services could one day fall victim to their own deemphasizing of soft news. They should not ignore the regular, quiet research and countless meetings that lay the ideological groundwork for the more inflammatory public conferences. Such coverage would better prepare both the reader and the correspon-dent to understand the critical junctures in the future of this evolving struggle.

The Council's tally of U.S. press coverage of UNESCO/Belgrade comes at a moment when communication researchers increasingly ques-tion whether the news media promote intelligent decision making. Some researchers conclude that the institutionalization of news reporting leads to the reliance on official sources and powerful social, economic and political leaders. Such "reliance" was noticeably suspended during the latter days of the Vietnam war, Watergate and the counterpolitics of the sixties and early seventies. Yet a British communication specialist turns with apparent hope to "research showing that the national liberation movements in the third world may be bringing forth a new information order." That, he suggests, would help the public "understand the deeper social process and manipulation of social power behind the events."[9] Journalism should indeed probe, where appropriate, the socio-economic origins of news. But press control posing as "liberation" is yet another Orwellian manifestation just three years early.

The Belgrade conference presented a clear sign that the compromises of the 1978 mass media declaration and the West's commitment to transfer media technology to the third world would not deter the hardliners from continual demands for increased governmental monitor-ing and direction of the press (under whatever guise). It is an attack that will never be turned back by ignorance or inattention.

## NOTES

1. Tom Stoppard, "Night and Day," Grove Press, p. 66.

2. Leonard R. Sussman, "Freedom of the Press: Problems in Restructuring the Flow of International News," in *Freedom in the World, 1980*, pp. 53-98.

3. A strategy conference for this purpose was scheduled for May 1981 at Talloires, France under the sponsorship of the Fletcher School for Law and Diplomacy, Tufts University, and the World Press Freedom Committee.

4. Vladimir Hudec, *Journalism: Substance, Social Functions, Development*, 1978; S. V. Tsukasov, *The Organization of Work in an Editorial Office*, 1979; Mikhail Minkov, *Radio-Journalism*, 1980; and Slavoj Haskovec, *The News Agency in the System of Mass Media*, 1980. These booklets are published by the International Organization of Journalists, Prague.

5. This section is based on an Op-Ed article published in the *New York Times*, October 23, 1980.

6. *Many Voices, One World*. Report of the International Commission for the Study of Communication Problems, Sean MacBride, *et al.* (New York and London: Kogan Page; London/Unipub, 1980, p. 264 (English version).

7. This author urged the MacBride Commission to acknowledge that two distinctly different journalistic systems operate in the world—one government-controlled, the other independent of government—based on different political realities; and there should thus be two separate analyses and no effort to produce a universal standard for news media. Published as Commission paper 18, *An Approach to the Study of Transnational News Media in a Pluralistic World*, UNESCO/Paris.

8. *The New York Times*, October 9, 1908, p. A7.

9. Robert A. White, in "Contribution of Research to News Reform," *Communication Research Trends* (London), Winter 1980 (I, 1).

# PART III

# Supporting Freedom in Muslim Central Asia

# Foreword

On November 14-15, 1980, a conference was held at Freedom House on "Supporting Freedom in Muslim Central Asia." This conference was the second in a series that began with the conference "Supporting Liberalization in the Soviet Union" reported in *Freedom in the World 1979* (pp. 83-197).

The purpose of the conference and the general issues to be addressed were sketched in the first paper, included below, "American Support for Freedom in Muslim Central Asia: General Policy Considerations." This is followed by eight papers delivered in summary form at the conference. With each paper are included the discussion it inspired. A personal summary and conclusions by the editor conclude the presentation.

In addition to the editor the participants were:

*Mumtaz Ahmad*, formerly Senior Instructor at The National Institute of Public Administration, Karachi. He is an authority on administration, modern Islam, and social change, particularly in Pakistan.

*Edward Allworth*, Professor of Turco-Soviet Studies at Columbia University. He has published especially on Central Asian languages and literatures, as well as the relation of nationalism to Russian rule.

*Richard W. Cottam*, Professor of Political Science at the University of Pittsburgh. He is a lifelong student of Iranian nationalism and American foreign policy.

*Michael M. J. Fischer*, Associate Professor of Anthropology at Harvard University. He is a leading authority on Middle Eastern society, social change, and contemporary Iranian religious institutions.

*William E. Griffith*, Professor of Political Science at the MIT Center for International Studies. He has published widely on U.S. foreign policy and diplomatic history.

*Teresa Rakowska-Harmstone*, Professor of Political Science at

Carleton University of Ottawa. She is an authority on Soviet society, Soviet nationalities, and especially Soviet Central Asia.

*Selig S. Harrison*, Senior Associate of the Carnegie Endowment for International Peace. He is a journalist especially concerned with the situation in South Asia and the problems of minorities.

*Paul B. Henze*, with the staff of the National Security Council at the time of the conference. An authority on Central Asian languages and politics, he is presently engaged in private research and consulting.

*Farhad Kazemi*, Associate Professor of Politics and member of the Center for Near Eastern Studies at New York University. An Iranian expert, he has been particularly interested in the relation of poverty in Iran to politics and revolution.

*Zalmay Khalilzad*, Associate Professor of Political Science and a member of the research staff of the War and Peace Institute and Middle East Institute at Columbia University. His specialty is national security policy, particularly in the Middle East and South Asia.

*A. Nabawi*, an Afghan scholar who was personally involved in the social and political affairs of Afghanistan until recently.

*Eden Naby*, Associate at the Harvard Center for Middle Eastern Studies. An area specialist, she is an authority on the minority peoples of Central Asia.

*Richard S. Newell*, Professor of South Asian History at the University of Northern Iowa. He has published on the current political history of Afghanistan and India.

*William L. Richter*, Professor of Political Science and Director of the South Asia Center at Kansas State University. He has written widely on Pakistani and Indian politics.

*Howard Wriggins*, Professor of Political Science, Director of the Pakistan Center, and formerly Director of the South Asian Institute at Columbia University. His government service included positions on the Policy Planning Staff of the State Department and the National Security Council. He was ambassador to Sri Lanka.

# American Support
# for Freedom in Muslim
# Central Asia:
# General Policy Considerations

A merican foreign policy must serve a variety of domestic and international interests. Among those interests are the defense, preservation, or extension of freedom in terms of political and civil rights and the self-determination of peoples. We desire that all peoples be free and also believe that a free world is more likely to be a peaceful world.

It is evident that in the Middle East and Central Asia advancing freedom is both an important and difficult task. The difficulties inhere in our previous policies in the region, in the intervention and presence of the USSR, and in the internal weaknesses and contradictions of the forces supporting freedom. The purpose of the following discussion is to consider the problems support for freedom faces in the area and to begin to sketch some of the options we might choose in response.

## MUSLIM CENTRAL ASIA

The area between Turkey and Iraq on the west, Russia in the north, and India on the east has long occupied a critical role in human history. The meeting place of many civilizations, Central Asia became identified with Achaemenid and successor Iranian civilizations. After the Islamic conquest it became the center of the new Persian-Islamic culture that is associated most closely with the fabled cities of Bokhara and Samarqand, the courts of Harun al-Rashid, Tamarlane, of the Moghul emperors of Delhi, and the Safavid kings of Esfahan, and with the scientist Avicenna and the poet-scientist Omar Khayyam.

Persians, Turks, Arabs, and Mongols gave their imprints to the region's culture. More recently Central Asia became a frontier area in which the Russian and British Empires contended for influence until they roughly divided the region across the middle of Iran and the north of

Afghanistan. In the twentieth century the northern competitor completed and filled out its conquests up to the modern borders of Afghanistan and Iran: below this line colonialism gave way to the large, but essentially weak nation-states of Iran, Afghanistan, and Pakistan. The role of conqueror and then protector slipped from the British to the Americans and now seems to have effectively slipped from the American grasp as well. Proud of their past, regional leaders began to assert in the post-World War II era of increasing wealth and fervent nationalism that they needed no protection. But Pakistan's repeated humbling by India and continuing poverty, Afghanistan's occupation by the USSR, and Iran's self-destruction of its military establishment has postponed this dream at least into the next century.

## THE STRUGGLE FOR FREEDOM

The struggle for freedom in Central Asia has taken two forms. In terms of self-determination the dominant "Islamic nationalism" of the region has been challenged for centuries. Iran almost succumbed to Soviet and British pressure in the nineteenth and twentieth centuries. Soviet Central Asia was occupied in the nineteenth century by Russia and finally integrated into its foreign society in the twentieth. The United Kingdom ruled what is now Pakistan for over a century and occasionally extended its sway into Afghanistan.

Within Islam there have always been wars. Tribe fought tribe, Shi'a fought Sunni, sect fought sect, but the modern idea of ethnic or state nationalism developed and only imperfectly became accepted by the peoples of the area in the twentieth century. The concept that territorial groups defined by language, government, customs, or religion should form separate units for self-government came so late that the formal states of Iran, Afghanistan, Pakistan, and (previously) the emirates of Bokhara and Khiva have hardly had more reality in the minds of their citizens than their threatened successors (Kurdish, Azerbaijani, Baluch, or Pathan tribal states) or real successors, the Soviet-inspired Uzbekistan, Tajikistan, Turkmenistan, and Kazakhstan. (This is not to deny that Iran and, more loosely, Afghanistan are historic states on a par with those in most of the world.)

Nationalism in the modern sense was introduced into Central Asia directly and indirectly by the Russians, English, and Europeans who came to play a dominant part in its life. Along with nationalism came the liberal democratic ideals of political democracy and civil rights under modern law. Because the British presence was longest and most secure, these ideals became perhaps most firmly ingrained in what is now Pakistan. But civil and political rights became widely known by the literate population of the whole region. The Iranian constitutionalist movement of 1905-06 established them firmly as an urban standard, if seldom operating reality, in Iran. Constitutionalist innovations from above in the 1920s in Afghanistan, though ultimately rejected, gave liberalism a currency that Afghan liberals repeatedly revived. In Soviet Central Asia a faint spark of liberal thought flamed at the time of the first World War, and then went out, although in some areas, for example scientific education, the advancement of women, and economic equality, liberalization according to Western models has surely proceeded further in Soviet Central Asia than in the more traditional south.

Had we considered freedom in most of Central Asia ten or even five years ago it would have been the struggle for freedom in terms of liberalization or modern nationalism that would have absorbed our attention. Today the struggle for freedom in the area represents primarily a struggle defined in terms of the older sense of self-determination. The Iranian Revolution that many expected would be a renewal of the much deferred constitutionalist struggle against authoritarian tyranny, or perhaps a socialist struggle for a one-party state on the Middle Eastern model, has witnessed the emplacement of a traditionalist and populist theological regime. The struggle has become more than the obvious struggle to replace an oppressive regime; it is the struggle of Islamic civilization against Western modernism. "Nationalist" we may label it, but it is not the imported brand; it is a universalist Shi'a or Muslim claim to revealed and unlegislatable truth.

In Pakistan a new authoritarianism has been imposed by the military in the name of a less radical mixture of modern nationalism and Islamic legitimacy. Since its inception as a Muslim state led by nonreligious modernizers, Pakistan has been bedeviled by the problem of legitimacy. Democracy never took root as in neighboring India, yet democracy has remained a significant part of the political culture of Pakistan. Today it once again has been forced underground in an attempt to justify military rule by a return to Islamic authoritarianism.

Afghanistan's conquest by small communist parties and then by the USSR has in this context awakened both modern nationalist and Islamic nationalism. The latter has been found most useful by the guerrilla forces for a number of reasons. Islam is more salable to potential outside Middle Eastern supporters; the communist, atheist takeover easily excited popular religious feeling; and the disunited tribes and peoples of Afghanistan can unite more easily around Islamic symbols than around national symbols often associated only with the Pushtu speaking people.

In Soviet Central Asia, too, it is Islamic civilization (if not Islam) that most easily identifies and describes the citizen seeking to differentiate himself from the ruling and intrusive Slavs. The modern nationalisms centering around linguistic differences are important, but they are ill formed and their political expression largely fraudulent. The history and cultural heroes of Soviet Central Asian peoples overlap one another and are common to peoples on both sides of the Soviet border. Loyalty to Islamic custom is also furthered by the fact that ethnic religious expression even in an aggressively atheist society is still much less subject to repression than political expression deviating from the all-Soviet line.

## AMERICAN SUPPORT FOR FREEDOM IN CENTRAL ASIA

Americans have two major reasons to support the freedom of Central Asian peoples. First, we believe all peoples have a right to self-determination. Self-determination means self-government, whether it be Islamic, tribal, liberal constitutional, or socialist. Self-determination in the American definition also implies that civil and political liberties be developed that allow people to become sovereign over their own affairs. Self-determination by peoples attached to authoritarian traditions may clash with popular democracy, but the evolution of constitutional monarchies and Catholic republics suggest that the apparent contradictions of the concept can be overcome.

Secondly, we support the freedom of Central Asian peoples because the region represents a dangerous area for the expansion of fundamentally antidemocratic and anti-self-determinative systems. Indian democracy and the return to democracy in Turkey are threatened by continued antidemocratic success in Central Asia. Such success would also thwart possible democratic evolution elsewhere in the Middle East. In part this threat to freedom simply derives from the persistence or expansion of nondemocratic models in Central Asia that legitimize repression in neighboring states. In part the threat is that the Soviet Union will eventually incorporate the whole region into its sphere of control, with the subsequent patterning of regional regimes in Moscow's image.

In terms of the Soviet threat, the United States and its allies would be interested in the continued independence of the southern states of Central Asia even if we had no interest in their freedom. The expansion of the USSR particularly into the petroleum springs of the Middle East could hardly be taken lightly. This consideration helps to focus attention, but it will not be the basis of analysis here. Interested in freedom, we must go beyond assuring simply the independence of countries in the region, or, more distantly, supporting independence movements in Soviet Central Asia, to concerning ourselves with the degree to which independence in any part of Central Asia might be made to support enhanced freedom.

## U.S. POLICY DILEMMAS

This sketch of American and Central Asian interests suggests major dilemmas for U.S. policy.

The major danger to the freedom of the peoples of the area is communist expansion or the acceptance of quasi-communist models. In Afghanistan and Soviet Central Asia this expansion means the virtual suppression of self-determination in any sense. One can imagine nationalist communist states emerging in the area, but the immediate presence of Soviet troops across the border makes this an unlikely prospect, except possibly in Pakistan. The political systems of communist or one-party socialist regimes (such as those of Iraq or Libya) deny essentially all political and civil liberties. The possibility that communist regimes might go further than present regimes toward meeting the nationalist aspirations of non-state nationalities, such as the Kurds or Baluch, should not be dismissed. However, except on a symbolic plane, the self-determination such peoples would attain within communist systems would be minimal.

The communists appear to have a strong hand. First, they are backed by the USSR: they are directly in power in half of the region because of this backing. In Iran they have long been a major part of the opposition, and in spite of repressions and the present Islamic fervor they still have strength, particularly among minority peoples such as the Kurds. A tightly organized communist movement is dangerous under the near anarchical conditions that reign in, or threaten, much of Iran. Fortunately, the communists of Iran are broken into several groups. In addition, the very fact of Soviet support weakens their appeal—particularly that of the pro-Soviet Tudeh party in Iran and the ruling parties in Afghanistan. In Pakistan the communists seem presently to be relatively weak.

The primary danger of communism in the noncommunist states is that in the absence of actual communist rule, Marxist-Leninist ideas have become a major part of the political understanding of modern intellectuals and the more modernized workers. This lays the groundwork for one-party socialist or communist movements attaining power and makes cooperation between local modernists and Americans or other Westernizers in a common struggle for freedom more difficult. Even many educated people whose class interests are clearly conservative find it difficult not to regard American, or other Western influence in the area, as "imperialist" and, thus, more dangerous than more obvious and immediate dangers.

In this atmosphere the main bulwark against communist expansion is traditional Islam. The active atheism of communism is well known to Muslim leaders, regardless of the claims to moderation sometimes raised.

The modernism of communism is almost equally suspect, especially in regard to the role of women, the nature of education, or the law. The Muslim clergy are themselves a class (or estate), and communist rule threatens both their obvious class interests and deeply held ideology. Items of communist thought or practice (for example, the equality of men and asceticism of leaders) can be incorporated in Islamic regimes, as in Libya, but in general communists are seen as enemies by Muslim leaders. Alliances with communists may be made, for example to oust the Shah, but they are purely tactical.

Muslim power exists in spite of the absence of an organized hierarchy on the model of the Catholic Church. There are two main versions of Islam and many competing sects. Religious leadership in Iranian Shi'ism is vaguely organized, but religious leaders are largely independent of one another throughout the region. Islamic strength is based on the near universal adherence of regional populations to Islam.

How deep beliefs actually go is hard to know. It has always been socially dangerous to deny Islam and may today be fatal in much of the region. But Islam requires only that the professed believer *say* he believes to be accepted into the community. Certainly in recent years large numbers of Iranian intellectuals (down perhaps to high school graduates) had little but contempt for the Islamic clergy, and many had little or no faith, at least in traditional Islam. The sudden religious conversion of this class in the early days of the Iranian Revolution appears likely to have been most superficial. The urban success of the Parcham and Khalq parties in Afghanistan also indicates the rapidity with which regional intellectuals may move away from Islam. However, in the face of external threat Islam remains a self-defining symbol system of importance to modernized intellectuals and even to partly Russianized Soviet Central Asians. It is a haven of last resort. For less educated Central Asians religion may play a larger role. Here religious leaders have often been intermediaries between citizens and governments. In some tribal and rural areas such leaders have even developed their own militias and become alternate focuses of political loyalty long before the Iranian Revolution.

Whatever its strengths and internal weaknesses, Islam remains the most effective opponent of communism in the region. This is most evident in Afghanistan where the guerrilla war is seen as a holy war against the infidel and where many of its leaders are religious. The role of Islam in the struggle is also seen in the willingness of Iran and Pakistan to support the Afghan struggle verbally, and, at least to a limited extent with arms, in spite of the dangers this support represents. After an early honeymoon the Iranian Islamic Republic has increasingly striven to eliminate communist or leftist influence from its political and educational life. In Soviet Central Asia adherence to Islamic custom even among communist leaders is seen as an expression of nationalism.

Supporting the Islamic resurgence in Central Asian countries becomes an imperative if America is to play a positive role in the region. However, the objectives of currently powerful Islamic movements coincide with ours only in the narrowest sense of self-determination. It is argued that if Islamic peoples want Islamic governments, that is what they should have—this is "true democracy." Yet the level of abstraction is too high, and the variety of possible Islamic governments almost infinite. Unless a people is offered alternatives at regular intervals under conditions of reasonably free discussion, outsiders have no right to conclude that a people wants or does not want any particular Islamic government, or even an Islamic government at all. (Catholic Mexico, for example, is bitterly anticlerical, as apparently is more democratic Spain.)

Islam as promoted today in most of Iran, Afghanistan, and Pakistan, and probably Soviet Central Asia does little or nothing for the promotion of political and civil rights and may operate as a substantial barrier to their further advancement. It is true that there are many religious leaders in the area who either support modern liberal democracy or believe religious leaders generally should stay out of politics. Some of these have achieved large followings. But there is a definite temptation for a politically inclined religious leader to use Islam to legitimize authoritarian rule. This tendency is reinforced by the identification of constitutional democracy as just another aspect of the hated Westernization that the Islamic leader sees himself battling against in the social or economic sphere—represented by interest payments, drugs, alcohol, the exposure of women, movies, and rock music. It also should not be forgotten that traditional Islam is a relatively tough, hard religion. Its doctrines emerged from a violent political struggle (and Shi'ism emerged from a continuation of that struggle). A spirit of compromise or a willingness to separate spiritual and material governance are simply less a part of the tradition of Islam than of comparable world religions. It will not be impossible to achieve in Central Asia the compromise between religion and liberal democracy that characterizes many societies, but it will be difficult.

We would prefer to support groups that desire liberal democracy with freedom to express divergent views privately or in the media, with periodic free elections, and with freedom from political imprisonment, execution, and torture. A liberal democracy need not be libertarian, but it should grant essential equality to the sexes and to minority groups of whatever kind, at least for their private activities.

Liberal democracy defined in this way has had and will have a hard time taking root in Central Asia. Yet, as indicated above, there has been considerable regional experience with the forms and, to some extent, the reality of such democracy. Before the coming to power of the Ayatollah Khomeini millions of Iranians lived in a Westernized manner. Women had achieved some independence. Knowledge of Western forms was common—Iran had more students being educated overseas than any country in the world. (Paradoxically this may still be true today.) Several times in this century Iran has seen periods with significant freedom of the press and discussion and has had significant elections and parliaments. In 1978-1980 these freedoms were revived in various forms and for varying periods, but increasingly their legitimacy has often been denied by Iranian leaders.

Afghanistan has seen several experiments. In a ten-year period between 1963-1973 an important degree of freedom was introduced into the political process. It was a period of achievement unfortunately little remarked in an outside world inclined to emphasize the incompleteness and inefficiencies of the attempt. Since World War II, however, Pakistan probably had the strongest experience with democracy, especially in the area of civil liberties where a relatively strong modern judicial system was able to operate and political organizations achieved a mass base unattained by parties in the other countries in the area.

Liberal democratic forces suffer from a variety of weaknesses. First, they are confined to each country individually, with little or no connection to their neighbors. While Islamic and communist movements are concerned with and, to a limited extent, support one another across borders and even across sectarian lines, liberal democratic parties in the area do not. In spite of accusations to the contrary, libral democratic parties or forces are also seldom supported by outside Western governments or organizations. Unfortunately, anticommunism has generally been the touchstone for receiving such support. This emphasis has led us too often to support autocratic generals or kings and to ignore democratic parties. This outside effort compares poorly with the consistent Soviet support of the region's communist parties, *as well as* support for autocratic generals or kings for immediate benefit.

Ideologically, liberal democracy also suffers from the undermining of its natural constituency by a Marxist ideology that justifies elitist intellectual domination of a society in the names of equality, anti-imperialism, and economic growth, and by a Western developmentalist ideology that justifies much the same type of domination in the names of modernist goals such as development, education, improvement in the position of women, population control, or environmental protection.

In the harsh Central Asian environment liberal democracy also suffers from the fact it is not a fighting ideology. It is easier to get people to risk their lives for an eternal truth such as Islam or Marxism, a national symbol such as Iran, or a charismatic leader holding such a truth, than it is for a democratic process that demands compromising the interests of such absolutes. Hatred of an oppressor can be whipped up enough to overthrow a regime, but hatred has relatively little sustaining power.

Liberal democracy requires both an elite willing to struggle to defend its freedoms and a general populace with enough experience with the possibility of such freedoms to be willing to respond to appeals for their defense. The majority in both groups must be unwilling to accept the legitimacy of nondemocratic regimes. Although embattled, Turkey, India, and Sri Lanka have elites and general publics able and willing to take part in this struggle. Even were liberal democracies established or reestablished in Central Asia, it would take years to develop equivalent democratic strengths. Obviously their attainment will be halting, and only with sustained effort and, probably, outside support.

The second dilemma the United States faces is that self-determination cannot be advanced as the basis of our Central Asian policy without also supporting the claims of lesser peoples against the very governments we would support against the USSR. In Soviet Central Asia our position is relatively clear: we support increasing the operational meaning of the theoretical independence of the Soviet Republics. But south of the border, do we mean to support the Baluch, Turkmen, Kurds, and so on? Or do we intend to suggest to Pakistan that the Pathans of the Northwest should have their own state?

The claims of these Central Asian nationalities cannot be lightly pushed aside. There are millions of Kurds, and they have been struggling for generations against a variety of governments. The mosaic of peoples inhabiting Afghanistan deserves at least an effective federal system that allows for a measure of self-determination. To ignore the movements of Pakistan's ethnic groups will reap a rich harvest of enmity for the United States and add to the legacy of mistrust that works against democratic development. Yet Marxist, Islamic, and modern nationalist opinion among the majority peoples in any state will interpret any effort we make to support the interests of such "subnational" peoples as imperialist meddling, as an attempt to weaken their nation so that we might better control it.

The importance of developing a policy toward nationality movements as a part of an overall international human rights policy makes Central Asia a testing ground for new concepts. Americans are equally challenged on the nationalities issue throughout Asia and Africa. We simply do not have a workable policy. To look at states such as Ethiopia or Zaire as indivisible entities is indefensible in a human rights policy concerned with self-determination.

## UNITED STATES POLICY ALTERNATIVES

To consider what our policy should be in defense of freedom in the region we need to briefly consider what it has been. First, U.S. policy has been to ignore nationality claims. We supported the Kurdish insurrection for years out of support for Israel and Iran. Apparently a purely devious effort, we never supported Kurds in Iran. Naive Western interest in ethnic variety has perhaps had a mildly supportive relation to the development of ethnic identity south of the Oxus. There has been almost no interest in the continued denial of self-determination to Soviet Central Asians.

Secondly, our policy has been to oppose communism and the USSR. We have done this largely by trying to support anticommunist governments whatever their other problems or to balance Soviet aid in the case of Afghanistan. (This policy meant de facto support of Pakistan against India in earlier years.)

Support has meant military aid and economic aid for development viewed quite broadly. The economic and technical effort was made to support democracy; it was felt that support for education, improved administration, a healthier people, as well as expanding contact with Americans, would ultimately make possible the democratization of these societies. Land reform was pressed on the region partly for this reason and partly with the optimistic hope that more equality and less poverty would make communism less appealing.

The most counterproductive part of the effort was that our government-to-government aid increased the repressive abilities of armies and governments, particularly in Iran, without being able to enhance the long-term stability of favored regimes. We supported liberalization in Iran on a number of occasions, but by sticking to the Shah we also undermined his legitimacy. By helping develop his secret police we undermined our future effectiveness: regardless of the extent of our actual involvement in the repression, our association with its perpetrators and our unwillingness to disassociate ourselves from the regime because of supposedly higher national interests will long be remembered.

Today we are cut off from Iran, out of Afghanistan. We provide minimal aid to the Islamic guerrillas of Afghanistan and make a modest effort to shore up the repressive, ostensibly Islamic rule in Pakistan. We have united the noncommunist Muslim states of the area against the USSR by our boycott of the Olympics. We are increasing our Indian Ocean forces and bases and trying to develop closer ties on the Gulf. We presumably aid the opponents of Khomeini, at least those outside the country. Our aid is probably not very effective—and perhaps given in ways that identify us more as anticommunist and anti-Islam than is healthy in the long run. What more should we be doing? What more useful policies might we support?

One approach would be an integrated campaign in regional languages explaining to the peoples of the region our vision of what the future might be for Central Asia. This should include an explanation of political and civil liberties as we understand them. Economically it should point out that we stand for neither capitalism nor socialism, but for every people to control its economy according to the changing interests of its democratic majority.

Specific messages would vary. Religiously the campaign should provide outlets for the expression of a liberal, tolerant Islam. (There are numerous liberal Islamic sources, both ancient and modern, and modern advocates.) In regard to national movements, we should develop a vision that offers a compromise between the interests of the present states and their constituent peoples. Beyond the nation-state we might promote regional unions of like-minded Islamic states, harking back to the Saadabad grouping of the thirties. We could point out how similar groupings such as the European Economic Community (EEC) help their members, and that this might be the key which would allow the Islamic peoples of the region to become completely self-reliant.

Another American initiative might be support for human rights organizations for each country, with the organizations subsequently linked together by common interests. A human rights organization exists in Pakistan and did at least until recently in Iran. Such groups should be organized with both internal and external sections to keep pressure on the oppressive systems of the day. This initiative is one that could be taken by private groups completely outside the government.

A third initiative would be to greatly increase American support for the guerrilla war in Afghanistan. If delivered in sufficient quantities, advanced technology weapons that can be carried by one or two men and are effective against tanks and planes (at least helicopters) would make the Soviets more anxious to withdraw. Making it feasible to attack critical bridges would make a significant difference in the outcome. Encouraging the guerrillas to expand their contacts into neighboring Soviet areas on an Islamic basis could lead the Soviets to reconsider their adventure, or, alternatively, lead them to meet more of the desires of Soviet Central Asians. An American promise of immediate air support in case of a Soviet attack on Pakistan might prevent the Pakistanis from being coerced into closing the sanctuary that now makes the guerrilla war possible. Alternatively, if we have no theory of how the guerrilla war can succeed, perhaps we should encourage the guerrillas to abandon it and try other approaches.

The issues in Central Asia for American foreign policy are many and conflicting, particularly if we define that policy as one devoted to promoting freedom and human rights. Against the background of this discussion, the conference participants were asked to develop the following papers and criticism.

# Prospects for Political Freedom in Iran

Richard W. Cottam

Iran in the fall of 1980 is not a totalitarian society. Indeed for much of the Iranian population the range of political freedom far exceeds their inclinations to express themselves politically. Yet for others, and this surely includes a majority of the most politically attentive ten percent of the population, restrictions on their freedom of action are greater than under the Shah. This is not a paradox. As it has evolved the Iranian revolution is a peculiar manifestation of populism. Were its charismatic leader, Ayatollah Ruhollah Khomeini, so inclined and temperamentally able to become an absolute leader, Iran could be described as fascist. Far from being an absolute leader, Khomeini in fact tolerates intensely competitive political activity by several groups and dozens of ambitious politicians. Yet his interventions in politics have led to an exclusion from Iranian political society of virtually the entire secular element of the Iranian populace. Khomeini's broad tolerance extends only to the faithful. He has allowed a cultural revolution to develop that is purging Iranian institutions of all who fail to measure up to the qualifications for leadership in an Islamic state. The Shah denied his people any independent political activity, but for anyone who would accommodate to his absolute leadership, participation in an ordered political society was permitted.

To an extent that may be unparalleled in history, Khomeini gives definition to Iranian political society. He is able to do so because of a charismatic attraction he exerts on the great mass of Farsi-speaking urban lower and lower middle class and because of a totally dedicated, ferociously loyal core element of the highly attentive public. His supporters are followers of whatever line the Iman advances and they appear to care little that Khomeini's Islamic ideology is impenetrably vague in terms of programmatic expression. They share his dislike and contempt for their countrymen who, in this view, have discarded the rich Islamic/Iranian culture for the culture of the "oppressor states." And their total support provides the instrumental basis for Khomeini's control of those who do not support him. The very massiveness of his support makes resistance internally extremely difficult.

Khomeini's charisma also impacts negatively on the possibility of the appearance of leaders with popularity that does not derive from the Imam's favor. The lack of alternative leaders reduces in turn the potential for independent political activity. There are leaders with some independent support. Most important is Ayatollah Kazem Shariatmadari, a lifetime rival of Khomeini for spiritual leadership in Iran. Shariatmadari is, with Khomeini, one of the five leading figures in contemporary Shi'a Islam and is generally considered a more outstanding thinker than Khomeini. But his support is largely parochial—confined to the Azeri Turkish speaking element of the Iranian population. Within Azerbaijan his support is probably greater than Khomeini's. In December 1979 when a confrontation developed between the followers of the two great ayatollahs, Shariatmadari withdrew into seclusion. Yet he remains a potential rallying point for future opposition activity.

Mehdi Bazergan, first revolutionary prime minister and the leader of the Freedom Front, clearly did have a following independent of the Imam. However, that following tended to be middle class and professional and much of it secular. Bazergan's willingness to serve Khomeini even though the latter was sanctioning the exclusion of Western-minded elements reduced Bazergan's base of independent support almost to the vanishing point. With the defection of his followers, many into exile abroad, Bazergan's own leverage atrophied until he became, like his colleagues serving the Imam, a leader by virtue of the Imam's beneficence.

A third emerging leader with clearly independent support is Massoud Rajavi, the leader of the organization Mujahidin-e-Khalq, to be discussed below. Rajavi is a young man but his personal appeal is strong, and he is proving to be a good political tactician. Although Rajavi clearly recognizes the limited basis of his support, he must be viewed as a potential rallying point for future opposition political activity.

A number of Iranian politicians living in exile whose core support is to be found in the exile community can also claim support inside Iran. Shapur Bakhtiar, the last Shah-appointed prime minister in Iran, is probably the exile leader with the largest following. His following is confined to middle and upper-middle class secularists. Bakhtiar's contempt for the Iranian mass was made clear by his interviews and speeches while he was prime minister and by his inability to recognize Khomeini's enormous popularity. But his followers regard Bakhtiar as a liberal, a man of great courage and the one leading Iranian who saw clearly the approaching religious dictatorship in Iran.

For the first year and a half of the revolution, Khomeini by his periodic interventions in political affairs perpetuated a strange, dualistic set of governmental institutions. Even before the revolution had finally been successful, Khomeini appointed Bazergan prime minister of Iran. And Bazergan in turn selected a cabinet, largely from the old boy network of secular and liberal religious laymen descendant from the Mossadeq administration. But because of the collapse of the police, the military, and the judiciary, the revolutionary regime set up revolutionary institutions that could provide the basis for internal security, security against external aggression, and the administration of law and order. Bazergan's hope and assumption at first was that these revolutionary institutions would be dissolved or at least integrated into their formal governmental institutional counterparts as these counterparts were reorganized and stabilized. Repeatedly Bazergan sought Khomeini's agreement for merging the two sets of institutions, and more frequently than not Khomeini agreed. But the revolutionary institutions generated their own vested interests in their perpetuation, and this new elite soon proved to have superior access to the Imam to that of Bazergan. Not only did Khomeini reverse himself on his promise to Bazergan, increasingly he referred to the need to maintain the influence base of a strong revolutionary element to balance the reformist and non-revolutionary governmental officials. In this way, Khomeini, probably more inadvertently than otherwise, developed an increasingly dominant revolutionary cadre which has steadily reduced the boundaries of free political activity. Although victims of this development see strategic and tactical consciousness in Khomeini's behavior, testimony by Iranian officials as to Khomeini's decisional style indicates far more an evolutionary process. But the results are the same; quite obviously Khomeini was more comfortable with his revolutionary lieutenants than with Bazergan reformists. The taking of the American hostages on November 4, 1979, proved to be a critical moment in this power struggle; it marked the clear ascendancy of the revolutionary arm.

Political party fortunes in the first year and a half of the revolution mirror the state of political freedom in Iran in November 1980. There were three political groupings that stood at the apex of the revolutionary leadership. Two of them represented different wings of the Mossadeq movement. There was the secular, liberal nationalist National Front, top heavy with the leading personalities that surrounded Mossadeq. These individuals were aging and had long before been enervated by the seeming hopelessness of the task of overturning the royal dictatorship.

However, when the revolutionary momentum developed, these elderly gentlemen were more than willing to offer themselves as its leaders. Shapur Bakhtiar and Karim Sanjabi were among its most prominent members.

The new generation of secular intellectuals opposed to the regime had by and large turned to other groups, particularly the far more dynamic Freedom Front, led by Mehdi Bazergan. Composed of liberal religious and lay activists, the Front's most significant accomplishment was to maintain a close and regular relationship with Ayatollah Khomeini in his years of exile. But the Freedom Front was indeed a "front" rather than a "party," and the philosophical range of its members was a broad one.

A third group, the Radical Movement of Iran, was smaller but activist and more revolutionary than the Freedom Front in tactical preference. Its spokesman, Rahmatollah Moghadam Maraghei, had served in the Majlis in the late 1950s and had spoken out courageously against the increasing oppressiveness of dictatorial control. His associates came mainly from the Justice and Education Departments.

These three groups together with prominent independents furnished the membership of the Iranian Committee for Human Rights and Liberty which functioned almost as the high command of the revolution inside Iran. It was formally associated with the International League for Human Rights, although that organization was not fully aware of its prominence in the revolutionary movement.

By October 1980 the National Front was largely defunct. Many of its leaders were in exile, some in active association with Shapur Bakhtiar. A few attempted to become members of Iran's new parliament. Some were elected but parliament refused to seat them. The Freedom Front was also largely defunct; yet many of its former members are in parliament and not a few in the new goverment. Prime Minister Mohammad Rajai and Ayatollah Mohammad Beheshti had some association with the Freedom Front in the years in which it was a semi-underground operation. In December 1979, Rahmatollah Moghadam was forced to flee Iran. Others of the Radical Movement fled or were jailed. They had been exploring an electoral alliance with the Muslim Peoples Republican Party which looked to Ayatollah Shariatmadari at the time of the government crack down on them.

The revolutionary left consisted of a number of groups most of them active among students studying abroad. Within Iran two leftist groups, the Fedayan-e-Khalq and the Mujahidin-e-Khalq, had turned to violence, operating guerrilla groups that mounted a few successful operations, and succeeded in enraging the Shah. As the revolution approached, they attracted a large percentage of revolutionary youth—especially in the universities. The Fedayan was Marxist, anti-Soviet and attractive to the kind of youth that a generation earlier had joined the National Front.

The Mujahidin was much attracted by the writings of Dr. Ali Shariati and looked especially to Ayatollah Mohammad Taleqani with reverent respect. Their image of the future was far more Marxist and far less theocratic than that of Khomeini. Since both groups seized arms from the Shah's army as it began disintegrating, they have some capability for armed insurrection.

A year and a half later the two groups survive, but are under increasing governmental disfavor, even suppression. Neither was willing to support the official referendum endorsing the Islamic Republic and the constitution. Massoud Rajavi was, until disqualified for not having supported the Islamic Republic referendum, a presidential candidate for the Mujahidin. Then a Mujahidin slate was put forward for election to the Majlis and attracted a respectable vote, especially from north Tehran. The organization, even suffering from official disfavor, can, and occasionally demonstrates that it can, bring crowds in excess of 100,000 into the streets.

The Fedayan is less successful. It has suffered significant defections from its membership to the Soviet-supported Tudeh Party. The defecting members apparently believe the efforts of the Tudeh to ally with Khomeini are an effective tactical move.

A major anomaly on the Iranian political scene is the Tudeh Party. It is generally regarded as the best organized by far of Iranian political parties, although it suffers from the association with the Soviet Union. The good to excellent relations the Shah maintained with the Soviet Union and, even more, with Eastern Europe, reduced the appeal of the Tudeh Party to Iranian leftists. When the revolution occurred the Tudeh remained close to the Soviet line which was favorable to the Khomeini regime. The Tudeh called upon its friends and allies to vote for the Islamic Republic and in favor of the constitution for the Islamic Republic of Iran. Since most Marxists see that constitution as a blueprint for a theocratic dictatorship, this tactical position was not one likely to improve the Tudeh's standing with the leftist, secular rank and file. In spite of consistently harsh verbal treatment by the Khomeini regime and the very strongly negative response from Iran to Soviet acts in Afghanistan, the Tudeh stood by its position. In the fall of 1980 that decision appeared to be paying off. The defections toward the Tudeh of Fedayan-e-Khalq members suggests that many leftist intellectuals agree that the left must not dissociate itself from a regime with such great popularity within the urban mass. The party's newspaper *Mardom* is published, and its leader, Nureddin Kianuri, a grandson of a great religious leader who was executed for his anti-revolutionary activities at the time of Iran's first revolution, is apparently able to speak rather freely in Iran.

Finally there is the Fedayan-e-Islam, a religio-political organization that was responsible for the assassination of Prime Minister Ali Razmara in 1951, an act that ushered in the second Iranian revolution led by Mohammad Mossadeq. Clearly marginal in the Mossadeq period and suppressed by the Shah, the Fedayan-e-Islam is now far closer to the mainstream. But to prosper the Fedayan-e-Islam must anticipate and adhere to Khomeini's line. This prevents the Fedayan-e-Islam from projecting a unique identity. However, the organization could well become in the near future a rallying point for the clerics and religious laymen most opposed to any secular manifestations in Iran.

The political parties and groupings that have appeared since the revolution have had to do so within boundaries set by Khomeini's charisma. By far the most important of these groupings is the Islamic Republic Party. The IRP initially represented a formalization of the overwhelming revolutionary alliance of clergy and the bureaucracies that administer the mosques and religious affairs. Directing the party is the organizational genius of the religious arm of the revolution, Ayatollah Mohammad Beheshti, but in ideology and political platform, the IRP is an umbrella organization that shelters individuals who range from one end to another of the political spectrum. They are united primarily in their support of "the line of the Imam." The necessity to appear true to that line leads to a misleading impression of homogeneity and to descriptions of the entire party as "hard line." In late October 1980, when there was something of a show down between radicals and moderates on the hostage issue, the IRP membership split, the largest number siding with the moderate pragmatic position. When Ayatollah Khomeini chastised the radicals for preventing a vote on the hostages, most of them quickly fell into line. However, they had clearly indicated the factional tendencies that exist within the parent organization and the quick regrouping that is likely to occur if Khomeini, for whatever reason, should withdraw from active participaton.

The rival Muslim Peoples Republican Party was in most respects parallel to the IRP. It was also cleric-mosque bureaucracy based, ideologically diverse, and personality focused. The leader was Ayatollah Kazem Shariatmadari, and its popular base was largely Azerbaijani. The confrontation in December 1979 between the followers of Khomeini and Shariatmadari, the withdrawal of Shariatmadari, and the collapse of the MPRP mirrored clearly the state of freedom of action in Iran. A major rival of Khomeini could not be tolerated; presumably with Khomeini's agreement, this challenge was dealt with brutally.

More symbolic of possible future political party developments than important in its own right is the Mellat Party of Dariush Foruhar. Foruhar was a member of Mossadeq's National Front, and his Pan Iranism party occupied the nationalist populist extreme end of the

National Front spectrum. Foruhar has a natural understanding of the fundamentals of change in the Iranian revolution and is obviously more than willing to serve as one of its leaders. The party he organized crosses many levels of political support—from working class to intelligentsia. Nationalism, Islam, and social justice are the symbols focused on. Foruhar, in sharp contrast to Bakhtiar, sees the future of political parties in terms of the ability to appeal to a newly awakened and active mass. For now success also requires excellent access to Khomeini, and Foruhar's access does not appear sufficient for party success.

In the power struggle that reached a new level of intensity with the arrest of Sadeq Qotbzadeh on November 8, 1980, the IRP was in open confrontation with President Bani Sadr and his followers. Bani Sadr had defeated handily the IRP organization in the presidential election. He did so in part because of the strong hints from Khomeini's family that Khomeini favored Bani Sadr's election. But also he had put together a loose coalition of literally hundreds of small groups—Bani Sadr has said 1,800—that did not survive the election. However that alliance was only in degree less unified than the IRP. In his November 1980 power struggle Bani Sadr obviously has had difficulty maintaining the alliance and thus is very much dependent on help from Khomeini in holding off the IRP challenge.

The parameters of political freedom in Iran at the time of this writing are fairly easily described. In the journalistic world, the boundaries of freedom are defined by the bitter fighting between the newspapers *Jamhouri-ye-Eslami* and *Enqellab-e-Eslami*. The former is the organ of the IRP and reflects a fairly radical theocratic view. The latter, close to Bani Sadr, is relatively liberal and definitely pragmatic. It would welcome a return of the secular element to political life and finds it possible to say that obliquely. *Mardom*, the organ of the Tudeh Party, obviously pulls its punches and makes the pretense of being dedicated to Islamic values. It diverges sharply from the governmental line concerning Afghanistan and Kurdistan. It openly argues the case for Soviet friendship even though the regime is critical of and hostile toward the Soviet Union.

There are a number of papers, such as *Kar*, that reflect a more secular viewpoint and that are semi-underground. However important critical journals, such as *Ayandegan*, that appeared to be nationalist, secular, and both willing and able to ridicule the regime have been suppressed. The National Front is consistently denied a journal.

Another indication of the state of freedom is the election campaigns. Control over who can and cannot be a candidate is explicitly maintained, and some successful candidates have had their credentials denied after election. Still the range on the spectrum of permitted political competition is fairly broad. While competition within the permitted media is vigorous, media assistance is denied to many candidates and groupings. Parliamentary debates and activities, as illustrated above, are sporadically intense. There remains the unseen requirement that the various sides not be too far from the Imam's line.

Prospects for political freedom in the immediate future are highly dependent on the course of the power struggle which, at the time of writing, is fiercely engaged. The radical Muslim groupings, including both members of the IRP and non-party allies within parliament, wish to see a continuation of purges and purification in terms of Islam of the many Iranian governmental institutions and political life. They would like to strengthen a trend toward exclusion of any manifestation of the secular, national, liberal West. The Bani Sadr grouping, on the other hand, would strengthen the long standing trend toward secularism in Iran. The Iraqi invasion should be of considerable help to the Bani Sadr faction. In order to conduct a war against a technologically superior foe, the government should turn to its military officers and technocrats who have been excluded. The price these secular elements would exact for their help would surely be a return to a position of some influence in political and social life.

There is in addition a clear trend toward independent political activity by ascriptive leaders of ethnic, tribal, and social elements. This activity, however, is largely covert and may be of more relevance to revolutionary than evolutionary change. The Kurdish rebellion is most symptomatic of this trend. Restiveness within the Qashqai, Bakhtiari, and other tribal elements should also be included.

Possibly most important if the prospects of enhanced political freedom are to improve is the emergence of leaders with independent bases of support. As indicated above, two leaders already in this category are Massoud Rajavi and Ayatollah Shariatmadari. If there is to be an evolutionary movement in the direction of political freedom, leaders with important roles in this regime must gain popularity not simply derived from Khomeini's charisma. President Bani Sadr understands this point and is making every effort to gain independent popularity by virtue of his role, sanctioned by the Imam, as commander in chief of the military. Bani Sadr surely wishes that if war heroes are to appear in Iran that he be the most prominent among them. Of the IRP members, Ayatollah Beheshti is unlikely to bid for personal popularity but can be expected to work for the political fortunes of such men as Speaker of the Majlis Hojatul Islami Hashemi Rafsenjani and Prime Minister Mohammad Rajai. But the IRP leaders are associated with the trend toward narrowing rather than expanding the political base of free activity and, thus, are more associated with coercive than popular control. There is hence little prospect that any of them will gain independent popularity. Far more likely is the appearance of a man directly from the military who might capture the popular imagination.

The Iraq invasion may have ended the prospects for revolutionary change in political leadership from the exiles. Both General Gholam Ali Oveissi and Shapur Bakhtiar have close ties with Iraq and must pay the price of an alliance with Iran's external tormentor. Were they to be successful, prospects for political freedom would be at best poor. General Oveissi almost certainly would establish a Pinochet style military dictatorship. Bakhtiar would wish for broadened political freedom, but he could only come to power through an alliance with Iraq and tribal elements such as the Qashqais in Iran; his mentors would surely place little or no value on political freedom. Two other exile leaders, Hassan Nazih and Ahmad Madani, have thus far avoided the foreign connection and both favor an essentially free political society. The scenario by which they would achieve power is difficult to imagine.

The most likely avenue of revolutionary change is a military coup. The demands of the war with Iraq are such that a strong military must develop if there are to be any prospects for success. Whether that military will be a product of an integration of the regular military and the revolutionary guards or will reflect the competition between the two is uncertain. Obviously the kind of military coup and the government set up by it will vary enormously depending on the outcome of the struggle of the revolutionary guard and the regular army. In any case an internal military coup would lead to a more populist-coercive regime than a movement led by General Oveissi.

For a leftist coup to occur in the immediate future, the precondition must be central government disintegration. The Mujahidin does have some prospects for leading a popular movement in the largest cities. But it is most doubtful that it, the Fedayan, or the Tudeh could gain power without a collapse of central authority. And in the event of a leftist coup, establishing control beyond the cities would be a difficult enterprise. One likely prospect would be the urban areas controlled by leftist elements and much of the rest of the country resorting to control by ascriptive regional, ethnic, or tribal elements.

In conclusion, the state of political freedom in Iran varies enormously depending on the factor of religiosity. But sharp change in this factor as well as many others is likely given the shock of the war with Iraq, an increasing economic deterioration and profound psychological malaise. The number of scenarios for change that have some inherent credibility is very large. Trends are contradictory and external events could easily prove to be the decisive factor in determining the direction of change with regard to the boundaries of political freedom.

# Comments and Discussion

A fter Cottam's summary of his paper, *Kazemi* suggested that part of the blame for the fundamentalist success in the Revolution should be placed on the secularists themselves. He thought that Bazergan and those around him did the greatest disservice to the secularist Iranian professional class that anyone could have done. They paved the way for Khomeini's group to take over by persisting too long in the belief that they could bring them to appreciate liberal guarantees. He also thought it was important to remember that the Tudeh party has gone through a number of important tactical changes. Whenever they felt that the time was right, they have changed their tactics—in the 1940s, the 1950s, and later. Now they have decided that it is best tactically to support Khomeini until the time comes to suppress him. This has paid off, at least, in the short run.

Referring to Cottam's comments on Shariatmadari, *Allworth* thought that the discussion should talk more of ethnic equality, ethnic freedom, and the role they play. He thought that for all groups in Iran that have been disenfranchised for many decades, personal and other freedoms lay in the direction of satisfying their desire for self-determination. He wondered whether Shariatmadari would not be the man to help the situation go that way.

*Cottam* replied that one of the sad aspects of the current situation was that exile plots involved these groups. The two main plots that are still alive involve the Qashqais and the Bakhtiaris. Yet he thought the point was important. The history of the Kurds since the revolution suggests that there is a real possibility of political freedom in Kurdistan. They have well-defined parties, independent leaders, and a good sense of where they want to go.

The unfortunate interaction of this movement with the revolution has been compounded by the strangeness of Khomeini. While most Iranians remain strong nationalists at heart, Khomeini himself considers nationalism evil, and has difficulty remembering there is such a thing. When he sees a struggle between the Kurds and his government, he thinks somebody is trying to drive a wedge between Sunnis and Shi'as. (He doesn't exploit the Shi'a-Sunni split, though some of his entourage may.) From this viewpoint he sees Kurdish leaders merely as counter-revolutionaries causing troubles between Shi'as and Sunnis.

So Khomeini cannot be expected to take seriously into account the yearnings of a people for self-identity or to work out a sensible autonomy program. Cottam placed most of the blame for the continued lack of a solution on Khomeini. As the struggle goes on it has led to a feeling of hopelessness among the Kurds, and a tendency to become tied in with Iraq and Oveissi. After this, any successful Iranian government, even if fairly liberal in granting freedom to the Farsi-speaking majority, will find it hard to grant rights to the Kurdish people.

*Gastil* suggested that the National Front had never really developed a concept of a federal state in which different peoples were granted special rights, but *Cottam* saw progress under Mossadeq, the only time they had responsibility.

*Naby* saw hope in the new constitution for the ethnic minorities. It did not overtly suppress propagating their cultures. However, it did not create any institutions for propagating them either, nor was it clear it would allow such institutions to actually function. She wondered whether it was a step in the direction of recognizing these minorities, at least culturally. *Cottam* agreed, but added that even the first draft was vague as to how the country would deal with ethnic groups. The proposals people like Foruhar were giving the Kurds would have given them an autonomy far beyond anything in recent history. But more recent events and the final constitution were less promising.

Foruhar had met almost all Kurdish demands in regard to newspapers, use of language, and full expression in terms of arts and literature; he had made major concessions in terms of local councils in which they would be able to choose the local people. But the Kurds wanted to establish a Kurdish province, and once establishing a Kurdish province they wanted to move for a provincial assembly and a governor who would have a major share in making provincial appointments. This was a very natural way for the negotiation to move, and Foruhar might have been able to handle it. Unfortunately, Khomeini became angry and sent Khalkhali to Kurdistan, and the pictures came out of Kurds being lined up and shot. From that point on the discussion became confused. But the thrust had been clear: The agreement was going to be close to what the

Kurds had obtained from the Iraqis. *Naby* suggested that the Iraqi agreement had turned out to be largely a paper agreement.

*Harrison* wondered what Foruhar had provided for by way of powers for provincial councils, or assemblies. For example, in the Pakistan debate over Baluchistan the Baluch spoke of five powers that would rest with the center. The center was to have defense, foreign affairs, including foreign trade, communication, and currency. Everything else was to be provincial. Provincial leaders differed over what they wanted to surrender to the center. *Harrison* wondered whether Cottam could conceive of any scenarios for Iran in which that kind of a federal solution would be politically or psychologically acceptable to the center. *Cottam* thought it was possible and that the Freedom Front had had a statement on this. The most explicit support for a federal solution had come from the Mujahidin and Tudeh parties.

*Newell* saw a contradiction: on the one hand Khomeini has no particular enthusiasm or interest in building a strong central structure, while on the other, he is adamantly opposed to devoiving power to the periphery. *Cottam* repeated that Khomeini apparently knew nothing of the idea of ethnic autonomy. Several participants agreed that ethnic nationalism was a very secular notion.

*Khalilzad* asked which of the potential ideological contestants for domination of Iran would have the best chance of bringing about freedom. *Cottam* thought that Iran was going to have to bring secularists back to survive in the war and economically. On the other hand, he has become very discouraged with bourgeois intellectuals in recent years. They want ultimately to do away with mass participation, restore order, and allow business to go on. A likely successor government would be a pragmatic regime, less free politically than the current regime. It would probably involve the military and be a more technocratic and familiar government. The best possibility of an evolution toward liberal democracy would be under Bani Sadr, if he could attract real popularity. He is a liberal and would try to produce democratic institutions and bring secularists back in. If the Mujahidin became leaders of the country they would be compelled, whether they wanted to or not, to establish a very tight dictatorship; this is true of all of the left. Although the Soviet Union is very sluggish, a terrible scenario would be the Soviet Union responding to an invitation from such a group. If the Tudeh came to power, they would have to invite the Soviets in to preserve power.

*Harrison* wondered whether the Mujahidin would ally with the Tudeh, or whether there were such ideological differences they couldn't. *Cottam* said that although they do not like the Tudeh, they might ally for political advantage. He could see them allying together to defeat Oveissi.

*Gastil* wondered about the idea of an "Iranian mass." His experience in Iran suggested that it was very hard to know how many supported a particular movement, in spite of the appearance of unanimity. Closer examination might reveal large proportions of the population were either not participating or participating for reasons different from those of actual support. Since it is so hard to know what the average lower-middle class or peasant Iranian thinks, it is hard to predict what he might do in a changed situation. *Cottam* responded that since political scientists define the masses as those that are not attentive to politics and do not have strong or sustained interests, in a way this must be true for all situations. But he thought that the most lasting result of this revolution and what made it critically important was that Iran was now a mass society. Mass politics in Iran means that there is a very large number of people capable of sustained political activity.

In regard to the question of this new politics, *Fischer* wondered why at critical points Shariatmadari or Taleqani were not able to command this mass base. Shariatmadari represented the idea of widening the polity— allowing representation to different interest groups. Fischer thought Shariatmadari represented a following far beyond Azerbaijan. He is widely regarded as a greater theological authority than Khomeini. He seemed to have the potential at the time of the debate over the constitution of starting a civil war if he had wanted to go that far. He clearly pulled back. Fischer wondered why at such critical points has Khomeini been able to mobilize more mass support than Shariatmadari. *Cottam* replied that people very close to the situation told him last December that the support that Shariatmadari has outside of Azerbaijan is only among the politically attentive. Outside of Azerbaijan, Khomeini has the mass support if a crunch comes between the two. What Shariatmadari did not want was to have this situation crystallized, because if it crystallized it would mean that the non-Turkish speaking masses would definitely consider Shariatmadari bad and the Turkish-speaking would consider Khomeini bad. Neither Shariatmadari nor his supporters wanted to have his base of support limited to Azerbaijan. In part this was worked out very well, although some of his people had to flee the country.

*Fischer* pointed out that the problem went beyond Shariatmadari. There were conflicts in towns like Shiraz where the two leading Ayatollahs were struggling with each other, or in Yazd where a Khomeiniite Ayatollah and his allies are widely resented by the populace because, for example, they allegedly executed two boys on immorality charges of which they were later found to be innocent. The executions were done rapidly without following proper procedures—particularly upsetting was the execution of minors while their parents were out of town. Fischer wondered why that kind of discontent is not organized and drawn upon to shift support away from Khomeini within the system. *Cottam* thought that Khomeini had better access to the people.

*Nabawi* asked whether Cottam saw a coalition developing between the Tudeh and some of the minorities. *Cottam* pointed out that in the Democratic Party of Kurdistan there is a Tudeh section, so there is a coalition already. The problem for both the Soviets and the Tudeh is that although their major strategy or tactic is to identify with the central government, they are also very important with the Kurds. They cannot take too strong a position. But Cottam agreed with Kazemi that if it looked advantageous to them, they would ally with the minorities tomorrow.

*Rakowska-Harmstone* suggested that it appeared to her as an outsider that of all the groups, the Tudeh was best suited to mobilize the masses. With their organizational advantages the Tudeh might be best suited to build the coalition, for they appealed to both minorities and the secular element. She wondered if there was a possibility of their being able to use the appeal of Shariatmadari, and whether there was contact between his Azeri people and the official Muslim Azeri Board in the Soviet Union. (No one knew.)

*Kazemi* responded that the history of the Tudeh in Iran and the pervasive anti-Tudeh feeling among the masses made their success improbable. There was a strong, underlying fear of the Soviet Union. Any regime or any group that is too closely allied with the Soviets risks losing out among the masses. The only way for Tudeh to play a key role is through coalition with other groups that have a better legitimacy. An alliance with the Mujahidin was possible in the distant future.

*Gastil* saw a contradiction between Cottam's description of a secular trend in Iran and the fact that the general public appears to be highly religious or at least very attracted to religious symbols for the moment. He wondered whether there had been a dramatic shift in the last few years in an anti-secular direction that would be maintained, or whether this shift has to do primarily with symbols. Perhaps the average Iranian is by no means as involved with, or interested in, religion as he appears to be. *Cottam* thought we should think of the secular trend in terms of an arithmetical progression. There is a much larger group of secularists today than in Mossadeq's time, but in terms of political participation, there is a geometric progression. About fifteen percent of the population was participant in Mossadeq's time while eighty-five percent is today. This means there is a very large group of newly participant people who are not so much anti-secular as not secular. This is one reason the present episode may be illusory. The mass is religious but the politically attentive are secular. When the mass returns to its more natural state of inattentiveness, then you will see Iran looking very secular again. *Wriggins* noted an analogy to Sri Lanka. A few years ago there was an enormous mass enthusiasm around religious symbols, and now it is largely gone.

*Fischer* brought up the modernist, anticlericalism of Ali Shariati. He thought that the religious symbolism that is mobilized was not an undifferentiated symbolism. Many people newly conscious in the political arena are extremely religious but are at the same time as cynical as they have always been. There is a deep strain of anticlericalism among villagers and urban working-class people that can reinforce the new modernist strain associated with Shariati.

*Richter* said that it had struck him in Pakistan, and was his impression for Iran and other areas, that individuals who three or five years ago had all the appearance of being secular or technocratic now had the appearance of being religious. They were starting to attend meetings discussing the Quran, and more generally attempting to reestablish their Islamic roots. Richter wondered to what extent he was correct in perceiving such a phenomenon, and to what extent this tempered the assessment that recent Iranian events represented only a temporary deviation from a general trend toward secularism. *Cottam* referred back to his example of Foruhar's party. He did not think we would again see in Iran the disregard of religion among political figures and people writing for a broad audience that was common in the past. Islamic fundamentalists cannot be ignored, just as Americans cannot ignore Christian fundamentalists. He said he saw the psychological process Richter mentioned occurring in many of his friends. Confronted with a movement of this magnitude, people who he thought were atheists suddenly became religious. *Naby* wondered if he was talking about people searching for their Islamic roots or creating an Islamic image of themselves. *Cottam* said that since he believed in psychological balance theory he didn't see the contrast. He thought that in order to live with themselves, his friends had to adopt a more religious position.

*Kazemi* referred back to the differences described between members of the Islamic Republican Party and those on the left. He wondered if they didn't have a great deal in common in terms of the groups they wanted to appeal to and their conception of the world. Didn't they have similar views of who are the important political actors outside Iran? Some people point out that both think imperialism is associated with capitalism. He thought that Islamic Republicanism was a new mixture. *Cottam* thought this a valuable point. Both groups shared a clear image of the source of all evil. Both Muslim fundamentalists and the left shared the Zionist-imperialist picture, and he thought they now shared a common dislike of the bourgeoisie. It was also brought out that their attitude toward the regular army was similar. They both made a clear distinction during the revolutionary period: when they talked about brothers and sisters in the military they were talking about enlisted men. (Cottam pointed out the parallel of our own right and left in that they both see the Trilateral Commission as a source of evil.)

# Prospects for Political Freedom in Pakistan

William L. Richter

Freedom has many meanings in the contemporary world, some of them mutually contradictory. Even within the Western liberal democratic tradition it is possible to distinguish at least three broad categories of freedom concepts:

(1) Individual freedom—the right and capacity of individual citizens to pursue their own perceived values relatively unimpeded by arbitrary governmental authority. This usage is perhaps best summarized by the phrase "political rights and civil liberties" which has served as a subtitle for the *Freedom in the World* series.

(2) Ethnic Self-determination—the right and capacity of significant groups within the society to pursue their perceived values relatively unimpeded by either governmental authority or the actions of other groups.

(3) National independence—the right and capacity of the nationstate to pursue self-determined goals unimpeded by outside powers. This implies not only formal political independence but also the elimination of military, economic, and cultural forms of dependence.

While most of this paper is concerned with the first of these categories, it is important to note that all three types of freedom may be intricately related. An absence of individual or political freedom may be a prime motivation for the coalescence of ethnic demands for self-determination. Dependency relationships may reinforce internal forms of authoritarian domination or secessionist conflict.[1]

Pakistan, more than most countries, has been plagued throughout its more than three decades of national independence with a relative lack of freedom in all three of the above categories: with authoritarianism, ethnic domination, and international dependence. For more than half of the period since Pakistan was created in 1947 the country has been under the rule of the military or a military-bureaucratic combine (1958-1971,

1977-present). Even during the two periods when civilians held the reins of power (1947-1958 and 1971-1977), the political system fell far short of guaranteeing full political participation, freedom of expression, or many other basic civil and political rights.[2] The persistent denial of the rights of the Bengali majority in East Pakistan led to the disastrous 1971 civil war and the emergence of independent Bangladesh—the only successful case of secession in the twentieth century. The domination of the Punjabi majority within post-1971 Pakistan and governmental insensitivity to regional concerns and aspirations have continued not only to alienate the Baluch, Pushtun, and Sindhis, but also to crystallize more diffuse identities, such as those of the Siraiki speakers of central Pakistan. In the international arena, Pakistan's military and economic dependence upon the United States and Western-dominated international financial agencies like the World Bank has been persistent despite notable policy differences in recent years. Within the past decade, new dependency relationships have developed between Pakistan and some of the oil-rich Muslim countries of the Middle East. All of these factors would need to be taken into account in order to make a complete assessment of the prospects for freedom in Pakistan. The scope of the present inquiry, however, is necessarily restricted, primarily, to the first of the above categories of concern, involving individual freedom, representative and judicial institutions, channels of political expression, and related aspects of political freedom.

## ISLAM AND FREEDOM

Before proceeding with an investigation of the contemporary political situation in Pakistan, we should consider the relation of Islam and freedom. The issue impinges upon the subject of freedom in Pakistan in a variety of ways, and underlies discussion of freedom in any Muslim country. The relationship is particularly relevant for Pakistan, created in the name of Islam and presently undergoing processes of social change that have been variously characterized as Islamic resurgence, revival, revolution, and recovery of identity.[3] From a liberal Western perspective, freedom and Islam might appear to be mutually incompatible forces. Islam, after all, means *submission*, seemingly the direct opposite of freedom. Modern Western concepts of freedom have developed in part in reaction to religious authority. This tradition is preserved most clearly in the doctrine of separation of church and state or of secularism, but many other liberal assumptions concerning freedom also reflect this heritage of "liberation" from the confines of revealed truth. Giovanni Sartori, for instance, questions whether a competitive and stable pluralistic party system can be viable in a country which does not have a "sufficient separation of the various spheres of life—religion, politics, wealth—and a sufficient protection for the individual as such.''[4]

However, it might appear highly ethnocentric and unfair to apply liberal Western models of freedom and of free institutions to countries with another significant political tradition. If separation of "church" and state is a *sine qua non* of freedom, for instance, then Islamic states would by definition be unfree, and there would be no further room for dialogue on this point. By the same token, practices of one society which another finds shocking should not necessarily, on that ground alone, be considered unfree. The "harshness" of Islamic punishments, such as the amputation of hands for theft, and the role of women in Muslim countries are two subjects which frequently arouse considerable concern among Americans and other Westerners, but societies in which there is considerable support for capital punishment and opposition to equal rights for women might hesitate before casting too many stones.

At the risk of gross oversimplification and possible misrepresentation, let us characterize a few of the more obvious distinctions between liberal and Islamic concepts of freedom. First, while the liberal notion of freedom is fundamentally secular, humanistic, and rationalistic, the Islamic understanding places freedom within the context of revealed law and justice. The Quran provides guidance for all of human existence, not just for the "religious side" of people's lives, and therefore provides some limits to political and economic freedom. Because freedom is perceived to have revealed limits does not mean that there is no scope for freedom at all. On the contrary, human beings are considered free to pursue and enjoy the fruits of their livelihood, to formulate and express their opinion on public matters, and even to revolt against injustice and an unjust political order. There is some disagreement among Muslims concerning the specific political institutions appropriate to an Islamic state, but many find firm ground for the legitimacy of political parties, elections, popular assemblies, and other familiar democratic institutions, though often in forms which would diverge from Western practice.

Secondly, liberal concepts of freedom are *individualistic*. Individuals are perceived to be endowed with rights to life, liberty, and property, and these rights are often regarded as near-absolute. Islam provides scope for individual freedom, but conceives all rights as derivative from God. Property, for instance, is held in trust by the individual, who is expected to share the benefits of that property with the rest of the society. Individual rights are tempered by social responsibilities.

Finally, it must be noted, Islam shares two important features with liberal political thought: both are fundamentally egalitarian and both are realistic or "this-worldly." That is, both place emphasis upon behavior in historical, real-life circumstances rather than upon withdrawal from the world into monastic seclusion or philosophical speculation. In this respect, Islamic political thought is closer to that of Machiavelli and his successors than to Plato and the preponderant tradition of classical and medieval Western political philosophy. Freedom—in both orthodox Islamic and Western liberal thought—involves freedom *in* the world rather than from it.

While these brief comments on Islam may serve to caution us against too hasty condemnation of certain Islamic practices unfamiliar to our own cultures, they should not preclude consideration of questions such as the relative extent of freedom in a country like Pakistan. In many respects, political rights and civil liberties valued in Western liberal societies are not incompatible with those derived from Islam. Tyranny, censorship, and injustice are abhorrent to notions of freedom in both traditions.

Unlike Iran, Pakistan has not gone through an "Islamic Revolution." The Constitution of 1973, with its parliamentary structure, federalism, and other Western-type political features, still theoretically remains in effect despite numerous modifications by the current military regime. Thus, while it is important to be cognizant of Islamic political values, it is still appropriate to evaluate Pakistan's current levels of political freedom in terms of its constitutional provisions for representative institutions, political parties, elections, and other features of liberal democracy, such as an independent and fair judiciary and the freedoms of speech, press, and assembly. Yet neither Pakistan's past nor present provides much cause for optimism concerning the future of political freedom.

## PAKISTAN UNDER ZIA

The current phase of military rule in Pakistan began July 5, 1977, when Army Chief of Staff General Zia-ul-Haq deposed Prime Minister Zulfikar Ali Bhutto. Bhutto had come to power in December 1971 in the wake of the Bangladesh war and had done a remarkable job of "pulling the country together" after the shock and humiliation of that conflict. But he had also centralized political authority in his own hands, outlawed the major opposition party, jailed political opponents, manipulated the news media, undermined the independence of the judiciary and the neutrality of the bureaucracy, and created special paramilitary forces for his own political benefit. When elections were held March 7, 1977, incidents of malpractice were sufficiently widespread to raise a strong protest of "rigging" against the government. This protest grew into an anti-Bhutto movement, which, by mid-April, had virtually immobilized Pakistan's economy and polity. The government and the opposition Pakistan National Alliance (PNA) began a negotiated settlement of their differences but, before the agreement between them could be concluded, the army stepped in with its own solution to the problem. General Zia announced that new elections would be held "within ninety days" and that power would then be returned to popularly-elected representatives. "Operation Fairplay," as this military intrusion into the political arena was ironically labeled, did not succeed as planned. Two weeks before the scheduled mid-October elections the polls were called off, apparently because the deposed Prime Minister and his Pakistan People's Party (PPP) were too strong an electoral threat, particularly in the Punjab, Pakistan's most populous province.[5] Several criminal cases were registered against Bhutto and his associates and the most serious of these culminated in Bhutto's conviction for involvement in a 1974 murder. Despite extensive clemency appeals from both within and outside Pakistan, the self-styled Quaid-i-Awam (leader of the people) was unceremoniously executed by hanging early in the morning of April 4, 1979. With Bhutto's fate sealed, Zia again scheduled national elections, for November 1979, and again found it necessary to cancel them at the last minute because of his assessment that they would not yield "positive results." In the most recent cancellation political parties were also banned, their leaders arrested, and stricter censorship imposed on the press.

General Zia had originally retained President Fazl Elahi Chaudhuri and the 1973 Constitution—except for those portions "held in abeyance" —in order to provide some semblance of continuity and to underwrite his claim that the coup was merely a temporary action to restore order and balance to the political system. In 1978, however, he replaced Chaudhuri as President and his repeated modifications of the Constitution, by no authority other than his own mandate, make that document increasingly unrecognizable.

Present political conditions in Pakistan allow little scope for popular political activity. National and provincial assembles were dismissed at the time of the coup in 1977. Political parties have been banned since the cancellation of the 1979 elections. Party and union leaders have been jailed and punished (even flogged in public) for engaging in non-violent protest activities. Some newspapers have been closed, many others extensively censored, and some reporters arrested for writing material objectionable to the military authorities.

Even the judiciary—the most independent element in the Pakistani system—has had a mixed record of providing protection to individual liberties under the present military regime. In delivering its judgment on a case brought by Begum Nusrat Bhutto challenging the constitutionality of the martial law order under which her husband was being detained in late 1977, the Supreme Court of Pakistan decided for the government and against Mrs. Bhutto. However, it did so on the basis of the "doctrine of necessity" rather than upon the much broader theory of "revolutionary legality" which government counsel had argued. By choosing the narrower justification of the coup, the court not only retained for itself the right of judicial review (however inadequately exercised in subsequent cases) but also decreed that the legitimacy of the miliary regime was dependent upon the fulfillment of certain conditions, the most notable of which was "the earliest possible holding of free and fair elections for the purpose of restoration of democratic institutions under the 1973 Constitution."[6] Despite the passage of approximately three years since that judgment, however, little progress has been made toward fulfillment of that condition.

Moreover, other governmental actions have been taken to weaken the effectiveness of the courts. A report issued by Amnesty International in April 1978 objected to the widespread use of military courts to try civilians for political offenses under martial law regulations.[7] Amnesty International also objected to the use of flogging, amputation, and executions as cruel and unusual punishments.

Some Pakistanis look upon General Zia as a deliverer of the country from the despotic rule of Bhutto. Others regard Zia as the tyrant and Bhutto as a martyr. Despite the above comments concerning the limitations on freedom in Pakistan, it has not been totally annihilated. Civil courts continue to operate and to dispense justice within the confines of martial law. Local government elections were held in late 1979, on a nonpartisan basis, and officials elected at that time have been given authority and funding to develop their own local programs. Most newspapers and news magazines continue to publish, even some moderately critical of certain governmental policies, although frequently with blank columns where criticism or innuendo exceeded the bounds of the censor's standards. During periods of relative calm political leaders are released from detention and some political parties at least are able to hold small meetings despite the technical illegality of parties. Nonetheless, political freedom in Pakistan may still be considered severely restricted by the arbitrary actions of an unrepresentative military regime. Further difficulties result from the external threat presented by the war in neighboring Afghanistan, including Pakistan's provision of shelter for more than a million Afghan refugees, and by the fact that no clear plan has yet emerged for an orderly return to civilian rule.

## PROSPECTS FOR FREEDOM: ALTERNATIVE SCENARIOS

Pakistan's future depends upon what sort of solution is found to the complex political puzzle which was created with the July 1977 coup.

General Zia has repeatedly assured his countrymen that the army cannot remain in power permanently, that he himself has no political ambitions, and that the people of Pakistan must ultimately have a government of their own making. But when will this restoration or transformation occur, and what will be the nature of the resultant political order? It seems clear that Zia himself has no definite answers to these questions, but that he is willing to consider a number of alternatives, some of them more conducive to political freedom than others. A review of six possible scenarios might provide some clue to the future.

*Scenario 1: Restoration of Parliamentary Democracy.* The most desirable, yet perhaps the most unlikely, prospect for Pakistani politics would be a return to the parliamentary system which was set aside when the army seized power July 5, 1977. The primary avowed purpose of the military intervention was the holding of fair elections by which such a restoration might be effected. Despite the two cancellations of general elections, the Chief Martial Law Administrator (CMLA), General Zia, has reiterated this objective upon numerous occasions. Moreover, there is widespread support among political leaders for a return to the system embodied in the 1973 Constitution. During mid-1980 Pakistani newspapers conducted a general forum on this subject and found a broad consensus among both PPP and PNA political leaders—with the sole exception of Maulana Kausar Niazi, Bhutto's former Information Minister—in favor of the reestablishment of parliamentary democracy under the terms of the 1973 Constitution.

If everyone favors this course of action, why is it so difficult to bring about? The answer is to be found in the reasons for the cancellations of the 1977 and 1979 elections. In both instances, the government gave clear indications that the anticipated results of the elections would have been unacceptable, that is, that the candidates of the Pakistan People's Party would have been too sucessful. If the PPP had returned to power, Zia and his military and civilian associates would have fared badly. Zia is thus caught in something of a catch-22 situation: elections cannot be held because of the appeal of the PPP, but the longer the military holds on to power, the greater the disaffection from its domination is likely to be. Other parties face similar dilemmas in this regard as well. If they co-operate with the military in joining a civilian government, as several of the PNA component parties did in 1978, they might argue that they are helping to bring about conditions for elections, but they run the risk of being labeled collaborationists and tools of the military and thereby losing public support. On the other hand, if they position themselves against the military rulers in order to maintain public appeal, they run the risk of forcing the military to postpone elections indefinitely for fear of what they might do if elected.

It is perhaps inappropriate to speak of "restoration" of democracy in Pakistan, because many would argue that what existed there from 1971 to 1977 was a system that was only superficially democratic. Bhutto's own repressive actions and institutions placed severe limitations upon political freedom even during Pakistan's "most democratic" period. However, if some sort of transition from military to parliamentary government could be achieved, the 1973 Constitution—backed by a broad-based national consensus and shorn of the controversial modifications introduced by Zia—might provide a framework within which representative institutions and political freedom could mature and thrive for the first time in Pakistan's history as an independent nation. Unfortunately, it may be the case, as the New Englander is supposed to have said, that "you can't get there from here."

*Scenario 2: Transition to a Basic-Democracy Type of Policy.* As the difficulties of restoring the pre-coup status quo have become more obvious, General Zia has cast about for alternative arrangements which might provide the current regime or some civilian successor with popular legitimacy. One such alternative arrangement which has been explored is to build a system of representation on the "local bodies" officials elected in September 1979. Zia has frequently commented that democracy in Pakistan must be built "from the ground up." Despite objections from party leaders, he insisted on holding the local bodies elections prior to the general elections to national and provincial assemblies (later canceled). In March 1980, an All-Pakistan Local Bodies Convention was held in Islamabad for 300 chairmen and vice-chairmen of District Councils and Municipal Committees, Mayors and Deputy Mayors of Municipal Corporations, and other local officials. Zia hailed the meeting as "the first step towards the establishment of a representative Government," and assured the delegates that they were "the real representatives of the people—duly elected." The convention considered issues not only of local interest but of foreign policy, defense, and other national issues as well.[8]

Much of this is reminiscent of the Basic Democracies System which prevailed in Pakistan during most of the Ayub Khan decade, 1958-1969. Under this system, incorporated into the 1962 Constitution, local officials, termed "Basic Democrats," selected higher-level councils and even served as the electorate for selection of provincial and national assembly members and of the president of Pakistan. Although Zia has not yet indicated any intention of investing local officials with such an electoral college function, his emphasis upon this local "base" for national politics not only leaves open that possibility but appeals to the sentiments of significant portions of the bureaucracy, military, and others who look upon the Ayub decade as an era of stability and prosperity.

The Ayub years, however, were also a period of growing economic disparity and political frustration within Pakistan. The Basic Democracy system proved inadequate to the task of channeling the popular discontent which emerged in the late 1960s and ultimately led to Ayub's resignation and scrapping the 1962 Constitution. It seems difficult to believe that the present regime would seriously contemplate reestablishment of such a system. Whatever consideration is being given the subject is no doubt by default: nothing else has worked and the local officials are available as a potential resource. Unlike Ayub, Zia apparently entered office with no clear masterplan, other than perhaps a well-meaning intention to hold elections three months later. The failure of "Operation Fairplay" has left the regime in a continuous state of drift and indirection, with a locally-based system of representation one not-very-promising possibility for direction.

Even if a Basic Democracy system were acceptable to political leaders, which it is not, it would not hold much prospect for enhancement of political freedom in Pakistan. The Ayub model, at least, demonstrated too much possibility for manipulation of the political process by the president and the bureaucracy.

*Scenario 3: Transition to an Islamic Type of Polity.* The other alternative to parliamentary democracy that has received some attention and encouragement from the present regime is the creation of an Islamic order more in keeping with the Quran and Islamic traditions. Because of the historical circumstances, the relation of Islam to politics has been an enduring issue in Pakistan. President Zia-ul-Haq, however, is the first ruler of Pakistan who has given wholehearted endorsement to the principle of *Nizam-i-Mustafa* (Order of the Prophet) or *Nizam-i-Islam* (Islamic Order). The current phase of Islamic resurgence in Pakistan, it should be noted, did not begin with the military coup, but rather had been building for some time. The PNA had raised the Nizam-i-Mustafa slogan in the March 1977 election campaign, and Bhutto had enacted some "defensive Islamization" measures in April 1977 in an attempt to weaken the protest movement against his government.[9] But the major thrust came after the coup. Beginning with the announcement of Quranic punishments within days after the takeover, Islamization had increasingly become a top priority of the present regime. Steps have been taken to introduce the collection and disbursement of Zakat and Ushr taxes, to abolish *Riba* (interest) in the banking system, and to establish a set of Shariat benches in the country's high courts to judge the conformity of laws to the Shariah (Islamic law). Election laws have also been changed, providing for separate electorates for Muslims and non-Muslims.

Most of these Islamic reforms have dealt with policy rather than structure, but Zia has also suggested on several occasions that a "new political system" might be created more in accordance with the principles of Islam, and in such a system there would be "no provision for Western-type elections." In October 1979 he appointed a twelve-member committee of "scholars, jurists, ulema, and prominent persons from other walks of life" to formulate recommendations concerning the structure of such an Islamic governmental system. While the recommendations of the committee are not yet available, some have argued that such an order should be partyless, utilize separate electorates (if elections are held at all), specify educational and reputational qualifications for both voting and candidacy, and vest full power in an *Amir* (ruler), advised by a *majlis-i-shura* (consultative assembly). In late 1979, retired Justice B. Z. Kaikaus filed a case with the Lahore High Court Shariah Bench charging that the entire system of parliamentary government embodied in the 1973 Constitution is un-Islamic. Although the court eventually decided against Kaikaus, his case was indicative of the contours of one very influential body of legal thought in present-day Pakistan.

During the last week of August, 1980, a two-day conference of ulema was held in Islamabad under the sponsorship of the Government in Pakistan. Like the local bodies convention six months earlier, the Ulema Conference considered a wide range of political issues and presented a formal charter of demands to the government. Zia utilized the occasion to announce the formation of an Ulema Board, whose members would rank as presidential advisors, and to say that he would consider the appointments of ulema to Shariat Courts and as representatives on federal and provincial councils. He also told them that, until such time as a national parliament came into being, the ulema would serve as his majlis-i-shura.[10]

Such comments should be considered in the context of a regime eager to exploit any linkages to the public available to it, but even this ulema conference had mixed consequences for the military government. The conference was primarily representative of one school of Islamic thought —the Hanafi school of Sunni Islam. In protest a group of ulema of the minority Shi'a sect assembled a few days later in Islamabad to present their own demands to the government. There was reportedly a police firing and a few of the Shi'a demonstrators killed. Although the government later attempted a reconciliation of Sunni and Shi'a interests, the incident demonstrated once again some of the difficulties inherent in attempting to aggregate majority and minority concerns in Islamic reforms.

There have also been other signs of resistance to the type of Islamic system suggested by the Kaikaus brief and Zia's fleeting comments.

Former Chief Justice Muhammad Munir, among others, has taken issue with the way in which "the State has drifted into the hands of an orthodox element which claims that they will make Pakistan a totally Islamic State, as it was in the days of Nizam-i-Mustafa."[11] Certainly, any further attempt to translate Islamic ideals into practice will need to take into account the differing perspectives of Sunnis and Shi'as, ulema and pirs,[12] as well as differing interpretations of what types of political institutions are acceptable to Islam.

The Islamic resurgence in Pakistan carries with it threats to personal and political freedom, not because of any prima facie priority of Western over Islamic values, but rather because religion can often be used as a cloak for political exploitation. Whether or not flogging is an appropriate punishment for certain criminal acts, its use in Pakistan against political dissidents appears to be a clear infringement of freedom. The fact that Islamic reform is being introduced in Pakistan by an unrepresentative military dictator further undermines its legitimacy and engenders opportunities for its misuse.

*Scenario 4: Another Military Coup.* With the present government of Pakistan unable to restore parliamentary democracy under present conditions, and unclear on how far or how fast to proceed in any other direction, speculation has arisen on whether some less orderly transition might occur, the most obvious of which might be another military coup. Speculation concerning such a possibility has gone on for some time, encouraged in part by General Zia's indecisiveness and less-than-inspiring public image. As Zia himself has noted, the longer the army stays in power in Pakistan, the worse it is for the reputation of the army. It might be possible that another general could either provide the country with the sense of direction or the political changes which Zia has been unable to do. For example, in 1969 General A. M. Yahya Khan was able to displace Ayub, scrap the basic democracies system, and prepare the country for parliamentary elections.

Some such coup was apparently attempted, or at least considered, in March 1980. Information concerning what happened is extremely scarce, but General Zia responded by retiring several of his more ambitious colleagues from military service and by removing command duties from the Deputy Martial Law Administrators involved in the administration of government at the provincial level. Zia appears to be quite aware at the present time of the dangers of displacement from within the military and, therefore, unlikely to allow conditions to develop that might permit such an outcome.

The consequences of another military coup for political freedom would depend largely upon the policy preferences of whoever replaced Zia.

*Scenario 5: Mass Protest.* Another alternative break from the status quo might be the development of a mass protest movement against the Zia government. The precedent for such activity is well-established in recent Pakistani political history. Such a movement brought down Ayub Khan in 1969 and another against Bhutto in early 1977 set the stage for the July coup. There are certainly many Pakistanis who regard the present regime as illegitimate and who would like to avenge what they perceive as the murder of Zulfikar Ali Bhutto. Yet attempts to mobilize anti-Zia protest, even following Bhutto's execution, have been singularly unsuccessful.

One reason for the relative absence of protest has been the government's use of effective, and often harsh, methods of preventive detention and punishment for proscribed political activities. But Pakistanis have previously risked their lives and freedom to bring down political leaders through mass protest. The threat, or even the reality, of arrest, flogging or even death, would seem inadequate to explain the relative calm of Pakistan.

A second explanation involves the health of the Pakistan economy, which has been rather strong under Zia. Production and exports have increased, many of the economically unproductive programs of the Bhutto era have been eliminated, and other steps have been taken to strengthen the economy. Perhaps the greatest single factor, however, has been the extensive migration of Pakistani labor to Persian Gulf and other Middle Eastern states, and the concurrent return of remittances from these countries to families remaining in Pakistan. This has had the dual effect of removing excess labor, which might otherwise form a potential pool of discontented demonstrators, and of increasing prosperity at home. Remittances from overseas Pakistanis (even counting only those which are officially reported) have become Pakistan's largest single source of foreign exchange.

If the Middle East migration should happen to slacken or even reverse, or if the Pakistan economy should for some other reason suffer a sharp downturn, the country might be ripe for a repeat of the events of 1967-69 or 1977. Short of that, this scenario is unlikely to materialize.

*Scenario 6: Persistence of the Status Quo.* It is also possible that nothing will change fundamentally in Pakistan in the near future. Unless some of the foregoing discussion of alternative futures for Pakistan is incorrect in its perception or analysis, this would seem to be the most likely prediction for the coming months, possibly years. While it may seem difficult to imagine that a regime with only a temporary mission and without any clear sense of direction or popular mandate could stay in power even as long as it has, the absence of feasible alternatives suggests that the political drift is going to continue. The domestic impasse is reinforced by recent international developments. The build-up of Soviet forces in Afghanistan and the intensification of the Afghan war after December 1979 has not only resulted in more than a million refugees on Pakistani soil, but has presented Pakistan with an external threat which tends to override internal discontent with military rule. Despite his political shortcomings, General Zia has proven himself skillful in responding not only to Soviet pressures from one side, but also to American influence from the other.

If this prognosis is correct, the prospects for a significant improvement in political freedom in Pakistan in the near future are dim. Indeed, the situation may worsen as military rule persists and the generals find themselves unable to respond adequately to pressures from the politicians to restore parties and elections, or from spokesmen for regional (for example, Baluch) or minority (for example, Shi'a) interests.

## WHAT MIGHT BE DONE TO ENCOURAGE POLITICAL FREEDOM IN PAKISTAN?

How might individuals, institutions, or outside governments encourage the preservation and expansion of civil liberties and political freedom in Pakistan? While the scope for American and other Western influence is greater in Pakistan than in any of its immediately adjacent Muslim neighbors (that is, Iran, Afghanistan, or the Soviet Central Asian republics), it is still considerably less than was the case even a few years ago. Pakistan is no longer the "most allied of America's allies" (as Ayub Khan once affirmed) and has in fact withdrawn from American supported alliances (SEATO and CENTO) to seek membership in the Non-Aligned Movement. Sensitive to the important role which American aid and advisors played during the 1950s and 1960s, and highly suspicious of American involvement in such crucial events as Bhutto's ouster, many Pakistanis now regard American advice with much greater skepticism than was once the case. The clash between Pakistani nuclear aspirations and American nonproliferation policies have further embittered relations between our two countries. In short, Pakistan has belatedly arrived at a point reached earlier by a number of other third world nations, of resenting "outside" interference in domestic politics. In the Bhutto case, outside appeals for clemency came from virtually every major country, including several other Muslim states, with no visible effect. The hangman's noose was not a matter for international consideration.

Given the modest limits within which they might have any positive effect, the following strategies might be pursued by government, individual activities, and scholars:

1. On the governmental level, the United States should avoid overcommitment to General Zia in overreaction to developments in Afghanistan. The urge to rush into a crisis situation with a ready-made arms aid solution runs the risk not only of becoming Zia's obvious external patron, but also of permitting the military to stifle internal dissent with externally supplied strength. The example of the Shah in Iran should be an instructive parallel.

2. To the extent that human rights remains an element in United States foreign policy, American officials should diplomatically encourage the full restoration of civil liberties and the broadening of press freedoms. This would entail (a) minimizing and if possible eliminating preventive detention; (b) releasing of political prisoners; (c) eliminating corporal punishments (such as flogging) for political "crimes"; (d) eliminating military trials for civilians; (e) relaxing and possibly eliminating censorship of the press.

3. Within the narrow confines previously discussed, American officials should encourage the exploration of ways and means of reestablishing representative government based upon the framework of the 1973 Constitution. This might involve (a) discouragement of further modification of that framework through executive fiat; (b) encouragement of continuing dialogue between the government and political party representatives, including the Pakistan People's Party; and (c) encouragement of continuing dialogue between the government and regional political leaders, particularly in the minority provinces.

4. American policy-makers should give thorough and serious reconsideration to our relations with the countries of the Middle East, our perceptions of Islam, and our assessments of the broad and diverse set of phenomena roughly characterized as Islamic resurgence. To continue to respond to developments in Southwest Asia (or indeed anywhere in the third world) as merely an aspect of big-power global competition will blind us to accurate assessment of both the motives and actions of people in the region.

5. On the level of individual and private organizational activity, the first step would be to maintain the monitoring functions of such organizations as Amnesty International. While AI appeals do not always receive favorable response from the government of Pakistan, they at least serve to inform the broader public quite specifically concerning governmental infringement of personal and political freedom.

6. Individual appeals are also important. While these proved fruitless in the case of Bhutto, they have been more effective in securing the

release of individual journalists arrested for writing stories judged objectionable to the regime.

7. Finally, on a scholarly level, there is need for much more complete analysis and understanding of the dynamics of Pakistani politics. Among the more obvious subjects to which scholars ought to be directing attention are: (a) the difficulties of establishing a workable electoral process in Pakistan; (b) the political role of the military;[13] (c) problems of political party development and organization; (d) federalism and the role of ethnic and regional minorities; and (e) values (for example, trust, honesty, tolerance) potentially supportive of democratic institutions. There is also a need to translate the findings of research on these and related subjects into language that can be disseminated to an informed public.

## NOTES

1. See Johan Galtung, "A Structural Theory of Imperialism," *Journal of Peace Research*, 1971, No. 2, pp. 83-84; and E. Wayne Nafziger and William L. Richter, "Biafra and Bangladesh: The Political Economy of Secessionist Conflict," *Journal of Peace Research*, 13, 2 (1976), pp. 91-100.

2. The fullest (however biased) documentation of this for the latter period is the series of White Papers issued in 1978 and 1979 by the Government of Pakistan on the conduct of elections, misuse of media, and the general performance of the Bhutto regime.

3. Among the rapidly expanding body of writing on this subject, see William L. Richter, "The Political Dynamics of Islamic Resurgence in Pakistan," *Asian Survey*, 10:6 (June 1979), pp. 547-559; Ralph Braibanti, "The Recovery of Islamic Identity in Global Perspective," in Bruce Lawrence, ed., *The Rose & the Rock* (Durham: Carolina Academic Press, 1979), pp. 159-198; and G. H. Jansen, *Militant Islam* (New York: Harper & Row, 1979).

4. Giovanni Sartori, *Parties and Party Systems: A Framework for Analysis* (New York: Cambridge University Press, 1976), p. 17.

5. For greater detail on these developments, see William L. Richter, "Persistent Praetorianism: Pakistan's Third Military Regime," *Pacific Affairs*, 51:3 (Fall 1978) pp. 406-426.

6. *Supreme Court Judgment on Begum Nusrat Bhutto's Petition* challenging detention of Mr. Z. A. Bhutto and others under Martial Law Order 12 of 1977 - Lahore, 10 November 1977, Government of Pakistan.

7. *Short Report of an Amnesty International Mission to the Islamic Republic of Pakistan* (20-25 January 1978) (London: Amnesty International, April 1978), pp. 14-16.

8. *Overseas Weekly Dawn*, 5:11 (March 15, 1980), p. 1.

9. These and other background factors are treated at length in Richter, "The Political Dynamics of Islamic Resurgence in Pakistan," *Asian Survey* 1976, pp. 547-557.

10. *Overseas Weekly Dawn*, 5:36 (6 September 1980), p. 1.

11. Muhammad Munir, *From Jinnah to Zia* (Lahore: Vanguard Books, 1979), p. vii.

12. A "pir" is a leader by virtue of his spiritual charisma. His position may be hereditary, and he may be the leader of a Muslim religious brotherhood. He is to a widely varying extent a mystic.

13. The best available work, now outdated by events, is Hasan Askari Rizvi, *The Military and Politics in Pakistan* (2d ed. Lahore: Progressive, 1976).

# Comments and Discussion

*Richter* added to his paper the comment that we were dealing with four different areas—three outside the Soviet Union plus the Soviet Central Asian areas. They had some of the same elements, but the elements were mixed so differently that simply drawing comparisons between them was difficult. We cannot deal with them in isolation: what happens in one area affects what happens in the others, as well as affecting the Soviet-American competition. This is what he refers to as the big picture—little picture dichotomy. The big picture is the superpower competition as it is affected by events in the area, while the little picture considers local issues, such as Baluch or Pathan nationalism, or the Iranian revolution on their own merits. Unfortunately, our tendency is to see events in Central Asia or other regions in terms of the big picture and to fail to see what is equally important in the little picture. This led, for example, to the American actions in the Bay of Bengal in 1971.

He added that his paper intentionally ignored two things that are part of the question of freedom in Pakistan. One is the international dimension, the threat to Pakistan's freedom from the Soviets in Afghanistan or from any other threats that they may feel. Second is the issue of ethnic freedom that Selig Harrison's paper covers (below).

*Ahmad* suggested that in discussing freedom in Islam we must consider "whose Islam." Fundamentalist Islam is of course much more politically significant in Pakistan, and we should look carefully at the publications of the fundamentalists, especially those of Maulana Maudoodi, the founder of the *Jamaat-i-Islami*. (Pakistani fundamentalists claim they have influenced the Iranian Revolution through their literature. They say the influence of Maudoodi on Khomeini was tremendous; in fact, most of Maudoodi's works were translated in Qom in the 1960s.)

127

Maudoodi holds that genuine freedom can only be attained within the framework of Islam, the literal meaning of which is submission or peace. In this context he advocates a metaphysical definition of freedom according to which an individual or society can only attain freedom by submitting to the laws of God and accepting God as sovereign. When Maudoodi speaks of civil liberties, he often quotes the example of communist societies. He points out that in communist political systems freedom is defined within the framework of the basic goals and objectives of society and so he says it must be in all societies.

Ahmad said that the opposition of the Pakistan National Alliance to Bhutto was supposedly against the repressive, authoritarian, and dictatorial policies of the Bhutto regime. However, when General Zia-ul-Haq came into power, and became allied with the fundamentalists, press censorship was approved. During this time the Minister of Information was from the Jamaat-i-Islami. The new government posted other restrictions on different occasions. They argued that since certain newspapers were writing what they regarded as against the basic values of Islam, they had to impose restrictions. The classic case, however, was during the Ayub Khan time when the Ulema were launching a campaing against Ayub Khan's authoritarian regime. Ahmad recalled a resolution passed by the Ulema that essentially said, "Freedom of expression should be a right, and Fazl-ur-Rahman's books should be banned." The difficulty for the fundamentalist regimes in Iran and Pakistan is reconciling this contradiction.

*Kazemi* said it was important to recognize the different between procedural and substantive freedom. If one takes for granted that within Islam there is some substantive freedom, it is equally or more important to consider procedural freedom. It is important to ask questions such as: Can a person be taken from his home at three in the morning and shot at five, or not? Are cases decided on the basis that a person is a true Muslim or not? Addressing these issues would be preferable to addressing more general questions of whether Islam is a free religion or not. *Ahmad* replied that Maulana Maudoodi had been quite explicit on both substantive and procedural issues of justice. Maudoodi believed that the ideas of civil liberties in Anglo-Saxon tradition originally came from Islam. He would not approve of an arrest without specific charges and notification of these charges.

Ahmad disagreed with Richter's claim that General Zia had not expressed clearly where he was going. On many occasions he was very clear. When he came into power in July 1977, he said he wanted to achieve two things: 1) to lay down the basic groundwork for the Islamization of society, and 2) to restore order and hold general elections. He seemed to have forgotten the second task, but he is persistently pursuing the first task. He knows what he is doing. He has to establish the institutional framework for what may ultimately be an Islamic system. He hopes to establish institutions that no future regime can undo.

*Richter* agreed that these were two of his goals, but a third had emerged. His first goal was the very limited one of holding elections. When he addressed the nation on the evening of July 5, 1977, on television, he said his primary goal was to hold elections and return power to the elected representatives of the people, and nothing would dissuade him from his goal. In the same speech he praised the spirit of Islam that had motivated the masses to rise against Bhutto, and said that a country established on the basis of Islam could never leave Islam. At that time elections were the goal, and Islam seemed only a mode of expression. Immediately after that he did indeed start taking actions that suggested he was not just a caretaker with limited objectives, but that he had ideas of transforming Pakistan in the direction of an Islamic state. The third goal was accountability (people would have to be responsible for what they had done). These three goals have persisted, with Islam being the most persistent of the three.

On whether freedom was consistent with Islam, *Richter* admitted that he was tempted to look at it in more theoretical terms than might be appropriate. But if we can do without separation of church and state in our definition of freedom, then there are aspects of Islam conducive to freedom. One is the rule of law—there are legal protections. Another is the pragmatic element in Islam that says everyone is free to choose within the context of what is given to him. Not everything is laid down by the religion. Thirdly, there is an element of consent in regard to Islamic conceptions of political rule. This offers a basis for freedom, whether or not these conceptions are actually applied in any Islamic system. If we assume that cutting off hands or allowing religious figures to have a major voice in politics is unfree, then we have already answered the question of the role of freedom.

*Gastil* commented that we have to look at any tradition both in terms of its theoretical discussion and its historical experience. Islam carries as its possibilities, or burden, all the centuries of its history going back to early caliphates. Christianity carried a similar burden, and in so far as Christianity determined political behavior several hundred years ago in the West, it was not based on anything Jesus Christ had said, but on what had happened in between. When we think about what Islam is today, whether it supports freedom or not, it is all those things that happened in between that have a great deal of effect on it, as well as the particular possibilities of the Quran, the hadith, and the various schools.

*Harrison* thought Richter should add scenarios having to do with the minority peoples of Pakistan, maybe an Eight, Nine, and Ten. He also thought that the Zia regime differed from previous military regimes in Pakistan in that the military was being introduced into the administration of the country in a more direct way than ever before. Ten percent of the civil service vacancies, as they come up, go to the military. This is at all levels of the administration, by formal directive, and has been in effect since almost the beginning of the regime. There is also a widespread belief that it is now a very corrupt involvement. Reliable sources certainly report corruption. In any event the fact that the belief in extensive military corruption is widespread and accepted by the politicized public and many civil servants is very important.

Harrison felt that Richter's Scenario Six may have validity for another couple of years because Zia, although not a man who conceptualizes intellectually, is a cunning person who knows how to let the top military people who are in his in-group share the loot. Harrison felt that the Ayub regime lost its solidity in the late sixties when Gohar Ayub, his son, retired from the military as a captain and in partnership with another military man became a millionaire in six months. That the military should again, and more seriously, fall into disrepute is important because looked at in historical perspective the military in Pakistan has been an instrument for rescuing the weak federal system from its many contradictions. It might be disastrous for the military to lose its capacity to play this role in the future by becoming too involved in administration and administrative corruption.

*Richter* replied that while he thought there was criticism of the regime for corruption and administrative involvement, he did not think it was different in kind from the criticism of Ayub during the later 1960s, or from the personal criticism of the corruption, drinking, and carousing of Yahya Khan that, along with the results of the Bangladesh war, led the military to lose respect for him. Richter wondered if Harrison thought this would lead to a decline in military prestige below the level of 1971 or the beginning of the Bhutto regime. *Harrison* said he found today a more severe debilitation of psychological support for the very continuation of Pakistan than in the past, a basic lack of confidence that the society can solve its problems. In a poor country corruption is the litmus paper of a viable or unviable society. Once there is widespread belief that the leaders are corrupt, they are no longer regarded as patriotic or "national." One can draw many parallels. Although the loss of confidence in Pakistan after Bangladesh was serious, the image of the military as a nationalist force was not completely undermined. Of course, it was not completely undermined now, but the systematic introduction of the military into the administration makes a difference that should be noted. Where this will lead and how fast is unclear.

*Richter* added that Zia and other military leaders were aware of the dangers of the military staying in power. They fear administrative entanglement, but more generally they feel the military becomes a less effective instrument of national security the longer it rules. Zia has made statements on this publicly and apparently privately. *Gastil* added that the Shah's regime was widely thought to be corrupt and it stayed in power for a long time.

*Naby* wondered whether Richter accepted Harrison's claim that there has been a systematic introduction of the military into the administration. Some claim that the bureaucracy has prevented a revolution or a mass movement in Pakistan. If the military is entering the bureaucracy, then there is a basic shift in the type of elites that run the country. The implications are unclear. It might mean that a combination of bureaucratic and military forces would prevent any kind of deep social change and, eventually, come into conflict with fundamental Islamic ideology.

*Richter* thought that the breakdown of the bureaucracy had begun under Bhutto. Bhutto assiduously set about not only cutting the military down to size, but also cutting the bureaucracy down to size by providing for lateral entry and in other ways. If he did not dismantle its steel framework, he at least made it more amenable to political influence. Many believe that Bhutto ruined the bureaucracy by his political manipulation and dismissal of officials. However, the military and the bureaucracy have found it easy to live together since the early 1950s—and they still do. What has been reestablished is a not-so-strange bedfellow situation. Although the military has taken over positions as Harrison describes, the bureaucracy has remained very important in determining state policy—particularly people like Agha Shahi and Ishhaq Khan, and a number of civilians who have been brought in who are neither a part of the military nor the bureaucracy. There is kind of a tripartite coalition in which the military and the bureaucracy are the major partners.

*Wriggins* added that military people were brought into the bureaucracy under Ayub. What was new was the demoralization and growing scepticism about the viability of Pakistan. This seemed far more consequential than having a few more military people in bureaucratic positions. He did not understand all the components of that discouragement, but there was the Baluch problem, the Afghan problem, the Indians, and the stagnating economy. He disagreed with Richter's favorable view of the economy: it was in bad shape, and the leaders really did not know what to do about it. The way they have land structured, plus the legacy of Bhutto and his ill-considered nationalizations make it very difficult. On questioning, Wriggins agreed the economy had improved since Bhutto was cast aside, but he thought it had very far to go. People ask why after twenty years there has been so little gain and wonder whether they have the courage to carry on. This mood was not common before, even under Bhutto—except for the first year and a half. Bhutto's political genius turned that around for a while, but then things began to slide again.

*Richter* thought the general malaise was not so much a reflection of corruption as of historical events. *Wriggins* agreed. *Richter* thought the fact that Pakistan split apart once makes it easier to conceive of its splitting apart again. Pakistan's hopes have been dashed so many times that it is possible to imagine that there is no way out.

*Ahmad* thought that in the last days of his regime Bhutto made the bureaucracy part of his coalition; it became a docile instrument of his support. Under Zia in the initial days after the July coup of General Zia, the civilian bureaucracy tried to reassert itself through the help of the military. There was a revival of the Civil Service of Pakistan (C.S.P.— the elite cadre with British Indian traditions.). During Bhutto's time 1,300 top civil servants were dismissed. After his fall most were reinstated; all but one or two CSP officers have been reinstated without going into the charges. In the Central Secretariat at Islamabad, almost all civilian secretaries are now from the CSP, but during the Bhutto period there was hardly any CSP secretaries in the central government. There is a rumor is Islamabad that all foreign policy decisions have been left to Agha Shahi, all economic issues to Ghulam Ishaque Khan, and Aftab Ahmad Khan takes care of agriculture. So the country is in the hands of these three civil servants. In spite of this cooperation, as Harrison has pointed out, the institutional rivalries are now coming into the open between the military and civil service as a result of the increasing introduction of military officers into the civil service. Almost every day one reads that some general, commodore, or admiral has been appointed chairman or managing director of one or another public corporation or educational institution. The Vice-Chancellor of the Baluchistan University is also a brigadier.

Ahmad added that in many public corporations as well as government controlled agencies, civilian officials encourage and spread rumors of corruption by the generals and other military officers. This has a positive impact on the prospects for freedom in that the institutional conflict between the civilian bureaucracy and the military is weakening the Zia government. The civil service is not cooperating when the military wants to show its teeth. For example, during Shi'a demonstrations in Islamabad in July 1980, it was quite evident that the civilian administration had withdrawn and they let the Shi'as surround the civil secretariat building. In recent demonstrations in Karachi when the lawyers marched in the streets, the deputy commissioners knew about it, but didn't do anything—the police simply withdrew.

*Newell* asked about the tone and direction of the Islamic quality of the regime. He had the impression from earlier information that the bureaucracy and the military were the centers of modernist secularism. He didn't see anything comparable to the social base for Islamic revival there is in Iran, as has been discussed, or even an elite religious leadership now that Maudoodi was gone, to provide a leader like Khomeini for Pakistan.

*Richter* replied that Zia represents a new military. This was probably one reason Bhutto originally boosted him above the heads of several other more senior generals to make him army chief of staff. He was something of an outsider, not as much of an old boy of the sort that Ayub or even Yahya Khan was. The situations are also different in that a good part of what has happened in Pakistan in the way of movement toward an Islamic system has been imposed from the top. So it does not represent the same base as in Iran. There was a mass movement that can be identified in Pakistan as being roughly similar to what happened in Iran in the anti-Bhutto movement of early 1977 (April-May). Still it was very different from Iran in at least one sense. There was not any single individual in the whole PNA (Pakistan National Alliance) movement who had the kind of status Khomeini had in Iran. It was much more a coalition of forces. Maulana Mufti Mahmood, president of PNA, was no more than one among equals. This may have to do in part with differences between Sunni and Shi'a Islam.

*Ahmad* added that there had been a change in the social basis of the military officers. In the 1950s most of the military officers came from upper and middle class rural families. Ever since the 1960s this has changed. The expansion of technical support services within the military, such as the engineering corps, medical corps, education corps, and communication and computer services required highly skilled, educated people. They have come from the middle and lower-middle class urban population, and these social strata are precisely the strata identified with Islamic fundamentalism and with the influence of the Jamaat-i-Islami and Maulana Maudoodi. This partially explains the support of the military for fundamentalist politics.

*Newell* remarked that it appears modernization in the sense of social mobility produced a greater potential for Islamic fundamentalism; *Richter* pointed out that the same thing has occurred in Kansas.

*Khalilzad* followed up the discussion by noting that in the past the Pakistan military had intervened as a unit. Since these social changes have taken place, he wondered whether the military might cease to act as a unit, with resulting fragmentation and divided loyalty. The result might be the kind of coups that occur elsewhere, with junior officers or those closest to the weapons making the decisions.

Khalilzad also wondered which factors might lead Richter to believe one scenario more likely than another. Did he know why mass dissatisfaction overthrew Bhutto, but now with the continued mass dissatisfaction there was not much protest? He suggested that there are fifty to sixty countries with lots of dissatisfaction, but only in some do we find mass protest. He wondered why. *Richter* suggested consideration of the general rate of inflation.

*Gastil* commented that the point was made, and is often made, that the most religious groups are the middle classes and lower-middle classes in the cities. This has been true of Islam since Muhammed. This group, the traders and craftsmen formerly has always been the most religious group. If so, then why are we so convinced of the Islamic fundamentalism of the tribes or the peasants, which still make up the majority of people in most of these countries?

He also pointed out that communist or quasi-communist leaders in third world countries seem to convert their peoples to communism even when the leaders are not originally communist. It gives them a way to legitimize staying in power. Fidel Castro was not a communist when he originally came in, but communism became a very attractive way for him to legitimize his rule. Most leaders like being in power and they like staying there. Competitive elections and civil liberties are dangerous to their positions. Communism or communist models offer legitimization without running these risks. By becoming communists or quasi-communists leaders can say that in the model of their new society parliamentary, bourgeois rights are not important: the leading party defines the people's interests. This provides them with a useful vocabulary of justification. Gastil now wondered if, with people like Zia, another kind of legitimization was becoming available. Zia can say that he does not need to give his opponents rights because the laws have already been written in the Quran, and all he needs is people to interpret them. He preserves the power, of course, to choose his own interpreters. Richter speaks of Islam coming from the top down in Pakistan. Perhaps this is because Pakistan's leaders are finding this an attractive alternative to a leftist, communist self-justification. Of course, people like Maudoodi and Khomeini had religious interests a long time back. What he was concerned about is people taking on an Islamic cover.

*Khalilzad* noted that Jamaat-i-Islami originally supported the Zia regime, while now they have turned very much against it. He wanted to know how they argued against the regime and how groups like this came to oppose Zia.

*Wriggins* said he believed Zia was a religiously serious man. Quite a few people in the army he knew believed he was a believing Muslim. He did not think his Islamic system was primarily expediency, or not more than twenty percent expediency. *Richter* also thought that to regard Zia as cynical in the same way one might have regarded Ayub is a misreading. *Gastil* pointed out there were different levels of belief. Fidel Castro is not simply a hypocrite. He had some knowledge of communism before he achieved power, and more now. But yet the usefulness of it to him as a legitimizing principle may have played a large part in his final decisions.

*Fischer* thought there was an interesting dynamic between the use by people in power of religious systems to legitimize themselves and the base that all of this is coming from—an educated urban middle class-lower middle class group of people who use the religion as a way of attacking that legitimacy. So the dialectic goes back and forth, and the question becomes, "Is there some way of encouraging the questioning aspect among the base in such a way that it encourages freedom, civil rights, or a tolerant Islam?" Fischer was not quite sure how to do that other than by holding up mirrors and talking constantly about these issues. But the opposition offers one kind of access.

*Ahmad* thought it extremely difficult to isolate factors of piety from factors of political expediency in Zia. The two things are intricately related. The Jamaat-i-Islami tells Zia: "We don't doubt that you are a sincere Muslim, but your Muslim piety has apparently nothing to do with your public conduct. There is oppression, civil liberties are being cur- tailed, and your personal piety has no impact on these public policies that run counter to Islam." Zia is trying to discover an Islamic system. Zia encouraged the press to initiate a public debate on the political-legal system of Pakistan within the framework of Islam. There are more than one hundred intellectuals who have participated in this debate, and each has an opinion on what is the Islamic system. On the other hand, Zia has definite ideas on what an Islamic political system is. There is to be a council ("Shura") without political parties that elects an Amir. If the Amir (ruler) wants to consult this council he can; if he doesn't, no one can compel him. In Zia's opinion Islam does not depend on majority opinion, but correct opinion. Even one person, if he thinks he is right, can disregard the opinion of the rest of the population.

*Khalilzad* pointed out that if you believe a ruler is pious, many funda- mentalists, including Khomeini, then believe that the ruler's legitimacy should not be questioned. This was Khomeini's basic criticism of Iran: the ruler was impious and corrupt, and therefore the whole state. How can the Jamaat, given they think Zia is pious and given the philosophical background that accepts that a pious leader makes for a pious system, criticize him? *Ahmad* replied that Zia was pious only from a very narrow point of view. He says his prayers, fasts, goes on Hajj. But he is criticized for not extending this to a true public piety in action. The Jamaat-i- Islami central executive committee recently issued a statement questioning Zia's Islamic legitimacy because of, among other things, his denials of freedom. They said, for example, that one man rule was against Islam; they particularly challenged his claim to the right to disregard the view of the majority.

*Cottam* thought legitimacy was a tough concept to deal with, as we often do not know what we mean by it. One test is: If you are a leader in a serious crisis, is it possible for you to generate the popular symbols that will allow you to ride through the crisis? For example, the Shah got into a fairly minor crisis (compared, for example, to Turkey) and tried to generate symbols. He tried hard, but could not, while Khomeini residing in another country did very well. One question is whether faced by severe inflation, Zia can use religious symbols to maintain his position. *Richter* expanded on his earlier comment concerning the relationship between inflation and governmental instability. Inflation and other economic ills can create serious political problems as in the late 1960s and the early 1970s. The relative strength of the economy was a support. If this gave way, he didn't think Zia could produce the sort of symbols that would be necessary. The critics could then get the masses into the streets. But without the economic crisis there wasn't the mobilization ability.

*Henze* brought up a question that has bothered Washington a good deal in the last year. While it would be good to have Pakistan playing a stronger role, it was frequently argued that, if you give Pakistan substantial aid without strings attached and without having an impact on what we find undesirable in its actions (and the Carter administration found a great deal undesirable), this would have a bad effect. He wanted to know if there was a formula by which we could be more generous militarily and economically to Pakistan and at the same time have a positive effect on Pakistan in terms of freedom and democracy.

*Richter* reiterated that we should avoid hitching our wagon too closely to General Zia, for both our interest and that of Pakistan. He saw real dangers in the small American offer made last January and which Zia, to his credit, rejected. Perhaps Zia's terminology was not appropriate, but the action was in tune with Pakistani public opinion. If we had made a very large offer perhaps Zia could have ridden out the criticism he would have received for being a tool of Americans. But then the question would have been the extent to which the general bent of the present regime would have resulted in detrimental effects, particularly for the problems Harrison addresses: the centralization of authority, repression of ethnic minorities, and thus the aggravation of centrifugal tendencies (below).

*Khalilzad* suggested that any decision on United States involvement in Pakistan has to be viewed in light of what our goals are in Pakistan and

the region—the large and small pictures. One has to think in terms of
both the costs of helping and the costs of not helping. We must ask
whether in making decisions on the margin, we are going to be better
off, have a more effective nonproliferation policy, by helping or not
helping. *Harrison* suggested that we would have to look at the question in a regional context. The question of American interests is intimately tied up with the impact on India of what we do in Pakistan.
A separate Pakistan policy is a mistake. Particularly with the present
situation in Afghanistan, separating the policies is even more unworkable than it has been over the years. From the standpoint of opposing the
extension of Soviet influence in South Asia alone, developing separate
policies for each country cannot work. We must have a starting point
that recognizes that there are two focal countries that should determine
policy in the region: Iran and India. American policy should treat relations with these two as its point of departure. This does not mean that
we cannot have a positive approach to relations with Pakistan. It is a
matter of priorities. Soviet-Indian relations must be a key concern, and a
community of Soviet-Indian interests in respect to Pakistan already
exists. Harrison believed any policy solutions must recognize the central
importance of our long-term relation with India.

*Henze* viewed the situation differently. While he would not rule out
the Indian aspect, it was important to realize that on the agenda of this
conference Pakistan was about the only country where we had any
leverage. In Soviet Central Asia we may have some if we broadcast
more, but that is a tenuous kind of leverage. We have almost no leverage
in Afghanistan; we certainly do not have much leverage in Iran—although there is a potential for creating it there—but we do have possibilities in Pakistan. Henze saw a new administration coming in now,
anxious to do something. This was a good time for reconsideration.
(*Richter* added that things could be worse, and if we were not careful,
they would be.)

# Baluch Nationalism and Soviet Policy

Selig S. Harrison

The expanding horizons of social consciousness in newly awakening traditional societies can be likened to a series of concentric circles. Initially, social awareness is defined by the inner circle of identity, but clan, tribal, linguistic, and regional perspectives gradually widen as rising economic expectations merge with a sharpening perception of the global environment. Confronted by the subcontinental dimensions of the United States, the Soviet Union, and the European Economic Community, the new nation-builders of the third world increasingly place a premium on size. The search for a satisfactory political expression of "national" identity often leads to the subordination of local particularisms within multi-ethnic states, which offer greater hope for economic progress and a greater sense of security against predatory neighbors than a narrowly conceived nationalism. As experience has shown, however, the larger, multi-ethnic unit is likely to be viable only to the extent that the constituent groups concerned belong to a common-communication universe delimited by broadly shared historical memories and socio-cultural patterns. In cases where multi-ethnic states have been established without regard for such communication boundaries, disaffected ethnic groups with real or imagined grievances against dominant rival groups are likely to take psychological refuge within their inner circle of identity and seek to develop a homogeneous nationalism.[1]

The case of the Baluch minorities in Pakistan, Iran, and Afghanistan presents a striking example of an ethnic group struggling to define an appropriate concept of nationality and nationalism against a background of growing regional political turbulence.[2] The Baluch tribal homeland is a vast area of desert and mountains, bigger than France, stretching for nearly 900 miles along the Arabian Sea. A small slice of the Baluch area reaches up into southern Afghanistan, but the majority of the five

million[3] Baluch are native to the Baluch areas of western Pakistan and
eastern Iran, though many have migrated in recent years from their arid
homeland to seek jobs in other parts of Pakistan and Iran as well as in
the Persian Gulf. Like the divided Kurds, with their dream of a unified
Kurdistan, many Baluch nationalists dream of an independent "Greater
Baluchistan" where the Baluch would be in a majority and would not
face what they regard as the indignities inflicted by dominant Punjabis—
in the case of Pakistan—and Persians in the case of Iran. Many of the
older generation of Baluch leaders, however, would prefer negotiated
settlements with Islamabad and Teheran granting the Baluch regional
autonomy within the existing Pakistani and Iranian political structures.
In addition to the potential economic advantages of identification with
larger polities, these Baluch leaders fear that the movement for a "Greater
Baluchistan" could all too easily become a focal point of destructive
superpower conflict.

## THE BALUCH NATIONAL MOVEMENT

The strategic location of Baluchistan has inescapably attracted growing superpower interest in the aftermath of Afghanistan. Thus, American
officials, warning of the historic Russian drive for warm water ports,
point to Baluchistan as the most plausible example of a possible Soviet
target. In the most familiar scenario envisaged by those who foresee
further Soviet expansionism, Moscow simply sends its troops and tanks
across Baluchistan to the Gulf, a distance of less than 350 miles, an-
nexing the Baluch area directly to a Soviet-controlled "Greater Afghanistan." But this worst-case scenario completely ignores the role of the
Baluch themselves and thus grossly oversimplifies the nature of the
Baluchistan problem. On the one hand, it obscures the political obstacles
that Moscow would confront in attempting to control the Baluch through
conquest. On the other, it underrates the danger that Moscow will pursue
its objectives more flexibly through a combination of political and military means, perhaps utilizing allied Baluch groups as proxies. For
example, while not ruling out the possibility of a naked Soviet thrust
comparable to the Afghan invasion, Pakistani and Iranian leaders are
more concerned that Moscow might help Baluch nationalist factions to
achieve their long-standing goal of an independent Baluchistan through
guerrilla warfare. In this scenario Moscow would give the Baluch
sophisticated weaponry, technical advisers, logistical support, and funds
but would seek to avoid the risks and costs of direct aggression. Alternatively, Moscow might seek to use the threat of a Baluch insurgency to
pressure Pakistan or Iran, or both into granting the use of Baluch ports
for military purposes.

Whether or not Moscow decides to play its "Baluch card," the Baluch nationalist movement has acquired a growing momentum of its own and is likely to have an increasingly significant impact on the course of events in Southwest Asia. The Baluch bitterly resisted their forcible incorporation into Iran by Reza Shah in 1928 and later into the new state of Pakistan left behind by the British Raj in 1947. In the case of Iran, the Shah's iron repression kept the Baluch largely under control with the exception of a brief, Iraq-supported insurgency. The Khomeini revolution led to a weakening of the central authority in 1979 and an outpouring of long-suppressed nationalist feeling. In Pakistan, by contrast, Baluch insurgents have waged on on-again, off-again guerrilla struggle ever since the departure of the British, culminating in a brutal confrontation with 80,000 or more Pakistani troops from 1973 to 1977 in which some 55,000 Baluch were involved, 11,500 of them as organized combatants. Casualty estimates during this little-known war ran as high as 3,300 Pakistani soldiers and 5,300 Baluch guerrillas killed, not to mention hundreds of women and children caught in the crossfire. At the height of the fighting in late 1974, Iranian combat helicopters (previously obtained from the U.S. by Iran), some manned by Iranian pilots, joined the Pakistani Air Force in raids on Baluch camps. The Baluch, for their part, did not received substantial foreign help and were armed only with bolt-action rifles, homemade grenades, and captured weaponry.

Significantly, when they started their poorly prepared insurgency in 1973, the Pakistani Baluch were not fighting for independence but rather for regional autonomy within a radically restructured, confederal Pakistani constitutional framework. By the time the shooting subsided in 1977, however, separatist feeling had greatly intensified. The wanton use of superior firepower by the Pakistani and Iranian forces, especially the indiscriminate air attacks on Baluch villages, had left a legacy of bitter and enduring hatred. Since nearly all Baluch felt the impact of Pakistani repression, the Baluch populace is now politicized to an unprecedented degree. In mid-1980, I found a pervasive mood of expectancy among the Baluch, a widespread desire to vindicate Baluch martial honor, and a readiness to renew the struggle when and if circumstances should appear favorable.

## THE HISTORICAL BASIS OF BALUCH IDENTITY

In order to assess the potential of Baluch nationalism as a flash point for intraregional tensions and superpower rivalry in Southwest Asia, it is not enough to focus on the political and economic conflicts of the recent past or even to search for the roots of Baluch attitudes in the stormy encounters of the Baluch with British colonial armies. It is first necessary to understand the strength of the deeply implanted historical memories that underlie Baluch nationalism, memories of a tempestuous struggle for survival stretching back for more than 2,000 years.

According to the most widely accepted Baluch legends, the Baluch and the Kurds were kindred branches of a tribe that migrated northward from Aleppo in what is now Syria shortly before the time of Christ in search of fresh pasture lands and water sources. One school of Baluch historians attempts to link this tribe ethnically with the original Chaldean rulers of Babylon; another with the early Arabs.[4] In any case, there is agreement that the Kurds headed toward Iraq, Turkey, and northwest Persia, while the Baluch moved into the coastal areas along the southern shores of the Caspian Sea, later migrating into what are now Iranian Baluchistan and Pakistani Baluchistan between the sixth and fourteenth centuries.

Western historians regard the Aleppo legends as unsubstantiated, but scholars in Baluchistan and the West generally agree that the Baluch were living along the southern shores of the Caspian at the time of Christ. This consensus is based largely on linguistic evidence showing that the Baluchi language originated in a lost language linked with the Parthian or Medean civilizations that flourished in the Caspian and adjacent areas in the pre-Christian era.[5] As one of the oldest living languages, Baluchi is a subject of endless fascination and controversy for linguists. While it is classified as a member of the Iranian group of the Indo-European language family, consisting of Persian, Pushtu, Baluchi, and Kurdish, Baluchi is a separate language and is closely related only to one of the members of the Iranian group, Kurdish. In its modern form, it has incorporated borrowings from Persian, Sindi, Arabic, and other languages, but it has retained striking peculiarities of its own.

The Baluch have been remarkably successful in preserving their separate cultural identity in the face of continual pressures from strong cultures in neighboring areas. Despite the isolation of the scattered pastoral communities in Baluchistan, the Baluchi language and a relatively homogeneous Baluch literary tradition and value system have provided a unifying common denominator for the seventeen major Baluch tribal groupings scattered over the 207,000-square-mile area reaching from the Indus in the east to the Persian province of Kerman in the west. Politically, however, the Baluch record is a mixed one, marked by relatively brief interludes of unity and strong leadership among centuries of fragmentation and tribal strife.

The most impressive demonstration of Baluch political unity came in the eighteenth century, when several successive rulers of the Baluch principality of Kalat succeeded in expanding their domain to bring most of the Baluch areas under one political umbrella. Mir Nasir Khan, who

ruled Kalat for forty-four years beginning in 1749, set up a loose bureaucratic structure embracing most of Baluchistan for the first time and got
the seventeen principal Baluch tribes to adopt an agreed system of
military organization and recruitment.

For Baluch nationalists today, Nasir Khan's achievements remain an
important symbol, providing some semblance of historical identity.
Indeed, Ghaus Bux Bizenjo, former Governor of Pakistani Baluchistan
and a leading nationalist, argued in an interview that Nasir Khan's
successors would have succeeded in creating an enduring polity if it had
not been for the deliberate manipulation of the internal divisions in
Baluch society by the British Raj. Playing off rival chiefs against one
other in the confused decades after Nasir Khan's death, Britain systematically divided the Baluch area into seven parts. In the far west, the
Goldsmid Line gave roughly one-fourth to Persia in 1871; in the north,
the Durand Line assigned a small strip to Afghanistan in 1894; and in
British India, the Baluch areas were divided into a centrally administered
entity, British Baluchistan, a truncated remnant of Kalat and three other
smaller puppet principalities.

In Bizenjo's view, the Baluch suffered this unhappy fate because they
happened to live in an area of vital military importance to the British, in
contrast to the more fortunately situated Afghans. It was historical
accident, he explained, that gave the Afghans the opportunity for independent statehood denied to the Baluch. Thus, it served the interests
of the British to foster a unified Afghanistan under their tutelage as a
buffer state that would shield their Indian Empire from Russia. Conversely, it was necessary to divide the Baluch in order to assure unimpeded control of the resulting imperial frontier with this Afghan buffer.
Nasir Khan's Baluchistan might have emerged in a buffer-state role
instead, Bizenjo contended, if the Russians had moved southward
sooner and if they had swallowed up Afghanistan before Britain em-
barked on its nineteenth century "forward policy."[6]

## THE HOPES OF BALUCH LEADERS AND PAKISTANI RESPONSES

Viewing recent developments from their own particular angle of
vision, Baluch leaders are increasingly persuaded that the Soviet occupation of Afghanistan could prove to be as opportune for the Baluch cause,
in one way or another, as the arrival of the British was for the Afghans
two centuries ago. They are attempting to use the implicit threat of a
Soviet-supported independent Baluchistan as a bargaining lever to win
regional autonomy for the Baluch within the existing Pakistani and
Iranian constitutional structures. What they are demanding, in concrete
terms, is a division of powers under which Islamabad and Teheran

would retain control over defense, foreign affairs, communications, and currency, while the Baluch would have unfettered local authority over everything else, including the exploitation of natural resources and the allocation of development funds. If Islamabad and Teheran should reject these demands, the Baluch leaders are confident that geopolitical factors will nonetheless work in their favor. Even if the Soviet Union is slow to support an independent Baluchistan, in their view, other powers are likely to do so in order to forestall the possibility of Soviet action.

How realistic are these hopes and expectations?

On the basis of extensive conversations with General Zia and other Pakistani officials, I see little chance that Islamabad will make the concessions necessary to reach an accommodation with representative Baluch leaders. Zia typifies the attitudes of Pakistan's dominant Punjabi majority. The Punjabis constitute fifty-eight percent of the population and are reluctant to grant local self-rule to Baluch, Pushtun, and Sindi minorities whose ancestral homelands cover seventy-two percent of Pakistani territory. It is particularly galling to the Punjabis that the Baluch, who make up some four percent of the population, assert a proprietary right over forty percent of the land area of the country. The very idea of demarcating provincial units in accordance with ethnic homelands has been a persistent source of conflict since the inception of Pakistan. Dominated by Punjabi military and bureaucratic elites, a succession of authoritarian Pakistani regimes have identified their interests with the preservation of a unitary state and have thus resisted pressures for democratic government that have been linked, inseparably, with demands for provincial self-rule.

There is an unmistakable note of ethnic arrogance in the Punjabi attitude, a desire to show the "primitive" Baluch tribesmen who is master and a feeling that the armed forces could suppress the Baluch once again, if necessary, as they did in the case of the 1973-77 insurgency. This condescending posture is reflected in the almost complete exclusion of the Baluch from the political, bureaucratic, and military power structure of Pakistan.

The Baluch charge that their area is neglected economically and that Punjabi-linked big business interests in Lahore and Karachi are milking Baluchistan of its resources. They point, in particular, to the natural gas deposits at Sui, which have been used solely to build up industries outside of Baluchistan. Evidence abounds to back up these allegations, as well as parallel charges that Punjabi settlers are grabbing the prime farm land in Baluch areas, and that Punjabi real estate speculators are buying up properties in Quetta, the principal urban center in Baluchistan. The Zia regime has responded to such criticism with increased economic development spending, especially on roads, and has promised to pipe some of the Sui gas to Quetta. But Zia continues to channel development funds through the Punjabi bureaucracy, ignoring Baluch pleas for local control over development decisions.

Although he occasionally consults several "Uncle Tom" Baluch politicians and businessmen for cosmetic purposes, Zia refuses to negotiate on the autonomy issue with the three Baluch leaders who command the overwhelming support of the Baluch populace: Bizenjo, Ataullah Mengal, and Khair Bux Marri. These are the leaders who emerged triumphant in 1970 when the Baluch had their first—and last—opportunity to elect their own provincial government. It was the dismissal of this government by the late President Bhutto that touched off the 1973-77 insurgency.

Despite Zia's refusal to hold new elections and to negotiate on the autonomy issue, he sharply criticizes Bhutto for "needlessly inflaming the passions of the Baluch" by summarily removing their elected regime. Zia says that he will be careful to avoid comparable frontal assaults on Baluch pride. Given the proper mixture of benign neglect and "non-provocative" firmness, he maintains, the Baluch problem will gradually subside. Thus, he has ordered Army units in Baluchistan to maintain a low profile, and he has appointed a suave, non-Punjabi military intellectual, Lt. Gen. Rahimuddin Khan, as Governor of Baluchistan. At the same time, Zia has clamped down firmly on political activity in the Baluch areas along with the rest of the country, forcing most nationalist activity underground.

Disgusted with what they see as Zia's obduracy and fearful of arrest if they challenge him openly, Ataullah Mengal and Khair Bux Marri have recently gone into political exile in Europe. Mengal and Marri are both the hereditary chieftains of large tribes collectively numbering some 200,000 people, but they emerged during the 1973-77 insurgency as "national" leaders. Nominally in Europe for medical treatment, they are quietly exploring the prospects for winning Baluch independence with foreign help, whether from the Soviet Union, China, the United States, India, the Arab world, or a combination of these. At the same time, they are keeping the door open for negotiations with the Zia and Khomeini regimes. Nationalist groups in both Pakistan and Iran are keeping their powder dry while Mengal and Marri continue their search for foreign help, but these groups are quietly building up their organizational strength in the interim in preparation for a possible resumption of hostilities.

## BALUCH COMMUNISM AND SOVIET NATIONALITIES POLICY

Given the widespread assumption that Moscow has its eye on Baluchistan and the strength of pro-Soviet sentiment there, it is surprising to find that there have never been effective Soviet-oriented communist organizations in the Baluch areas of either Pakistan or Iran. This is primarily because Soviet policy has consistently stopped short of supporting the concept of an independent "Greater Baluchistan." While defining the Baluch as a separate nationality and upholding their inherent right of secession, Soviet ideologians have until now advised against invoking this right, calling on their Baluch sympathizers to work with other "progressives" for overall communist victories in Pakistan and Iran as a whole.

The multi-ethnic Soviet Union utilizes a cynical form of ideological sleight of hand to justify strong centralized control of its diverse constituent republics while making a ceremonial bow to their separate "national" identities. On the one hand, communist nationality doctrine affirms the right of every nation to self-determination, including the right of secession; on the other, it stipulates that only the proletariat, whose will is embodied in the Communist Party, can decide whether it is in the interests of a particular nation to exercise this right on a given occasion. This doctrinal flexibility has been peculiarly suited to shifting communist tactical priorities in the multi-ethnic South Asian environment.

Even before Independence, the communists in undivided India were well aware of the relevance of Soviet nationality doctrine for the Indian scene. The draft program of the nascent Indian Communist Party declared in 1930 that only an "Indian Federal Soviet Republic would be capable of insuring to national minorities their right to self-determination, including that of complete separation."[7] Later, when Hindu-Muslim conflict overshadowed all Indian political life, communist theoreticians turned to Soviet nationality doctrine in formulating their stand on the demand then being put forward by the Muslim League for a separate Muslim state of Pakistan. This demand was anathema to the Hindu-dominated Congress Party led by Gandhi and Nehru, and its religious rationale made it initially repugnant to the communists. Seeking to exploit their organizational strength among Muslims, however, communist leaders made the fateful decision to support "what is just and right" in the Pakistan demand. "The rational kernel of the Pakistan demand," wrote the party's leading theoretician on nationality, G. Adhikari, is that "wherever people of the Muslim faith living together in a territorial unit form a nationality . . . they certainly have the right to autonomous state existence just like other nationalities in India."[8]

In its memorandum to the British Cabinet Mission in April, 1946, the Communist Party called on Britain to turn over power not to the provisional central government headed by Nehru but to seventeen sovereign regional constituent assemblies, each to be empowered to decide whether or not to join the projected new Indian Union "or remain out and form a separate, sovereign state by themselves, or join another Indian Union."

Four of these assemblies were to have been in Muslim-majority areas that later became part of Pakistan (Western Punjab, Sind, Baluchistan, and Pushtunistan) and thirteen others in areas that were to constitute the Indian Union.[9]

Despite the fact that it made nominal allowance for the formation of "separate, sovereign" states, the memorandum had the practical effect of supporting the Muslim League by envisaging "another Indian Union." By all indications, Moscow encouraged communist support for the creation of Pakistan, believing that India would be weak and disorganized, and would eventually be fragmented in the process of achieving independence. After Partition, however, when it became clear that India and Pakistan were both well-established, Soviet policy had to adjust to this new reality. In 1953, Moscow formally signaled its acceptance of the Indian state by decreeing that "though for India, too, the principle of self-determination means and naturally includes the right of separation, it is inexpedient for Indian nationalities to exercise the right."[10]

In the case of Pakistan, Soviet ideologians were initially less explicit, and as late as 1964, Yuri Gankovsky, a leading Soviet writer on nationality problems, wrote that "the dismemberment of India into two dominions along religious lines did not solve the national problem in Pakistan." To be sure, he conceded, "the slogan of Pakistan, albeit in an indirect, deformed way, expressed the striving for national autonomy and self-determination" of the homogeneous Muslim regions in the subcontinent, Baluchistan, and Pushtunistan, as well as of "the Moslem parts of the Bengali, Punjabi and Sindhi peoples." But since Partition, he said, reactionary landowners, theologians, and businessmen had distorted the original intention of Jinnah and the other League founders, who had "emphasized that the areas encompassed in Pakistan would be autonomous and sovereign." Gankovsky did not directly challenge Pakistan's legitimacy or its continued right to exist, but he presented detailed historical analysis to show that it consisted of five distinct nationalities whose right to national autonomy had yet to be recognized in the Pakistani state as it was then constituted.[11]

The Baluch, Gankovsky wrote in the *The Peoples of Pakistan: An Ethnic History*, "are the only one of Pakistan's major peoples who had not been consolidated into a bourgeois nation by the time when the colonialists left the Indo-Pakistan subcontinent." Baluchistan's economic dependence and backwardness were even greater than in other areas of British India during the colonial period, which had "a negative effect on the ethnic processes at work in the country, curbing the development of capitalist relations and arresting the rise of bourgeois-society classes and social strata." British neglect of Baluchistan economically drove many Baluch out of Baluchistan into neighboring Sind and other provinces in search of work, and "this territorial dispersion did and does make the Baluch national consolidation exceedingly difficult." Nevertheless, he concluded, despite these handicaps, "the rise of the Baluchi nation is under way. . . . The national consolidation of the Baluchis is still on the move in our day." Pointing to Baluch literary and political activity, he declared that "the Baluchi proletariat is growing and the bourgeoisie and intelligentsia are taking shape. The birth of Baluchi national consciousness is in evidence."[12]

Gankovsky's 1964 study marked the first public Soviet scholarly treatment of the Baluch with the exception of a 1959 economic treatise. As an historical tome, focused mainly on the pre-independence period, it did not offer specific policy advice to the nationalities in Pakistan, pointedly avoiding the debate then developing in Pakistani communist ranks over the right of secession. By 1967, however, in a book devoted to post-independence "national movements," Gankovsky made clear that Moscow was opposed to separatist activity. He praised the "democratic movement" in Baluchistan for concentrating on the economic grievances of peasants and workers while also seeking the administrative unification of the Baluch areas into a single provincial unit which would enjoy "complete autonomy." At the same time, he directed vitriolic attacks at the "openly separatist position" of the Khan of Kalat and his uncle, Sultan Ibrahim Khan, who wanted to create an independent Baluchistan as a means of perpetuating their feudal special privileges.

"Imperialism and internal reaction do everything possible to sow suspicion and hatred among ethnic communities of multi-national liberated states," Gankovsky concluded, "and to make their cooperative struggles for social progress impossible." He called for "incessant work" by all "progressive, patriotic forces interested in consolidating the independence and unity of their countries to prevent the spread of separatist tendencies and moods."[13]

Soviet unwillingness to support the Baluch aspiration for independence has cast a continuing pall over communist organizing efforts in Baluchistan ever since their inception. "At first, in the thirties, our prospects looked extremely promising," recalled Kadir Bux Nizamani, who served as secretary of the Sind-Baluchistan branch of the Communist Party from 1935 to 1941. The party had recruited Ghaus Bux Bizenjo, a rising young political activist who was later to become Governor of Baluchistan, and Mohammed Hussain Unqa, one of the most popular Baluchi-language poets of the day. As the independence of the subcontinent approached, however, Bizenjo, Unqa, and other Baluch "progressives" were thinking increasingly in terms of an independent Baluchistan, and the communist decision in 1941 to support the Pakistan movement "had a very bad effect, a very demoralizing effect, cutting the ground out from under us before we could really get started."

The communist stand in support of the Pakistan movement reflected the marginal position of Baluch and Pushtun comrades in pre-Partition party councils and a corresponding dominance of party leaders from other parts of the subcontinent that has persisted since Partition. Both the Baluch and Pushtun regions were homogeneous Muslim areas where there was little fear of Hindu domination and little interest in the Pakistan cause. The Muslim League was not a dominant force in these areas, drawing its principal support, instead, from the Muslim-minority provinces, especially the populous Ganges Valley state of Uttar Pradesh, which happened to the major centers of political life under the British Raj.

After Partition, many of the wealthier, better-educated Muslims in the Muslim-minority provinces migrated to Pakistan, where they assumed powerful positions in the bureaucratic and business worlds. As allies of the dominant Punjabis, these "Mahajirs" (refugees) or "Hindustanis" became unpopular targets of the minority Baluch, Pushtuns, and Sindis. The communist leaders who migrated to Pakistan were also suspect as "Mahajirs" in the eyes of many of their locally rooted party comrades, but this did not prevent them from promptly asserting their claims to leadership of the new Pakistan Communist Party.

Looking back on this period, K. B. Nizamani, who has since broken his communist ties, wrote in 1979 that "since the areas constituting the western part of Pakistan did not have an effective Communist organization, the Pakistan Communist Party fell largely under the control of Punjabis and newly arriving Hindustanis who had no understanding of the most acute contradictions in the country. From the very first day Pakistan was formed, the primary contradiction in the country was between the dictatorship of the ruling class and the suppression of the rights of the smaller nationalities. But since the majority of the so-called Communists were Punjabis or Hindustanis, they considered this a secondary or minor contradiction."[14]

When communist organizers came to Baluchistan, Nizamani recalled, they were looking for industrial workers and landless agricultural laborers who could be rallied on the basis of conventional Marxist-Leninist class appeals. Confronting instead a nomadic tribal society, they generally hurried back to Karachi, concentrating their efforts on the migrant Baluch factory workers there.

In a definitive, hitherto-unpublished "Strategy Document" adopted at their Second Congress on May 1, 1976, Communist Party leaders declared that "the question of national rights has not been solved in Pakistan." However, it warned party members "to guard against the two erroneous lines found on this question in the country. The first line denies the existence of nationalities. The second line equates the struggle for national rights with the struggle for national states, leading to the breakup of the country into penny pockets which again, like the first line, serves the interests of reaction and imperialism as it divides the democratic struggle.''

Referring only obliquely to the insurgency then raging, item three in a list of seven priority political tasks called on party members to "participate in the just struggle of the people of Baluchistan" but enjoined them, at the same time, to "unite and connect the struggle in Baluchistan with the other democratic issues in the country." Imperialism and its agents "are trying to cut off the struggle of the Baluch people from the general anti-imperialist struggle in the country," it cautioned, "by propagating that the Baluch people are struggling for separation." Elsewhere, stressing that the party's struggle for national rights includes "the right of self-determination, so that national barriers may be broken and class consciousness may develop," the Strategy Document made a gesture to Baluch leftists by declaring that "if the struggle develops faster in some sectors or some areas, that specific contingent of the overall democratic forces will be of great help in throwing back the enemy all along the line and bringing nearer the emancipation of the whole of Pakistan."[15]

Despite the lack of a unified, tightly knit communist movement in Baluchistan, it should be stressed that the Soviet Union has more often than not had a favorable image over the years. Soviet support of the Bhutto regime during the insurgency and the 1979 Russian invasion of Afghanistan have tarnished but not fundamentally altered this image. In Baluch eyes, Washington has been consistently and directly identified with the repression of the Baluch by successive Islamabad regimes through its military and economic aid, while Moscow, which has been arrayed against every Pakistani regime, except Bhutto's, represents a potentially liberating alternative. In addition, the Baluch, like many third world peoples, tend to identify the Soviet Union as a friend of the underprivileged, in contrast to the United States, with its multinationals, which is seen as a source of support for exploitative local capitalists. As for the Soviet occupation of Afghanistan, Akber Y. Mustikhan, one of the leading Baluch businessmen, explained that most Baluch regard descriptions of Soviet atrocities in the Western press as "greatly exaggerated. They are reluctant to believe that the Russians, whom they don't know first-hand, could be worse than the Punjabis, whom they do know all too well. We talk to them of freedom, but they say, 'what freedom do we have to lose? We never had freedom like the Afghans.' "

As a result of this readiness to give Moscow the benefit of the doubt, there have always been a goodly scattering of active individual pro-Soviet "progressives" in Baluchistan linked with assorted leftist factions in Karachi and Lahore, some staunchly pro-Soviet but most of them free-wheeling Marxist-Leninist groups with a vaguely Soviet-inclined program. In the 1960s, it should be noted, there were also a few pro-Chinese groups, but Peking's identification with Islamabad and later the normalization of Sino-U.S. relations have put these elements on the defensive in the Baluch areas.

In the aftermath of the Soviet occupation of Afghanistan, there have been some indications of Soviet efforts behind the scenes to stimulate indigenous Baluch communist organizations in both Pakistan and Iran, but Moscow still stops short of supporting an independent Baluchistan.

The basic reasons for Soviet caution with respect to Baluch independence appear to lie in Moscow's overall assessment of short-term prospects in Iran and Pakistan. Soviet strategists recognize that although Baluch nationalism is boiling, it is still at a low boil. So long as there is a reasonable chance of increasing Soviet influence in Teheran and Islamabad, Moscow is likely to seek maximum flexibility in dealing with changing Iranian and Pakistani political developments. Soviet sources also allude somewhat ruefully to the high risks and costs that would be involved in sponsoring and sustaining an independent Baluchistan. Given the lack of an effective communist organizational base in the Baluch areas, Moscow would have to work primarily through non-communist nationalist groups if it were to promote independence in the foreseeable future. While far from negligible, these groups would need massive military aid, reinforced by sustained financial, technical, and logistics help, in order to conduct a successful insurgency. Moscow might well be called upon to intervene directly with its own forces if the going got rough. Yet, the need to rely on non-communist Baluch leaders would made the Soviet position inherently insecure even after the attainment of independence, unless it were to disregard Baluch wishes and attempt to make the new state a Soviet satellite.

Although there is some evidence of oil, copper, uranium, and other resources in Baluchistan, it would take multi-billion-dollar investments to determine their extent and to develop and exploit them. The development of Gwadar harbor alone for military purposes would require estimated outlays of two billion dollars or more to deal with desilting and other technical problems.

Some observers assume that a decisive factor deterring a Soviet adventure in Baluchistan is the likelihood that Moscow will be bogged down in Afghanistan for some time to come. Here one should think twice, for it is possible that Moscow might seek to relieve pressure on the Afghan front by stirring up trouble in Baluchistan. Just as Soviet hopes for winning greater influence in Teheran and Islamabad deter Moscow from encouraging a Baluch insurgency, so its desire to punish Iran and Pakistan for providing sanctuaries to Afghan resistance forces could well prompt Soviet retaliatory action in Baluch areas.

If the Soviet Union is able to consolidate its position in Afghanistan during the years ahead, Moscow's interest in Baluchistan would be likely to intensify. But Soviet calculations would still be governed by the evolving political and diplomatic environment in Pakistan and Iran. In a climate of growing Baluch discontent, Moscow would no doubt be tempted to pursue an adventurist course—especially if it confronted an entrenched anti-Soviet Islamic fundamentalist regime in Teheran and had written off its hopes for detaching Islamabad from its military ties to Peking and Washington. Conversely, given an accommodation between key Baluch leaders and either Islamabad or Teheran, or both, Moscow would find it more difficult to organize an insurgency and to legitimize an independent Baluch regime. There is still time, in short, for Pakistan and Iran to build their political defenses against possible Soviet pressures, but time is rapidly running out.

## Notes

1. For a more complete discussion of the interplay of nationalism and subnationalism, see Selig S. Harrison, *The Widening Gulf: Asian Nationalism and American Policy* (New York: The Free Press, 1978), esp. pp. 3-36.

2. An extended examination of the Baluch case is presented in Selig S. Harrison, *In Afghanistan's Shadow: Baluch Nationalism and Superpower Rivalry*, scheduled for publication by the Carnegie Endowment for International Peace early in 1981. Portions of this paper overlap with *In Afghanistan's Shadow* and with a forthcoming article, "Baluch Nationalism and Superpower Rivalry," scheduled for simultaneous publication in the December issues of *International Security*, published by the Harvard Center for Science and International Affairs, and *Politique Etrangere*, published by the French Institute of International Relations.

3. Estimates of the Baluch population range from less than four million to thirty million, depending on whether one extrapolates from official census figures in Pakistan, Afghanistan, and Iran, or accepts Baluch nationalist claims. The figure used here makes allowance for the political character of official census figures. It excludes those of Baluch ethnic origin who do not speak the Baluchi language but includes Baluchi speakers living outside of the Baluch homeland in other parts of Pakistan and Iran as well as in the Persian Gulf.

4. For example, see Sardar Mohammed Khan Baluch, *History of the Baluch Race and Baluchistan* (Quetta: Gosha-e-Adab, rev. ed., 1977), pp. 5, 16-17, and Ma'an Al-I'jly, *Baluchistan Diyal Al-'Arab* (Baluchistan: The Home of Arabs), (Bahrain, 1979), an Arab work citing Baluch sources.

5. J. H. Elfenbein, "Baluchi," in *Encyclopedia of Islam*, Vol. I, A-B (Leiden: E. J. Brill, 1960), p. 1006. See also Elfenbein, *The Baluchi Language: A Dialectology With Text*, Monographs, Vol. XXVII (Royal Asiatic Society, 1966): pp. 41-45, and Richard N. Frye, "Remarks on Baluchi History," *Central Asiatic Journal*, Vol. VI, No. 1 (1961): p. 49.

6. For a differing interpretation of Baluch history, see Brian Spooner, "Tribal Ideal and Political Reality in a Cultural Borderland: Ethnohistorical Problems in Baluchistan," Ethnohistory Workshop, University of Pennsylvania, 1978, esp. pp. 8, 15-16.

7. "Draft Program of Action of the Communist Party of India," International Press Correspondence, December 18, 1930, cited in *The Communist Party of India*, U.S. Office of Strategic Services, Research and Analysis Branch, No. 2681, August, 1945.

8. G. Adhikari, *Pakistan and Indian National Unity* (Bombay: People's Publishing House, 1944), p. 29.

9. *Memorandum* of the Communist Party of India to the British Cabinet Mission, April 15, 1946. See also P. C. Joshi, *For the Final Bid to Power—Freedom Program of the Indian Communists* (Bombay: People's Publishing House, 1946), p. 5.

10. "Questions and Answers: Nationalities and the Right of Secession," *Crossroads*, September 6, 1953, p. 10.

11. Yuri V. Gankovsky, *The Peoples of Pakistan*, English edition, (Moscow: Nauka Publishing House, 1971), p. 210.

12. Ibid., p. 208.

13. Yuri V. Gankovsky, *National'nyi vopros i National'nye dvizheniia v Pakistane* (The National Question and National Movement in Pakistan) (Moscow: Nauka Publishing House, 1967), p. 250.

14. "Pakistan's So-Called Left," *People's Front*, London, Vol. 3, No. 10, February, 1979, p. 2.

15. "Struggle for Independent National Democracy in Pakistan," Strategy Document II, Communist Party of Pakistan, 1976, pp. 44-45.

# Comments and Discussion

In his summary *Harrison* added to his paper a short discussion of the distinction between the Baluch problem as a manifestation of the conflict between tribalism and centralization and the Baluch problem as one of emergent nationalism. The Baluch problem has been presented by the Bhutto and Zia regimes as one of tribalism in conflict with central authority, of tribal chieftains trying to defend their feudal systems and privileges against the liberating effects of modernization. Of course, that was one of the elements of what is happening in the area and to the Baluch. But Harrison stressed that there has emerged a Baluch nationalism that transcends the mere reaction of a tribal leadership to the incursion of central authority. In both Pakistan and Iran the Baluch have been incorporated forcibly into the present states, and this has generated a reaction that in the case of the more politicized Pakistani Baluch began in the 1930s before the emergence of Pakistan.

This process of politicization has created a situation which is somewhere between tribalism and the development of a full-fledged modern nationalism of the kind developed by Bengalis in their movement for secession from Pakistan and the creation of an independent Bangladesh. The Bangladesh movement fit most definitions of modern nationalism. It was reasonably broad based, middle class; it has a highly developed literature which became a political literature, a press. Baluch nationalism is considerably less developed, but it sufficiently meets the test of a nationalist movement even though the aspirations of this movement are not necessarily, unconditionally, aspirations for an independent state.

On the possibility of Soviet involvement, Harrison added that Soviet use of the "Baluch card" by supporting independence, or a Soviet military adventure into Baluchistan, would have to rely on the Baluch nationalist leadership for local support—especially the three leaders he had mentioned (See page 145, above). Of them Mengal and Marri are not intellectually pro-Soviet. Marri has had a background as a romantic Maoist, and he talks about a national communist society for Baluchistan, but he is in no respect, intellectually or emotionally, pro-Soviet. Mengal is a nationalist equally critical of both superpowers. Bizenjo was a communist in his youth and is intellectually more at home with the left than the others. He has had continuing contacts with the left in Pakistan. But he is a political animal with all kinds of contacts. He got along with Bhutto well enough that Bhutto thought he could make him governor. Later since Bhutto could not handle the rest of the Baluch leadership, and they were moving in directions that made it impossible to continue the game without antagonizing his army supporters, Bhutto ditched Bizenjo and the Baluch and pursued policies that led to the present situation. Thus today, though Bizenjo is the closest to the left of the three, he is prepared to do business with Zia. Bizenjo could become the instrument of the Soviet use of the Baluch card—as could the others.

It is a tense situation. Zia recently called off a visit to Quetta (the largest city in Baluchistan) on a plea of indisposition after several bombs went off. Harrison emphasized that there is a legitimate leadership, and it is increasingly alienated and willing to do business with any quarter. The government has only one tribal chieftain in Baluchistan actively working with it—Doda Khan Zarakzai—and some people in the Zehri tribe. All the other tribes are passively or actively opposed to the government. The Russians may not touch the situation for years to come, but at any time they might.

The Soviets go for targets of opportunity rather than acting in accordance with inexorable historic drives. In the Baluch situation they can see a continuing deterioration in the relationship between the principal Baluch leaders and the governments of Iran and Pakistan. There is a declining probability of a settlement being reached, and a growing radicalization of the forces on the ground in Baluchistan. This is occurring at the same time as the Soviets may be despairing of change in the nature of the Pakistan regime. In their eyes Pakistan has a right-wing regime that continues to cooperate with an Afghan resistance that makes things hot for them. If they see Zia's left opposition failing, if they see the Afghan situation at a continuing impasse, if they see an entrenched regime in Iran that is increasingly anti-Soviet, they may play the Baluch card. If, on the other hand, there is movement toward a political solution in Baluchistan, if Bizenjo and Zia have talks, for example, then the opportunity would be less tempting. The noncommunist nationalists would be as difficult to handle as the Afghans.

Harrison did not think we could separate Baluch scenarios from our conceptions of where the Afghan situation is going. The most favorable environment for a relaxation of this problem and for a diminution of the danger of Soviet adventures is one in which there is a political settlement of the Afghan problem in the next several years. Such a settlement would include winding down the war in Afghanistan with some kind of a withdrawal of Soviet forces, and a neutralization of Pakistan and Iran in terms of Chinese and American relations with Pakistan and American relationships with Iran. A regional environment capable of supporting peace in Afghanistan would be the environment most compatible with federal settlements in Pakistan or Iran that would permit the Baluch to remain within the present states. Baluch independence is unlikely to come in the forseeable future unless it comes under the sponsorship of the Soviet Union. Therefore, it is clearly in the American interest to work for an overall solution in which this option does not become viable. The problem cannot be approached simply in terms of what do you get the Zia regime to do for the Baluch. It has to be included in an overall regional approach that recognizes the interdependence of the Afghan problem, the Baluch problem, the future of Pakistan, and American policy in the whole region from India to Iran.

*Henze* asked what was the present situation in Baluchistan in regard to Baluch education and cultural life, and what the relation of this was to the dissidence. He wondered whether the movement was merely a reaction to oppression or had a positive side. *Harrison* replied that it was ironic that many students have become politicized because of the efforts of the Pakistan government to establish colleges and junior colleges as part of a liberal policy. (By contrast, in Iranian Baluchistan education was very Persian-oriented, and the psychological pressure of the situation tended to keep many Baluch from wanting to be even in the environment of the Iranian schools. Partly as a result, there is a very small number of educated, politicized Baluch in Iran compared to Pakistan.)

It is hard to get at the numbers of politicized Baluch in Pakistan, but there are some indicators. The Baluch Student Organization is one of the elements of the nationalist movement—the one most penetrated by communist elements from outside of the movement. Membership has been running at about 6,000 since 1967. This suggests that something like 25,000 people have gone through this process of politicization, allowing for turnover and graduations. In Pakistan there is an actively politicized group of considerably more than these 25,000, perhaps 40,000 to 50,000 including some people who have come from the hinterlands into the movement, particularly since the 1973-77 insurgency. That doesn't seem like many. But when one realizes how small the Parcham party was in Afghanistan, it becomes clearer how a few people with some

perspective on what they think they are doing can made a big difference
—particularly when they have capable leaders. Harrison thought the
Baluch leaders were every bit as capable and sophisticated as other
leaders he had known in that part of the world. They do not fit the
common image of scruffy, tribal leaders.

The cultural side of the movement has basically been created by the
political movement. The Baluch Academy in Quetta has published more
than one hundred books at various times. There have been Baluch
journals on and off for the past twenty years. They rarely last very long,
five years or so, and they go out of business, and a new one is started.
Richard Frye recently came up with some rather discouraging conclusions on the cultural life of the Baluch. But he was not looking at the
politically generated literature, which is all underground. It is not publicly available at any bookstore or even at the Baluch Academy. You have
to get it from the BSO (Baluch Student Organization) or the BSO-Awami.
Both of these student movements have mimeographed monthlies,
quarterlies, and theoretical journals. Some of the content is quite literary,
what you would see in any third world country, and some of this is of
good quality. There are only veiled discussions of independence—no one
wants to get arrested, as many do.

Harrison added that cultural life is restricted to certain centers—
Quetta, Khuzdar, Karachi, Gwadar, Turbat; and in Iran, Zahedan,
Iranshahr, and Khash. Even if one goes to a town like Sarawan, a very
out-of-the-way place in Iranian Baluchistan, he will find a small group of
educated people well aware of what is going on in Pakistan and Baluchistan. There is a great deal of exchange of written material now between
the two Baluchistans.

The situation in Iranian Baluchistan is very sensitive, but this is a
recent development. Throughout the Shah's period, it was not very
politicized—SAVAK was extremely efficient. Under the new regime
there was encouragement at first of open expression in all the minority
areas. Then some things were published by the Iranian Baluch that
alarmed the people in the Khomeini group. The lid was put on, and now
it is all underground again. Still the center is Pakistan. If there is
another serious Baluch insurgency it would have to start in Pakistan,
and the Iranians may get behind it.

*Wriggins* asked about the Omani Baluch on the Gulf. *Harrison* replied
that there was considerable political interest among them. He said there
are two groups in the Gulf. The "Old Baluch" consist of those who
came hundreds of years ago. Many are Arabized and well-to-do—part of
the power structure. There are also some tribes on the Gulf among the
Old Baluch who are related to Baluch tribes across the water in Iran. He
interviewed a Baluch Sheikh in Bahrain. The Sheikh was a strong Baluch

nationalist, a very wealthy man, and related by marriage to the royal family in Bahrain. He spoke of Mengal and Marri as his leaders, but he was annoyed that they would not learn Arabic and make Baluchistan a part of the Arab world. The "New Baluch" are pretty much like other Pakistani Baluch; there is a Baluch nationalist movement among them.

On the relation between the Baluch and the Afghans in Afghanistan, *Nabawi* said that prior to the April 1978 coup the governments of Afghanistan and some political figures attempted to contact people in Baluchistan and the Northwest Frontier to develop a relation with them in support of Pakhtunistan. In this period the Baluch were contacted through the Pushtuns. Afghan governments almost never tried to contact Baluch leaders directly. Even when Akbar Bugti came to Kabul himself in an attempt to develop closer relationships with the Kabul government, the government tried to contact him through a Pushtun from the Achakzai tribe. The government would use the Pushtun Wali Khan of the National Awami party as a means of contacting the Baluch in the NAP (National Awami Party). When they wanted to contact Marri, they would go to Afzal Bangash, a Pushtun, since he also was thought to be close to the Chinese communists.

Nabawi added that after the "communist" coup, especially in the first nine or ten months when Taraki was feeling stable, the Afghans had a great influence on the leftists in Baluchistan and the Northwest Frontier, and even on the leftists of the Punjab and Sind. As they say in Persian, "The drum sounds better from far away." They did not know what Taraki or his system was doing, but they were very impressed. They thought the greatest thing in the world had happened.

In about the ninth or tenth month of Taraki's government there developed for the first time a direct relation between the Afghan government and the Baluch in Pakistan. The Afghan government paid more attention to the Baluch than to even the Pushtuns or the Northwest Frontier. A group of leftists from Baluchistan were given the assignment of translating Taraki's works into Baluchi and disseminating them in Baluchistan. In Kabul, some pamphlets were published about the Baluch leaders. They focused mostly on Bizenjo with whom the Kabul government was trying particularly to develop a relationship. In addition Afghan exiles who were staying in Baluchistan were harassed many times by leftists at the instigation of the Kabul government.

Later, after the incident between Amin and Taraki and once the rebel groups started a serious campaign, Kabul became preoccupied with the rebels and no longer sent missions back and forth to Baluchistan. Nabawi knew of no significant move to open these contacts again since the Russian takeover. But the potential remains.

*Rakowska-Harmstone* asked whether Harrison had information about

Soviet training of young Baluch. She had heard a report that a considerable number of young Baluch had been trained in the Soviet Union. The Russians were burned in the last ten to fifteen years by nationalist leaders, who are notoriously unreliable. Now they much prefer to use agents whom they have actually trained—although these may also be unreliable. In Baluchistan their efforts have not been going that well, and they may be training an alternative leadership. *Harrison* had no confirmation of this. The principal organized guerrilla force, already armed and trained in Baluchistan, is a group called the Baluch People's Liberation Front. It is based primarily in the Marri tribe and its principal cadres left Pakistan during the latter stages of the 1973-74 insurgency and began operating from base areas in Afghanistan. The Daud regime, in the name of traditional Afghan hospitality to the Baluch tribes, decided to designate them as refugees. They gave them rations and permitted them to set up camps. One was really a refugee camp with older people, but some were simply guerrilla base camps. Harrison had seen many captured weapons in the camps. These Baluch were given a subsidy by the Daud regime; it was continued by the Amin regime; and it is still being continued by the present regime. It takes $750,000 a year just to feed them. Although the Pakistani government has put out stories that they have all come back, most remain in Afghanistan (perhaps 5,000), and the great majority of the leadership is still there. But Harrison had no information that these people were being trained in the Soviet Union. He thought they were now in a very ambiguous position.

Harrison added that the Baluch were pretty close to Amin at first. Bizenjo liked the regime. He viewed the Khalq correctly as a nationalist-communist, very Pushtu, communist party. As a Soviet scholar once said to Harrison, "The Khalqis are a strange ideological cocktail, fifty percent Pushtun nationalism and fifty percent Marxism-Leninism." Amin thought of himself as somebody using the Russians, and Bizenjo, Marri, and others thought of this as the kind of communism they could get along with. As Nabawi said there was an enthusiastic Baluch response. They are not enthusiastic now; they can see what has happened. They may still do business with the Kabul regime, but they don't like it.

Amin officially recognized the leadership of the Baluch People's Liberation Front. As a good example of what Nabawi was saying, the Pakhtunistan celebration, held every August in Kabul for many years, became under Amin "Pakhtunistan and Baluchistan National Day." The principal leader of the BPLF in Afghanistan, Mir Kazar Ramkhani, read a message at the celebration.

Harrison added that if the central governments of Iran and Pakistan developed sophisticated policies toward the Baluch that didn't stir things up, the chance of activating a serious nationalist movement would be greatly reduced. To that extent Zia has been much smarter than Bhutto. He learned the basic lesson: "Don't go in there with the helicopters." His governor-general, Rahim-ud-Din, speaks softly, and doesn't insult them. This can buy time, but Harrison did not think it could do more than that. For there is now established a momentum that over a period of years is bound to become much more of a problem. Any real resolution requires granting a degree of autonomy.

As to what the United States can do, Harrison thought the situation offered little opportunity for a positive contribution. American leverage would be unlikely to induce concessions by Zia sufficient to bring about a political settlement. In the absence of such concessions it would be dangerous for us to have a policy designed to help the Pakistani government prepare itself for counterinsurgency activity against the Baluch; to attempt to deal with the problem through throwing money at it (for example, by building a road) without any political concessions; or a policy designed to give strength to a regime that does not have much domestic strength. These would all polarize the situation and add to the problem in a way that would eventually help the Russians. Some of his friends in the new administration think in terms of a big military program giving Zia what he wants. This would make matters worse. Harrison thought we should provide some economic inputs to make possible the functioning of a viable government in Pakistan. Beyond that a detached policy appeared the best policy in this regrettable environment where so many mistakes have been made.

*Naby* asked about the Pakistani Baluch perception of their co-ethnics in the Soviet Union. She wondered if they had exaggerated notions of their status and population, similar to those that the Soviet Turkmen and Uzbek have of their co-ethnics in Iran and Afghanistan. What role does their perception play in their attitude toward the Soviet Union and perhaps the nationality policy? Secondly, Naby wanted to know what was the relationship between the Baluch and the Pushtuns in Baluchistan, particularly in view of the growing Pushtun population in urban centers like Quetta and the fact that basically Pushtun refugee camps have been established in Baluchistan. She also mentioned the apparent attitude of some Punjabis that an exacerbation of the relationship of these two peoples in Baluchistan would be a way to solve the Baluch problem for the central government.

*Harrison* thought that only those Baluch who are intellectually interested in Marxism-Leninism think of the Soviet Union as a model with respect to nationality policy. He finds those who even mention their compatriots in the Soviet Union to be a very small number. And even these have little knowledge of how the 10,000 or so Baluch in the Soviet Union are treated. (To his knowledge no Soviet literature in Baluchi has come into the area.) What they do want to establish is the existence of a finger of Baluch territory going up through Afghanistan into the Soviet Union. They want a strategic border with everybody that counts, so the existence of the Soviet Baluch helps the dream of a Greater Baluchistan by providing a rationale for a border with the USSR. One Baluch, who puts out a paper in London and was formerly secretary of the Sind communist party, complains that other Baluch do not understand the importance of keeping this finger of territory. But Bizenjo will talk for a long time about Soviet internal nationality policy without mentioning the Baluch in the Soviet Union. However, the Baluch in Afghanistan are very much on the minds of Baluch leaders. They wonder how to deal with the possibility of adding a part of southern Afghanistan to their vision of a future state.

In regard to the second question, Harrison had initially assumed there was unity among the non-Punjabi nationality groups in their relation to Islamabad. He learned it was a complicated relationship. Today there is a rupture between the Pathan and Baluch autonomists. They do not like each other at all. (The Baluch and the Sindis get along well together culturally and politically.)

In the province of Baluchistan there is a strong Pushtun minority: there is disagreement on their precise numbers. Whole districts of northern Baluchistan and Quetta are heavily Pushtun. The Pushtuns have been more effective and aggressive both in agriculture and business, and now own a great deal of Quetta. The question of how to demarcate an ethnic Baluchistan vis-à-vis the northern districts is a problem for Baluch nationalists. They want Quetta, but do not expect to keep the northern districts of Baluchistan. They want a linguistic redemarcation of Baluchistan either within Pakistan or otherwise. They say they will let the Pushtuns keep their lands and rights, and treat them as brothers for they need Pushtun enterprise. But they want to have a state with a clear Baluch majority. The Pushtun refugees coming down from Afghanistan, many very wealthy, buying land and shops aggravate the situation. This opposition is exploited to some extent by the central government as Naby said. In Pakistani Baluchistan there is also a small but significant Punjabi influx, some Parsees, and a few Hazaras (a small community but important in smuggling supplies to the resistance—the Hazara mercantile network is influential in both Afghanistan and Pakistan). One of the main reasons the government can still function in the province is the cooperative relationship it has with the local Pushtun leaders.

*Khalilzad* asked whether the majority of the people in Baluchistan were Baluch or non-Baluch. He (and other participants) had seen estimates of only forty-two percent. *Harrison* replied that although it was a disputed point, he believed the majority of the residents of Baluchistan were Baluch. Most Pathan leaders would not claim to have a majority. Mr. Barozai, the former chief minister and a Pushtun, said in 1977 that the Baluch had a majority—about fifty-five percent. But no one really knows. The census data is extremely inadequate; the current influx of Pushtun refugees could lead to a Pushtun majority if they remain and acquire political rights.

*Kazemi* asked about the non-Baluch ethnic population of Baluch areas in Afghanistan and Iran. *Harrison* replied that in Iranian Baluchistan, from the census figures for the provinces known as Seistan and Baluchistan, the overall total is officially 650,000. About 100,000 of these would be Seistani; there are perhaps 5,000 Persian officials and businessmen. (Some Seistanis are of Baluch origin but no longer tribal. The same is true in the Punjab where there are detribalized Baluch who are no longer culturally or politically Baluch.) These figures are hotly contested. The Baluch believe the figures are doctored, pointing to the many areas to which Baluch have migrated and to areas that have been gerrymandered out of Baluchistan. They give incredible figures. Harrison estimates, after going through claims and censuses, that 1,000,000 would not be out of line as an estimate of Baluch for Iran as a whole. In Afghanistan there are 100,000 Baluch in the southern strip of the country, which also includes some small pockets of Aimak.

*Allworth* asked whether it would be useful to set up a Baluchi language center at Columbia so we could do more about the problem, or should we not worry about the five million people because they are just a drop in the bucket. *Harrison* replied that there is only a handful of anthropologists and linguists who know anything about the Baluch. There are very intelligent people in various parts of the U.S. government who have tried to become acquainted with the situation. When asked at Columbia once if there should be courses in Baluchi, Harrison replied that while he was in favor of Americans having more sensitive relations with many parts of the non-Western world, including Baluchistan, if Columbia had a choice of teaching Baluchi or Marathi, for example, he would prefer Marathi as the more developed and important language. Columbia should not set its priorities in terms of the shifting priorities of the U.S. government. The U.S. government should be putting the money into support for teaching Baluchi as part of an upgraded program relating to all non-Western cultures.

*Khalilzad* questioned Harrison's statement that the Soviets respond to opportunities. He did not believe the Soviets just waited around for opportunities, but that they created, actively sought, and promoted them. Whether they seek or promote particular opportunities has to do with many things, including their capability. If they pacify Afghanistan, the Soviet's ability to promote opportunities will increase enormously. Without Soviet promotion the Baluch problem may be a minor problem, although on humanitarian grounds we should encourage the Pakistanis to try to come to terms with it. Militarily the Pakistanis might be able to handle it without outside assistance, perhaps by exacerbating the internal differences in the province.

If we believe that the Baluch security problem is unlikely to be serious without Soviet assistance, that Soviet ability to intervene in Baluchistan will greatly increase if they pacify Afghanistan, and that the Soviets take advantage of and make opportunities, then Baluchistan appears to be an important place where the Soviets would be likely to promote opportunities. Still, Harrison recommends a policy not to help Pakistan, and not to assist Afghan resistance (which would imply the Afghans will be defeated). How then will we make it so costly for the Soviets on the ground in Afghanistan that they won't interfere in Baluchistan? Why should they accept a compromise on Afghanistan if it is not expensive enough? If the Afghans accept the Russians, why should they get out? Therefore, to make it costly for the Russians in Afghanistan we have to have the resistance movement. To have the resistance movement we have to help the Pakistanis because without the Pakistanis the Afghan resistance cannot get much help. So in these terms, the policy of doing nothing looks worse than the policy of doing something to avoid the Russians gaining a foothold in Baluchistan, which in turn would not be in our interest in terms of the big picture of Iran's reaction, the Gulf, or oil security. So Khalilzad thought the premise of Harrison's analysis—that the Soviets only respond to opportunities and do not actively seek and promote them, and do not have a picture of what they would like to see happen—was not appropriate. If we think they will seek opportunities, then our prescription must be different.

*Harrison* replied that he supported active involvement in the Afghan problem, but argued that we were not going to get the Russians out with a policy based solely on military pressure. (See discussion of Afghanistan below, pp. 188-90.)

*Ahmad* felt that the policy of doing nothing to help Zia to overcome his problems in relation to Afghanistan, the Soviet Union, and India makes it difficult for Zia to negotiate regional solutions with the Baluch or other groups. A strong and self-confident Pakistan government is more likely to enter into a political settlement with ethnic minorities than a government that is insecure because of external threats, is politically and psychologically alienated from both big powers, and feels a constant paranoia that Pakistan is going to disintegrate. Removing the insecurity would be helpful. On the other hand, there is a real danger that if you start sending in military equipment it will be used against the insurgents. Ahmad did not know the balance, but thought some help was essential. *Wriggins* added that we must have some way to demonstrate to Pakistan's leaders, and not just Zia, that we have not forgotten Pakistan.

*Ahmad* added that he saw a trend in Pakistan since Bhutto introduced his constitution in 1973 and during and after 1977 toward cooperation between the Punjabi political parties and the National Awami Party (NAP). (At that time the Baluch and Pushtun political factions in the NAP were together.) The Jamaat-i-Islami and other centrist political parties supported the demands of Bizenjo and other regional leaders that additional autonomy be incorporated in the constitution. In exchange, Bizenjo did not object to the Islamic provisions in the constitution. In the process of the movement against Bhutto, personal friendship evolved between Bizenjo and Mengal from the Baluch side, and on the Punjabi side Professor Ghaffur Ahmad, SherBaz Mazari (a Baluch), and many other Punjabi leaders. In 1977 as a matter of solidarity with the Baluch leadership, the PNA did not nominate a single candidate in Baluchistan.

On this basis Ahmad thought that there was a possibility that if a centrist, civilian regime replaces Zia, it might be able to enter into a political settlement with Baluch politicians. He thought that the military regime was incapable of comprehending the seriousness of the Baluchistan issue. There was no realization among the top military and even civilian officers that there is such a thing as the problem of Baluchistan. Recently they inducted a large number of young, educated Baluch into the bureaucracy. They apparently believe that it will help if they introduce more young Baluchs into the civil service and give more development aid to Baluchistan.

*Cottam* wondered about the Iraqi role, and whether they were better informed about Baluch than others. *Harrison* said that, as part of their approach to Iranian minorities, the Iraqis became interested in the Baluch in the 1960s when they picked up some emigré Baluch leaders. They supported some insurgent activity in 1969-73, but it was not a large operation. They had a broadcasting service and printed material, but it was a marginal episode in Baluch history. Since they did not want to compromise their relations with Pakistan, the Iraqis finally backed away from it. Harrison did not see evidence the Iraqis were very serious about the Baluch now. In their present struggle even their rhetoric has not focused much on the Baluch. *Cottam* said that they were mentioned in recent Iraqi materials.

In conclusion *Harrison* made the point that his paper had tried to describe the point of view of Baluch nationalists, and to suggest their alienation. He was not saying he shared the Baluch view. If we look at the territory occupied by particular population groups and match up percentages with the area, we will not find many federations in which such a small percentage occupies such a big, strategic, and resource-rich part of the country. In Pakistan the Punjabi reaction is understandable. Zia says, "Why should a people who are less than the population of Lahore control all of our resources?" Much the same problem affects Iranian Baluchistan, which contains one of the most significant under-developed copper deposits in the world.

Harrison said he wanted to adopt a somewhat more detached posture and to make clear that as far as he was concerned what the situation represents is a struggle of two perspectives, two sets of actors. His modernist Pakistan friends believe in the greater good for the greater number, and believe Pakistan should have access to these resources for its development. But the Baluch think in terms of equity. We should not award merit badges in dealing with nationalisms. People feel a certain way, and we have to deal with that. The rights and wrongs are not terribly clear.

# Prospects for Freedom in Afghanistan

## Richard S. Newell

It is impossible today to conjure freedom for Afghanistan. The loose social consensus that had held its diverse and fragmented society together for two centuries under the monarchy has been shattered irrevocably by feckless Marxists ruling with political incompetence, vicious factionalism, and gross insensitivity to the society they are committed to transform. Their failure brought on the Soviet invasion that has plunged Afghanistan into a war of pacification. During such a struggle no one is free, not the Soviet soldiers who cannot leave their camps except in force, not the officials of the Parcham government who take their orders from Soviet advisers and must be protected from Afghan citizens, and certainly not the Afghan people who are subject to curfews, political indoctrination, arbitrary arrest, strafing and bombing from their government, and ambush, kidnapping, highway robbery, murder, and requisition of food, animals, and supplies by desparate resistance groups. War, tyranny, and anarchy are simultaneously tearing apart the fabric of routine, habit, security, and group cohesion. Afghanistan in 1980 is ruled by terror and destruction.

There is no immediate prospect that this physical and moral turmoil will end. The fighting has taken on definite patterns since the spring of 1980 when Soviet units began a series of punitive campaigns into the regions of most obvious resistance. They have refined their operations, finding that the bombing and strafing of mud-walled villages even when accompanied by armored assaults do not bring about permanent pacification. The population flees, much of it becoming refugee, escaping to Pakistan if possible; a sizeable male minority stays behind to repossess their villages or to retreat to higher valleys or the hills overlooking their homes waiting to launch raids under the cover of night. Except where the Soviets or the remnants of the Afghan army are deployed in force, the countryside remains under the control of the resistance. Government officials and school teachers are virtually restricted to the cities which themselves are increasingly penetrated by resistance groups. Herat is reportedly a no-man's-land: the Soviets refuse to take the casualties that pacifying it would require, and local Afghan army and police units are incapable of doing so. The city has fallen into the anarchy of struggle between rival gangs aimlessly struggling for control of its neighborhoods.

As the war is being waged, neither side is capable of eliminating the other. The human cost of a guerrilla war seems likely to continue indefinitely. Under such conditions there is little prospect of establishing a level of human rights acceptable to any of the protagonists.

A discussion of the prospects for freedom in Afghanistan necessarily requires taking a longer view. The effort can have value regardless of how or when the present struggle will end. The various outcomes that might bring the conflict to a close have implications for the degree and kind of freedom that Afghans may eventually experience. Even though such a discussion requires making conjectural projections from a confusing present, it offers opportunities for exploring the dimensions of freedom that are at stake in Afghanistan. Victory for the Soviets and their clients in Kabul will clearly impose a different meaning of freedom than would a victory by the resistance. It could also be argued that neither side could establish a regime compatible with freedom. Such possibilities require examination of the propensity of Afghan culture to provide the political and social prerequisites for freedom.

## MOST LIKELY OUTCOME
### AFTER SUCCESSFUL PACIFICATION SOVIET TROOPS WITHDRAW; THE PARCHAM GOVERNMENT CONTROLS THE AFGHAN SATELLITE

Pacification would mean that the Afghan armed forces supplemented by a Marxist militia would have been able to control the population. It can be assumed that the Soviet Union would commit itself to provide sufficient economic aid to enable the government to begin reconstruction and development of the economy devastated by the war. Much of the initial effort would involve resettling on the land the large number of refugees who had squatted in the cities to avoid raids and fighting in the countryside. Much attention would also have to be paid to the rebuilding of roads, irrigation systems, schools, and basic government facilities.

Following closely would be an intensive effort to develop agriculture, both cereal crops for subsistance and market crops—fruits, cotton, sugar—for export. The latter crops would be monopolized by the Russians as a means of ensuring repayment of assistance loans. The Soviet Union would emphasize investment in extractive industry, especially now that it is known that Afghanistan has world-class deposits of chrome, copper, iron, and possibly uranium. There is geological evidence for greater reserves of natural gas and oil than Russian survey teams have reportedly yet discovered. The pace of developing the extractive industries will be governed by Soviet needs, but the effort will require the presence of many, perhaps 10,000 or more Russian or East European technicians and skilled workers. Given the heavy equipment and massive raw materials shipments associated with mining operations, the construction of a rail network in Afghanistan will almost certainly take place. To reach the deposits it will penetrate large sections of the Hazarajat and some of the mountainous regions adjacent to the Pakistan border. These have always been among the most difficult regions for Afghan governments to control.

The political implications of such developments will include the massive employment of Afghans in construction and mining, largely under foreign supervision. Past Soviet experience with heavy construction efforts in frontier physical settings suggests the use of conscripted or forced labor perhaps housed in heavily guarded camps. Such arrangements would provide opportunities to "re-educate" recalcitrant segments of the population. In any event, elaborate security measures would be necessary to assure protection of the large foreign population that would have to be housed away from the cities.

While forced draft attempts are being made in mining and transportation, a softer more diffusely focused policy is likely to be applied to the rural economy. The Parcham Party under Babrak Karmal has committed itself to gradual reforms in agriculture. In the wake of a successful repression of rural resistance, most of the prominent landholders will have fled or been eliminated. The circumstances should permit the government to complete the general redistribution of land which was bungled by the Khalq Party under Taraki and Amin. Because of the government's limited cadre of trained and experienced officials and its many other priorities, it is likely to delay an attempt to collectivize agriculture. Some prototype state farms might be organized near the cities. Considerable attention would be paid to servicing agriculture through credit inputs, fertilizer distribution, and small irrigation schemes organized on the basis of government directed cooperatives. In the early stages farmers may be left a good deal of freedom to market their crops in order to gain their participation or acceptance of other aspects of the new order.

Similar permissiveness may govern policies toward most Afghan traders. During its first weeks Karmal's government announced a relaxed policy of controls over private foreign trading. This replaced the nearly total choking off of private activity under the previous Khalq regime.[1]

These accomodative policies would be accompanied by more fundamental moves to gain control over Afghan society through reorganization
and re-education. Marxist experience and practice elsewhere provide a
guideline for action. In fact, Russian and East European and perhaps
Cuban cadres will probably be prominently involved in the early stages
because of the shortage of Afghan Marxists capable of carrying out
the required programs.

The re-engineering of the society for Marxist purposes will require a
comprehensive indoctrination of the population through state education
for all children and a variety of mass participation/education organizations
for adults. Great emphasis upon inculcating Marxist values in the elementary grades (up to grade ten in the Soviet system) is likely to form
the crux of this strategy. For adolescents and young adults conscription
into the military (an established practice under the monarchy), recruitment
into a Marxist militia, or mobilization into labor brigades will be aimed
partially at producing acceptance of revolutionary social goals. After the
induction of males is secured, a phased extension to females can be expected. For older adults, literacy programs and the mass organization of
women, minority groups, nomads, city workers, and so forth will be
created for purposes of control, re-education, and deployment for development.

Much attention will be paid to minorities on the model of catering to
their linguistic and cultural identities already established in Soviet Central
Asia. Soviet specialists in minority languages were among the most active
of the advisers brought in to recast Afghan educational and cultural
programs shortly after the 1978 coup. In contrast to previous policies,
the new Marxist government began to implement teaching and radio
broadcasts in minority languages, especially Uzbek, Turkmen, Nuristani,
and Baluchi.

The Parcham government has announced plans for the formal institutional framework within which such efforts to control and reshape the
society and economy will operate. In his first speech after his appoint-
ment as head of the Parcham government Babrak Karmal characterized
the Democratic Republic of Afghanistan as based upon a "national united
front under the leadership of the working class." The country's conditions and state of development precluded radical change. "It is not our
direct duty to practice socialism." Instead, he offered reconcilation and
establishment of "revolutionary tranquility." Arbitrary arrest, imprisonment and execution were to cease, political prisoners are to be released,
and Islam was to be respected. Freedom was to be reestablished so long
as it met the demands of the "New Model Revolution," that is, citizens
would be allowed to "form progressive and patriotic parties."[2]

The goals of the new government were spelled out more fully in a set of "Fundamental Principles" on the occasion of the second anniversary of the April 27-28, 1978, coup. The principles make it clear that government is to be organized on the classic Marxist model. It is to be totally subject to the control of the Peoples Democratic Party of Afghanistan which is the vanguard committed to completing the "second phase" of the revolution. In deference to Afghan tradition, the party is to call a Loya Jirgah, or grand national assembly, to ratify a constitution drafted by the party's Revolutionary Committee.[3]

The principles reiterate the party's decision not to impose "socialism" during the "second phase" of the revolution, but they make clear that all aspects of society are subject to revolutionary change and to the party's authority. A "vast national fatherland front" is to provide the basis of the party's power. The front consists of "workers, peasants, tradesmen, nomads, the intelligentsia, women, and representatives of all nationalities."

The personal rights and obligations of citizens are described in some detail. All are subject to the authority of the revolutionary vanguard. Rights are to include: equal status before the law; a guarantee of security of domicile, personal communications and property; freedom of religious practice, employment, health protection and social insurance; expression of grievances, due process, access to education and knowledge. On the other hand, personal expression and behavior are to conform to the dictates of the revolution. Rights to education and information are bound by the objectives of the revolution and the effort to develop "progressive" national education.[4] Private ownership of land is recognized, but is made subject to "democratic changes," a vague allusion to the land redistribution attempted under Taraki which the new government is determined to achieve more gradually. Grazing rights held by nomads are also subject to government confiscation. Nomads are "guaranteed" the right of "unhindered passage in national territories" and the use of pastures "free of charge" which suggests withdrawal of private rights to pasturage.[5]

Personal rights are thus securely tied to state policy. Their enjoyment is to come from the fruits of successfully completing a social, economic revolution and marked economic progress.

However it defines freedom, the promises and assurances of the Parcham are essentially meaningless during a civil war in which its cause is almost totally controlled by its Soviet sponsors. Its promises are designed to be attractive to a generally impoverished population and especially to the often abused minority ethnic communities. Altogether the latter constitute close to one-half of the population. Yet the principles have fallen on deaf ears. Parcham's revolutionary appeals have curdled in the face of the government's complete dependence upon Soviet troops for survival. The failure of the invaders to control most of the rural population and even some of the cities calls into question the ability of the Marxists to carry out their revolution. Their identification with the Soviets has invalidated whatever appeal their programs of economic betterment and elimination of social privilege might have had. A judicious mixture of carrot and stick may eventually bring the survivors around after a long war of attrition. The very process that would bring a Marxist victory would be likely, however, to destroy the features of Afghan life which give meaning to the roles of individuals and groups, or to their religion. At best the Marxist alternative offers eventual material improvement at the cost of personal integrity and freedom as defined and protected by Afghan tradition.

## SECOND OUTCOME
### CONTINUED WAR WITHOUT DECISION

By the summer of 1980 the fighting in Afghanistan had settled into a stalemate. The resistance forces had no means of expelling the Soviet forces; the latter could destroy or scatter resistance groups at will, but did not have the ability to subdue them completely. Total pacification would probably require at least the quadrupling of Soviet combat troops trained for counterinsurgency operations.[6] The costs in manpower and economic resources are great enough, apparently, to act as severe restraints on Soviet strategy. Military and political commitments elsewhere on the USSR's vast frontier, continuing economic stagnation, and popular resentment over mounting casualties in an unsatisfactorily explained war keep the Soviet government from acting with a free hand in Afghanistan. Consequently, there is a strong possibility that the level of Afghan resistance can be maintained, perhaps indefinitely.

In some essentials the resistance to the Russians is a continuation of ingrained hostility toward any central authority in Afghanistan on the part of tribes, communities, and ethnic enclaves that have been habitually jealous of their autonomy. But now the dialectic of a modern war of pacification/extermination is exerting unprecedented pressures upon the opposition. It is dependent upon outside support to survive at a level that makes possible more than minimal nuisance raids on weakly defended government and Soviet positions. Light, hand weapons, high-velocity, anti-helicopter machineguns, basic medical supplies, simple communications equipment, and ammunition form the bare minimum of what they must import. This requires either the support or the benign complicity of Afghanistan's neighbors; these depend in turn upon a strong stand by the Muslim community or Western backing of a regional security effort.

The prospects for a collective regional response appear to have been ruinously disrupted by the war between Iran and Iraq, although it is likely that the struggle in Afghanistan will continue long after the Persian Gulf war is settled. In any event regional developments in 1980 have added chronically to the rivalries and enmities which offer a bleak prospect for a concerted effort to aid the Afghan resistance. It will have to make do with the trickle of weapons and money it appears to have gotten from the Gulf states and perhaps China and Egypt and, hence, indirectly, the United States.

Therefore there is a strong possibility that neither side will be able to escalate their war effort sufficiently to destroy or to force the withdrawal of the other side. The Soviets and their Kabul clients should be able to continue to hold the cities, key military and infrastructural installations, and the main roads during daylight. However, the Parcham government will be denied the opportunity to expand the social base of its control. There will be too few youths to draft and far too few schools to operate to create a foundation for a permanent social transformation. Instead, the resistance can be expected to create its own institutions of control over the countryside, including regularizing theft and forced requisition into taxation, converting reprisals into makeshift judicial arrangements, and systematizing the recruitment and training of Mujahidin to begin the formation of quasi-permanent armed forces. In short, two incomplete governments will strengthen their hold on Afghanistan's divided landscape and people. The twentieth century offers many examples of people who have learned to cope with protracted stalemates, but such contests allow little scope for personal freedom. In this outcome the resolution of Afghanistan's national self-determination would be indefinitely deferred.

### Third Outcome
### The Resistance Movement Succeeds; Soviet Forces Withdraw

This result is by far the least likely to occur given Soviet strength, the divisions between the resistance groups, and their great inferiority in weapons. Even so, the possibility remains that after a protracted struggle a combination of developments, perhaps changes in the Soviet leadership, a growth in opposition on the part of the Islamic nations, a coalescence of military and political force among the Mujahidin groups might cause the Soviet Union to withdraw under some face-saving formula that guaranteed genuine Afghan nonalignment and nonbelligerence toward the USSR, on the Austrian model. One immediate result of this unlikely event would be the almost certain collapse of the Marxist government in Kabul. Its successor would have been determined by the military/political process that had brought victory to the resistance. Among the groups contending for control a wide spectrum of ideological models would be represented, extending from Maoism through Western liberalism to several Islamic modernist variations to strict interpretations of Islamic fundamentalism. The course of the struggle against the Soviet forces would have had a great bearing on which of these ideological approaches would have the strongest political claimants.

At this writing the best organized, financed and led of the resistance groups are the Hizb-i-Islami and the Jamiyat-i-Islami, both fundamentalist oriented. The former, under Gulbuddin Hekmatyar, is the most dynamic and dogmatic. Yet the competition between these organizations and their more moderate Islamic rivals led by Sibghatullah Mujaddidi and Sayid Ahmed Effendi Gailani is largely a struggle for outside attention and support. Hekmatyar and Burhanuddin Rabbani, the Jamiyat leader, have attracted between them the lion's share of foreign Muslim assistance. It remains unclear how effectively they have been able to convert this financial and military aid into the control and supply of Mujahidin groups actually carrying out hostilities inside Afghanistan. The continuing ability of guerrilla groups to harass Soviet and government forces can be attributed as much to their functional autonomy and self-sufficiency as to improvements in coordination and supply from organizations quartered in Pakistan. Even so, several months after the invasion evidence of better logistical arrangements and a stronger command struggle were becoming apparent.

Should victory be achieved it will probably be linked to the emergence of one of these groups, or a coalition, to dominance over the others. Evidence of movement in that direction so far suggests that a persisting pattern in Afghan politics is repeating itself, the dominance of Pushtuns over the minorities. Yet, unless a formula is found for inclusion of the minorities, an insistence on Pushtun control of a postliberation government could lead to a new round of fighting. Regionally based ethnic groups, especially the Tajiks in the northeast and the Panjshir Valley, the Hazaras in the central mountains, the Persian-speaking peoples centered on Herat, and the Nuristanis, have contributed too much to the resistance to accept Pushtun overlordship docilely. The refusal in May of the Pushtun dominated groups operating out of Peshawar to support an attempt to establish a government in exile, based upon a provisional Loya Jirgah representing all the areas and peoples of Afghanistan, is a disquieting indication of the rivalry that could once again develop between Pushtuns and non-Pushtuns.

Particularism thus remains a dangerous threat to the slender prospect of a return of Afghan self-rule. Afghanistan's many communities— ethnic, sectarian, nomadic, peasant, and urban—share a tendency toward giving scope for self-assertion to the individual within an overall pattern of conformity to basic norms. The Islamic Sharia law reinforces this tendency toward personal freedom bounded by informal pressures to observe legal/cultural standards. For Afghan men, and especially women, the autonomy provided by this concept of freedom cannot be equated with the rights which have evolved in the liberal, Judeo-Christian, industrial West. Each of these communities remains jealous of the uniqueness of the particular package of habits, styles, and beliefs that it retains. The crux of the problem for leaders of a liberated Afghanistan would be how to federate these groups into a mutually acceptable political system. Without such a solution, freedom from the Soviets is not likely to remove tyranny from Afghanistan.

## POSSIBLE AMERICAN CONTRIBUTIONS TO THE PROSPECTS FOR FREEDOM IN AFGHANISTAN

American responses to the Afghanistan crisis have been based upon a serious miscalculation. Control over the country was conceded to the Soviet Union immediately after the invasion. This error has limited American policy to symbolic gestures and measures that have not addressed the aggression directly. The embargoes have imposed further discomfort upon the already troubled Soviet economy; the Olympic boycott brought home to the Soviet people evidence of worldwide resentment against the invasion. The Soviet leadership has been put on notice that it has set back detente to the point where there is again the real possibility of an uncontrolled arms race. The reactions of the Carter administration were, however, so wide ranging in scope and so soft in focus that in the same breath it could be accused of both overresponding and underresponding.

What American policy has lacked has been a clear commitment to support the Afghan liberation struggle. This reluctance might have been reasonable in the first weeks after the invasion when most diplomatic sources inside Afghanistan predicted a quick and total Soviet seizure of the country. By April 1980, it was obvious that this expectation was wrong.

By that time, however, American policy was set. Carter's rhetorical and political investment in a new hard posture toward the Soviet Union did not include a line of action directed specifically at changing the situation inside Afghanistan. Some assistance may have been sent to the resistance forces through Pakistan. The facts are not available. Evidence from the testimony of Mujahidin leaders, and from press reports of the fighting and the circumstances of Afghan emigrés in Pakistan strongly suggests that the military aid reaching the resistance has not been sufficient to have a significant effect on the struggle.[7] Some aid has come from the Arab oil states and shortly after the invasion a few light weapons may have been supplied by the Chinese and the Pakistanis.

This lack of support for the Afghan liberation forces could have pivotal consequences for neighboring states in the Middle East and South Asia. Successful resistance against the invasion is the best guarantee of security against future efforts by the Soviet Union to penetrate or dominate the region. Its preoccupation with the resistance has undoubtedly added to Soviet caution in responding to the regional paralysis created by the Iraq-Iran war and it has probably had a restraining effect upon Moscow's handling of the labor crisis in Poland. Should Afghan resistance cease, an opposite effect can be expected. The crushing of resistance there could serve as an object lesson to other peoples who may eventually be forced to choose between resisting or submitting to Soviet power.

The situation offers the United States a rare opportunity to demonstrate that it is able to effectively support the integrity of the region and the self-determination of its peoples. This requires operating as a countervailing force to the expansionism of the Soviet Union. This cannot be achieved by acting unilaterally, or by relying upon military arrangements to install strategically placed bases within the region. American military bases tend to discredit and thus destabilize the very governments we wish to support. The alternative is to promote regional collective security by acting in support of joint defense arrangements as established between the governments of the region themselves. This line of policy requires much greater diplomatic virtuosity than finding opportunities for bilateral military aid. For most of the governments of the region it is the only line of approach that will lead to acceptance of the United States as a positive factor in the defense of the region. Otherwise, we will continue to be viewed as an imperialist predator interested mainly in oil, Israel, and the cultivation of a few Muslim clients. That image makes the United States no more acceptable in the region than the USSR.

Finding the means of getting enough aid to the Afghan resistance to raise substantially the cost of pacification is an activity ideally suited to demonstrating American bonafides as a superpower with benign interests in the region. It would require joint action by the United States and the Muslim governments who have already expressed strong opposition to the Soviet presence in Afghanistan. They have found that the denunciations issued by the Islamic Conference in January and May have had little or no affect upon Soviet behavior. In a joint effort, the American role could be openly avowed but kept indirect. Neighboring governments acting to reinforce Pakistan would funnel the actual aid to the resistance. American participation could be restricted to providing supplies and perhaps some training. This collective effort would demonstrate that military pressure can be exerted on the Soviet Union without a high profile American military/naval presence in the area.

The successful working out of a such a joint means of supporting the

Afghan resistance struggle would have the effect of helping to unify the defense of the region without activating regional fears that we intend to intrude or to dominate. It would also demonstrate American willingness to cooperate with Islamic states whose political systems have recently been energized by religious revival movements. It could contribute to the eventual restoration of friendly relations with Iran. Above all, it would indicate American support for the national self-determination of all peoples, regardless of their location, state of development, cultural traditions, or definitions of personal freedom.

## NOTES

1. Liz Thurgood, *Manchester Guardian,* February 10, 1980.

2. *Kabul New Times,* January 1, 1980.

3. Text of the "Fundamental Principles of the Democratic Republic of Afghanistan." Unofficial translation from the Afghanistan Mission to the United Nations. Published in the *Newsletter* of the Afghanistan Council of the Asia Society, June, 1980, pp. 48-52.

4. Ibid. Chapter Two, Articles 28-33.

5. Ibid. Chapter One, Articles 19 and 20.

6. *Asiaweek,* May 30, 1980, p. 32.

7. Marvine Howe, *New York Times,* May 23, 1980, p. A10.

# Comments and Discussion

*Newell* added that in a long-term struggle new, presently unknown leaders may emerge within Afghanistan that will become dominant. He thought that almost all the fighting had been locally generated and directed with little effective supervision by outside groups.

Russian troop levels at 300,000 would be expensive while supplying guerrillas sufficiently to force the Soviets to this level would not be expensive. The weapons supplied to the Afghans would not be of use to the Pakistan government against India. However, the Baluch unfortunately could use the weapons against Islamabad. International guarantees to Pakistan might be exchanged for some kind of autonomy settlement with the Baluch.

As far as freedom in Afghan-ruled futures was concerned, Islam had historically not been a powerful force in ruling the country. The tribes had generally been the centers of power. As a result, in spite of all of the talk of Islam as a motivation for resistance, the institutions being used to try to resist the outside intervention have not essentially been Islamic. Hekmatyar, Gailani, and Mujaddidi are all religious figures, but it is not clear any one of them will dominate the resistance if it survives. Newell thought so much would happen to the country in the course of victory that it would be hard to estimate what the Islamic element would be in the outcome.

Newell argued that if the Russians leave they will have to be dealt with, and this will probably involve dampening of the Islamic content. This is another reason a future regime is unlikely to be fundamentalist. What happened in Iran is not a model; the institutions and the demography are entirely different. He noted that Afghans were quite sensitive to questions of civil freedom in Western terms when they tried them. It is true that their major experiment (1963-73) may have failed or collapsed, yet if they were given an opportunity later it is likely they would be sensitive to civil freedoms again. These freedoms are congruent with the overall sense of autonomy or personal self-assertion that is characteristic of most of Afghan society, and is consistent with the way Afghans have lived with the Shari'a and Islamic civilization generally.

In regard to Newell's second scenario, *Rakowska-Harmstone* noted that *The New York Times* reported the current struggle was allowing the Afghans to overcome their ethnic and tribal divisions. She wondered how important Islam would be in underpinning a new Afghan unity.

In regard to Newell's first scenario, Rakowska-Harmstone also thought the model of Soviet Central Asia is of much greater importance than people generally realize. What is going on is like a rewrite of the history of the early 1920s; it is likely the timetable will be very similar. At first the government will make concessions allowing traditional institutions to continue, for example, in agriculture. Then there will be a gradual tightening and reforms will be introduced to completely change the social fabric. The education policy and the policies toward Islam will be as crucial as they were in Soviet Central Asia. The Soviets see what they have done in Central Asia as applicable to the third world in general. They might colonize Afghanistan in line with their model. This is the big brother aspect, the help extended by the Great Russian People, without which success is thought impossible.

Rakowska-Harmstone did not believe it is likely that the Soviets will ever withdraw. However, negative internal feedback from Afghan operations may go deeper than most suspect. She had heard of the coffins coming, with reverberations in the Baltic Republics and Moscow. This is coupled with the Polish case and other Eastern European problems. Yet they will not withdraw without a regional arrangement, and we will need an activist policy to build up pressure behind a withdrawal that adds to the pressure of their own internal difficulties. There is a breaking point: the Soviet Union cannot support interventions everywhere. In answer, *Newell* did not think Islam, although a given, was a very significant unifying factor, particularly for the ethnic groups. However, the struggle itself may give it this role. He had seen little analysis or data relating to whether the opposition is split between the Pushtuns and the rest. It is a fact that many minority groups are involved in the guerrilla war in the country, while in Peshawar the groups are all Pushtun. This is a major factor the resistance will have to overcome. The Kabul regime is largely Pushtun and may also have this problem. *Khalilzad* agreed (see his paper below). A Russian withdrawal might lead to internal ethnic conflict. *Newell* saw a possibility of federation as the solution.

*Newell* added that if the present regime achieves victory, they will go about setting up an ambitious educational scheme similar to that in

Central Asia. But if they do not have more than just the cities under their control, they will be lacking about ninety percent of the population. On that basis education will be a long-term problem as it was in Central Asia.

*Nabawi* remarked that within a year after the 1978 coup the atrocities, illegitimate actions, executions, and the subordination of the government to the Soviet Union became obvious to everyone, and most of the people turned against the government. In addition, the fact that the People's Democratic Party was devoted to Sovietism rather than to communism caused other Afghan communists to denounce it as well. He summarized the anti-government activities that began to take shape in four categories:

(1) Armed struggle, conducted by well-organized groups continuously and consciously, led both from bases in neighboring countries and underground centers and strongholds within Afghanistan. Most groups operate independently of each other and to a large extent independently of political circles outside Afghanistan.

(2) Spontaneous violence by individuals or small groups not related to organized groups in or out of the country. They attack Russians, the institutions of the government, or the members of the Khalq and Parcham parties.

(3) Nonviolent resistance by almost the whole nation, except for those whose life depends on the presence of the Russians in Afghanistan. This resistance now includes a large number of the Khalqis. (Incidentally, the enmity of the Khalqis and Parchamis has reached the point that it can be utilized if one knows how.) It includes spreading news, information, or rumors in favor of armed struggle against the government and the Russians, giving covert support to the armed struggle, and taking part in organizing strikes, demonstrations, or riots. Even many who appear to be progovernment denounce the regime as soon as their office doors are closed. When Nabawi left Afghanistan almost all offices were essentially on strike—nobody was doing any work to speak of. People were just sitting around, exchanging news and information, and condemning the Russians and the Parchamis.

(4) External activity in foreign countries such as India, the Arab countries, Europe, and the United States, where many Afghans are involved in one way or another in trying to work for the cause of their country and to help the freedom fighters.

If we put these elements of the liberation movement together, we will see that the armed struggle is only one element in the liberation struggle. It is difficult for the armed struggle to continue, especially in its present form. The people will finally get frustrated and disappointed. Once they are disappointed, they will feel they have lost the war. Our history shows that once Afghans feel they have lost a war against an enemy, they will not only stop fighting, but for some years they will not easily go against the same enemy. So it is very important not to let the armed struggle fail.

The armed struggle, if rendered effective, can be one important element in convincing the Russians to consider a political solution. Of course, there are many shortcomings in the armed struggle that must be overcome if the Afghans are to continue for a relatively long time. The result of an effective long-term resistance would be that the Afghans would convince the Russians that they cannot feel secure or establish a stable puppet government in Afghanistan. However, no matter how effective the armed struggle becomes, it alone cannot force the Russians to withdraw or even to negotiate. But if more effective resistance is coupled with international pressure, and if the other elements of the liberation movement also become more effective, then the Russians will at least reconsider their position in Afghanistan, and might talk. We must look for political solutions. Any specific initiatives or proposals should be preferably initiated by Afghans— the proper Afghans—or by or through the United Nations and the non-aligned countries.

As an example of the shortcomings of the armed struggle, there is no coordination of action among the rebel forces. Their operations are an amalgamation of isolated phenomena. The results are usually uneconomic and undesirable. One view is that it is better for the Afghans not to be coordinated. If each group operates separately, the Russians will not know where the headquarters are, and so be unable to destroy the movement as a whole. Another view is that unless there is a single leadership the resistance will not succeed. However, Nabawi looked for something in between. He wanted unity of action, not a single leadership but a single center to coordinate the operation of the different groups with their different leaders.

We cannot bring the Afghans together and tell them to have a single leader at this point. That would be next to impossible. Everybody thinks he is a leader. The best thing would be to leave each group under its own leaders. A military council consisting of engineers or experts on guerrilla warfare and the representatives of the different main groups of fighters should coordinate the struggle. It should be made clear that there is no desire to change the leadership but only to help the operation of all the groups. They should be shown that coordination would be of value to their cause. This approach might not work, but unity of action on this basis seems more likely than through establishing a leadership hierarchy.

The tendency of superficial hierarchies to fall apart in the Afghan context is illustrated by the communists themselves. The Khalq and Parcham were supposedly united before the communist coup in Kabul, but their unity was superficial and dishonest. The main element in each movement was in the military, but neither let the other know what was going on. Even after the coup the Khalq party tortured some Parchami to give them the list of the Parcham party in the army. They resisted, for they knew all those identified would be killed.

As an example of another area of need besides weapons, consider the information dissemination ability of the freedom fighters. There is a strong campaign in Afghanistan in favor of the Soviet Union. The mass media are now devoted to this. The freedom fighters may have a radio station, but it cannot be heard in many parts of Afghanistan. Obviously they should have a strong radio station with several frequencies.

Unless you are strong on the battlefield you cannot be strong at the negotiating table. However, even in the area of weapons, help should be provided with discretion. For example, to provide the freedom fighters with all kinds of weapons immediately would encourage adventurism. Once they go to that, everybody will be killed and very little will be gained. Weapons should be introduced under strict conditions. For example, an anti-gunship rocket should be used only to defend strongholds, and not for offensives resulting in direct confrontations with the Russian army. The traditional hit and run methods that the freedom fighters know best should be accepted as the principal tactic of the struggle even if weapons are made available. Weapons could be provided with the understanding that unless they are so used no more will be forthcoming.

The resistance movement also needs to adapt its warfare to the present situation. What is needed right now is mostly sabotage and, more important, urban guerrilla operations. Nabawi said that until the time he left Kabul there were almost no urban guerrilla operations in Afghanistan. Once two Russians were shot by freedom fighters. There were other incidents when individuals became angry, but there was no evidence that there were any operations carried out by trained urban guerrillas. Under the present circumstances, with 85,000 Russian troops in the country, the freedom fighters must adapt to the situation. Instead, in many instances the freedom fighters are still doing the same things as they were doing against the Afghan army. The freedom fighters, whether in or outside of Afghanistan, cannot afford to produce literature for educating people in the principles of modern guerrilla warfare. A contribution from outside could be to write or translate pamphlets about guerrilla warfare and to send them to the freedom fighters. There apparently has been no help of this kind.

Another weakness in the liberation movement as a whole is that in the United States, Europe, and Arab countries there are a large number of Afghans who are not mobilized, many of whom are people who represent a potential for being organized on the basis of a national and democratic program, but who will give up their hope of a free Afghanistan and be lost to Afghanistan forever if they are not mobilized and involved soon.

Nabawi would propose that a small group of politically conscious, militantly democratic Afghans should be helped to undertake the mission of mobilizing these Afghans now.

There also needs to be a reliable source of information and material on issues relating to Afghanistan. To provide this, Nabawi proposed that a research group be established distinct from the above-mentioned political group, consisting of three to five individuals, mainly Afghans, as the core, to study systematically and publish authoritatively on the economic, political, and cultural issues relating to Afghanistan. Its members should be carefully selected primarily on their academic merits, especially relating to their understanding of Afghanistan. Such a group would be invaluable in presenting a realistic, well-rounded, and objective picture of the situation as a whole.

*Ahmad* understood that for the disbursement of Middle Eastern funds for the guerrillas there was at least informal coordination—about three or four months ago the freedom fighters held a meeting leading to this agreement. At the same meeting they said they would help each other in the field, and they would keep each other informed of operations. When the second Islamic summit was being held in Islamabad, the question was who should represent the freedom fighters in this conference. Ultimately Iran decided to coopt the Afghan delegation. But before that could be formed, there was pressure from Saudi Arabia and other countries that they should form a united delegation. There are some indications that such informal coordination might work. Although the armed struggle may be weak, he disagreed with Nabawi's assessment of the danger of disappointment and passivity if victory does not come soon. There is a Pushtu saying, "A Pathan who takes his revenge after one hundred years says he took his revenge soon." This is repeated by some of the freedom fighters in Peshawar. They say, "It is not we who are impatient, but the Russians. It is our country so we can wait."

*Gastil* asked whether the reports of guerrilla groups fighting one another were significant. *Naby* said a British journalist who went into Paktia reported this in January on a PBS program. He claimed to have seen members of one group (perhaps Gailani's) fighting with, or at least not coordinating with, another group. Many people pick this up, and say, "See what happens." Naby thought that even if we credit this report, we have to take into account that the report relates to a period before the Soviet invasion. The picture has changed dramatically since that invasion, not only in terms of coordination. The Afghan bureaucracy through the Taraki, and to some extent Amin, period tried to survive and not make too many waves. Since the Soviet invasion this has changed. The refugees and Mujahidin are also different. As an example, when Naby was in Kama (which now is invaded by Soviet forces) the fortifications had been taken with the cooperation of two groups that in Peshawar were quite separate politically.

*Khalilzad* added that he had seen a recent report that a religiously oriented group, apparently Hekmatyar's, attacked some of the Afghan Mellat forces. The report came from one of the leaders of the Mellat group in New Delhi. But on the whole, although there have been tensions, there has been very little fighting of that sort among the Afghans since the invasion. It has been surprising, given past conflicts, that there has been so little intra-Afghan fighting among the partisans.

Khalilzad added that the Afghan opposition certainly had many shortcomings. It was ill equipped, both politically and militarily. There are attempts at unity. Five major groups are in an alliance. The majority of the fighting has taken place independently of these groups inside Afghanistan, but these groups send in arms. They sell them sometimes. At other times they give them only to those who pledge to accept their leadership. Aside from the political and military problems is the problem of food. The national price for wheat established a few years ago has been destroyed. In areas such as Badakhshan where there were reports of a great deal of fighting initially, there are great shortages of food, and the prices of wheat and flour have gone up substantially. Part of the aid from the outside could be in the form of canned food or other imperishable foods that could be easily transported.

Pakistan plays a very important role in all of this. The Pakistanis can try to force the groups to unite or use the groups against each other. Apparently they are trying to undermine those involved in the fighting by bringing together a group of former Afghan officials who have not been involved in the fighting to represent the Afghans at the upcoming meeting of the General Assembly. Clearly the government of Pakistan can use the Afghans for its own purposes. Even the alliance of the five groups is in trouble; they have warned each other that unless everybody puts their military forces under a central group under the leadership of Sayyaf, the central leadership will force the disarming of those who will not go along with it. An attempt will be made soon to impeach Sayyaf because of reports he had been sending away a million dollars to a special account instead of using it to buy arms.

In spite of these problems, we must still ask what are the alternatives, the goals, and how one might go about achieving them.

*Newell* added the observation that the presence of a million and a half refugees in the Northwest Frontier will produce something comparable to the Palestinian problem in almost any scenario except an early Afghan victory. It will provide a base for continual conflict, no matter how the Pakistanis handle the situation. There are compelling reasons why the Afghans may feel it is frustrating to continue the fight, but when there are a million and a half refugees with no place to go, there will be pressures for the conflict to continue. So even if there is a lessening of resistance inside the country, the constant goading of the refugee situation will lead to renewed fighting. It may be sporadic. The Afghans might be paid off and quieted for a time, but it will not mean it is over. The Russians may find they just turned their back at the wrong time. So, the second scenario seems most likely—continuing, protracted resistance. *Khalilzad* (and others) added that there are about 1,500,000 refugees with over 300,000 of these in Iran. Many are unregistered and more are coming in regularly.

*Gastil* asked if "Tajik," an expression applied to the Persian-speaking Afghans, actually identified an ethnic group in the sense that they identify themselves as opposed to other groups, organize "Tajik" military units, and so on. *Newell* interjected that there are two particular areas of concentrated resistance: the Panjshir valley and Badakhshan. Both are basically Tajik. *Gastil* said they happened to be Tajik, but is there a "Tajik" ethnic sense? Do the Tajiks in Kabul for example cheer when the Tajiks in Badakhshan have victories? *Khalilzad* suggested that even some of the Pushtuns may not think of themselves as Pushtuns. There are some Pushtuns who do not even speak Pushtu.

Khalilzad added that although we think of Pushtu being the dominant language, the language of the bureaucracy as well as major universities has been Persian. At some level there is a sense people are Pushtuns. Some Afghan citizens have thought "Afghan" only meant Pushtun. Some people in Mazar-e-Sharif where he spent some time told him they were not Afghans, but something else—Tajiks, Uzbeks, or members of some other group.

*Rakowska-Harmstone* noted that in the USSR the "Pamir Tajiks" are not really Tajiks, but Iranian groups speaking mutually unintelligible languages. Tajik is their *lingua franca* now, but originally they had a great deal of trouble with the Tajik language because it was not their language. The same thing might be true across the border.

*Henze* thought the discussion had brought up an option we have to be alert to the Russians playing in Afghanistan: deliberately setting one group against another. When we look back at the history of Soviet Central Asia in both a crude and sophisticated way, this was a dominant theme. Turkestan was divided up, so that the people who lived a little higher up were divided from those lower down, and so forth. Initially, at least, the result was perceived as very artificial. In Afghanistan, trying to sort out ethnic groups would be so difficult it would be unlikely to happen soon. But if Newell's scenario involving a full Soviet victory became reality, the divisions would be used to keep people busy. That is what they did in the Caucasus after the revolution. In the second scenario there is the vicious and appalling option of the Soviets deliberately trying to set everybody against everybody else. If the situation deteriorates into a stalemate, we have to anticipate that.

Henze added that a subject as interesting as the Tajiks was the status of the Turkmen and Uzbek, because they are much more directly related to the peoples across the border.

*Naby* found it interesting that the Afghan government ignored the Tajiks in their nationality policy after the 1978 coup. Instead they played up the Uzbek, Turkmen, Nuristanis, and Baluch; they tried to instill Pushtu as the interethnic language. But we have a new issue now, the report that the Soviets have annexed the Wakhan Corridor. If that were the case, then there may be a question of ethno-linguistic tradeoff: Panj-Deh would be a likely tradeoff.

If the Soviets are going to create a Mongolia, Bulgaria, or even a Finland, they are going to keep up the facade of a separate country, with a separate vote in the UN. But just as they did in Eastern Europe in 1944-45, they may make some little readjustments of the border. Now the Wakhan corridor first of all geographically might be called a natural extension of Gorno-Badakhshan. Second, it would give the Soviet Union a common border with the subcontinent. Even if not usable, it is psychologically a possible source of intimidation. The Soviets are building at least a helicopter pad, if not an airstrip in the Wakhan Corridor. The Wakhan Corridor connects China with Afghanistan, although the Chinese do not use the corridor but come through Pakistan on the Karakoram Highway.

*Henze* was doubtful the Soviets would actually annex the Wakhan Corridor. He found only one precedent in Soviet history in Asia. They established Tanu Tuva, the Tuvinian Autonomous Region, then quietly annexed it in the 1930s. They officially annexed it in 1944-45. Otherwise the Soviets have been very sensitive to this sort of thing. The situation in Eastern Europe at the end of World War II was quite different. He thought they might take de facto control of the Wakhan, but that they would legally incorporate it into the Soviet Union seemed extremely unlikely. *Rakowska-Harmstone* disagreed. She argued that using the Polish example they could simply have a referendum. They incorporated eastern Poland by referendum in 1939. She had observed her parents when they had to vote. Everyone had to vote for the incorporation of their area into the western Ukraine or western Belorussia.

*Henze* thought that we should assume that the Soviets would move very quickly to block off the Wakhan Corridor. Since there is nothing the Soviets are more sensitive to than the Chinese, the fact the Chinese have a link to Afghanistan through the Pamirs is obviously a problem for them. The Wakhan Corridor, just one big valley, lends itself to easy occupation. *Naby* added that Afghan objections might not be so strenuous. They did not want the Wakhan Corridor to begin with. *Henze* suspected they wanted it badly now.

*Harrison* returned to the larger question of aid to the guerrillas. He thought that the essential problem is where the aid goes and therefore which groups emerge most powerful in the resistance. The religious fundamentalists have had a definite position on the far right of the spectrum. They represent the only politicized element that opposed the consensus on which a noncommunist Afghanistan had been tolerated or accepted by the Soviet Union from 1955-1973. Some fundamentalists were already exiles before the insurgency began, while others, such as Gailani, whose religious approach is more moderate than the others, left after the 1978 communist coup. The people who organized the insurgency in the first instance, and who preside over the groups in Peshawar, come from these same fundamentalist and other religious groups. These groups are trying to use the resistance struggle to reach a position in the society that they did not have before. While Harrison agreed it was not necessary to have a coordinated resistance in order to have a resistance worthy of our support, the problem in channeling aid is discriminating between those elements of the resistance that, if they became the leaders of the resistance, would complicate and delay a political settlement, and those elements that would not. It is not entirely clear where the commanders on the ground would come out politically. Now they are all bitterly anti-Soviet because they are fighting against them. But differences can be detected. The foreign policy of the Loya Jirga group is much more conciliatory than that of the fundamentalists. The Loya Jirga was not itself a resistance group, but it was a gathering together of various local groups, some of which are involved in the fighting, that do not accept the leadership of the major Peshawar groups. As has been pointed out, some are allied with the less fundamentalist Gailani, who has his base in the tribal areas. In any event the first element of an effective political-military policy will be to differentiate in giving aid between the fundamentalist and the tribally-based elements of the resistance.

Since the Soviets are not going to want to deal with a group that has been fighting them for fifteen years, supporting such a group seems unrewarding. If Hekmatyar wants to carry on the fight, that is an asset, but the Saudis, the Kuwait Department of Religious Affairs, and the Jamaat-i-Islami of Pakistan are going to feed money into Hekmatyar whatever one does. Other people involved should recognize that the place to put money and support is not with the groups that are going to make it more difficult to implement any diplomacy you try to devise to help resolve this problem.

The goal of this diplomacy is what Harrison calls "Finlandization"— something much closer to the Soviet Union than what they had before 1973, but less than an occupation.* These terms would be considered appeasement by many, but are political realism. Obviously, the actual terms have to come from the field commanders, from the people who emerge as the real leaders of the resistance.

If we have a policy based just on the objective of making it hot for the Russians, tying the Russians down, increasing the pressure, we will be repeating some of the same mistakes we have been making in Afghanistan for the last decade. If we simply up the ante, they will up the ante, and we will have more Afghans killed, and nothing will be resolved. If we combine military pressure with a political and diplomatic posture that makes sense, then we have a policy that is not just a prescription for killing more Afghans and tying down the Russians. Our policy should not reflect the attitude of Deng Xiaoping who advocated "tying them down until the inevitable world war comes" (in his interview with Oriana Fallaci). We should rather approach this in Afghan terms first, regional terms second, and in global terms third. As for Afghanistan itself, we should place as much emphasis on attempting to negotiate with the Russians as on building up pressure. We should operate concurrently on the diplomatic and military fronts. We should make clear that we do not want to make Hekmatyar czar of a centralized Islamic dictatorship that will be anti-Russian and anti-tribal.**

This gets back to Newell's point that Islam has not been the most basic or powerful force in Afghanistan. This was a society in which tribal autonomy was the essence of the political process, and Kabul made its peace with many autonomous power structures. The Loya Jirga in Peshawar emphasized tribal autonomy. Yet Hekmatyar talks about erasing tribalism, which is incompatible with Islam. This ideological distinction is fundamental because, if we strengthen groups that are not able to relate to the tribal leadership or the Russians, we do not have people who will contribute to our ultimate objective.

*Cottam* said that if this means the United States should give support differentially, he would disagree. *Harrison* replied that any American aid or other aid we stimulate or encourage to the resistance forces should:

---

* Harrison reported having said to a Soviet scholar who came last year with a group to Stanford, "You are going to make it into a Central Asian Republic, aren't you?" He replied, "No, no, if you must compare it to anything, compare it to Mongolia." Harrison repeated this to a high Soviet official at the UN, who said, "Mongolia, Mongolia is practically a province of the Soviet Union. Perhaps we should say Bulgaria."

** Harrison develops his position more fully in his article, "Dateline Afghanistan: Exit Through Finland?", *Foreign Policy,* No. 41, Winter 80/81, pp. 163-187.

(1) only by given if it is coupled with a simultaneous and carefully thought-out diplomatic posture toward the Russians, and

(2) be given to the people on the ground who are doing the fighting and not to people who will contribute to a further distortion of the political situation. The question of how change occurred from 1970 to 1980 is of course central to this discussion. In his *Foreign Policy* article (cited above), Harrison believes he has shown how anti-Soviet forces had provoked and aggravated the Russian desire to intervene in Afghanistan.

*Khalilzad* had no question about the desirability of being discriminating in our assistance so that we might increase the chances of those who are more sympathetic to our views and would make a compromise possible. In any event without increasing Soviet military cost substantially, it is unlikely they would agree to compromise.

Among the groups in Pakistan, at least three of them—those of Hekmatyar, Rabbani, and Khalis—want an Islamic Republic. That is what they are struggling for, and they appear to have substantial support in Afghanistan. Historically they have not been very important, but they are more important now than ever. Modernization, interaction with the outside world, has led to a variety of responses, even among the intellectual elite in Afghanistan. One response is that we have to search for a more Islamic solution to the country's problems. Those three groups have said on many occasions they do not believe they can solve the problem only through military confrontation. They also say that though they support an Islamic Republic, the form of Afghan government will be decided subsequently. The people will be given several options. Gailani has even said that he will accept the monarchy back if the people of Afghanistan want it. (In fact he wants the monarchy himself.) Mujaddidi as well as Nabi have said that they will accept the king if the people or the tribes want him back.

The possibility of a solution depends on what Russian ambitions in Afghanistan are. We have talked about what the Afghans can do. But no matter what the Afghans do or offer, it is unclear that the Soviets will accept. If they really came into Afghanistan because they thought there was the threat of an imminent overthrow of Amin and the establishment of a hostile government, then there is any easy solution. Several foreign powers as well as the major leadership of these three groups have proposed the neutralization of Afghanistan. But Khalilzad knew of no signal from anyone, to the United States government or to the representatives of European governments, that the Soviets are interested in anything like that. *Henze* agreed. The problem with Harrison's argument was that there was no evidence of forthcomingness on the Soviet side. Their position is hardening all the time, so while Harrison builds a beautiful structure, Henze thought it had no foundation. *Harrison* agreed there were no clear signals yet, but still thought it was the only way to get the Russians out, if any way existed.

*Rakowska-Harmstone* asked two questions of Harrison. First, how did one know which group to help and which not in terms of subsequent behavior? Second, if one dilutes the resistance, could he not be subverting the whole resistance? If you give to some groups and not others, couldn't one defeat the whole thing? *Gastil* pointed out that in World War II we switched from Mihailovich to Tito without weakening Yugoslav resistance.* (*Wriggins* and *Rakowska-Harmstone* agreed.)

*Cottam* supported Rakowska-Harmstone's point. He thought Harrison wanted to have his cake and eat it too. As the situation develops it will be just exactly as she says, the question of which ones to support will not be as clear to everyone as Harrison believes. There will be advocates of each group, especially if we assign personnel to liaison with each group. These people will come to have vested interests in their groups. Arguments will be made for every group; compromising them will lead to increasingly sucking the United States into doing exactly what we do not want. Since this will add to Soviet paranoia about a Sino-American alliance, it makes the possibility of changing the Soviet position less. On the contrary it will produce exactly what we are afraid of. We will be fighting a superpower 9,000 miles from our base, and they will be able to pay the priority price to win, whatever it is.

*Wriggins* asked what Cottam's conclusion was. *Cottam* said he was the dove in this group. He did not want to send any aid to any group. *Harrison* wondered if Cottam thought the Soviets would react that way if we had a diplomatic posture that said their withdrawal could be over a period of years. *Cottam* said that if he were them, he would not believe it. If he saw clandestine aid to a group, he would never believe it was not Chinese or American. In the face of American aid the Soviets could not withdraw.

*Newell* agreed with Cottam on clandestine aid. He thought United States aid should involve as many of the Muslim countries of the region as want to help. This may require careful orchestration if they find themselves too exposed to do it individually for themselves. He thought as long as the aid is not monopolized by Hekmatyar or anyone else, we should not worry about distinctions among groups. If one group has a policy that is antithetical to Afghan instincts then it will collapse in the process of competition. We should let the chips fall where they may. He had been thinking about the Yugoslav analogy as well. In 1942 if we had said it was going to be Tito we would not have given aid.

---

* For political reasons, of course, it may have been an error.

# Religion and Nationalism in Soviet Central Asia*

## Teresa Rakowska-Harmstone

In the last two decades national self-assertion of the Uzbeks, the Kazakhs and other Central Asians has emerged as a dominant theme in the life of Soviet Central Asian republics, and it is Islam which has been the touchstone and an integral part of their new sense of modern national identity. This mutually reinforcing linkage between nationalism and religion has been a characteristic feature of modern nationalism also in other cultures and societies. Central Asians' new nationalism fits well into the traditional Muslim concept of the unity of the sacred and the secular, even though, paradoxically, it has evolved under the impact of extensive modernization and secularization policies, and has been embraced by modern Soviet-educated Muslim elites. Its roots are in the historical developments both preceding and following the 1917 Revolution; it was sparked by an Islamic reform movement led and initiated by the Tartars and, interacting with a imperial alien power, it was carried on by the early Muslim communists, whose heirs are the modern elites.

### BACKGROUND

*People.* There are five Muslim republics of Central Asia, each named for its titular ethnic group: Uzbekistan, Turkmenia, Tadzhikistan, Kirgizia, and Kazakhstan. In 1979 their population numbered 40 million people, of whom 28 million were the Muslims and the rest were immigrants, mostly Slavs from European Russia. Of the six major indigenous groups

---

* This paper was derived from a broader study, "Central Asia and Kazakhstan," prepared by this author for Alexandre Benningsen et al., *Islamic Communities Under Communist Rule*, to be published by George Allen & Unwin, Ltd., 1981.

the Uzbeks, with 12.5 million people are the largest; all, except the Tajiks (Tadzhiks) are of Turkic ethnic origin and speak Turkic (Altaic) languages. The Tajiks are Farsi-speaking Iranians. All of the indigenous groups are Muslims; most of Sunni of the Hanafi rite. Smaller Muslim groups include the Uighurs (Turkic) and the Dungans (Chinese), refugees from the Chinese Sinkiang, and the Iranian-origin Baluch, Afghans and Kurds. Exceptions to the Sunni creed are to be found only among the Tajiks of the Pamir, who are Ismaili of the Nizari rite, and among scattered Iranians and Azerbaijani who are Shi'ites.

European immigration into Central Asia began in the 19th century, but the main influx came between 1927 and 1959. The Russians are the key group; in 1979 there were nine million of them in the five republics. Among the immigrants there are the unwilling deportees such as the Volga Germans, the Crimean Tatars and the Koreans, and representatives of almost every other Soviet national group. Non-Muslims tend to cluster in the cities and at industrial sites. This demographic mix makes Central Asia one of the most "internationalized" parts of the Soviet Union, but the appearance is misleading. Non-Muslims tend to Russify, and the cities are predominantly Russian in character. The countryside (with the exception of northern Kazakhstan) is Muslim, and there is little interaction between the two communities.

The settlement pattern and demographic trends reflect the profound cultural alienation between the two communities. Muslims do not migrate out of their original area of settlement and are reluctant to leave their traditional rural habitat. Consequently their rate of urbanization is low and they constitute a minority in their capital cities. The Muslims' demographic pattern is a typical rural pattern characterized by unlimited birth rates, low death rates and low mobility. Their crude birth rates (except for the Kazakhs) have been in excess of thirty per thousand in the seventies, which made for the highest natural growth rates in the Soviet Union. This (combined with the decline of fertility among Soviet European groups), has resulted in the Muslim population explosion attributed by Soviet as well as Western scholars directly to ethnic and cultural factors.[1] The results of the last two population censuses strikingly illustrate the high fertility rates as well as low mobility of the Muslims. In the 1970-1979 period the numbers of the Muslim groups increased by over thirty percent (except for the Kazakhs), but the republics' urban population showed at most a five percent increase (in Uzbekistan), no increase (in Turkmenia), and a two percent decline (in Tadzhikistan). The Muslim population explosion has caused serious imbalances in the distribution of Soviet manpower (for economic as well as military purposes) and has had important political implications: in the reversal of a trend prevalent in the 1926-1959 period, the Muslims' share in the population of their republics has been growing while that of the Russians (and other Europeans) has been decreasing. This has enhanced the Muslims' political importance, but the simultaneous domination of urban and industrial centers by the immigrant elements has also raised the potential for ethnic conflict.

*History.* Islam came to Central Asia in the seventh century with the Arab conquest, and the region's indigenous people, a mixture of descendants of successive waves of Mongol-Turkic nomads and original Iranian settlers, are the product and inheritors of a frequently illustrious but turbulent history. The seat of a splendid medieval Perso-Arabic Islamic civilization, the region came under the Russian rule in the 18th and 19th centuries in the demarcation of the spheres of influence between the Russian, the British, and the Chinese Empires, and remained within the new Soviet socialist state after the upheaval of the 1917 October Revolution. But, although Tatar reformism made some inroads among educated Muslim elites there, the bulk of the Muslim population entered the modern era under communist rule still tradition-bound and economically backward, lacking a sense of separate national identities beyond loyalties to a particular family-clan-tribal group and a common perception of a membership in the universal *Umma*, the community of all believers.

The Civil War period in Central Asia and Kazakhstan was characterized both by the struggle between the Whites and the Reds fought within the Russian community there, and by the Muslim resistance movement, the Basmachi rebellion, triggered by the suppression of traditional Muslim institutions by the victorious Bolsheviks, who proved to be as colonial in their attitudes vis à vis the Muslims, as their Tsarist predecessors. The Basmachi were suppressed only in 1921, by a combination of new conciliatory policies and vigorous military action, and Muslim "progressives" were invited to participate in the building of a new socialist society. Many of them did, forming the nucleus of a Muslim communist cadre.

Four distinct policy phases followed the end of the Civil War. Each corresponded to the requirements of what the leadership perceived as paramount needs of the time from the point of view of the long-range integration of the region into the new Soviet state, periods of concessions alternating with attacks on Muslim society and traditions. Within the overall framework of the nationality policy applicable to all of the non-Russian peoples of the Soviet Union, Moscow's policy in Muslim areas was adjusted to take into account specific conditions there.

The policy of *korenizatsiia* (nativization of the apparat), and of partial restoration of traditional Muslim institutions (*waqfs*, Muslim schools, and *shariat* and *adat* courts), was adopted in 1921 within the framework of the NEP (New Economic Policy). But an effort to break the region's Pan-Turkic, Pan-Islamic unity began in 1924 with its delimitation into the five republics, and with the introduction of cultural policies designed to develop each main subgroup's languages and cultural traditions separately as a vehicle for the common integrative socialist message.

The need for an accelerated social change, and a decision to collectivize agriculture and to begin industrialization of the country signalled a shift to assault tactics. In Central Asia the assault started in 1927 with a head-on attack on Islam and all of its institutions and on the traditional system of social relations all of which were proscribed. The collectivization followed, with its attendant extreme sacrifices and economic dislocations. New socioeconomic structures were consolidated through the thirties. Massive purges of Muslim leaders, accused of "bourgeois nationalism", accompanied the changes, and resulted in a return to a *de facto* direct Russian rule.

The German attack on the Soviet Union in 1941, which forced partial concessions to accomodate national and religious needs of the people in the interest of survival, ushered in a new policy phase. In Central Asia (and in other Soviet Muslim areas), it meant a momentous reversal of the previous policy of forced secularization. Islam was legalized through the establishment, in 1943 in Tashkent, of the Muslim Spiritual Directorate for Central Asia and Kazakhstan (one of four new Muslim directorates in the USSR). The setting up of an official hierarchy, unprecedented in Islamic practice, was an essential condition for the party to be able to maintain control over reviving Islam. The price of official approval for the newly registered "official" clergy has been the support for Soviet domestic and foreign policies and the accceptance of severe limitations on their activities. The Directorate manages a small network of "official" mosques (about 200 in the late 1970's) and deploys a small number of clergy; it has not *waqfs* to administer and no *shariat* courts, and it cannot collect the obligatory *zakat*. But it attends to spiritual needs of believers, collects voluntary offerings, issues a few religious publications, and runs the only two schools in the Soviet Union that train Muslim clergy.

The concessions inititated in 1941 were partially rescinded after the war, but Stalin's death in 1953, and the resulting struggle for power in Moscow opened up new opportunities for the assertion of local demands in Central Asia as elsewhere; a new momentum was created by Nikita Khrushchev's de-Stalinization campaign of 1956. It marked the start of a new phase in nationality policy, that of *sblizhenie* (rapprochement or "ever growing closer together"), which has retained its validity through the Brezhnev era. The policy combines two key elements: an accommodation to national pressures, *but* with their subordination to an overall goal of integration. Tactical shifts of emphasis between the two elements of the policy have been characteristic of its implementation. The initial "Thaw" of 1956-1959 gave way to a push for a merger *(sliianie)* of all Soviet nations into a single whole. But with the ouster of Khrushchev in 1964 (with national pressures a factor in his removal), the "merger" was shelved, and "flowering" *(rastsvet)* which allows for the development of the national characteristics of each group while they are all "coming closer together" became a dominant theme. By the mid-seventies, however, the pendulum began to swing back again toward integration, still a dominant theme for the eighties. Policy lines which reflect this emphasis have been the promotion of demographic mix through migration and intermarriage (the so-called "internationalization"), and an effort to equalize fertility rates between regions, a new major effort at linguistic Russification, and an effort to substitute "international" Soviet "customs and traditions" for national customs and traditions, particularly those marked by religious content. The 1977 Constitution did not affect the status of the republics, despite efforts of the centralists as seen in the behind-the-scenes debates of the sixties and seventies. But there is evidence (from information supplied by H. Carrere-d'Encausse and Alec Nove) that the centralists are now mounting a new effort to erode republican powers by shifts in jurisdiction in state and economic management and in economic planning.

*Behavior.* The Muslim community of Central Asia has come into its own in the last twenty-five years despite constraints imposed by the system, vacillations in nationality policy, and the maintenance of political and economic controls from Moscow. Several major elements in the nationality policy have contributed to the emergence of a distinct identity of Soviet Muslim nations, and to the crystallization of their national self-perception. The formal federal structure has given each republic a territorial, economic, and institutional base and a structural framework to aggregate demands and to articulate ethnocultural identity; the concomitant cultural policy became a vehicle for a cultural renaissance based in the region's cultural heritage; the ideological framework, while postulating a class-based merger has allowed for an interim development of national identity, thus legitimating national self-assertion; the policy of modernization not only has improved the socioeconomic indicators and stimulated the formation of new Muslim political and cultural elites, but also created conditions for the intensification of ethnic conflict and for the Muslim population explosion, with all of its attendant consequences. The requirements of Soviet foreign policy, finally, benefited Soviet Muslims by forcing a higher level of tolerance for their cultural characteristics, inclusive of Islam, than might have been the case otherwise.[2]

Last but not least, the emergence of the new national identity has become rooted in the common Muslim heritage, the revival of which took place under the umbrella of "official" Islam regardless of difficulties in the performance of the customary five pillars, (*zakat* and *hajj*, are, in effect, forbidden). There is overwhelming evidence that the performance of religious or religion-related practices is almost universal among Central Asian Muslims, even though formal religiosity declined in comparison with the pre-Revolutionary period, and the Islamic clergy no longer exercises total control over the life of the Muslim community. The fast and the prayers are still widely observed, and Shariat norms, while no longer enforceable in legal terms, survive as moral norms that are still widely adhered to by the people and have acquired the character of "national customs." Their observance continues to be vital for social group acceptance and peer approval not only in the case of rural masses but also among the new Soviet-educated Muslim intelligentsia and party and state officials.[3] The latter function throughout their official life as nonbelievers, but most sources agree that on retirement they rejoin the community of believers, when religion no longer interferes with their professional career.[4]

Among religious life cycle rituals male circumcision is universally followed, because it is seen as obligatory for all Muslims, and is supported by the whole weight of public opinion. A Soviet scholar complains that a statement that: "he who is not circumcised is not an Uzbek (or a Turkmen, or a Tajik, etc. as appropriate)" is heard not only from illiterate elders but from educated young men.[5] Traditional marriage customs are also widely observed as a national as well as a religious obligation and the traditional view of women's role in the family still largely survives. Central Asians feel that marriage should be contracted early; and that it is a sacred duty to have many children; the attitudes that are reflected in their fertility patterns. The payment of *kalym* (bride price) not only occurs, but has revived as the measure of the family's standing in the community. Ethnically mixed marriages are generally frowned upon. Muslim males do marry European females (a practice allowed by the Shariat) but marriage by Muslim females outside Islam—a practice forbidden by the Shariat— is extremely rare. Tradition prevails almost universally in death and burial rites, which combine Islamic with pre-Islamic customs deeply rooted in the region. Community rites observance is also widely spread: religious holidays (particularly *Uraza Bayram* and *Kurban Bayram*) are celebrated widely and on a lavish scale and are also regarded as part of national traditions. Pilgrimages to holy places *(mazars)*, are made by numerous believers as a substitute for *hajj* and because they are a survival of pre-Islamic cults of spirits and ancestors. The *Ramazan* fast is widely observed, although most believers content themselves with the observance of only three days of fast (a practice blessed by official Islam). Religiosity, as well as alienation from the non-Muslim community, are reported to increase in general in the Ramazan period, and during the observance of religious holidays. Participation in religious rites is not limited to elders and women, but includes many children and young people, and members of the intelligentsia.

The almost universal character of religious rites and customs in family and social life of Central Asian Muslims requires daily presence of a clergyman, a requirement that cannot be met by officially registered clergy because of their small numbers. This implies a vast network of "unofficial" clergy and "unofficial" mosques. Their existence, albeit officially illegal, is well documented in Soviet sources, mostly through criticisms and complaints of "religious survival". Evidence also exists, although less direct, that the Sufi brotherhoods, outlawed and considered to have become extinct, have nevertheless survived, and may be more influential than is generally supposed.

## MUSLIM PERCEPTION OF SELF-IDENTITY

The one major theme that emerges from the examination of religious practices and social perceptions of Soviet Central Asian Muslims is the process of formation of a new national identity of which Islam is an integral component. As in the case of the explosion of nationalism in the third world—of which Central Asia is a part—the presence and the policies of an imperial power have been the catalyst, and have supplied the very concept of nationalism around which new self-perception has been built.[6] In order to fill the concept with content that would be meaningful in terms of their own cultural identity, Central Asians turned to their history where Islam was the one element that could provide a common integrative force for a crystallization of a modern sense of national identity. It is Islam as a common culture rather than Islam as a religion that is at the base of Central Asian Muslim's new national self-perception, of which active religious faith is just one component. It is still the touchstone for the masses but for the modernized elites it has become a formal, if crucial element. One question that remains is whether, as the nation-building process develops, the universalistic essence of the *Umma* that disregards political boundaries will contribute to a Soviet Muslimhood and a resurrection of old unity of the region as a whole (with doors open to other Soviet Muslims), or whether the policy of delimitation has taken roots strongly enough to result in an emergence of five Muslim nations, conscious of common bonds vis-à-vis the Russians but competitive in particular interests. Soviet Muslimhood has had its beginnings in the perceptions and activities of Sultan Galiev, a Tatar, the highest ranking Muslim communist in the twenties, and an advocate of a Muslim-Turkic Soviet republic, who was purged by Stalin. It characterized many first generation Muslim communists, and it is explicitly assumed to be there already by Soviet critics of the phenomenon. Practical experience else-

where in the Muslim world would indicate that fragmentation into particular nationalisms is a likely course in the long run as soon as the catalyst—an imperial power—begins to withdraw. This is manifestly not
the case in the Soviet Union, although elements of tactical retreats—
interspaced with renewed pressures—have occurred, both acting as stim-
ulants to Muslim national integration. Moreover, while the systemic
framework and political dynamics of the relationship with Moscow
favour the development of the five nations, they are, in effect, artificial
entities; the cultural and socioeconomic unity of Turkestan (Soviet Central
Asia) on the other hand, is a product of a millenium and is the natural
base for the development of Soviet Muslims' separate and increasingly
militant national identity.

*Religion-Nationalism Linkage.* The most thoughtful, valid and, from
the point of view of Soviet aims, the most devastating analysis of the
linkage between nationalism and religion is offered by a prominent Islamic scholar, T. S. Saidbaev in the discussion of what he defines as the
integrative role of Islam, which still survives:

> Because of the widely held perception in the psychology of society which
> identifies the religious with the national sense of identity, Islam is a force
> that unites believers and nonbelievers into one nation, and creates a feeling
> of unity between the representatives of various nations which professed
> Islam in the past. This Muslim unity has nothing in common with the unity
> which currently exists between the nations of the Soviet Union. But it should
> be noted, the more so because it manifests itself in daily life.[7]

Saidbaev disagrees with other scholars and commentators who maintain that the linkage exists only in the case of active believers, because it
is precisely the integrative power of Islam that unites the believing and the
non-believing parts of the Muslim nations, with the participation in
religious activities and support for the mosques seen as a national duty by
members of the Muslim community in general, inclusive of the intelligentsia.[8] As Saidbaev explains in his analysis, the integrative power of
Islam goes far beyond its purely religious significance, because it stems
directly from the cultural cohesion of the region and its people in the
development of which Islam played an integral part.[9] With the exception
of the Tajiks, the people of Central Asia speak related and mutually
intelligible Turkic languages, and both the Turks and the Tajiks share
characteristics of psychology, customs, and traditions bred by their common
history and socioeconomic conditions, the characteristics that were
integrated into Central Asian Islam and thus make it appear national.
This is the key factor that is at the source of the Muslims' resistance to the
atheistic and "internationalist" Weltanschauung. Taking advantage of

this fact the official clergy now poses as the "guardian of national traditions" but its influence alone is not strong enough to explain the community's perception that Islam is the determinant of its national identity, or to account for the high levels of preservation of religious practices and for the participation in them of national intelligentsia. The religion-nationalism linkage is deeply imbedded in the works of many Islamologists and forms a part of the self-perception of the Soviet Muslim community in Central Asia as elsewhere. The structural-functional features of the Muslim society contribute to the preservation of the linkage: their low level of urbanization and of participation in the work of the socialist sector; the survival of two- or three-generation family structure and its strong cohesion as well as the large number of children. Of special significance is the fact that the overwhelming majority of rural settlements are uninational and have little if any contact with the non-Muslim milieu, which means that traditional socialization predominates in the upbringing of children. This means that as the children grow up the religious habit becomes a social necessity even as they acquire education and join the ranks of intelligentsia.[10] Saidbaev sees the family setting as crucial; the figures he quotes for ethnically mixed families in the four republics (5.7 percent of the total in Uzbekistan, 3.4 in Turkmenia, 6.5 in Tadzhikistan and 11.9 in Kirgizia)[11] present an eloquent if unintended testimony to a virtual non-existence of "internationalization" in these republics.

An unintended but equally damaging exposé of the failure and counterproductive effects of the policy of nationality rapprochement *(sblizhenie)* in Central Asia emerges from Saidbaev's review of the reasons for the revival of religiosity, the message of which is, in a nutshell, that any effort at secularization is perceived by "some" Muslims to be a threat to their national identity.[12] This threat has become credible for some individuals who are unable to view national processes scientifically, says Saidbaev, because of the trends that set in as a result of *sblizhenie* and the merger of Soviet nationalities. In their view these include not only a loss of "outmoded forms" but also of valid forms and essential characteristics of national identity, promote tendencies towards levelling of economic and cultural national differences and awaken fears that nations will disappear, and national characteristics, customs and traditions will be lost. Individuals who share these fears consider the preservation of Islam crucial to the preservation of their identity and feel that without Islam there is no national past and no future national spiritual development. These attitudes, continues Saidbaev, are behind some members of the intelligentsia's support for the clergy and for the restoration of historical monuments of religious significance, and breed a sense of alienation toward non-Muslims and toward the "friendship of the people." They also introduce elements of "national narrow-mindedness" and "ethno-centrism," and a revival of the old simplistic dichotomy dividing the world into believers and non-believers. Thus, "even for a contemporary Muslim the basic attribute that divides or unites representatives of one or many nations is largely the profession of faith."[13] The linkage of religion and nationalism has been stimulated, adds Saidbaev, by inept propaganda promoted by some issues of mass political literature and some cultural organizations, by the ineptness of efforts to introduce new Soviet customs and traditions and by failing to include in them a national (but presumably non-religious) component.[14]

In the final analysis the religious character of Muslim nationalism is a "natural," both in terms of historical and ethno-cultural setting and in terms of the imperial role that the Russians have historically played in Central Asia, and still do in the guise of "Elder Brother." From the information provided by Saidbaev it appears that at the family, village, and clan level, the linkage is instinctive, but for the intelligentsia it is a conscious act. For the latter the important thing is not to be personally religious, but to appear to be so in public. Other Soviet sources are equally explicit in the acknowledgment of the religion-nationalism linkage, but most of them attempt to minimize the depth and breadth of the phenomenon, and none provides a comparable scholarly analysis of its nature and origins.[15] Needless to say the linkage undercuts the very basis of the policy of *sblizhenie*, Moscow's effort at integration; the linkage's importance and conscious utilization for the elites is increasing.

*Muslim Elites and Attitudes.* The post-war policy of renewed emphasis on the education of local cadres and their placement in the power structure has brought a major change in the position of Muslim elites and in the relationship between the Muslim and European communities. The lines of direct control from Moscow remain, secured by the placement of central cadre (mostly Russian in ethnic origin) in the key positions in the republics' party and government hierarchies and by the centrally-controlled KGB (security) network, and Russian (European) management of the economy remains largely intact. But the local power structures are now dominated by Muslim political elites. Moreover, as noted above, Muslim leaders now have representation in the All-Union decision-making bodies, and thus have their own lines of communication to Moscow. This has been reflected not only in cultural policies, one aspect of which is the revival of Islam, but also in the loss of the old privileged status by the European community in the Muslim republics. The change is well summed up in verbatim comments made by interviewed Volga Germans long resident in Kazakhstan and other Muslim republics: "Formerly, the Russians were putting the screws on Kazakhs, but now it is the other way round," and variations on the theme "they are the masters of their own house" and it is "their republic."[16] The change is the more remarkable because the position of Muslim elites now appears to be as strong in the republics where the titular group is in the minority (Kazakhstan and Kirgizia), as in the three other republics where they numerically dominate the population.

Despite the fact, underscored by all available indicators, that the pace of modernization has been slow, this has not been the case in terms of Muslims' attendance of educational institutions, even though the number of students per capita in middle and higher schools is lower for the Muslim groups than for most other national groups in the USSR.[17] They make up the deficiency in proportion by the sheer weight of numbers; Muslim school graduates rapidly swell the size of the Muslim intelligentsia from which new elites are recruited. Suffice it to say that between 1950 and 1970 the number of "scientific workers" (presumably with higher education) among the five major Muslim groups increased 13.2 times (from 1,974 to 26,130),[18] and that in the 1972-73 school year there were 572,700 Muslim students (members of the five groups plus Karakalpaks) enrolled in higher educational institutions (VUZ'y) and middle technical schools—double the enrollment in 1962-63 and 2.9 percent of their total numbers in 1970.[19] It is characteristic of the Muslim group that a higher percentage of students attend VUZ'y (60 percent of total in 1972/73) than technical schools (40 percent), a reversal of the ratio that obtains for comparable Western nationalities such as Belorussians or Lithuanians. Availability of Muslim cadres, and their promotion within the system has been a matter of central policy, which has been maximized by the practice of local leaders to promote "their own," and it has resulted in the shift of proportion between the Muslim and European cadres within the power structure of the republics referred to above.

Muslim elite members are almost exclusively of peasant origin because of the specific characteristics of the Muslim community.[20] Thus, their attitudes are the product of traditional socialization, and they retain strong ties with the traditional community. (But some of the relatively small group of children of the urban-based current elite Russify.) The elite's other important characteristic is that more of them tend to have humanities-social science that science-technical educational background, because of the language problem (most science faculties and technical schools have had Russian as the language of instruction) and partly by preference for entering faculties where they can study their own national heritage." Both of these characteristics contribute to their strong resistance to assimilation to Russian "Soviet" culture (a trend among political elites of some of the Western republics), and to their promotion of Muslim national identity. This is a matter not only of conviction, but of conscious utilization of their heritage for the maximization of their political power and for the maximization of the republics' importance within the All-Union context.

The new self-confidence of the elites has been stimulated by the Muslim population explosion. The republics' importance as producers of food and raw materials will also increase, as well as probable investment inputs for the development of processing industries, made imperative by the sole availability there of surplus labor and despite central planners' obvious reluctance to commit scarce capital to the peripheries and to run the political risk of further maximization of the Muslims' importance. The requirements of Soviet foreign policy in the seventies, and likely for the years to come, also have contributed to Muslim leaders' perceptions of their increased value to Moscow (see below). This new sense of power has been reflected in the higher profile of the national element in their policies and demands, although in the case of top leaders it is the deeds (in support of and compliance with more explicit lower ranks) rather than words (where toeing the party line is an obligatory requirement) that are the measure of the new nationalism. In political life the promotion of local cadres at the expense of the "others" has been the subject of recurrent criticism from the center, and a characteristic of "national exclusiveness," "national chauvinism," "localism," "mutual protection," and similar deadly sins. The practice of extending preferential treatment to their co-nationals by the leaders is reinforced by Muslim cultural traits, which impose an obligation to take care of one's relatives, members of one's clan and tribe, and one's own ethnic group. Another aspect of political self assertion has been a vigorous promotion of formal constitutional and legal rights of the republics. The debate over the meaning and definition of the term "national statehood" *(natsional'naia gosudarstvennost')* as it relates to rights and duties of union republics and lower level autonomous units (including the right to secession), was carried on vigorously by Central Asian scholars in the sixties and seventies preceding the adoption of the new constitution.[21] It may be inferred that the influence of the republics, including the Muslim republics, contributed to the absence of change in the federal structure under the 1979 constitution. Local rehabilitation of the most prominent among "bourgeois nationalists" purged in the thirties, such as Turar Ryskulov, Faizullah Khodzhaev, and Akmal Ikramov,[22] are also indicative of the trend.

The notorious "lax" attitude toward religiosity in the life of the republics by Muslim officialdom is symptomatic of the new approach. Soviet sources abound in complaints of "permissive" attitudes of officials toward religion and religious rites; active participation in them by members of the intelligentsia has already been discussed. The Kazakh First Secretary Kunaev, for example, is quoted issuing a blanket condemnation of party workers in four oblasts of Kazakhstan (Gur'ev, Aktyubinsk, Semipalatinsk and Alma-Ata) for religion-nationalism linkage, as well as singling out for specific criticism a raykom secretary because he expressed a sentiment that "religion does not do any harm."[23] This is typical of the criticism that has been repeated over the years at republican party congresses, in scholarly studies such as those quoted in this work, and in thunder from Moscow in the form of Central Committee CPSU resolutions and denunciations in the central press, all with little visible effect and no particular penalties visited on the offenders.

Tacit acceptance of religiosity is a part of the general reinstatement of "national heritage" in the place of honour in the cultural life of the region under an obvious patronage of political elites. In linguistics, a vigorous campaign has been carried out in the last decade to "purify" Central Asian languages, which means substitution of locally derived terms for the extensive terminology borrowed from the Russian, a direct reversal of the linguistic policy of the thirties. The magnitude of the task may be gauged by the fact that, as reported by a Kirgiz scholar, 70 to 80 percent of socio-political, pedagogical, and scientific-technical vocabulary in the languages of national republics is derived from Russian.[24] This has been a local initiative, criticized by the centre. In 1979 a Kazakh scholar recommended in a Kazakh language newspaper that the Arabic alphabet be taught to young Kazakhs, because without Arabic "our knowledge of the ancient written heritage is extremely inadequate," which is "a basic cause of our sometimes being ignorant of the history and culture of the peoples who have been related to us since time immemorial, who come from the same roots, who have the same interests—the Kirgiz, Uzbeks, Turkmen, Tatars, Bashkirs and Tajiks." He points out that "the written heritage is not the repository of old ideas, as some think superficially" but "if you clean the surface it is a valuable thing, and . . . the wisdom in it is great."[25] The last statement is typical of the general trend, which is referred to as *mirasism* (the quest for rehabilitation of the national heritage). The trend goes beyond the language campaign, to affect literature, the arts, and historiography. "*Mirasism's* main themes are the pride in the history and culture of the region; love for the Homeland *(Vatan)* (a word variously applied to denote a particular republic or the region as a whole, but never the "Soviet Motherland"); emphasis on the Eastern link of Soviet Muslim culture; and emphasis on the value of traditional customs and traditions as expressions of national identity in a modern setting, as contrasted with ignorance of one's heritage and uncritical aping of Western (read Russian) models. In historiography the trend has long involved reinstatement in the national pantheon of leaders and events previously consigned into a "reactionary" limbo, and sporadic efforts to chip away at the still sacred canon that the Russian conquest of Central Asia was the most fortunate event in the history of the region. As a result Muslim historians have been criticized repeatedly for departing from Lenin's "two streams" approach. In literature and arts the problem has been, in Moscow's view, the "retreat" into and "glorification" of the past, and a failure to portray adequately the socialist reality. (The number of publications in local languages is extensive and readership is broad even in villages. There is now nearly universal literacy, a real achievement of the Soviet system.)[26]

In their promotion of *mirasism* Muslim intelligentsia and political elites skillfully utilize the Marxist-Leninist ideological matrix. They argue for "national self-determination" and "equality" in terms of impeccable ideological double talk, reinforced by numerous quotations from Lenin and laudatory references to the policy in the early Soviet *korenizatsiia* period, presented as the Leninist heritage, as well as the praise for achievements under the Soviet system. The Eastern-Muslim-Turkic dimensions of the argument are less explicit but nevertheless present, as are the unacknowledged shadows of Sultan Galiev and other purged early Muslim leaders in the background.

The position and attitudes of Muslim top political leaders is ambiguous. They are a part of the system, identify strongly with its achievements (such as economic and social development), and act as spokesmen for and implementers of centrally-determined policies, the local popularity of which is frequently questionable. But they have been able to carve out for themselves an area of influence and flexibility that allows for the manipulation of these policies for the best advantage of their Muslim constituency, with which they identify strongly in cultural terms. This provides them with a national political base. They resent their Russian alter egos, but have learned to live with them, to collaborate with them on the basis of common interests (to make the republic look as good as possible to the centre), and to undercut or by-pass them if necessary. They are politically loyal, but in return they expect influence in Moscow, freedom to run things at home, and tolerance for what they consider their national heritage, of which Islam is a part. They are impatient to develop their republics further and thus increase their relative importance. They petition Moscow for higher investments, while at the same time pushing their constituency to modernize faster.

A recent article in *Pravda* (23 May, 1980) by the Uzbek First Secretary Rashidov, and typically entitled "On the Path of Unity and Brotherhood" is indicative of these attitudes couched in the obligatory party line. It is designed to refute prevarications of Western bourgeois "falsificators" of Central Asian reality. The article starts fittingly enough with an eulogy to Lenin and to the second program of the party (1919), of which Lenin was the author and which provided the basis for the *korenizatsiia* policy of the twenties. Rashidov stresses the principle of equality of all Soviet nations that was articulated in the program (equality is mentioned three times in one paragraph), and continues with a statement that such equality has already been achieved under the current policy of *"rastsvet* (flowering), *sblizhenie,"* and "mutual enrichment" (in that order). The rest of the article stresses the economic development of Uzbekistan (a point of great pride) and tolerance towards Islam in Central Asia, (inclusive of the existence of the Muslim Spiritual Directorate); it explodes the "myth of Russification," stresses the importance of the Russian language as the language of communication among the nationalities, and makes an obligatory genuflection toward the leading role of the "great Russian people." As for the Russians in key positions in the republics—yes we have them, we are proud of them, but they do not enjoy any special privileges.

Political mobilization of Muslim elites and their participation in the power structure not only has stimulated the growth in national self-assertion but also has increased the potential for ethnic conflict. The resentment of the European community over the growing numbers and influence of the Muslims has been enhanced by an increasingly competitive situation in the educational system (it appears that admission to educational institutions is clearly subject to informal preferential quotas in favour of local nationalities)[27] and in the market place, especially in political and administrative jobs which are under the jurisdiction of Muslim-dominated local party organizations. When Muslims begin to compete more effectively for jobs in the socialist sector, as predicted, the conflict will intensify further. Moreover, the change in the relative standing of the two communities seems to have had little effect on their relationship and attitudes. Formally united in "friendship of the people" and "fraternal love," their almost total social and cultural alienation is a matter of record. Europeans cluster in the cities and Muslims dominate the countryside; Europeans work in the socialist sector, economic management and administrative infrastructure; Muslims till the soil, concentrate on subsidiary private economy and craft-related production, saturate local party and state administration, and have a majority in the republics' decision-making bodies inclusive of top positions.

The two communities are separated by culture, including religion and language, by biological traits,[28] and by historical memory; the "assault" period is well within the living memory of the Muslim older generation. The Russian colonial attitude of the early twenties, and their sense of civilizing mission in a backward land has persisted and has rubbed off on other members of the European community; but the Europeans now feel discriminated against and their resentment grows.[29] An American scholar recently on a study tour in Tashkent reports the continuation of the "colonial outpost" mentality among resident Russians:

> They view with discomfort the increasing Uzbek numbers, confidence, competitiveness and competence, and find increasingly less valid the former stereotype of an Uzbek as being 'someone who picks cotton, eats melons, and sings and dances.'[30]

The Russian nickname for the Uzbeks is reported to be *chushka* (from the Uzbek *chochqa*—pig) referring to their refusal to eat pork, the Uzbek's nickname for the Russians is *kalinka* or *samarskii* (neither is meant to be complimentary).[31] Muslims resent past treatment and periodic assaults on their culture. They resent their subservience to Moscow in matters of policy, and the unwritten rule which still holds in party and state administration that every Muslim in a top position has to have a Russian deputy. Racial overtones in the relationship between the two communities are strikingly revealed in the Volga German survey cited above, in which spontaneous references emerge to "black nations" (Muslims) and "white nations" (Europeans), in comments such as: "the black nations have their own cemeteries, and the white nations theirs"; a Russian said, "that is terrible, the black race takes over," or "now the blacks take over everywhere."[32] These reveal the racist attitude, the resentment, and the change in relative position of each community. A hint of a similar attitude on the Muslim side is contained in a 1972 Uzbek novel set during World War II in which a party secretary inveighs against oppressors with "white bodies."[33]

Ethnic conflict occasionally erupts. A student riot was reported in Alma-Ata in 1978, with Kazakhs attacking Russians over alleged discrimination (against Kazakhs) in admissions to higher education.[34] A major riot took place in Tashkent in 1969 (Pakhtakor affair), at an occasion of a soccer match between a local and a Moscow team, the leitmotiv of which was the Uzbeks telling the Russians to "go back home, we did not ask you to come here." The riot spilled into the streets; Uzbeks stopped traffic and pulled out and beat up anyone who looked like a Russian. It is reported to have involved casualties and was suppressed by MVD troops. The handling of the aftermath of the riots is indicative of the relationship between the two communities, and between the republics and Moscow. The event was initially covered up jointly by the first secretary (Rashidov) and the Russian second secretary (Lomonosov) of the Uzbek party, for fear of repercussions if its true nationalist dimensions came out; it was dismissed as "petty hooliganism." But complaints from local Russians to central party authorities forced reopening of the case twice, and it ended in 1974 with a personal involvement of Politbureau member Mikhail Suslov, and a removal of some key Uzbek personalities (implicated also in corruption scandals), and of Lomonosov, for his participation in the cover-up.[35]

All the evidence points to national integration of Soviet Muslims on a regional basis. But it would be wrong to leave this discussion without a note on some ethnic tensions within the Muslim community. The Uzbeks are unquestionably the strongest and the most important among the five major groups, and unquestionably play a leading role; their tendency to be condescending towards other groups is occasionally resented. There are also tensions between Uzbeks and Tajiks dating to the Uzbeks' ruling position in the old Bokhara Khanate, and a degree of competitiveness between the two. Crimean Tatars who were deported to Uzbekistan retain a very strong sense of group identity, are far more modernized as a group than the Uzbeks, and have been very troublesome to the authorities in their efforts to be allowed to return to Crimea. Their activities have been resented by Uzbek authorities and occasionally suppressed.[36] The Kazakh elite is equal, or perhaps superior, to the Uzbeks in their modernization level and national self-assertion, but their ethnic base is small, and because of their history and location they tend to be marginal to the main Muslim integration effort and cannot compete with the Uzbeks for the leadership.

## FOREIGN POLICY DIMENSIONS

The new importance of Central Asia in Moscow's foreign policy came to the fore in the sixties and seventies, with the quest for influence in the third world, specifically in the Muslim Middle East, and with the quarrel with China. Central Asia is important in general as a showcase of a socialist model of development and a training center for future leaders of the third world; specifically Soviet Muslims play a role in contacts with the Muslim world and countries contiguous to the area, and in an effort to destabilize Chinese borderlands. Central Asia is Muslim; it is strategically located at the gateways to the Middle East, to the Indian subcontinent, and to Chinese Sinkiang; its people form sizeable minorities all across the borders. For all these reasons Central Asians' contacts with the third world have multiplied, and Central Asian elites and "official" Muslim clergy participate readily in support of foreign policy ventures which, while serving Soviet interest abroad, enhance their importance at home.

*A Model of Socialist Development.* Central Asia as a success story in communist nation-building and economic development—the catch phrase is always "thanks to the assistance of the great Russian people"—is an important theme in contacts with representatives of third world countries.

The foreign policy link is explicit. The late Alexei Kosygin, addressing the Kirgiz party and government leaders on the occasion of the 50th anniversary of the Kirgiz republic, said:

> "The experience of socialist construction in regions formerly underdeveloped and the experience of having solved the national problem, which has been accumulated by Kirgizia and other republics, has enriched Marxist-Leninist science and opened up a revolutionary perspective for the majority of mankind: the nations of Asia, Africa, and Latin America." (*Pravda*, 3 Nov. 1974)

Three aspects of the model are of particular importance in the efforts to convince Asians and Africans that they should adopt it: economic and social achievements; political success (the "solution" of the national problem and bypassing of the capitalist stage of development); and the Soviet (Russian) link as the necessary catalyst of success. Economic and social achievements (such as economic indicators of production and consumption, health, education and literacy statistics, and cultural development) are impressive and undeniable, particularly in comparison with neighbouring Muslim countries. They are the best selling point. The claim to political success appears fully credible, particularly to those committed to the socialist idea. Muslim elites are demonstrably and visibly in command in their republics (with Russian assistance and cooperation); a Leninist type of socialist society has been built, and the distinct cultural identity of the region has been retained. The existence of "official" Islam strongly supports this impression. The most difficult to convey, however, has been the notion, crucial for Soviet policy purposes, that none of these developments would have been possible, but for the leadership and help of the Russians, and that the success of the model elsewhere would necessarily involve the assistance by the Soviet Union and other "fraternal" socialist countries.

Practical aspects of Central Asian inputs into Soviet foreign policy include the development of cultural contacts with foreign countries (mostly Afro-Asian or "socialist"), sponsorship of numerous international conferences, and training provided at Central Asian universities for foreign students. Uzbekistan is the most important among the republics in performing these functions and Tashkent is a major base for international exchanges. Proceedings of a 1972 conference in Tashkent reported that at the time Uzbekistan had ties with 107 foreign countries, which involved organization and sponsorship of major symposia, seminars and conferences with foreign scholars (twenty such conferences were organized in the fifteen years preceding 1972), including an important conference held in the early seventies on the experience of socialist transformations in the USSR and their international significance. The number of foreign students who received a diploma from Uzbek higher educational institutions in the 1962-1972 period was reported to have been 1,200; there were 620 foreign students from 31 countries enrolled there in 1972/73.[37] The value of the exchanges is seen to be extremely important not only from the point of view of the political education of foreigners, but equally so from the point of view of the "internationalist upbringing" of Central Asian students.

The picture that emerges indicates that Central Asia, Uzbekistan in particular, is indeed of great importance in Soviet relations with the third world, and even gives substance to hitherto empty constitutional provisions that the republics have the right to engage in foreign relations, or at least gives a good facsimile thereof. Of all the Soviet republics Uzbekistan (and other Muslim republics to a lesser extent) alone has been able to develop extensive foreign contacts. This has Moscow's blessing because they are Asian and Muslim and the third world has acquired priority in Soviet foreign policy. Soviet Central Asia's unmistakably Muslim character is, in this context, a definite asset. This goes far to explain the tolerance by Moscow both of the revival of religiosity and of Muslim national self-assertion, and justifies Muslim elites' visible sense of self-confidence. It is yet too early to assess the effects that the exchanges and the training have had on the build-up of a reservoir of friends of the Soviet Union in the third world, and its political implications. But the investment has been massive, the stakes are high (in terms of a domestic fall-out as much as in foreign gains), and Soviet Central Asian Muslims have been crucial to the effort.

*Islam and the Middle East.* The requirements of the Soviet policy in the Middle East have also contributed to the sense of self-importance of Soviet Muslim elites and to the prosperity of the four Muslim Spiritual Directorates, the representatives of which act as loyal spokesmen for Soviet interests abroad. As the oil crisis developed and the militancy of Islam increased contributing to destabilization of the region, so did the opportunities for Soviet penetration. But the new militancy also made Soviet Muslims more vulnerable to "infection." To turn a potential disadvantage into an asset, the role of official Islam as the prime agent of Soviet influence has been upgraded, thus giving it a direct stake in collaborating with Moscow.

The Muslim clergy's activities abroad aim at three important objectives: 1) to convince foreign Muslims that Soviet Muslims have achieved both prosperity and religious freedom under socialism; 2) to gain a position of influence in the international Muslim community (basing their claims to leadership on the medieval glory of Islam in Turkestan); and 3) to mobilize support for Soviet foreign policy in its overall aim of "universal peace and social progress," and in all of its current objectives.

The Muslim Spiritual Directorate of Central Asia and Kazakhstan has played a key role in these efforts, and the star of the show is Mufti Babakhanov, who travels extensively and, as a member of the World Supreme Council of Mosques, is a respected member of the international Muslim community. The Directorate has developed broad foreign contacts; its publications are disseminated abroad; its officials make frequent visits to Muslim countries and in return receive numerous foreign Muslim religious delegations. They participate actively in Muslim congresses abroad and organize many such congresses at home. *Pravda* (July 14, 1980) reported that six such international meetings were organized in the last few years, with two in 1973 (in Tashkent and in Dushanbe).

It is difficult to measure the degree of influence that the Directorate's officials were able to gain, or the effects of their rather crude propaganda, despite the fact that the Muslim states' line-up behind Soviet-sponsored policies is at times impressive. But there is a standing contradiction between the Soviet clerics' claim that they are faithful to the sacred rules of the Quran, and their actions as agents of an avowedly atheistic power and as proponents of a secular communist society. Scepticism toward their claims that Islam flourishes under communism has been expressed many times in foreign Muslim literature. Foreign Muslims' support for Soviet policies has more to do with politics, and the pursuit of their own objectives, than with the acceptance of Soviet claims at face value, even among Islam's militant left. There is little doubt, however, that the Soviet Union reaps much credit overall for its support of the Palestinian cause and for its "anti-imperialist" stand.

Soviet Muslim political elites have not played a direct role in Soviet foreign policy comparable to that assigned to the Muslim clergy, perhaps because as a part of the system they can lay no claim to represent an entity different from it. But, as members of Soviet official delegations, of technical assistance teams, and of education, cultural and scientific exchanges, they have been a walking advertisement of the success of Soviet nationality policy. Their ethno-cultural characteristics have given them an ability to communicate with kin groups in neighboring countries.

In an exception to the general pattern, Soviet Muslim elites, particularly Uzbeks, and Tajiks have been directly employed in Afghanistan since the Taraki coup in April 1978, as teachers developing the educational system, and as advisers in government agencies.[38] According to various Western press reports Soviet Muslims also featured prominently in the Soviet invasion of Afghanistan of December 1979, as soldiers in reserve units of the Central Asian Military District that entered Afghanistan in the first wave of Soviet troops. Their participation in the invasion has been interpreted variously as an outcome of a hasty decision (the only troops available), or a result of a miscalculation (they were expected to be greeted as "brothers" and "liberators"). Whatever the reason, the units have since been withdrawn and replaced by regular troops where there is no visible Muslim component, the move also variously interpreted as triggered either by Soviet Muslims' fraternization and desertions (of which cases were reported), or by the reserves' lack of counterinsurgency training, possibly both. Central Asian civilians, however, are said to be practically running the infrastructure of Babrak Karmal's government.

If true, the reports confirm a difference in attitudes between Muslim elites and Muslim rural masses that emerges from the examination of the previous evidence. The elites, inclusive of the official Muslim clergy, perceive a major advantage to themselves in acting as a vanguard of Soviet penetration across the border. In the case of the clergy their political loyalty in furthering Soviet aims abroad is an excellent guarantee of their survival at home and contributes to the unusually high level of tolerance of religiosity in the republics. As long as it is important to convey an image of "flourishing" Islam to Muslims across the border, official clergy will prosper and religious repressions are unlikely. A similar argument can be made for the elites. Although the re-emergence of Muslim elites in political life is a result of many factors, Central Asia's importance as a showcase of Soviet development is an important element in the elites' status and influence. Moreover, the Muslim elites' new role in Afghanistan offers an opportunity to strengthen their domestic position: not only are they an asset in the consolidation of Soviet power there, but, by helping to bring Afghanistan into the Soviet orbit they add to the overall Muslim power base and consequently to their weight in Union councils.

Should an occasion arise they may be just as willing to play a similar role in Iran, Pakistan, or elsewhere, and for similar reasons, as long as the Soviet Union deals from the position of regional and global strength. But their loyalty is based on a strict *quid pro quo*. Should conditions change, so may the perception of their self-interest. Influence flows both ways as contacts develop, and comparisons with the outside world are not necessarily favourable to the USSR. A new wave of internal repressions à la Stalin, an internal upheaval such as a famine, or—most important— a shift in the balance of power adverse to the Soviet Union, may transform Muslim nationalism's current push for greater autonomy into a bid for independence.

Rural Muslims' commitment to Islam as a religion is much stronger, and thus their degree of responsiveness to fundamentalist Islamic message is higher. Also, they have less of a stake in the preservation of the *status quo*, despite economic and social gains that contrast favourably with conditions among foreign Muslims. Islam's appeal is emotional. Although little direct evidence is available, rural Muslims retain a perception that a part of their community lives just across the border, including refugees from the period of "assault." They are aware of the new trends developing there. Air waves carry foreign programs in familiar languages and with familiar culture content, and there are listeners in rural areas. A Soviet source reports that in Turkmenia religious broadcasts from pre-Khomeini Iran were not only heard but taped, and the tapes were passed on and played at religious gatherings.[39] Finally, the survival and broad activities of conservative unofficial mosques, as well as the continued presence of Sufi brotherhoods, provide a receptive environment for the fundamentalist Islamic message.

How vulnerable are the republics overall to the appeal of militant Islam and to outside influence in general? The official clergy is politically loyal and, having modernized, has departed from the true faith in the eyes of the orthodox. But appearances may be misleading. As Bennigsen and Lemercier-Quelquejay point out, Islam in Central Asia has "two faces—the official and the unofficial," the combined action of which has enabled it to survive a half century of oppression.[40] It has shown great flexibility in taking advantage of changing circumstances. The elites may not respond to a purely religious appeal but are highly receptive to the nationalist message especially when combined with religion. Moreover, they have retained stronger cultural ties with their constituency than has been characteristic of modernizing elites elsewhere.

An official perception of a threat from outside definitely exists, and the new integration efforts aim once again at undercutting the roots of traditional Muslim community, this time by persuasion and social engineering. A growing concern over the impact of outside forces has been reflected in the multiplication of attacks against Western analysts of the Central Asian scene.

*The Conflict with China.* Muslim minorities on both sides of the Sino-Soviet border have been an important weapon in the struggle between the two communist powers to subvert each other's efforts to integrate their border regions. Chinese Sinkiang (previously known as East Turkestan) and Soviet Central Asia are historically a part of one cultural entity, Muslim in religion and ethnically Turkic (except for the Dungans). Approximately five million Uighurs live in Sinkiang, in the area designated as the Uighur Autonomous Region, and a Kazakh minority of approximately 500,000, located primarily along the border with Soviet Kazakhstan. On the other side, as noted above, there is a Uighur and a Dungan minority. Neither Russia (Soviet Union) nor China has been a constant pole of attraction. Rather, Muslims from each side surged across the frontier to escape repressions that alternately affected Russian and/or

Chinese-controlled territory as a result of policies originating in Moscow and/or Peking. In the 1979 census the total number of Uighurs in the USSR was listed as 211,000, of whom 70 percent were in Kazakhstan, 14 percent in Kirgizia with 16 percent probably dispersed. The treatment of the Uighurs appears to bear a strong correlation to the state of Sino-Soviet relations; it has been favourable in periods of hostility, but subject to usual minority restrictions in periods of friendship. The correlation is shown in an interesting study by Rasma Silde-Karklins,[41] particularly as reflected in cultural policies.

The propaganda battle has been waged by both protagonists, in print and on airwaves. The Soviet Union significantly upgraded the number of hours broadcast to Sinkiang from Alma-Ata and Tashkent in the Uighur language in the seventies. Publications designed to discredit the Chinese treatment of the Uighurs and Kazakhs have been emphasized in periods of peak hostilities. Efforts at the penetration of Chinese territory apparently also continued, even though the border has been closed by the Chinese since 1958.

As demonstrated by past cross-border migrations, Uighurs and Kazakhs move (if they can) to the side where conditions appear to be better at the moment. In the sixties and seventies conditions were undoubtedly better on the Soviet side, and it appears that for the present at least, Chinese efforts to discredit the Soviet nationality policy in the eyes of Soviet Muslims find little response, particularly in the republics closest to Sinkiang. This is not to say that a change may not come in the future, should the current Soviet integration drive accelerate, or if there is an improvement in the Chinese minorities policy under the new leadership.

For the Soviet Union the stakes are high and exceed by far the regional tug of war. Apart from the importance of the issue of nationality policies in the competition with China for the influence in the third world, the campaign is a part of an overall effort to destabilize China.

## NOTES

1. Viktor Perevedentsev, *Metody izucheniia migratsii naseleniia,* Academy of Sciences of the USSR (Moscow: "Nauka," 1975), and Murray Feshbach, "Prospects for Out-migration from Central Asia and Kazakhstan in the next Decade," pp. 656-709, in *Soviet Economy in a Time of Change; A Compendium of Papers Submitted to the Joint Economic Committee, Congress of the United States,* (Washington, D.C.: GPO, 1979). More generally for the demographic information in this section see USSR Central Statistical Administration, "USSR National Economy in 1970" (in Russian) (Moscow: Statistika, 1971), pp. 15-21; USSR Central Statistical Adminstration, "Population of the USSR Data from the All-Union Census" (in Russian) (Moscow: Izd. Politcheskoi Literatury, 1980) pp. 23-30; and B. M. Ekkel, "Definition of the Index of "Mosaicity" of the National Composition of Republics, Regions and Provinces of the USSR" (in Russian), *Sovetskaia Etnografiia,* no. 2 (March-April) 1976, p. 38.

2. For further development of these themes see this author's "Ethnicity in the Soviet Union," pp. 73-87, *The Annals of the American Academy of Political and Social Science,* "Ethnic Conflict in the World Today," v. 433 (September, 1977).

3. T. S. Saidbaev, *Islam i obshchestvo; opyt istoriko-sotsiologicheskogo issledovaniia,* (Moscow: "Nauka," 1978), pp. 225-227.

4. *Ibid.* p. 191; also in A. Bennigsen and Ch. Lemercier-Quelquejay, *Islam in the Soviet Union,* (New York: Praeger, 1967), pp. 178-183; and Rasma Karklins, "Islam; How Strong is It in the Soviet Union? Inquiry based on oral interviews with Soviet Germans repatriated from Central Asia in 1979," pp. 65-81, *Cahiers du Monde Russe et Soviétique,* XXI (I), jnv.-mars 1980.

5. N. Ashirov, *Islam i Natsii,* (Moscow: Politizdat, 1975), p. 63.

6. See the classic study by Rupert Emerson, *From Empire to Nation: The Rise to Self-Assertion of Asian and African Peoples* (Cambridge, Mass: Harvard University Press, 1960).

7. Saidbaev, *op. cit.*, p. 193.

8. *Ibid.*, pp. 194-5, and 207; See also Ashirov, *Islam i natsii . . .*, p. 63.

9. Discussion in this and the following paragraph is based on Saidbaev, *op. cit.,* pp. 193-204.

10. Confirmed also in the observed behavior of the intelligentsia by N. Ashirov, "Islam i natsional'nye otnosheniia," pp. 34-38, *Nauka i Religiia,* no. 2 (February 1974), p. 37.

11. Saidbaev, *op. cit.,* p. 199. It is not specified whether the families referred to were Muslim-Muslim, Muslim-European, or both.

12. *Ibid.,* pp. 204-206.

13. *Ibid.,* p. 205.

14. *Ibid.*

15. This includes works of Ashirov and others quoted here.

16. Rasma Karklins, *Nationality Power in Soviet Republics;* Final Report to National Council for Soviet and East European Research, (N.D.) (forthcoming in *Survey*), pp. 7, 11 and passim.

17. See M. Mobin Shorish, "Who Shall be Educated: Selection and Integration in Soviet Central Asia," pp. 86-99, Edward Allworth, ed., *The Nationality Question in Soviet Central Asia* (New York: Praeger, 1973).

18. Calculated on the basis of data in *Narodnoe Khoziaistvo SSSR v 1970 g.* (Moscow, "Statistika," 1971), p. 658.

19. *Narodnoe Khoziaistvo SSSR v 1972 g.* (Moscow: "Statistika," 1973), p. 651. No ethnic data were released after 1972.

20. K. Akmuradov, "Izmenenie sotsial'no-klasovoi struktury obshchestva v Turkmenistane," pp. 160-177, *Velikii Oktiabr i sotsial'no-ekonomicheskii progress v Turkmenistane,* (Ashkhabad, "Ylym," 1977), pp. 170, 172.

21. See for example, proceedings of a conference on developments in state and law in Central Asia and Kazakhstan held in Alma-Ata in May, 1974, *Voprosy natsional'no-gosudarstvennogo stroitel'stva v Srednei Azii i Kazakhstan,* AN Kazakhskoi SSR (Alma-Ata: Izd. "Nauka," 1977).

22. See Allen Hetmanek, "National Renascence in Soviet Kazakhstan: The Brezhnev Era," pp. 295-305, and James Critchlow "Nationalism in Uzbekistan in the Brezhnev Era," pp. 306-315, in George W. Simmonds, ed., *Nationalism in the USSR and Eastern Europe in the Era of Brezhnev & Kosygin* (Detroit: University of Detroit Press, 1977).

23. Saidbaev, *op. cit.,* p. 195.

24. T. K. Karymshakov, "K voprosu o razvitii i sblizhenii iazykovoi zhizni sovetskikh sotsialisticheskikh natsii," pp. 11-28, *Natsiia i natsional'nye otnosheniia,* (Frunze: "Ilim," 1966), pp. 25-27.

25. *Sotsialistik Qazaqstan* June 19, 1979, quoted in John Soper, "Kazak Scholar on Teaching the Arabic Script," RL Turkic Department Program Backgrounder, 1/8/79.

26. For the discussion of the various aspects of *mirasism,* see E. Allworth, *op. cit.* passim; Alexandre Bennigsen, "The Crisis of the Turkic National Epics, 1951-1952: Local Nationalism or Proletarian Internationalism?," pp. 463-474, and E. Allworth, "Mainstay or Mirror of Identity—The Printed Word in Central Asia and Other Soviet Regions Today," pp. 436-462, in "Russian and Soviet Central Asia," *Canadian Slavonic Papers,* V. XVII, 2 & 3, 1975; Hetmanek and Critchlow in Simmonds, *op. cit.;* and William Fierman, *Uzbek Feelings of Ethnicity: A Study of Attitudes Expressed in Recent Uzbek Literature* (prepared for the Department of State as part of its external research program; N.D.).

27. See Karklins, *Nationality Power.*

28. See James Critchlow, "Uzbeks and Russians," pp. 366-373, *Canadian Slavonic Papers, op. cit.,* pp. 371-372.

29. See Karklins, *Nationality Power . . .* and Michael Rywkin, "Religion, Modern Nationalism and Political Power in Soviet Central Asia," pp. 271-285, *Canadian Slavonic Papers, op. cit.*

30. David C. Montgomery, "The Uzbeks in Two States: Soviet and Afghan Policies Toward an Ethnic Minority," pp. 147-173, in Wm. O. McCagg and B. D. Silver, eds., *Soviet Asian Ethnic Frontiers* (New York: Pergamon Press, 1979), p. 158.

31. *RFE/RL, Soviet Area Audience and Opinion Research, Background Report 20-79,* "Notes on Life in Uzbekistan," October 26, 1979, p. 3.

32. Karklins, *Islam . . .,* p. 10 and Karklins, *Nationality Power . . .,* pp. 10, 23, and passim.

33. Quoted by James Critchlow, "Minarets and Marx," pp. 47-57, *The Washington Quarterly,* V. 3, No. 2 (Spring 1980), p. 53.

34. Karklins, *Nationality Power . . .,* p. 26.

35. *RFE/RL, Soviet Area Audience and Opinion Research, Background Report 19-79,* "Crime and Corruption in Uzbekistan," October 26, 1979.

36. See Montgomery, *op. cit.,* pp. 158-159, and this author's *Russia and Nationalism in Central Asia: The Case of Tadzhikistan,* (Baltimore: John's Hopkins University Press, 1970), pp. 16, 179-180.

37. Kh. S. Shukurova, "Znachenie kul'turnykh sviazei Uzbekistana z zarubezhnymi stranami v internatsional'nom vospitanii trudiaschikhsia," pp. 224-229, and K. S. Sadykov "Ukrepliat' druzhbu sovetskikh narodov," pp. 167-172, in *Bratstvo narodov i internatsional'noe vospitanie* (Tashkent, Min. Vyssh. i Sred. Spets. Obrazovaniia Uzbek SSR, 1974).

38. Personal communication from M. Mobin Shorish who visited Afghanistan in 1979. See also Critchlow, in *Washington Quarterly,* p. 54.

39. Allen Hetmanek, "Spillover Effects of Religious Broadcasts in Iran on Soviet Muslims," *RFE/RL, Radio Liberty Research, RL 142/80,* April 14, 1980.

40. A. Bennigsen and Ch. Lemercier-Quelquejay, "Official Islam in the Soviet Union," pp. 148-159, *Religion in Communist Lands,* V. 7, no. 3, 1979, p. 157.

41. Rasma Silde-Karklins, "The Interrelationship of Soviet Foreign and Nationality Policies: The Case of the Foreign Minorities in the USSR," unpublished Ph.D. Dissertation, University of Chicago, 1975.

# Comments and Discussion

*Henze* thought that an interesting light on the issue of Chinese-Soviet relations in Central Asia was shed by the Victor Louis book, *The Coming Decline of the Chinese Empire* (published by the *New York Times* with a dissenting introduction by Harrison Salisbury). Among other things Victor Louis goes so far as to revive the old concept of Manchu nationalism that the Japanese pushed in the 1930s.

Henze also pointed to some useful recent work on the significance of Central Asians in the Soviet armed forces. The Rand Corporation has made a study of ethnic factors in the armed forces projecting the percentage of Muslims to the end of the century. This becomes a serious problem for the Soviets, particularly considering that the Soviet armed forces are not the leveling institutions that many people think. The Soviets treat the non-Slavic nationalities, and especially the Muslims in the armed forces, very much the way we treated blacks in our armed forces up to World War II. An Uzbek does not ordinarily aspire to be an airplane pilot or to get into the more exciting modern part of the armed forces. He is likely at best to be a foot soldier, and more likely a support soldier in the quartermaster corps, or in an engineering or construction battalion. The Soviet armed forces are not organized on a national basis, yet in effect there are Central Asian units, because engineering battalions and quartermaster corps are up to ninety percent Muslims. This situation is worth attention, and may have a great deal to do with the attitude of Central Asians over time. *Rakowska-Harmstone* added that the reserves are organized according to where they live. That is why the initial units in Afghanistan were so heavily Central Asian.

*Naby* added information on the racial factor from her own experience in Soviet Central Asia and the western part of the Soviet Union in the winter of 1979 right after the coming of Khomeini to power in Iran and in the stormy aftermath of the Taraki regime's establishment in Afghanistan. As a Middle Easterner she felt strongly that she was treated as a "black." No one directly told her to go sit in the back and be quiet, but that seemed the reaction to her presence whenever she did not indicate that she was a foreigner. It was assumed that she was merely a Central Asian and treated accordingly. However, this led the Uzbeks with whom she was traveling to take her into their midst and share their food with her. They proceeded to regale her with details of their family life and relationships, which she had not solicited. It led her to wonder whether this Muslim identity was not really a negative identity, a reaction to racial and other discrimination.

*Wriggins* asked whether that made any difference from an affirmative identity. *Naby* thought a negative identity would be weaker in the face of a lessening of Russian chauvinism. This lessening will not necessarily occur, but it may. A negative Islamic identity would also be more likely to decline as the Central Asians come to see more clearly who they are and have less need for it.

*Rakowska-Harmstone* agreed there was a negative element. However, she pointed out that third world peoples go through similar stages. First they attempt to identify with the metropolitan culture. Then when the third world "native" finds he is still not accepted, he turns back to his own roots and builds them up. Starting as a negative phenomenon this process tends to become a positive phenomenon. In the USSR one choice is to become a second-rate Russian. You can never go further: you are never quite as good as a Russian no matter how hard you try. The other choice is to turn back and find things in one's own background to be proud of. After all, in the great days of Samarqand and Bokhara, or Ibn Sina, where were the Russians?

She had asked in her paper what was the basis on which the Central Asian nationalism integrates. This is something we have not really determined. Bennigsen feels there is a supernational basis, a Muslim nationalism aggregating on the old Turkestan basis, which is open ended for other Muslims such as the Tatars. Below this are the artificial "nations" the Russians have created by subdividing the area along lines of linguistic difference. Below this are the old tribal lineages and village identities. The evidence seems to support Bennigsen's regional aggregation. On the other hand, Rakowska-Harmstone said she could not quite get away from the feeling that although the republics were artificial, they have existed for forty to fifty years, and they did have some historical basis. There was historical antagonism between the Tajiks and the Uzbeks. There must be resentment of Uzbek ascendency, although as long as the Russians are there the Muslim peoples will probably pull together.

The peoples compete with one another, and the Russians play on this in their assignments of positions or projects in Central Asia, and in deciding who gets into the Politburo. Generally clusters of smaller republics are represented by candidate members in the Politburo. The Caucasus "cluster" generally has one representative; Central Asia has one; the baltics do not quite rate. For Central Asia the Uzbeks have the institutionalized role: Kunayev is the frosting on the cake. (The Kazakh Kunayev is a full member, but this has to do with Kunayev having been Brezhnev's second in command when Brezhnev was the first secretary of Kazakhstan.) But there has not been a Turkmen or a Kirgiz. Should the imperial presence be removed, which is not likely, there might be a lot of squabbling in the area. Today there is a feeling of oneness vis-à-vis the Europeans.

*Henze* said this worked both ways. In the armed forces the Russians look on all Central Asians as one group. They are called "the yellows;" they talk of the yellowing of the Soviet Union. This must pull Central Asians together. *Rakowska-Harmstone* added that the surveys among the Balts who have come out suggest that in the army the Muslims are even less acceptable to the Balts than are Russians.

*Allworth* thought that if Rakowska-Harmstone had been talking to this group five years ago she would probably not have used the term Muslim to identify Soviet Central Asians. She would have talked about the nationalities. He also thought that she would not have been talking about a "new sense of national identity" in these terms. (However, Allworth noted that at the end she pointed out the personal caveats she had in regard to this interpretation.)

The interpretation Rakowska-Harmstone presented initially is the fashion, especially among European scholars, and particularly the French, who now have a vested interest in promoting the idea that Islam is the unifying factor in Central Asia and other areas like Tataristan or Azerbaijan. They see the ethnic factors as secondary. This approach is only a new fashion for us: French scholars have been pushing the idea for decades.

Allworth did not think it very helpful. There was nothing new about the pervasive importance of Islam in the area, and no new component from Islam added to what might be called a nationality identity. On the contrary, new official nationalities have been grafted onto whatever was already there. He did not see how this added up to a "revival" of Islam. We are more sensitive now about what is there, and talk about it more, but for Soviet Central Asia it has no systematic policy or intellectual implications. It is impressions, allusions. It seems particularly interesting to some people in the United States government, in the International Communications Agency. They talk about it a lot. The notion of Islamic revival in Soviet Central Asia feeds itself and becomes "something."

The position is artificial to a large extent. Perhaps Soviet anthropologists have a natural tendency to play down Islam in writing about the rural areas of Central Asia. Nevertheless, their evidence is what we have to deal with. We cannot take surveys. They methodically discuss the evidence of Islamic belief they find in community after community. They write of the virtual absence of clandestine or organized neighborhood mosques. They say even those old people who say they are Muslims do not know the rites. They do not know the meanings of important terms in Muslim hagiography, nor do they know how to conduct a service.

Allworth then told of a theologically educated Uzbek he knew in Turkey. The man had contact with a distant relative, a young, reliable informant from Andijan in Soviet Central Asia. They talked religion. The man from Andijan said: "Oh, if we only knew something about Islam. Why don't you come to Central Asia and teach us?" His distant relative in Turkey told him that was out of the question. But the Andijan relative insisted, saying, "We would protect you." This was only an anecdote. Yet a man from the depths of Uzbekistan, the most densely populated part of the region, speaks outright about the fact that they know nothing about Islam and they need help from the outside to understand their own religion.

Allworth had seen the rituals; he had seen funeral processions on the streets of Samarqand. But the question of Islam is religious as well as cultural. We focus too much on the cultural.

Allworth said he agreed with Rakowska-Harmstone's later statement that whatever integrative force Islam may have, the ethnic force is stronger. He had seen nothing to contradict that. In fact he thought it inexact to use the term Muslim to describe Central Asians. He did not think they were Muslims in any sense that has any religious connotation. Then, to refer to Central Asians as Benningsen does as an integrated group in the 1970s and 1980s is as preposterous as in 1924 when the Kazakhs and Uzbeks nearly came to battle over who would possess Tashkent. If one speaks with Mobin Shorish (University of Illinois) or others who have a Tajik view of the area, he will discover the tremendous amount of friction between Uzbek and Tajik, not just latent but very openly expressed. It is encouraged by the Soviet government.

*Fischer* thought the question as to whether ethnic or Muslim identity is more important may be beside the point. People have multiple identities, and they are mobilized at different times. So the question is more the context of mobilization than which is more important. He was worried about the distinction Allworth had drawn between Islam as religion and Islam as cultural identity, because what seems most important in our discussion is the cultural identity. He had found that precisely the same sort of lack of religious knowledge is manifest among Jews in the Soviet

Union as Allworth ascribed to Muslims. Yet today we see Jews coming out having a tremendous amount of interest in regaining the lost cultural heritage about which they know nothing. People come to the Passover services starting from scratch, looking at children's books, finding out who Moses was. (*Wriggins* agreed.)

*Griffith* asked to what extent the Soviets have been shaping their policy toward Central Asia on the basis of foreign policy needs. It is often argued (see discussion of Newell paper, above) that if it is made costly for the Soviets in Afghanistan, and a way is found for them to withdraw gracefully, they will withdraw. This implies they got into this simply in order to support a regime asking for their help. On the other hand, if you can confirm that they put an enormous effort over thirty years into building up their relationship with Central Asians as a device for helping their foreign policy ambitions, that tends to confirm the view that the invasion of Afghanistan is part of a long-run advance strategy into the Middle East and South Asia. He wondered what more Rakowska-Harmstone could say about the extent to which foreign policy concerns over the past twenty to twenty-five years have determined their internal policy.

*Rakowska-Harmstone* thought it was a significant determinant. Changing Tajikistan from an autonomous republic to a union republic was done with the hope of creating a Persian-speaking base to carry, if she remembered the quote correctly, "socialism abroad." This was the only justification she could find as to why they decided to raise the republic from an ASSR to an SSR or to include part of the Ferghana Valley inhabited by Tajiks in the SSR in order to give it sufficient size to warrant the upgrading. Right after World War II, a large number of poems were directed from Tajikistan to "British India" comparing their freedom with that of the Indians under the British yoke. This was just from Tajikistan. There was a similar effort in Uzbekistan and Azerbaijan.

She thought it was always intended that the area be an initial starting point. But its development was delayed in the internal context by the Muslim-communist nationalism of Sultan Galiev, the Tatar who felt they should all get together and create a Muslim republic. His assumption was that Russian workers were just as much colonialists as tsarist officials. Combined with Stalin's need to consolidate power, this threat led to a turning inward for many years. But the impetus to use Central Asia was there at the beginning. It was revived in World War II, and she believes it has been revived again recently.

# Turmoil in Central Asia

## Zalmay Khalilzad

The crises of economic development, national integration, political legitimacy, and big power rivalry have resulted in major political convulsions in the Central Asian countries of Afghanistan, Iran, and Pakistan. During the past two years Afghanistan's Presidents Daud, Taraki, and Amin, Iran's Premier Hoveida, and Pakistan's Premier Bhutto have been killed. An Islamic Republic has been established in Iran. In Afghanistan, a number of pro-Soviet Marxist-Leninist regimes succeeded each other, culminating in the direct Soviet invasion and occupation of that country. An Islamically oriented military regime has been ruling Pakistan.

The crises in the Central Asian countries have had serious implications beyond their borders as well. The Central Treaty Organization (CENTO), conceived as a cordon sanitaire between the Soviet Union and the Persian Gulf, is dead. Two Western allies in the region, Pakistan and Iran, have become nonaligned. Afghanistan, previously the only nonaligned Central Asian country, is in danger of becoming part of the Soviet satellite empire. The Soviet occupation has thus eliminated a buffer state; brought the Soviet forces to the Pakistani border; set a new precedent in massive use of Soviet forces in the area outside of the Warsaw Pact countries; and substantially reduced the distance between the Soviet forces and the entrance of the Persian Gulf, putting that region within the range of a large number of Soviet tactical aircraft.

The Iranian revolution dealt a devastating blow to the Nixon doctrine. Iran's armed forces, among the largest and best equipped in the world, have been substantially weakened. With this change in Iran's military capability and the overthrow of the Shah, its mission—checking the expansion of radical and pro-Soviet forces in the region—has been aborted. A major consequence of this has been a change in the balance of power in Iraq's favor in the Gulf region, a shift that contributed to bringing about the current war between these two traditional rivals. The outcome of this war may have still further profound impacts on the political and military situation in the area. American-Pakistan relations are strained because of many problems including conflict over Pakistan's nuclear program and the scope of future security relations between the two countries.

The crises in the Central Asian countries are not over. In varying degrees, each state in the region is politically fragmented at several levels; each contains many minorities, some of which are seeking increased autonomy, and many political groups with conflicting ideological beliefs. Although there are significant differences between Afghanistan, Iran, and Pakistan in the degree of popular support for the current regimes, all have many political groups opposed to the existing governments. These groups disagree among themselves in regard not only to the desirable political and economic order, but also on foreign policy and alliance questions. All three countries have serious economic problems and continue to experience structural dislocations. As in the past, crises in the area will continue to be influenced by the regional environment and the policies of the outside powers, especially the two superpowers. And the conflicts in the area will, in turn, have an impact on the international system and even on the domestic politics of the superpowers and on their relative capability to influence developments in the Persian Gulf.

On the whole, the recent crises in Central Asia have caught the international community by surprise, and the confusion has been reflected even at the highest decision-making levels of the world's capitals. Clearly, a more systematic understanding of the internal, regional, and global complexities of the politics of this region is required.

## THE INDEPENDENT CENTRAL ASIAN STATES

All three independent (or recently independent) Central Asian countries face serious internal security problems. In varying degrees and at general levels, each is fragmented. Each contains structural causes for instability not only because of modernization per se, but also by the way modernization has been implemented; and each contains many political groups with conflicting beliefs. These conflicts are further aggravated in many instances by the absence of a consensus on the manner of political competition. In each country no matter which group comes to power, it is likely to be challenged, at times violently, by others.

The overthrow of the Shah by a broad coalition of forces under the leadership of religious leaders, came as a shock not only to many policymakers around the world but to political modernization theorists as well. Many theorists operating on the assumption that economic growth would be accompanied by increased secularization and integration neglected the fact that political fragmentation often accompanies rapid economic development in third world societies. Since most of the theories assumed a general model of development, they were unable to sufficiently distinguish the different processes and sometimes contradictory constellations of groups and events in third world polities.[1] Operating within the frameworks of conventional theory, many analysts predicted stability for the region in general and for Iran in particular. For example, John Campbell argued in 1975 that "the Gulf States were generally enjoying such prosperity and economic growth that the regimes...seem to have a cushion against revolution."[2]

Prominent experts on Iran also predicted stability for the country and longevity for the Shah's rule. In 1964 George Lenczowski, praising the Shah's program of creating a modern institutional superstructure wrote:

Iran enjoys a few immunities likely to protect it from violent upheavals à la Iraq. These immunities may be listed as lack of ties with revolutionary pan-Arabism, the continuous threat of Soviet imperialism which tends to unify the national ranks when the pressure is great and obvious, and the historical continuity of the monarchical institutions.[3]

In 1968 Marvin Zonis had asserted that "now, at least, the throne appears secure,"[4] and a year later Leonard Binder argued that Iran "seemed clearly on its way to becoming a prosperous, stable, modernizing autocracy."[5] And as late as August 1978, the CIA stated in its proposed national Intelligence Estimate that Iran could not even be considered a pre-revolutionary society, and that "those who are in the opposition both violent and non-violent, do not have the capacity to be more than troublesome. . . . There is dissatisfaction with the Shah's tight control of the political process, but this does not threaten the government."[6]

In fact, extreme economic conditions and interactions with the outside world exacerbated existing problems, created new ones, and transcended others. In the case of Iran, the rapid increase in income, from the point of view of the Shah's regime, was a mixed blessing. On the one hand, it increased its ability to coopt potential opponents, initiating projects that the country could not afford before, including a substantial expansion of security forces for both internal and external use and greater international political and economic power. However, increased oil income and the rapid economic and social changes resulting from government programs unleashed powerful new forces and antagonized some older ones. Rapid growth was accompanied by social and cultural dislocations, greater inequality of wealth distribution, an increase in the degree and magnitude of corruption, higher inflation rates, and more dependence on outside powers, especially the United States. These policies antagonized some of the major social forces as well as those whose interests were negatively affected; yet there was a reluctance to make political modifications appropriate to the progressive changes taking place in the economy and society.

In Iran the following dramatic economic and social changes had taken place. In 1953, Iran's oil income totalled less than $34 million. By 1977 it came to more than $20 billion. Between 1953 and 1978 the cumulative income from oil amounted to more than $54 billion. During the same period, nonmilitary imports increased from $40 million to almost $12 billion. Per capita income increased from slightly more than $150 to more than $2,000, even though the population grew from 13 to 35 million. The number of industries of various sizes, including the large, capital intensive ones the Shah was especially fond of, increased from less than 1,400 to 8,000; the number of universities from four with 14,000 students, to sixteen with 154,315 students; the number of primary schools increased from 5,956 with 746,473 students to 23,476 with more than four million students. Technical schools increased from 36 to 800 and the number of students from 2,538 to 227,507. Tens of thousands of students were sent abroad. Iran's "urban" population increased from five to ten million between 1956 and 1966 and was expected to reach twenty million by 1980, making about fifty percent of Iranian population "urban." There was a construction boom. The educated middle class doubled in size between 1956 and 1976, growing from six to thirteen percent of the total employed population. If merchants and businessmen are included, the middle class constituted almost twenty-five percent of the population.[7]

At the same time, there were inadequate housing in the urban areas; high inflation rates, at times exceeding fifty percent; massive transportation problems in Tehran; gross inequities and the flaunting of wealth by the rich through conspicuous consumption; large-scale financial scandals; and what appeared to many, especially the religious oriented, as moral decadence in Iran's urban areas. The Shah's economic policies were also weakening the traditional forces of the Bazaar and strengthening big business, in which members of the royal family had direct interests. The Shah's legal and educational policies weakened the clergy.

It was a coalition of heterogeneous forces transcending class and ideological barriers that finally overthrew the Shah. Some of his opponents such as the leftists were against his domestic policies as well as his close relations with the West; others such as the Social Democrats opposed the Shah for his reluctance to share power; while the factionalized religious movement opposed him because they believed the Shah's policies were leading toward Westernization, secularization, and moral decline. The West's muted reaction to the 1978 Marxist-Leninist coup in Afghanistan, the encouragement from the Soviet Union, and Washington's vacillation and confusing signals also convinced many of the Shah's opponents that the international environment was favorable to a decisive move on their part.

Major structural changes have also taken place in Afghanistan and Pakistan since World War II, although not as dramatically as in Iran.[8] Structural changes and interaction with the outside world has led to the emergence of large numbers of political groups in the countries of the region. In some cases ethnic politics might well threaten their territorial integrity and lead to regional conflicts. Ethnic dissent is strongest among the Kurds in Iran, Iraq, and Turkey. Other ethnic groups seeking varying degrees of autonomy include the Baluch, Arabs, and Azerbaijanis in Iran. In Afghanistan, the population is composed of ethnic groups such as the Pushtuns, Tajiks, Uzbeks, Hazaras and Turkmen. The current fighting against the Soviet occupation forces, besides the Pushtuns, the dominant ethnic group, includes the other major groups. Afghanistan's various ethnic and tribal groups have traditionally been suspicious of their central government, especially those seeking to centralize the country. Traditionally, the Pushtuns, whether Persianized or not, have dominated Afghan politics not only because of their numerical advantage, but also because of greater military capability, including dominance in the state's armed forces. The recent turmoil in Afghanistan has encouraged the emergence of several new and ethnically based centers of military power that any future government will have to take into account. The minority ethnic groups are likely to push for a federal political system giving the regions a large degree of internal autonomy. Failure to meet such demands might well lead to conflict among the groups, threatening the country's integrity and providing opportunities for manipulation by external powers.

Pakistan, too, has serious ethnic problems. Punjabi domination of the state and society is resented by the other three main ethnic groups, especially in Sind and Baluchistan. Punjabis constitute some sixty percent of the population, eighty percent of the armed forces, more than eighty-five percent of the higher bureaucracy, and some eighty percent of the business activities.[9] Many Baluch leaders have been pushing for provincial autonomy, recognition of nationalities, and a weak central authority only responsible for defense, foreign affairs, and currency.

The Baluch nationalists, however, are faced with a number of difficulties. Unlike the Bengalis of East Pakistan, to whom they are sometimes compared, the Baluch are few in number and their area is territorially contiguous with the rest of Pakistan. While in the 1970 elections the Awami League won 288 out of 300 seats in Bangladesh, the Baluch are divided along many lines. In these elections Bhutto's Pakistan's Peoples Party won five seats in Baluchistan, the National Awami Party won eight, the Pakistani Muslim League (Qayyom Group) three, and the Jamiat-al-Ulema Islami (Hazarvi Group) won four seats in the area. Other parties winning seats included Jamaat-i-Islami (one), and National Awami Party (Pakhtun-Khwa) (one). Baluchistan's population is heterogeneous. Besides the Baluch, who constitute less than fifty percent of Baluchistan's population (but see Harrison: Comments and Discussion, above), other ethnic groups in the area include Pushtuns, Hindus, Punjabis, Sindis, Hazaras, and Jats.[10] The Baluch are themselves divided into more than a dozen tribes and a thousand clans. There are many rivalries and mutual suspicions among local leaders. For example, in 1973 after dismissing the elected government, Bhutto lured Akbar Bugti, one of the major tribal leaders in Baluchistan to assume the province's governorship. Even the 1973-1977 insurgency was confined to central Baluchistan, involving mainly the Mengal and Marri tribal armies. The Merkanis, for example, who occupy the coastal areas, did not participate in the insurgency. To develop a province-wide organizational network, the insurgents would have to overcome the problems posed by ethnic and tribal conflict and diversity.

Ethnic conflicts are accompanied by ideological conflicts in the region. The ideological groups competing for power and influence, either overtly or covertly, are many. In Iran they include the Marxist Fedayin, the Islamic Mujahidin, the pro-Soviet, Marxist-Leninist Tudeh, the various factions of Westernized moderates, the factionalized religious movement largely represented by the Islamic Republican Party (IRP), and many other smaller groups. Since the revolution, the IRP and the various leftist groups have gained at the expense of the moderate center. Despite their show of animosity toward the West and sympathy for a number of internal programs and external "causes," relations between the clerically dominated government and the leftist groups, especially the Mujahidin and Fedayin, have been antagonistic. This antagonism could lead to large-scale military confrontation between the left and the government. Ideological conflicts at times might be accompanied by or blurred with ethnic and sectarian ones.

Domestic changes in Iran, as in other countries of the region, could have serious implications for Iran's foreign policy. For example, the country's domination by Fedayin would be likely to lead to much closer relations with the Soviet Union. The Fedayin, who are said to have several thousand armed guerillas, have been active in the country's minority regions, such as the Kurdish area, and are supported by many intellectuals and insurgents. They have supported the Soviet invasion of Afghanistan, opposed any resumption of good relations with the West, pushed for the weakening of the armed forces because of "American influence in that institution," and suggested that Iran import weapons from the Soviet bloc.

The Mujahidin, who follow an eclectic ideology, drawing on Marxism and Islam, follow a political line similar to that of the Arab Baath Party in regard to the Soviet Union: pragmatic, inclined to be sympathetic, but not absolutely committed. The Mujahidin have not condemned the Soviet invasion of Afghanistan, and like the Fedayin, have favored the weakening of the armed forces, and continued hostility towards the West. This group has been gaining in support recently. The Tudeh Party, which is servile to the Soviet Union, has been opportunistically supporting Khomeini thus far. Because of this support, they have been subjected to fewer restrictions than the other two leftist groups. Although Tudeh is the smallest of the three groups, it has important support among the oil workers and among minority populations, especially those in the region close to the Soviet Union. Tudeh can be a valuable tool for the Soviet Union. It can influence domestic developments by such measures as prompting instability, and can disseminate pro-Soviet ideas. The current regime's failure to deal with the country's domestic problems or defeat in the war with Iraq could push more and more groups leftward.

In the case of Pakistan, General Zia's regime, with a political record including four postponements of scheduled elections, the manipulation of the press, the "suspension" of political parties, the public flogging of those accused of political and other crimes, and the execution of former Premier Bhutto, is opposed by all major political parties. The opposition groups include not only Bhutto's People's Party but also members of the Pakistan National Alliance such as the Jamaat-i-Islami, who organized the campaign of civil disobedience and participated against Bhutto, and later participated in the Zia government. Although the major parties disagree among themselves on issues such as the degree of political centralization, the role of political Islam, ties with the outside powers, and the internal economic policies, they are in agreement on the need for elections in the immediate future.

In Afghanistan, political fragmentation continues even in the aftermath of the Soviet invasion. A major Soviet goal since the occupation has been to harmonize relations between the rival Peoples Democratic Parties, Khalq and Parcham. Babrak Karmal, upon being installed as President, claimed the leadership of a united Parcham and Khalq. Several Khalqis, especially those loyal to Taraki, were appointed to high positions in the regime. These included the first Deputy Prime Minister and Vice President of Revolutionary Council, Assadollah Sarwary, Minister of Interior and Member of the Central Committee of the PDP, Said Mohammed Gulabzoi, Minister of Transport and Member of the Central Committee of the PDP, Lt. Colonel Sherjan Mazdoryar, and Minister of Communications and Member of the Central Committee, Lt. Colonel Mohammad Aslam Watanjar.

Fragmentation continues among the groups that led the opposition to the Khalqi regimes and the Soviet forces in Afghanistan. Although there are numerous groups involved in the struggle against Moscow, the best-known groups are those motivated by Islam and headquartered in Pakistan. At present the major groups with headquarters in Pakistan include the National Liberation Front, headed by Sebghatullah Mujaddidi, who is from an old and well-known Afghan family that played an important role in the overthrow of King Amanullah in the 1920s. Mujaddidi has spent several years on a religious mission in Scandinavia, and has strong ties with some of the members of the traditional Afghan power elite. Another group is the National Front for the Islamic Revolution of Afghanistan, led by Siad Ahmad Gailani-Affendi, who is a descendant of the prophet and who was an important businessman until recently, and has strong ties with the former monarch, Mohammad Zahir Shah. Like Mujaddidi, Gailani-Affendi has strong ties with elements of the traditional power elite. There are two factions of the Islamic Party, headed by Gulbuddin Hekmatyar and Mohammed Yunis Khalis. Hekmatyar has been in Pakistan since before the overthrow of Daud and opposed the former President, has strong ties with Pakistan's Jamaat-i-Islami and the Muslim Brotherhood Movement, and has a well-organized party and cadre. Hekmatyar's group has more and better weapons than the other groups. He claims to have the largest number of followers. The fifth group is the Islamic Association led by Burhanuddin Rabbani, a former theology professor at Kabul University, with a long record of involvement in the Muslim Brotherhood movement which had ties with similar movements in other Islamic countries. Another group with a small following is the Islamic Revolutionary Movement of Mohammad Nabi Mohammadi. The main Afghan partisan group with headquarters in Iran is the Islamic Movement of Afghanistan, led by Mohammad Asef Mohseny Qandahari, who claims to be the leader of the Afghan Shiites and is ideologically influenced by the Khomeini revolution in Iran. Small secular groups active against the Soviets include the National Socialists and Maoists. There are also attempts by some prominent politicians of the pre-1973 period such as former Prime Minister Mohammad Yusuf to become involved with those opposed to the Soviet occupation, hoping perhaps to become a compromise candidate for leading a future Afghan government if the Soviets withdraw.

Despite their common antipathy towards the Soviet Union and sympathy for Islam, even the major Islamic groups based in Pakistan have failed to form a united front. Under pressure from the Islamic world, especially Saudi Arabia, an Islamic Rescue Front consisting of the six major Pakistan-based groups was formed towards the end of January 1980. Rasul Sayef was accepted as the president of the new alliance. It was not long before Hekmatyar withdrew from the alliance. The longevity of the unity among the remaining members is uncertain because of major disagreements.

The reasons for lack of unity among Moscow's Afghan opponents are many. Besides personality conflicts, there are disagreements over leadership, the shape of a future Afghanistan, the potential role of the former king and high-level Afghan officials, and the type of relations with other political groups and countries. Both Hekmatyar and Gailani have claimed to have the largest number of supporters.[11] Hekmatyar, in particular, has argued his group has to be recognized as the largest and most powerful. Well supplied with weapons, he appears unwilling to share them with others without dominating the alliance. Hekmatyar's drive for leadership is opposed by the other groups, especially Gailani, Mujaddidi, and Nabi. Rabbani and Khalis, who is known to participate in actual fighting inside Afghanistan, are more sympathetic to Hekmatyar.

Ideologically, Gailani's group is the most liberal; Mujaddidi's, Nabi's and Rabbani's groups grow relatively more conservative; followed by Khalis; and then Hekmatyar is the most orthodox. The ideological differences among the partisans are most pronounced in regard to the shape of a future Afghan government, the role of the former king, relations with other countries, and prospects for a negotiated settlement of the Afghan crisis. Hekmatyar wants the establishment of an Islamic Republic in Afghanistan, similar to what has happened in Iran. He opposes any role for the royal family in the conflict with the Soviets or in a future Afghan government. He believes the ex-king Zahir Shah, who is in Italy, and his family to be at least partially responsible for the current crisis in the country. He, at times, talks about a possible trial of the former king and some of his associates if an Islamic Republic is established in Afghanistan. Khalis and Rabbani are sympathetic to these views.

The other three groups have not specified the shape of a future Afghan government. Concentrating on the need to get the Russians out of Afghanistan, they say that after that "the people of Afghanistan would decide what type of government they want."[12] Gailani is known to have close contacts with Zahir Shah and his family, and favors a political role for him in a future Afghanistan. Mujaddidi and Nabi are not opposed to this in principle, but have repeatedly argued that they are not fighting for the royal family.[13]

On relations with external powers and groups there are also major differences. Each partisan group is suspicious of the amount of financial aid the other groups receive from external sources, and what happens to that aid. Hekmatyar wants external support to come largely from the Islamic world. Rabbani and Khalis are sympathetic to him on this point as well. Gailani does not oppose assistance from and contact with non-Islamic powers. He has repeatedly called on Western powers to support the Afghans in their conflict with the West, and also has friendly ties with Saudi Arabia. Again, Mujaddidi and Nabi sympathize with him. The three more conservative leaders believe that there can only be a military solution to the Afghan crisis. They believe a peaceful resolution involving negotiations with the Soviets is unlikely and undesirable. Gailani and the other two leaders oppose "closing the door" on a possible negotiated settlement.[14]

While the Pakistani-based groups receive considerable coverage in the international press, most of the fighting in Afghanistan has been by poorly armed, local ethnic, tribal, and sectarian groups without much link with those in Pakistan and Iran. The externally based groups, at times, provide weapons to some of those fighting inside the country.

## REGIONAL INSTABILITIES AND CONFLICTS

Despite the fact that the countries of the region are all Islamic, which permits similarity of views on some international issues, there are many regional conflicts including border disputes, rivalry for regional dominance, interference in each other's domestic affairs, ideological conflicts, and degree and type of dependence on outside powers. In the current conflict between Iran and Iraq most of the above elements have been present.

Iraq and Iran have been rivals for the domination of the Persian Gulf for some time. Iraq has been seeking hegemony not only over the Persian Gulf but the Arab world as a whole. In the past Iraq made little headway because of Egypt's dominant position in the Arab world and the Shah's Iran in the Persian Gulf. It was largely Iran's military superiority that forced Iraq to enter into a settlement in 1975 which it had long opposed, including acceptance of Iranian sovereignty over the eastern half of the Shatt-al-Arab estuary, Iraq's only commercial outlet to the Persian Gulf. The Camp David accords and the peace treaty between Egypt and Israel leading to Egypt's isolation from the Arab world weakened at least temporarily Iraq's major rival in the Arab world. The Iranian revolution weakened its rival in the Gulf.

With the Shah's overthrow, the substantial degradation of Iranian military capability, and political disarray in Khomeini's Islamic Republic, the Baghdad regime also saw a potential risk to its position from Khomeini's ideology and his commitment to export the Iranian revolution. Khomeini appealed to Iraq's majority Shi'a population against the Sunni-dominated and Arab Socialist government of Saddam Hussein. To weaken Khomeini and Iran, Iraq encouraged the disintegration of Iranian armed forces and assisted Tehran's ideological and ethnic opponents while preparing for its own military action against Iran. Iran's isolation from its former allies and arms suppliers after the overthrow of the Shah, and especially once the American hostages were taken, further encouraged this tendency in Iraqi policy. Baghdad abrogated the 1975 treaty and sent its forces into Iran.

Other territorial conflicts involving Iran and the Arab countries have included Tehran's occupation of three islands near the Strait of Hormuz (Abu Musa, and the greater and lesser Tunbs), and Iranian claims over Bahrain. Although subsequently Iran recognized Bahrain's sovereignty the issue might well be raised again. Treaties and agreements in this area have been abrogated on many occasions. For example, in 1969, Iran unilaterally abrogated the 1937 treaty governing passage through Shatt-al-Arab which led to another agreement with Iraq in 1975. The 1975 agreement now has been declared null and void by Iraq. Despite the Shah's acceptance of Bahrain's sovereignty, after the Iranian revolution, a religious leader warned Bahrain that unless it accepts Shiite rule, Iran will annex it and impose an Islamic Republic.[15] (The religious leader was later reprimanded by Khomeini for this statement.)

Pakistan has had territorial conflict with Afghanistan and India. The Durand Line, drawn in 1893, "formalized" the thousand-mile border between Afghanistan and British India. Afghan rulers, however, expressed reservation about that border, with varying degrees of enthusiasm. In 1949 the Afghan Grand Assembly declared it did not recognize "the Durand or any similar line." The Afghan governments have expressed support for what they call Pashtunistan. It has not been clear what the Afghans mean by Pashtunistan. It is unclear whether they are talking about only the Pakistani Northwest Frontier Province or whether the concept includes Baluchistan as well. It is equally unclear whether they want the Pakistani provinces to become part of Afghanistan, form a separate state, or achieve greater autonomy within Pakistan. The Afghan rulers have expressed support for Baluch and Pushtun nationalists in Pakistan, but the degree and scope of that support has varied considerably depending on such factors as the personal commitment of the Afghan prime minister and the Pakistani activity in the disputed region. Although considerable progress was made in 1976 between Afghanistan's President Daud and Pakistani Premier Z. Ali Bhutto, the "Pashtunistan" crisis could once again affect regional security. With the Soviet occupation of Afghanistan the "Pashtunistan issue" has acquired additional significance which will be dealt with later.

Pakistan, in turn, has territorial claims against India in Kashmir. At the time of the partition of India in 1947, the majority of the people of Kashmir were Muslims, which formed the basis for the Pakistani claims over Kashmir. Kashmir, however, was controlled by a Hindu ruling class which opted for Kashmir's accession to India. The Pakistanis considered this accession to be illegal and sent forces to Kashmir. Subsequent clashes resulted in de facto division of Kashmir with India controlling two-thirds of the area and more than three-quarters of the population. Because of Kashmir, the hostile state of relations with India, and the Indian role in the Bangladesh crisis, many Pakistani leaders consider India to be their country's most dangerous enemy. This belief persists even after the Soviet invasion of Afghanistan. Some Pakistanis have argued that the "liberation" of "Indian Kashmir" was an absolute necessity for Pakistan's survival.[16]

The Indians, too, have on occasion expressed the desire to "liberate" the Pakistani-controlled Kashmir which, although of little economic significance, has considerable strategic value, especially in the context of Pakistani-Indian and Sino-Indian relations. The Indians have expressed concern that the Pakistani Kashmir may be used by the Chinese to attack India in case of a conflict between India and China.

Because of the Kashmir crisis and the history of relations between India and Pakistan, which includes two major wars, and the Indian role in the Bangladesh crisis, many Pakistani leaders fear that increased Indian military superiority, especially the acquisition of nuclear weapon capability, could encourage it to attack Kashmir and further dismember Pakistan. In order to keep up with India, the Pakistanis have been seeking both a plutonium and a uranium route for the acquisition of a nuclear weapon capability.[17]

Rival states in the region have taken advantage of ethnic, sectarian, and ideological conflicts. For example, the Shah directly supported the Kurdish nationalists against the Iraqi government until 1975. In 1973, it was discovered that the Iraqi embassy in Islamabad was using its diplomatic immunity for smuggling weapons to Pakistani and Iranian Baluch nationalists. Iran, under Khomeini, has been encouraging religious and other opposition groups in all other countries in the region, including Afghanistan and Pakistan. However, Iran has not been the only country attempting to encourage the overthrow of rival governments. Pakistan has been the headquarters of several Afghan opposition groups for many years, and external aid has been channelled to them through Pakistan. Afghanistan in turn has encouraged Zia's opponents.

## BIG POWER RIVALRY

Internal and regional conflicts are influenced by and provide varying risks and opportunities for outside powers. Which power is better able to take advantage of instabilities in Central Asia or at least prevent them from negatively affecting their own interests depends largely on its goals, its understanding of regional and internal problems, its possession of and willingness to use "relevant capability" to help friendly groups and contain the hostile.

The goals of Soviet forces (either short-run or long-term) towards the three Muslim Central Asian states have included the weakening of the Western alliance system in the region; detaching Iran and Pakistan from such alliances; bringing nonaligned Afghanistan into the Soviet camp; the extension of Soviet power and influence over these states; preventing the spread of Chinese influence in the area and encircling that country by friendly governments; the spread of Marxist-Leninist ideology and strengthening of servile Marxist-Leninist groups; access to the natural resources and airspace of the countries of the area; and trade. The Soviets have emphasized different goals at different times depending on factors such as the ideological predisposition of their ruler(s) and Soviet preoccupation with other parts of the world.

In order to achieve their goals, the Soviets have relied on both positive and negative incentives. Positively they offer each government economic and military aid, trade, a military alliance, help in resisting or pressuring regional rivals, support at international meetings, propaganda favoring the regime, support against domestic opponents (except pro-Soviet Marxist-Leninists), and encouragement of the local Communist Party to support the regime. Negative incentives have included propaganda, especially radio broadcasts criticizing the target regime; military pressure including overflights, large maneuvers close to the border (where applicable), armed invasion, providing arms for regional opponents, helping domestic opponents (financially and militarily, either directly or indirectly); encouraging the local communist parties to organize demonstrations and strikes against a target regime; suspension of aid; and suspension of trade.

The Soviets respond to opportunities that arise as a result of the instabilities common to the countries south of its borders and other third world nations. At the same time, however, they do not passively watch and wait but rather actively promote and seek such opportunities to extend their influence through systematic application of the means of pressure listed above. These opportunities can arise from a crisis in relations between any of the three countries and any or all Western states, especially the United States; from a crisis of national integration such as ethnic and religious conflicts; from a crisis of political and economic development, producing conflicts between groups with different ideological beliefs; from regional conflicts; from local nationalism when directed against the West; and from Islam when directed against pro-Western regimes.

The goals of the United States foreign policy towards the countries of the region have included access to Iran's national resources, especially oil, at reasonable prices, preventing the direct or indirect extension of Soviet or regional hostile state power and influence over these countries, increasing American capability to influence developments in the region, maintaining friendly governments in all three countries, encouraging Iranian and Pakistani alliance with the West and Afghanistan's nonaligned states, increasing the cost of Soviet intervention in Afghanistan, and the spread of democratic ideas in economics and politics to the people of the area. Like the Soviets the Americans have relied on positive as well as negative incentives and at times have responded to and promoted opportunities.

The United States position in the region has experienced a steady decline. This decline, becoming more rapid just as the region becomes internationally more important, has not been inevitable. It has resulted from a failure of military and diplomatic policy and from a long-term inability to develop a flexible system of adequate responses to the political conditions in the third world.

There are many indicators of this decline. United States prestige in the area is at an unprecedented low level. After World War II, while colonialism began to crumble, many countries in the developing world sought close economic, political, and military ties with the United States. Many governments and political groups looked towards the West, especially the United States for ideological inspiration. Today the United States has become largely irrelevant ideologically in Central Asia.

A fundamental problem in U.S. policy towards the region has been the comparative decline in American and allied capability to project military power, accompanied by the reverse trend of a significant increase on the part of the Soviet Union. While in the 1950s the United States could dominate the Soviets in projecting power even into the capital of Afghanistan, Kabul, at present in a number of plausible contingencies even in the Persian Gulf proper, the USSR could get there faster and would be able to bring more firepower to bear than the United States.[18] This decline has shadow effects, encouraging hostile powers and groups and discouraging the sympathetic.

In devising policy towards this crucial region the United States has often lacked a yardstick by which to decide between alternatives or even at times to determine what they are. Each crisis forces the United States to improvise under the pressure of events. This approach has made coherence of policy difficult and has damaged U.S. reliability. In dealing with societies such as those of Central Asia, faced with recurrent instability, the United States at times has had difficulty knowing whether a particular arrangement or plan enhances U.S. security or is irrelevant. Proposals are often developed as a compromise between competing groups without an overall sense of purpose.[19]

Another problem in U.S. policies towards the region has been lack of coordination with allies. The role of Japan and our NATO allies in influencing the developments in this area is still largely undefined. There have been many declarations of unity but they have not obscured the confusion with the allies. The response to the Soviet invasion of Afghanistan has been characterized by indecision and squabbling among the Western allies. Until NATO and Japan coordinate policies for the security of vital regions such as Central Asia, the disarray in the aftermath of Afghanistan might well be repeated.

The major problems in U.S. policy in the future for the area include how to increase U.S. credibility with sympathetic groups and governments, how to reverse the decreased American ability to influence developments in the region, and how to discourage Russian repetition of the Afghan invasion in other countries and constrain Soviet power. In framing policies towards these problems, the United States faces difficult choices and trade-offs.

One policy with varying degrees of bearing on all three problems is increasing U.S. capability for projecting power in the region. To begin reversing the military imbalance in the area the United States stationed two carrier task groups near the Persian Gulf in the aftermath of the American Embassy takeover in Iran and the Soviet invasion of Afghanistan. Some of these forces have been withdrawn from other areas. It is not clear how long these forces will be stationed in the region. These task forces, while useful, are not sufficient to establish a military balance in the area. One other means for effecting such a balance which has been frequently discussed is the "Rapid Deployment Force" (RDF). RDF has several limitations. For one thing, the force will not be in place for a few years. For another the Soviets are already deployed in the region. If the Soviets were to attack the Gulf region, they would be launching cross-border air and ground operations, while forces starting from the United States would be thousands of miles away and would have to be airlifted over lines of communication quite vulnerable to enemy attack and subject to overflight denial. RDF also involves prepositioning of materiel and equipment near the region either on ships or on land. It is not clear how the United States plans to defend these ships and land facilities against a possible Soviet attack. An additional complication is caused by the likely lack of any lengthy warning through Soviet use of deception to obscure signals from the United States as to the direction and extent of Soviet purposes.

Oman, Somalia, and Kenya reportedly have offered facilities for the use of the United States. These offers would reportedly preclude the stationing of a substantial number of U.S. troops in these countries but permit the prepositioning of equipment and weapons. While such facilities would improve U.S. power projection capabilities to respond in a timely fashion to possible Soviet intervention as well as other regional crises, they would not be as effective as a significant local land and air presence. However, due largely to the opposition from Iraq, Iran, India, and the Soviet Union as well as political groups at home, even sympathetic governments in the area are opposed to a major U.S. presence on their territories. Even countries such as Saudi Arabia, which wants U.S. firmness and presence in the area, refuse to accept a U.S. military presence on their territory. Many, including the Pakistanis, are doubtful about U.S. ability and resolve to assist them in the event of external aggression even if they moved closer to the U.S.

The increased U.S. naval presence in the area as well as initiating the use of facilities offered by Oman, Somalia, and Kenya might increase the confidence of sympathetic groups and governments that the U.S. is serious about the security of the region and might in turn encourage them to seek closer security relations with the U.S. including accepting more direct U.S. presence on their territory which in turn would increase U.S. power projection capability.

Governments such as that of Oman which have offered facilities for the U.S. face considerable internal opposition. Close association with the U.S. might lead to increased opposition as these opponents are likely to be encouraged by Iran, Iraq, and the Soviet Union to oppose any American presence. To improve U.S. power projection capability through a land presence in the area, the U.S. might have to become involved in domestic conflicts in the host countries in support of favourable, though not necessarily solely status quo, groups. Given the importance of improving U.S. capability in the area, such an involvement might be regarded as not too expensive a price to pay for increased security. However, if the U.S. is unwilling to risk any such direct entanglement in the internal conflicts of the countries in the area, an increased U.S. presence might well counterproductively result in a net increase in the vulnerability of friendly governments. On the other hand without substantially improved capability to project power in the area, the U.S. might, in order to defend the Persian Gulf, have to depend on nuclear weapons in the event of a major Soviet attack. Without improving the conventional balance in the region defense by escalation is unlikely to be credible. It is doubtful that the outcome of a limited nuclear exchange between the U.S. and the Soviet Union in the region would be desirable. In any case, defense through nuclear escalation is a posture that the U.S. should seek to move away from.

Improving power projection will require sustained effort. There are also a number of interim measures that need to be considered. One such measure concerns the controversial question of aid to Pakistan. Pakistan faces serious threats, both internally and externally, and its situation has been seriously exacerbated by the Soviet presence in Afghanistan. Pakistan is a U.S. ally of long standing. It was a member of SEATO as well as CENTO, and it allowed American facilities on its territory. In 1959 it signed an agreement with the United States, Article 1 of which reads:

> The government of Pakistan is determined to resist aggression. In case of aggression against Pakistan, the government of the United States of America, in accordance with the Constitution of the United States of America, will take such appropriate action, including the use of armed forces, as may be mutually agreed upon and as is envisaged in the Joint Resolution to promote Peace and Stability in the Middle East, in order to assist the government of Pakistan at its request.

This agreement was reaffirmed by President Carter after the Soviet invasion of Afghanistan. In spite of the wording of the treaty itself, some U.S. officials in the past have asserted that the agreement does not imply a commitment to use U.S. forces. (Analogous interpretations were

offered regarding the Shah's Iran, although Iran had a similar agreement with the U.S.) Such equivocation cannot remain without effect on
the stability of U.S. alliance structures or on overall U.S. credibility.
Other states can hardly fail to note, and draw conclusions from, the
difference in the commitment level of the two superpowers, one of which
does not stand behind even its clear statements of intent, while the other
acts on its much more vaguely worded "friendship treaties." That this
"action" takes place not only to support the governments the treaty was
concluded with, but on occasion has the purpose of installing still better
"friends," may not increase their level of trust towards the Soviet
Union, but it does not encourage any dismissal of that country's willingness to act.

In the case of the U.S., confusing signals continued to be sent even
after the Soviet invasion and President Carter's reaffirmation of the
commitment to Pakistan's security. For example, Clark Clifford stated
in India that any Soviet move towards the Gulf would mean war, while
Secretary of Defense Brown, testifying before Congress, was far less
clear on the actual degree of U.S. willingness to intervene in the case of
an attack on Pakistan.

In the recent discussion in the U.S. regarding military aid to Pakistan,
several key issues have emerged. The Indian objections, Pakistan's
nuclear effort, and the domestic situation in Pakistan are the major
obstacles to such an aid programme. While Saudi Arabia and China
favour military aid for Pakistan, the Indians do not. Prime Minister
Gandhi, whose country recently signed a military agreement with the
Soviet Union for more than 1.5 billion dollars, has objected to potential
U.S. arms shipments to Pakistan, arguing that these arms might be used
against India.

The intensity of Indian opposition is likely to depend on the type of
arms Pakistan receives. Indians are likely to be less hostile to Pakistan's
acquisition of mountain artillery, anti-tank and anti-aircraft missiles,
helicopters, and interceptors, than if she received longer-range strike
aircraft like the A-7s, the F-4s or the F-15s. They are also likely to object
strongly to the provision of heavy armour suited for the Punjabi plains.
Some of the weapons that Pakistan might need can be provided by
China. The Soviet occupation of Afghanistan, which borders China, is
regarded as a threat to their country by the Chinese leadership. The
Chinese, are therefore, likely to increase their assistance to Pakistan.

Opposing American arms to Pakistan is not necessarily in the interests
of India's security, either, since the prospect of Pakistan or parts of
Pakistan (such as Baluchistan) falling under Soviet control has negative
implications for India as well. India, too, is dependent on Persian Gulf
oil, and only Pakistan separates it from Soviet forces in Afghanistan.

Given the overwhelming Indian superiority in the area of conventional arms, there is little basis for worry that U.S. arms to Pakistan would significantly affect this balance. Limiting Pakistan's conventional arms might increase that country's incentive to acquire nuclear weapons; the Indians should be more worried about the prospect of a conventionally weak and irredentist Pakistan armed with nuclear weapons.

The issue of proliferation, in fact, is yet another illustration of the paradoxical policies followed by the U.S. Vis-à-vis the two potential nuclear rivals in South Asia, U.S. policy has been clearly discriminatory, cutting off all aid to Pakistan, a U.S. ally, for seeking a nuclear weapon option, and refusing to do the same in regard to India, a nonaligned country with a friendship treaty with the Soviet Union and a country, moreover, which has produced its nuclear device using U.S. material in violation of the conditions under which material had been granted. This does not mean that the objective of non-proliferation should be abandoned in the wake of the Afghan crisis. Rather, the U.S. should seek to encourage both India and Pakistan to declare South Asia a nuclear-free zone and to open their nuclear facilities to international inspection. The Pakistanis have come out in favour of such an agreement. While it is doubtful that the Indians will accept such a proposal, at least a clear statement of U.S. support would increase U.S. credibility with Pakistan. Greater U.S. engagement in the area and the provision of conventional arms to Pakistan are also likely to increase U.S. leverage to influence at least Pakistan's nuclear policies.

The third consideration causing controversy is the concern that in aiding Pakistan, the U.S. would be supporting another unpopular dictator who may use the weapons against his internal opponents rather than the Soviet Union. This is an important point; the U.S. will have to distinguish between supporting a country's capacity for self-defense and bolstering a particular regime. Arms supplies should be accompanied by cautionary steps; the government should be urged to hold democratic elections, and to come to terms with moderate regional opposition leaders, including Baluchs. The U.S. should make it clear it is supporting Pakistan and not endorsing a particular regime; for this purpose, contact should be established with opposition parties possessing a popular base. Providing aid to Pakistan at the present time is likely to alienate some political groups in Pakistan, but the desire to defend itself against a variety of possible external aggressions is an issue that transcends party politics, and in this goal the U.S. might be able to cooperate with many Pakistani parties. Without a credible defense relationship with the U.S., the Pakistanis are unlikely to allow anything but the most modest assistance to the Afghans in their resistance to Soviet occupation.

Another important measure with both interim and long-term dimensions would be increasing preparedness to take advantage of Soviet difficulties. Again, this would require coordination with the allies and careful analysis. The Soviets are faced with a number of critical situations in many parts of the third world which at times have been neglected by Western observers, who have paid attention to Soviet gains rather than seeing the accompanying risks and losses and the opportunities these provide for an active policy on the part of the industrial democracies. This is clearly demonstrated in the case of Afghanistan, where Soviet invasion and occupation is opposed by most political groups and the population, and resisted with various degrees of activism.

In recent private and public discussions on whether to assist the Afghan partisans, several arguments have been advanced against such aid. These arguments have included the following: that significant aid to the Afghans is not feasible because of Pakistani reluctance to allow such aid to reach the partisans; that even if allowed, providing such aid could be dangerous for the security of neighboring countries by encouraging further Soviet expansion; and that such aid would in fact be morally reprehensible because it would lead to little more than substantial increases in the Afghan loss of life by prolonging the conflict and raising its intensity.

The considerations involving assistance to the Afghans are complex, and the arguments raised against it have some justification. However, each one proceeds from a partial and fragmentary view of the situation. Often, they serve as rationalizations for doing essentially nothing in a situation which is politically and morally weighted in favor of support.

It is true, as the first argument stresses, that the Pakistani government has been reluctant to allow substantial American weapons from reaching the partisans. General Zia did demand a security guarantee from the United States in case Pakistan is threatened by the Soviet Union, but such a pledge is unlikely in the immediate future. The Pakistani nuclear program, the political situation within Pakistan, and the congressional attitude in Washington are all unfavorable. Providing aid to the Afghans, however, is a matter of political decision. None of the obstacles is insurmountable. For instance, Pakistan allows equipment of Russian origin to reach the partisans, since these weapons, if intercepted by the Soviets, can always be claimed to represent arms captured from Soviet occupation troops by the Afghan rebels. Russian equipment is available from several countries with friendly ties to the United States, including the anti-aircraft and anti-tank weapons most needed by the Afghans. There is also a substantial unofficial market for Soviet weapons, but the Afghans alone do not have the funds to purchase them. The United States itself or the Arab oil producers, with U.S. encouragement could assist the Afghans in this regard.

The second argument, that substantial aid to the resistance would increase the risk to the security of countries such as Pakistan who host the headquarters of several partisan groups, is of considerable relevance. However, the risk to Pakistani security from aiding the partisans has to be compared with the risk associated with failing to do so. An Afghan defeat leading to a pacified Afghanistan will greatly increase the Soviet capability to pressure and influence Pakistan. The internal conflicts in Pakistan certainly would provide the Soviet Union with sufficient opportunity for subversion. However, while the conflict in Afghanistan goes on, the Soviets can hardly spare much of their existing force for large ventures into Pakistan. And a Soviet withdrawal in the face of rising costs of their occupation would increase the security not only of Pakistan but of the entire region.

The moral argument against aid to the Afghans, on the ground that it could lead to greater loss of life on the part of partisans and population, is also of mixed merit. Wisely or not, the Afghan population has demonstrated its determination to face starvation and massive sanctions to resist an occupying army and defend itself against communism and foreign control. To recommend that they submit to domination because the invader is more powerful than they are is an argument that denies every political value this country stands for. To fight against oppression is, almost by definition, a fight against material odds; to advise a third world country to take its beating gracefully and come to terms with the aggressor presents moral dilemmas of its own. Whether the Afghans continue to fight does not depend on the quality of their weapons but on their will to resist. The weapons will, however, affect their prospects of doing more than making a heroically reckless gesture. The Afghans seem determined to go on fighting, even if all they have is homemade nineteenth century muskets and World War I rifles. Even with these, they are causing far more trouble than the Soviet Union had expected. External assistance could raise the costs of Soviet occupation enough to bring about a compromise solution. This, rather than a continuation of warfare and the expulsion of refugees, is required to save Afghan lives, for the continuation of the present level of opposition appears to be acceptable to the Soviets.

However, neither the decision to support nor the decision to abandon the Afghans is likely to be reached on primarily moral grounds. Supporting the partisans will increase the costs of the Afghan invasion to the Soviets. Some of this is reportedly being done already. With the continuation of the partisan warfare, a number of goals could be achieved without actually defeating the Soviets. The costs for the Soviet Union could include reduced capabilities elsewhere as a result of the commitment of troops, materiel, and funds to "the Afghan front," as well as domestic consequences in Muslim areas of the Soviet Union. The Islamic population of the Soviet Union might reach one quarter of the Soviet Union's population by the year 2000. Islamic consciousness continues to form a type of counterculture that may be susceptible to Muslim agitation if the Soviets continue the war with their ethnic and religious counterparts across the border. Continued war in Afghanistan may also lead to succession problems within the Soviet leadership as rising costs for the invasion exacerbate factionalism, and produce alliance strains vis-à-vis the Eastern bloc countries. More generally, hostility to the Soviets may increase among Muslim countries and groups.

The major setbacks of Western policies in the third world during the 1960s and 1970s have been due to errors that were bipartisan and alliance wide. The Soviet invasion of Afghanistan, while posing a potentially massive threat to the security of the industrial countries and to the independence of surrounding states, also marks a potential turning point in the course of American and allied policies in recent years. Constructively using this opportunity will require a balanced view and a sustained effort at implementing multifaceted courses of action including reversing the current military imbalance in the Persian Gulf.

## NOTES

1. See Alex Inkeles and David Smith, *Becoming Modern: Individual Change in Six Developing Countries* (Cambridge: Harvard University Press, 1974). Gabriel Almond and James Coleman (eds.), *The Politics of the Developing Areas* (Princeton, N.J.: Princeton University Press, 1960). Lucian Pye, *Aspects of Political Development: Essays in Heuristic Theory* (Boston: Little, Brown, 1970). Daniel Lerner, *The Passing of Traditional Society: Modernizing the Middle East* (Glencoe, Ill.: Free Press, 1958). For a critique of some modernization theories see Cheryl Benard and Zalmay Khalilzad, "Secularization, Industrialization and Khomeini's Islamic Republic," *Political Science Quarterly*, Summer 1979.

2. In Abbas Amiri (ed.), *The Persian Gulf and Indian Ocean in International Politics* (Tehran: IIPES, 1975), p. 55.

3. George Lenczowski, *The Middle East in World Politics* (Ithaca, NY: Cornell University Press, 1964), p. 232.

4. Marvin Zonis, *The Politics of Insecurity*, quoted in Leonard Binder, *Factors Influencing Iran's International Role* (Santa Monica: The Rand Corporation, 5968-FE, October 1969).

5. Ibid., p. 48.

6. Quoted in Abdul Kasim Mansur, "The Crisis in Iran," *Armed Forces Journal International*, January 1979, p. 28.

7. For studies of domestic changes in Iran as well as changes in its relations with the outside world see James Bill, "Iran and the Crisis of '78," *Foreign Affairs*, January 1979. Zalmay Khalilzad, "The Superpowers and the Northern Tier," *International Security*, Winter 79/80. Ervand Abrahamian, "Structural Causes of the Iranian Revolution," *MERIP Reports*, May 1980. Amin Saikal, *The Rise and Fall of the Shah*, Princeton: Princeton University Press, 1980. Shahram Chubin, "Repercussions of the Crisis in Iran," *Survival*, May-June 1979.

8. For details see Zalmay Khalilzad, *The Return of the Great Game:* . . ., prepared for the California Seminar on International Security and Foreign Policy, Los Angeles, 1980.

9. *MERIP*, September 1980, p. 25.

10. See Akbar Ahmed, *Social and Economic Change in Tribal Areas* (Karachi: Oxford University Press, 1977). A Embree (ed.), *Pakistan's Western Borderlands* (Durham, N.C.: Carolina Academic Press, 1977). *Pakistan Forum*, special issue on Baluchistan, Ontario, Vol. III, May-June 1973, No. 9.

11. *Dawn Overseas*, October 27, 1979; *New York Times*, December 8, 1979; *New York Times*, December 22, 1979.

12. For Iran, see Shahram Chubin's "Leftist Forces in Iran," *Problems of Communism*, July/August 1980.

13. *Foreign Broadcasting Information Service*, (*FBIS*), South Asia, Vol. VIII, June 20, 1980; p. cl.

14. Ibid., p. c2.

15. *The Christian Science Monitor*, September 18, 1979, p. 3, and October 5, 1979, p. 4.

16. Akbar Khan, *Raiders in Kashmir*, Karachi, 1970.

17. For a detailed discussion of Pakistan's nuclear program and its implications see Zalmay Khalilzad, "Pakistan and the Bomb," *The Bulletin of the Atomic Scientists*, January 1980.

18. Albert Wohlstetter, et al, *Interests and Power in the Persian Gulf*, prepared for the Director of Net Assessment, Office of the Secretary of Defense, Los Angeles, 1980.

19. Zalmay Khalilzad, *The Return of the Great Game:* . . ., for a historical treatment of this problem in the region.

# Comments and Discussion

*Cottam* began the discussion by saying the paper was good and persuasive within an old paradigm that should be discarded. It appeared the lessons of Iran have not been learned, and they are terribly important. He was not talking of Islam and the internal situation, but of American capability. What Iran shows is that American capability in South Asia is slight. Since we are overextended, an entirely different strategy is called for.

Cottom thought the persistence of the old paradigm was due to a couple of things. First, we implicitly treat the Soviet Union as though it were Nazi Germany, but in our policy responses we treat her again and again as if she were Albania. As an example, the exclusion of the Soviet Union from the negotiations of the Israeli-Arab dispute was incredible: The seven-thousand-miles-away superpower excluding one five hundred miles away. Another example is the incredible provocation of the Soviet Union involved in America's Kurdish operation in 1971-75 in Iraq. It is fully documented since Daniel Schorr stole the documents and published them in the *Village Voice*. We know what we did. We treated the Soviet Union as though we could kick her in the shins in her own backyard. We apparently confuse a sluggishness on the Soviet Union's part with impotence. She *is* a superpower, capable of being terribly but sporadically aggressive as we have seen in Afghanistan. Her foreign policy bureaucracy looks like her economic bureaucracy—noninnovative and paralyzed, even idiotic on occasion. But it will respond in some situations intensely, and in her own backyard effectively.

What happened in Iran reflects the fact that we are now confronted with mass politics in the Middle East. When we initially went in, it was to an area without mass politics. It was perfectly simple to intervene at levels such as we did, for example, overthrowing Mossadegh; unfortunately we are still operating under the surrogate paradigm, which Khalilzad has. A surrogate will be sucked into creation; he is not created out of rational calculation beforehand. Zia could have easily become one. Sadat is one, Qabus (of Oman) is one; we continue to follow the old paths, even though we are suffering the shock of the loss of the Shah.

It is terribly important to throw away all of the nonsense that is being advanced that we could have saved the Shah: we could not have. We tried desperately to save him. Cottam thought the Carter administration was vulnerable on human rights policy in Iran—he disagreed with Fischer on that. But he did not think it vulnerable on its efforts to save the Shah. Ultimately the only way to have "saved him" would have been to depose him six or seven months earlier. Even then, we probably lacked the capability, because he had built his access to military units with the thought of avoiding a coup. Iran was lost because it is now a mass politics state we can no longer control.

On the other hand, Soviet power is declining as well. As Newell suggested, the costs to the Soviets of Afghanistan will be fantastic if they have to go to 300,000 troops. Cottam asked Yazdi when he was foreign minister how he felt about the 1,600 mile border with the Soviet Union. Yazdi replied that he did not think about it at all, because "the Soviets would not be crazy enough to invade us." He knew that it would take over a million soldiers to occupy Iran on a permanent basis.

The moral of the story is that we should recognize the growing strength of the regional powers, especially if they work together. They are actually in a position of deterring the Soviet Union, although the Soviet Union can conquer them if she wants to pay the price. Barring that, the regional powers can make the costs of staying in Afghanistan very high. What our declining power should lead us to do is supply the regional powers with whatever is necessary to defend themselves and aid the Afghans. But we should not aid the Afghans ourselves. The problem this avoids is that the Soviet Union is so afraid of the Sino-American alliance—and it is as paranoid about China as we were—that any kind of direct action on our part will dangerously exacerbate their fear.

Cottam thought the Islamabad conference of Muslim states was wonderful. Islamabad showed the willingness of the region to stand up and embarass the Soviets. Concentrating on persuading the people of the area to develop this unity would be much better than adhering to an old paradigm that leads to sailing ships back and forth in the Indian Ocean. (Cottam had never understood what they were supposed to accomplish.) We must give up the notion of playing with surrogates. Iran shows we cannot defend them when they come under severe attack from their own people, and ironically, they will come under severe attack precisely because of our role in keeping them in power.

*Newell* agreed with Cottam's general points, but felt less optimistic about the results of Islamabad. He thought it was the Islamic counterpart of the Carter policy, a lot of noise and thunder and very little action in terms of the specific case, Afghanistan. Nevertheless, if America has a role, it would seem to be in helping to focus and support the regional collective effort at security against the obviousness of the Russian threat. Without that, Russian pacification of Afghanistan would lead to a pervasive intimidation of regional powers that without overt military movements will disintegrate whatever is left of regional security after the pacification.

*Griffith* suggested that we should change the way we divide up the area for analytical and policy purposes. We should abandon the term "South Asia" and talk about those areas that are primarily concerned with the problems of the Persian Gulf and the Israeli-Arab dispute. This goes from Kabul to Casablanca. It leaves out India. India as Khalilzad suggested is bound to be generally hostile to our interests. We have no reason to want to drive the Indians into the hands of the Russians; we probably could not if we tried, except perhaps by trying to invade them. In general we should listen to Indian views minimally and disregard them almost totally, because their interests and ours are contrary.

Griffith disagreed with Cottam's assertion that the United States does not have the capability to involve itself in the affairs of the region. Our naval and air power in the region is at the moment superior to that of the Soviet Union. He thought the question really was intentions and desires. He disagreed with Cottam's policy, but also with what he took to be the policy of the people now coming to power in Washington. Clearly, for the next four years Cottam's policy will be the politics of the impossible. He thought the Reagan administration would follow about as opposite a policy as they could. He had no doubt they would overdo it, for they will not view the problems of the region with sophistication. Still, Griffith felt it ill becomes this country, and requires us to believe the French should not have aided us in the Revolutionary War, to say that it is contrary to either our interests or moral duty to send arms to Afghan rebels if the Afghan rebels want arms. Griffith thought we would not have become independent without arms aid from the French and eventually French troops. If one is opposed to arms aid in principle, then America should have remained dominated by the British. It is our moral duty and in our national interest to offer aid; we should leave it to the Afghans whether they think they are going to win the war, or whatever.

*Cottam* replied that he was not making a moral argument. He thought the issue should be thought of in terms of national interest. To the extent a moral question was involved he would like to help the Afghans. He agreed that Reagan would take the course Griffith outlined. He thought we would get another shock like the loss of the Shah. The result will be a helter-skelter movement of policy in the direction Cottam had suggested. Unfortunately, this will be far worse. Our friends and allies in the area will really be upset if they get even a chance indication of how weak our capability is in terms of interventions—and it is the interventions rather than ships sailing up and down that are important.

*Khalilzad* agreed with much of the latter part of Cottam's critique of his paper, but not his overall discussion at the beginning of paradigms. Whether in an old or new paradigm, it is important to protect the countries of the area from the Soviet threat. There is a Soviet threat. One does not have to view the Soviets as Nazis to believe they are capable of invading other countries. They have done it and are now in the process of pacifying a country. One does not have to think they have a master plan to believe they are a threat to United States interests. Having the capability to contain Soviet power in the area has to be an essential element of superpower rivalry. Without that capability Soviet pressure on countries in the region is likely to increase. There is already substantial Soviet pressure against both Iran and Pakistan.

Khalilzad said that although the balance of power concept is old, it still has a great deal of relevance. This is a separate argument from Cottam's discussion of the danger of surrogates. Iran was a devastating blow to the Nixon doctrine. The idea that others will look after our interests for us, and by relying on them we can handle regional problems, has been shown to be false. It is likely the United States will go for greater self-dependence in maintaining a counter to massive Soviet moves in the region. The concept of a rapid deployment force is really a response to the experience in Iran. We cannot depend on others to do the job; we need a capability for timely action on our own.

Khalilzad had not proposed that we give Pakistan arms and say, "Now you take care of regional security problems for us." But it is very important to coordinate efforts with countries that have common interests with the United States and see the threats the same way the United States does. Events in the Persian Gulf might even threaten the survival of NATO. If Iran, to take an extreme case, were to come under Soviet domination— which would not be easy because that would require more force than Afghanistan—we are not sure what the response of Western Europe and Japan would be. It is an alliance problem; the Turks are part of the NATO alliance and can help in redressing the military balance in the Persian Gulf. If we can coordinate stategies for use of facilities in the region, so much the better.

*Ahmad* wished to comment on the relation of the nature of the regime and the desirability of the United States offering assistance. In regard to Pakistan three things should be remembered:

1) In spite of all he has said and done Zia's regime was not the most repressive regime in the world, nor the most unpopular. Although it was military, Ahmad thought it less repressive than the recent civilian regime of Bhutto. (*Wriggins* agreed.)

2) On the question of U.S. military aid, as Khalilzad has pointed out, almost all important political groups agree that Pakistan must acquire military aid from the United States to ensure its territorial integrity. Even the Peoples Party agrees. Probably the only opposition would come from the Baluch leadership.

3) Unlike Iran, which has recently achieved mass participation, Pakistan is not a mass society in that sense. The formal foreign policy decision-making structure has continued from previous regimes, giving a great deal of continuity and relative stability in foreign policy throughout the country's existence. There are shifts, but not rapid shifts. Pakistan is not Iran; the structure is formalized and dependable. So it is not likely that a "Shah" will be created in Pakistan through aid.

With regard to India, the recent article in *The MERIP Reports* by Eqbal Ahmad contends that ultimately Pakistan will be pacified and become a Soviet satellite. This will lead to a Chinese-American-Indian alliance in the region because India is the only third world country with an independent national bourgoisie. Then the Indians will line up with the United States, while Pakistan will be neglected. If this scenario of Eqbal Ahmad is correct, Pakistan would prefer not to have the status of an East European country but to be integrated with the Soviet Union along with Afghanistan because Muslims will then constitute a majority.

On the point about mass politics making it tough for us, *Wriggins* wondered whether this meant that if there is mass politics we just have to bow out. He was troubled by this implication, but yet puzzled with how to deal with other people's mass politics.

*Harrison* thought mass politics an absolutely central issue. He agreed with the basic thrust of Cottam's critique. It seemed to him, though, that moral issues and national security interests overlap. If the basis of a Reagan administration program of substantial visible aid to the Afghan resistance is clearly and overtly to bleed the Russians or tie them down, if we are in a sense using the Afghans as pawns in a superpower game unrelated to a serious, credible, regionally conceived program of winding down the war in Afghanistan—getting the Russians out through a settlement—then what we would be doing in an era of mass politics would be alienating ourselves from millions of politically conscious people. They may decide they do not like us; that they do not like us just as much as they do not like the Russians. As a result they will make it impossible for any American policy to succeed. A secure environment in Southwest Asia requires the people to perceive American objectives as superior to

Soviet objectives. A foreign policy that ignores power, that ignores the dangers posed by the Soviet presence and as a result allows them to consolidate their position in Afghanistan would be unrealistic, but it would be equally unrealistic to think that military power is the only thing that is powerful. It is exceedingly important how a mass, politicized population feels about us, how they perceive our objectives, and assess what we are trying to do.

In spite of the distinction Cottam makes between our doing it and letting a regional power do it, Harrison pointed out the weapons would have to come from somewhere, and some of them would have to come from the United States or at least be facilitated by the United States. If directly linked with diplomatic effort, he was for a covert program; he was against a program with the America flag on it. He also wanted to repeat that we should not go in there "gung ho" with a big program. But if we are going to help the resistance in a way that is directed toward getting the Soviets out, our policy cannot include a major American program of assistance to Pakistan. It certainly cannot include facilities or anything that would resemble an alliance. It has to be based on understandings with the Soviet Union with respect to future American non-involvement in Pakistan and Iran. Pakistan is a highly politicized society and its political life has been radicalized in the last ten to twenty years. Pakistani public opinion does not want an American presence, it does not want an alignment, and it does not want to be a pawn in the superpower game. To the extent a popular consensus is possible it would be for a neutral Pakistan.

Answering Wriggins' question, Harrison thought that the era of mass politics meant that we could successfully pursue our foreign policy interests only in terms of what is acceptable to the public opinion in a country. In the long run only these policies work, whether it is Japan and the presence of American bases in Japan, or whatever it is. It means a lower American posture in some cases and higher in others—depending on what the domestic politics of that environment will support. Such an attitude is just as *Realpolitik* as thinking in terms of military power.

*Ahmad* added as a matter of information that a recent public opinion survey in Pakistan showed that the majority of the people are in favor—and this includes the people of Sind, the NWFP, and Baluchistan—of American assistance. Secondly, a survey he had conducted in 1975 and repeated in 1978 on a stratified sample of Ulema from all these provinces showed about eighty-five percent of the Ulema to be in favor of having friendly relations with the West as against the Soviet Union.

*Gastil* suggested that the moral question should be taken seriously. We helped the Kurds for a number of years, resulting in many deaths, and then withdrew as part of a political agreement between Iran and Iraq.

He could see us doing the same thing in Afghanistan. After helping the Afghans for a number of years, for one reason or another we might decide to stop. It would be said, and many Afghans would agree, that we were just sacrificing Afghans for our other interests. This is a real possibility in the situation.

Secondly, Gastil thought it a mistake to consider the Russian troubles in Afghanistan a paradigm for the troubles they would have in some of the other countries in the area. The Soviets could go through Pakistan much more easily than has been suggested. Once they get their tanks rolling they could quickly take the major cities. Historically, in a conventional, open engagement most countries do not stand up to big powers like the Soviet Union. Morale is very low in these circumstances. Once the Soviet tanks started pouring into Pakistan, Pakistan would find it hard to hold its army together. The peasants in every hamlet will not be shooting at the Russians. Iran is also not Afghanistan. Afghanistan is very rural; Iran is now fifty percent urban. Going through it with a modern army would not be that hard. Holding it in the long term is another issue. But Germany held Europe in World War II very successfully against many resistance movements; even in Yugoslavia they did not have that much trouble. They did not hold all the mountain tops but they did not need them. Their troop trains went through regularly. For many Soviet purposes Soviet military operations in Pakistan and Iran could be rapidly successful. After that, once they had established their victory, they could pull back and handle the area rather like Eastern Europe.

The people of Eastern Europe now know that the United States is not going to come in and help them. If the Soviet Union could establish with a few military operations in the Middle East that the United States would not effectively come to the aid of regional peoples, then they could establish sufficient control of the area to make its states satellites. So let us not assume that the mass political mobilization of a nation means that a modern army cannot take it and do what it wants—after all European countries have been mass mobilized for fifty years.

*Henze* suggested that if one wants to be relevant in the policy process and wants to give the administration advice that has some effect, one has to concern oneself with what are the most likely possibilities in the Middle East and not the least likely. One of the least likely is that the Soviets are itching to march across borders and invade other areas. This does not fit the history of the Soviet Union: its troops cross borders very exceptionally and reluctantly. They have gone into Eastern Europe in the post-World War II period only when things have fallen out of control to the point where there was no alternative. Afghanistan is another example. He saw little indication the Soviets have a preset plan to march into any other country. They know that military power is to be used to achieve political aims without its employment. It is employed only in desperation. For this reason the Soviets have not put vast numbers into Afghanistan. They are saving them for other situations. They have armed forces sitting on the borders in the Caucasus. They might want to go in and help their Azerbaijani brothers; there are many contingencies. But the notion they would like to take over Pakistan by military invasion is grotesque. If they want to take over Pakistan they will use all sorts of wiles and guiles—that is what the Soviet Union has always done.

At the other end of the spectrum, Henze found it equally unrealistic to postulate agreement with the Soviet Union when there is no remote sign that this is a possibility. If we build up an elaborate structure on the basis of the possibility that somehow we are going to negotiate the Soviets out of Afghanistan, we are just fooling ourselves. We are not being relevant. This is why by far the most likely of Newell's scenarios for Afghanistan over the next ten years is that we will not get the Soviets out and the Afghans will go on fighting. Such inconclusive struggles have characterized other areas of interest to the Soviets. The Soviets do not have the capacity or necessarily the will to bring the affair to a conclusion.

Henze thought it important to understand that the Soviet Union has never abandoned its concept of expansion. Along with an ideology that requires expansion, the Soviet Union is an empire. It is the last of the empires that were formed in the past few centuries. But it is an empire with a particularly rigid ideology, and its leaders know that when it stops moving forward it will start moving backward. This is a serious preoccupation of Soviet thinkers.

To them what goes on in Poland has an intimate relationship to what goes on in Afghanistan. It is not accidental that the Poles are as interested in Afghanistan as they are, and that Afghans are increasingly aware of Poland. These interconnections must be taken into account in schemes for a negotiated settlement in Afghanistan. We must always consider the problem the Soviet Union has in maintaining its own momentum, its own controls.

*Gastil* replied that he, Khalilzad, and Cottam had been discussing the basic lines of the military equation in the area—the worst case scenario. The European defense system is based on the improbable scenario of the Russians crashing across the borders of West Germany. The balance there, and the idea the Soviets could go quickly to the Channel unless we placed sufficient forces in between, is the basic fact European strategy is built around. (*Henze* disagrees.) In the Middle East the same thing is the case. Of course, the Russians do not intend to crash through to Karachi or Abadan tomorrow. On the other hand, how countries in the world look at their political-military relationships is based upon what could be done. Iran has always said to itself, "If the Russians come in, of course, the Americans will come in. This is what keeps the Russians from coming in, so we do not even need to put our troops on the Soviet border." If this is no longer the case, if it can no longer be assumed the Americans will come in, then that changes the whole Iranian approach to the situation. Gastil's disagreement with Cottam was that he did not believe that the defense situation had changed radically because the Iranians have a new defense system based on a politically mobilized mass population.

*Nabawi* commented that it is sometimes said the United States could not give aid directly to the armed resistance. No one is asking the Americans to stand on the Khyber Pass with tanks and planes. Clearly the United States would have to use covert means of aid. It should use the least obvious channels, but the most effective. Such channels, for example through friendly third countries, can surely be found.

But the basic issue remains: the Americans must make up their minds whether they want to support the armed struggle decisively and sincerely or not. If they determine that the armed struggle is not desirable and that they will not support it, it would be most humane to let it be known to the freedom fighters that they should follow another course. But the most important thing is to have a policy of some sort.

*Richter* said that Khalilzad's paper suggested ways of doing something and yet not doing too much. This raises two questions: what is the nature of the gap between overcommitment and undercommitment, and is there one gap or two? Is there a level of proper commitment below a massive buildup of Pakistan? Is undercommitment not helping Pakistan enough and is overcommitment too big an American presence? Richter wondered how Khalilzad conceived the proper level of aid to Pakistan relative to the Afghan situation.

*Khalilzad* said that what was of greatest importance was that the United States develop a military capability to contain Soviet power in the Persian Gulf. He was not talking about the United States having the ability to govern the area, but that it should be able to defend the area against a massive Soviet threat. The area is very unstable and fragmented. Things could happen, alliances could change internally. Invitations could be offered to, or acquired by, the Soviet Union to intervene. If the United States can redress the balance, then the amount of aid to particular countries to counter lower-level threats, such as the modernization of the Pakistan armed forces, need not be massive.

On the discussion as to whether aid to the resistance movement should be direct or indirect, although under the Carter administration the clear security commitment the Pakistanis wanted was unlikely, it was still possible to provide covert, indirect assistance to the Afghan resistance movement. Egypt was one source of arms, but there were several others with substantial Soviet arms. The Pakistanis themselves have pointed out these sources in conversation. They have said, "If you want a resistance movement, why not this and that from here and there." They have seen American arms under the present situation as too provocative. They have asked, "What next? If the Soviet pressure on Pakistan increased, what would the United States do for us then?"

The black market or free market for arms is substantial. Weapons are offered—for example, a hundred SAM-7's in Africa or Southeast Asia are available at a certain price. It is a financial problem, and the Pakistanis are very much aware of it. Perhaps they take their own cut of the money that is spent for such weapons. It is constantly pointed out that we should just give money to the resistance movement. There is nothing wrong with such indirect support.

In reply to Henze's doubt that an invasion of these countries was imminent, Khalilzad said he had not said there was such a plan. But the Soviets have a persistant interest. They would like to bring the area under greater Soviet influence, make it more sensitive to Soviet security needs, and servile if possible. With the internal conflict and fragmentation that have taken place in the region opportunities have arisen for greater Soviet influence. This is what happened in Afghanistan. A similar chain of events is plausible for other countries in the region. If this happened in Iran or Pakistan it would be much more important than in Afghanistan. So the United States' ability to deter such an invasion is very important.

Having said this, enumerating United States policy mistakes would take a long time. It was a mistake always to back dictators or monarchs rather than being more decisively associated with those groups with which we shared a world view. For each country we have to examine what forces are liberal, but this does not take the place of the overall need for a security structure.

Khalilzad did not think the United States needed a theory of victory at the beginning of an undertaking to help the Afghans. Things change. People are now fighting. At some level of cost the Soviets will accept a compromise. Determining that level depends on what one assumes Soviet ambitions to be in Afghanistan. Why did they come in? People disagree. Many believe that it is not of absolute importance to the USSR that they rule Afghanistan to the extent they do today, when even the speeches of diplomats going to the United Nations are written by the Soviets.

Assisting the Afghans may be sufficient. There are Afghans who will accept a compromise. They are not all saying that they will fight to the end. Gailani has said on many occasions that he would be willing to accept a compromise with the Soviet Union. If the Russians were interested in a compromise perhaps they could get one. So far, there is no sign the Soviets want a compromise. *Naby* mentioned that Gailani has turned out to be the butt of criticism by the resistance movement because of this. And yet the Soviet press has particularly picked on Gailani to discredit the whole resistance.

*Newell* suggested that any degree of aid to Pakistan beyond that directed toward guerrilla warfare would be canceled out by the Indian reaction. In this situation, we almost have to develop regional auspices for getting any equipment at all into Pakistan. Only this would dissuade India that there was an American-Pakistan alliance directed against them. (Several disagreed, wondering what India would actually do if it had this opinion.)

*Harrison* thought a key question was whether in the long run the continued existence of Pakistan became so repugnant to both India and the Soviet Union that the many vulnerabilities we have discussed could become a basis for intervention or subversion. At the moment India is keeping its hands off the Baluch issue; they have not supported Pathan separatists, and they do not want the Russians to come down into Pakistan. But if we carry Khalilzad's scenario to its ultimate conclusion of a three billion dollar aid program and an alliance structure, and China is brought in, the people in India who do not want Pakistan to continue to exist will reemerge. Pakistan is a vulnerable and fragile state. Harrison said one of the reasons he had been so interested in the Baluchistan issue was that he thought there was a real danger that the Indian position and attitude toward the existence of Pakistan might change in response to growing Sino-American-Pakistani military cooperation. Such a polarization might lead India to identify its interests with the Soviet Union.

*Newell* pointed out that as we think of collective action such as the Muslim conference, it is well to remember India is still oil-dependent on the Middle East. This gives the Islamic world leverage that could be used without us in the forefront. This allows us to support a multilateral program for Pakistan while avoiding the unilateral support that sooner or later would be counterproductive. The dynamics of the Indian reaction are irresistible, even if the present Indian government resisted them. The Indians say the Pakistanis have been putting their equipment on the Indian border. That is what they assume would happen again if more equipment went in to replace the obsolete equipment. So the amount and kind of aid and how it is given to Pakistan become crucial variables—just as crucial as what happens in terms of our goals for the Afghan resistance.

On the possible Indian reaction to helping Pakistan, *Ahmad* said we were forgetting that an alternative India is developing. During the Janata regime of Desai the relationship of Pakistan and India considerably improved. There still is a committee, formed by the Janata parliamentarians, in support of the freedom fighters in Afghanistan. Some Indians are coming to believe that a strong Pakistan is in the interest of India. It may be that the Indian protest against aid to Pakistan has become little more than a routine, almost reflex action. *Khalilzad* felt that in spite of changes in India, coordinating United States aid to Pakistan with India should not be a deciding factor. Indians are opposed to even small aid agreements with Pakistan. Pakistan would be very distressed to see the basis of United States support be the satisfaction of India. In this case Pakistan might even prefer the USSR to India. In addition, the relationship he had proposed between India and Pakistan would not include the establishment of bases or lead to a decisive shift in the military balance.

*Cottam* added a consideration that Henze may have overlooked in his view of Soviet reactions and expansionism—the example of the Soviet pull-out in Azerbaijan. After studying it at some length, he found the usual explanations for it to be romantic and unsatisfactory—Iranians outwitting them, Truman sending the Sixth Fleet into the Persian Gulf, and so on. The general American view is that by standing up and showing determination we got them out. In fact they pulled out because of cost-benefit. The costs would have been the long-term hostility of many peoples in the area, the loss of any goodwill they had built up in World War II, while the gains were insubstantial. It was American diplomacy at its best. George Allen was a magnificently complex and careful negotiator. His detachment was important in reducing the sense of capitalist encirclement— he did not threaten them at all. It is not beyond the realm of possibility that this could happen in Afghanistan. If the Soviets do not see a reason that is compelling for them to stay, the costs of their being there (in what seemed to Cottam an absurd place for them to be) would be so high, they might get out. This would be especially likely if they did not think the United States and China would profit enormously from their withdrawal. *Wriggins* suggested this reenforced Harrison's point of being able to design an overall posture in the region that was not threatening.

*Gastil* thought we should not forget that the withdrawal from Azerbaijan occurred after a world war that left the Soviet Union with tremendous problems in Europe it had not worked out. Now they feel much stronger. *Rakowska-Harmstone* agreed that there has been a change in the balance of forces since 1945. This change may tempt the Soviets to act quite differently. Perhaps they see themselves at an apogee of power before the United States revives, and they must act now. At the same time they are distracted by many problems, and certainly Poland is the first among these.

# Supporting the Evolution of Modern Civil Society from a Traditional Base

## Michael M. J. Fischer

The Iranian revolution of 1977-80 and the Soviet invasion of Afghanistan provide important moments to re-evaluate the social and political evolution of Central Asia and the Persian Gulf region so as to formulate medium-range and long-term foreign policies that are flexible and not merely reactive to crises, and that support indigenous aspirations for justice, equity, freedom and sense of identity. A viable foreign policy requires a re-evaluation not only of the interpretations of the native intellectual classes and of local political slogans and ideologies, but also of the relation between governments and their changing social bases. Only by adopting a dynamic, sociological perspective can we hope to foster values of freedom and social progress that encourage the development of societies naturally allied with our own highest principles.

Until the 1977-80 revolution, a fairly clear contrast could be drawn between the ideologies of development that guided the West in its days of transformation from monarchy to democracy, and those that guided development in Central Asia and the Persian Gulf region. In the West, development was thought to depend on the expansion of enfranchisement of ever larger portions of society so as to give more people a stake in the stability of society; development was linked to a political ideology of contractual law, democracy and free enterprise. The great paradigm was that of the French Revolution, in which the monarchy and nobility were replaced by the bourgeoisie and in time, the bourgeoisie would yield either gradually or through revolution to the participation of the proletariat or the people at large. In Central Asia and the Gulf, by contrast, development was explicitly linked to a different ideology: "revolution from above", "tutelage of the masses", non-democratic organization "to prepare society", single party "command structures", and the inculcation of discipline (as opposed to the internal, anxiety-generated discipline of the Western "protestant ethic"). (However, in the Arab and Persian world the theater of manners, the duality of personality, and individualistic suspicion of government prevent realization of efficient dictatorial models.)

To complete the picture three further issues require attention: (a) an analysis of the working class situation in these countries leads to questions of control and conservatism on the part of the ruling strata; (b) the analysis of the rising new professional classes leads to questions of constitutional change and replacement of royal and shaikhly family rule by technocrats; (c) the position of these economies within the world economy leads to native evaluations of the limited potential for liberal democracies to restructure society, and leads to considerations of the use either of Marxism or of an appeal to Islamic populism to mobilize the masses against perceived injustice on both domestic and international levels.

The Iranian revolution provides a kind of prism for these questions. The revolution is analyzed in Marxist terms as an "insurrection" with little program or organization. In this analysis Islamic populism serves the interests only of either reactionaries (the ulema) or a-revolutionary liberals (the bourgeoisie), both of whom would re-establish a form of economy and polity that would be not much different from what went before. The Islamic leaders in Iran, however, claim to see the revolution as a mass movement demanding a restructuring of society, channelled by Islamic values into a form which will provide a more just arrangement than what went before. Other observers see the revolution as a combination of these perspectives: beginning as a bourgeois revolution, it radicalized the masses and changed the consciousness of a generation; it therefore provides the basis for a stronger new polity, whatever the surface features of the government in the next few years. The revolutionary generation is young, largely literate, pro-technology, anti-scholastic puritanism and fundamentalism, but with a feeling that Islam provides a moral superiority to the corruption of the materialist modern West. There are those who would argue that the revolution—because of these sociological features—could have been finessed, had the Shah either provided for political modernization (and particularly in the final years of his reign, funnelled some of the money being spent on arms in other directions), or had the Shah been eased out in 1978 and power transferred to the bourgeoisie.

Whether or not the last suggestion could have been accomplished, whether or not revolutionary experiments with democratic forms such as workers committees will survive, social scientists and policy makers should consider how larger and larger groups of people can be given a stake in the sociopolitical systems of the Central Asian and Gulf states, rather than simply concerning themselves with the short-term survival of current regimes and elites. Anticommunism is all too often used to oppose progressive programs fostering social democracy, and not just to oppose Soviet imperialism: the two things should be kept separate. Sympathetic understanding of the Islamic revival is crucial to dealing with the class, generational, and cultural tensions and divisions in the Islamic world. But to simply support Islamic revival because it is anticommunist will be disastrous for the goals of developing a liberal civil society in which non-Muslims and secular Muslims can participate as full citizens.

## THE IRANIAN REVOLUTION AS PARADIGM

A number of factors need to be remembered about the Iranian revolution. First it did not spring out of nowhere: it was the fifth time since 1873 that secular reformers and religious leaders formed an alliance that was able to either force a major policy change or a change in the government itself. The 1906 Constitution and the 1952-53 nationalist and republican effort under Dr. Mohammad Mosaddeq are the two most important of these five, and, together with the beginning phase of the 1977-80 revolution, they may be considered attempts at classic bourgeois revolution. But only in the current revolution did the intellectual leadership of the alliance fall to the religious leaders. Part of the explanation was the success of the Pahlavi regime in suppressing open political discourse in the 1960s and 1970s, thus forcing all criticism into the language of religion. Islam became an umbrella language for a variety of different and opposed interest groups.

Second, it must be remembered that it is still too early to fully characterize the revolution: it is still in process. The first phases of the revolution fit fairly nicely the phases outlined by Crane Brinton for the English, American, French and Russian revolutions. A society that experienced a period of prosperity and rising standard of living was hit by a recession or depression that caused a financial squeeze on the government. Attempts at reform included exactions from leading sectors of society, which then turned against the government, thus adding support to oppositional ideologies that called the government illegitimate. As it loses legitimacy the government becomes so paralyzed it can no longer employ the forces of coercion normally available. The result is a surprisingly easy initial victory over the ancien regime. There follows a second phase of terror, dual sovereignty (a public government and a secret power structure), and a series of political crises that narrow the social base of the revolution. Eventually there is a long and painful phase of reconstruction, out of which a stronger state emerges with greater public mobilization, participation, or loyalty.

In the Iranian case, the 1973 oil price increases led to reckless spending (so that within eighteen months the government was over-committed and had to borrow on the international capital markets), a construction boom (which brought large numbers of rural people to seek jobs at wages that quadrupled rapidly), and inflation. The inflation was countered with recessionary policies that hit not only the new construction workers, but the middle class' real estate market, the entrepreneurs' rules of business (changing laws on foreign capital participation and requirements about selling public shares), the civil service (a continued freeze on wages that had not risen in three years), and the bazaar (made a scapegoat for the inflation). In 1975 there was a much resented attempt to introduce a single party state in which all adults were required to participate. These grievances provided a platform for the use of Islamic rhetoric denouncing the government as illegitimate, and the clerics became spokesmen for sectors of society more important than themselves.

The Pahlavi state found itself in the now classic position of having enormous revenues from oil that made it relatively independent of the need to respond to the demands of its citizenry: there was no direct relation between taxation and politics, the state could be independent. Instead of being liberating this proved self-defeating: the citizenry increasingly found its interests being subordinated to those of making Iran a military guarantor of oil supplies to the West.

Thirdly, it must be remembered that Iran is undergoing a demographic explosion: one half of the population is under seventeen. This young generation is well-disposed towards modern education and technology, but is also the carrier of a popular Islamic moral code and a demand to be full participants in modern society, not subordinated to second class status. Although this generation responded to the rhetoric of the clerics, and especially to the rhetoric of the story of the Battle of Karbala which provided the symbolism of struggle against political corruption and tyranny, its hero was Dr. Ali Shariati. Shariati called for a renewal of Islam, for casting off the centuries of Islamic stagnation and corruption, for turning away from the ritualism and archaism of the clerics, and for each Muslim taking upon himself the responsibility of helping to reinterpret Islam in the context of modern society.

The inability or refusal of the Shah to modernize the political system and to gradually incorporate more and more groups into the political decision-making structure was to prove an important part of his undoing. The problems were in at least four areas: the technocratic class, the industrial labor force, agriculture, and commerce:

(1) Iran had one of the most sophisticated and best educated elites in the Middle East. Various indices can be adduced from the 150,000 university students in the country in the 1970s, plus almost that many

again abroad, to the educational levels in the bureaucracy: of 401 directors-general in 1970, only two percent had less than a secondary education, 90 percent had at least a B.A., and 20 percent had Ph.D.s. Among parliament members, by 1941-63, 36 percent had B.A.s; in the 1963-67 parliament fully a third were educated in foreign universities, as were 90 percent of the cabinet ministers between 1965 and 1974. There was a problem of rapid growth of people with academic degrees beyond commensurate expansion of jobs; at the same time there was an insufficient number of mid-level managers in industry. The technocratic class felt misused and often bypassed in favor of foreign experts. The attempt to create cells to debate policy within the state-controlled Mardom (later Rastakhiz) party was not felt to be serious nor a sufficient outlet for their creative energies.

(2) More important than the raw figures on industrial labor force growth, was the refusal to allow independent labor organization. Reliance was placed on government organized syndicates and paternalistic management. Productivity and quality control were sacrificed to these techniques of control. No effort was made to give industrial workers a political stake in their economic contributions. Connections with international union organizations were frowned upon. When strikes occurred the news media were not allowed to cover them, managers were forced to accede to workers demands, and strike leaders were jailed: political quiescence was the primary objective. An attempt in the mid-1970s was made to give workers a share in productivity by selling them public shares in major industries; however, this program turned out to be largely a sham, the shares being held in trust for workers by a state corporation.

(3) Investment in agriculture was funneled away from small producers toward large mechanized agricultural projects, dependent on large irrigation dams, that squeezed many peasants off the land. The most glaring example was the Dez Irrigation Project in Khuzistan. An alternative agricultural policy of raising producer prices and supplying credit to stimulate production might not only have avoided some of the massive imports of food, but more importantly might have given a political stake to a viable peasantry.

(4) Rather than expanding access to cheap commercial credit, policy was directed to structuring oligopolistic control of major foreign trade opportunities through licensing procedures, and of major industrial enterprises through a very conservative banking policy. Small businesses remained dependent upon the bazaar credit system. The bazaar in turn, rather than being honored for its important distribution and investment mechanisms, was attacked as something dangerous because it was not under direct political control. The attempt to set up a state-guided guild

system (through which the punitive price campaign of 1975-77 was organized) cannot but have helped stimulate the financing of the anti-Shah movement of the following year. Modern entrepreneurs also felt they were increasingly at the mercy of a capriciously changing business climate, when in the mid 1970s laws on foreign capital participation and on the sale of public shares were changed. At the same time levels of corruption began to escalate.

In sum, Iran displayed three patterns:

(a) an alienation between government and citizenry grounded in the freedom from accountability provided by massive oil revenues funneled directly to the government, rather than by way of taxation from productive activities. As in other oil producing countries, Iran suffered from the paradoxes that the oil industry provided relatively little multiplier effect or backward linkages into the domestic economy and employed relatively few people directly; yet it provided massive funding to the government.

(b) the vicious cycle in an authoritarian monarchy of innovation from above destroying local initiative and self-reliance on which self-sustaining economic growth and political maturity depend in the name of speeding development and protecting against reaction.

(c) an inability to institutionalize and domesticate constructive criticism of government policies so that they could become self-correcting and reduce the dislocations and alienations inevitable in situations of rapid change.

American foreign policy might have been able to help by insisting on considerations of political maturation and social criticism, rather than acceding to the Shah's demands for praise or silence. Most specifically the activities of SAVAK and the lack of due process should not have been ignored.

Reconstruction after a revolutionary explosion is always a difficult affair. American foreign policy might turn from considering revolution as simply a dangerous, uncouth activity likely to play into Soviet hands, and rather pick up the slogans of the revolution which were progressive. Among these were constitutional rule, decentralization, workers committees, regional autonomy, redistribution of wealth and land, due process of law, and rejection of subordinating Iranian domestic development to the goals of securing oil supplies to the West. Regarding the last, we should make it plain that we see the development of justice and equity in the domestic Iranian polity a crucial component of the security of the Gulf. We should encourage those international linkages that foster progressive social and economic development: associate membership in the EEC, association of Iranian unions with international unions, involvement of Iranian social democrats with European social democrats (the slap that former Prime Minister Callaghan gave the National Front in 1978 was unforgiveable), the strengthened association of Iranian and international human rights organizations, the monitoring of minority rights, the open discussion of means of increasing regional autonomy within a national union. If we are serious about supporting tolerant Islam, we might consider radio broadcasts that discuss Islam in a scholarly and informed way; if, however, it is used in a heavy-handed propagandistic manner, it will be used against us.

## THE PERSIAN GULF

Similar patterns are to be observed in even more dramatic, inequitable, and skewed forms in Saudi Arabia, Oman, Kuwait, Bahrain, and the Emirates: again the working classes (complicated by the overwhelming numbers of guest workers) are dealt with in terms of control rather than incorporation, and there is a slow shift to more technocratic decision making at the top of the system (away from single-family rule).

*Labor Organization.* So far most of the oil industries in the Gulf have successfully prevented the development of open union negotiations and often retracted offers of other forms of contractual arbitration. In Bahrain in 1954-56 the Committee for National Union led strikes for improved working conditions, unions, government reform, a lessened British role, and individual freedoms. The CNU briefly gained recognition from the shaikh to negotiate for the workers, and while this recognition was later withdrawn, the agitation eventually achieved the drafting of a labor ordinance in 1958. As soon as the government regained full control in 1956, the CNU was suppressed, its press closed, and three of its leaders exiled. Nakhleh argues that the refusal of the authorities to be more flexible toward their workers has driven labor to politicize its demands. Every labor strike becomes joined to calls for freedom of speech, assembly, press, release of political prisoners, removal of expatriates, and overthrow of the government. Labor leaders and journalists who support them regularly are jailed or exiled.

The two most liberal states are Qatar and Kuwait: Qatar allows workers' committees to help handle grievances; Kuwait allows unions, but only for persons employed in the same job at least five years; no non-Kuwaiti may be an officer. Very little study of labor organization has been allowed or made public. Both Iran and Saudi Arabia have used psychological tests to stabilize their oil labor forces, and there may well be interesting problems of social and psychological adjustment in training preindustrial labor for industrial jobs. In the Aramco case, however, at least as important seems to be that instead of using bedouin labor, the company turned to Shiite minority (more docile?) labor.

Much of the Gulf labor force is imported; it is argued that workers are given little security in order to keep them docile and to make them difficult to organize by leftists. High barriers on eligibility for citizenship and ownership of property by aliens characterize all the Gulf states. They fear that to liberalize labor negotiation procedures and citizenship requirements would lead to the takeover of the political arena by foreigners. In 1975 there were as many Yemenis working in Saudi Arabia as there were Saudi adult males; as much as a quarter or a third of the total population was foreign. Of Qatar's labor force, 40,000 of the 48,000 members are non-Qatari. Over one-third of the United Arab Emirate's total population is foreign, 64 percent of Abu Dhabi's population, and over half of Kuwait's; three quarters of the labor force in these places is foreign. Only 20 percent of Bahrain's population, but 37 percent of its labor force is foreign. Before the revolution Iran had well over 60,000 foreigners, and Iraq had some 30,000 Egyptians alone. Normal abuses of foreign labor are best documented for Kuwait: compelling illegal aliens to pay a percentage of their earnings to contractors so as not to be deported; crowding; deporting aliens for minor scrapes with the law; and restricting their access to the welfare system. State education in Kuwait is free, but only ten percent of the student body may be non-Kuwaiti.

*Constitutional Change.* If an analysis of the working class situation leads to questions of control and conservatism by the ruling strata, the analysis of the rising new professional class leads to questions of constitutional change and replacement of shaikhly family rule by technocrats. Rugh (1973) provides a summary of changes in the elite of Saudi Arabia. In the 1950s only one ministerial post was not held by a royal prince or a protege of the family: the Minister of Commerce was from a Jeddah merchant family. In 1960 King Saud gave five ministerial posts to commoners educated abroad (four in Cairo and one in Texas); five posts were held by princes and one by a member of the al-Shaikh family descended from the founder of Wahhabism. In 1969, under King Faisal, of 189 top bureaucratic posts (grade 2 and up), 45 had Western training, 111 had Arabic secular training, and only 31 had traditional religious education. In 1970-71, the Grand Mufti of the al-Shaikh family died and was replaced by a minister of justice from the ranks of the Jeddah judges. Only the Ministry of Education was still held by an al-Shaikh family member, but his two deputies were American educated (a B.A. and a Ph.D.).

The smaller Gulf states are also undergoing a transition from rule by shaikhly families, sometimes in concert with merchant families (as in Kuwait), to more technocratically trained elites, but they are further behind. The UAE has retained Jordanian, Sudanese, and Iraqi judges until local ones can be trained. Abu Dhabi relies heavily on Indian and Pakistani administrators, and Qatar's teachers are largely Egyptian.

These changes include pressures towards representative constitutional rule and away from more informal consultations by shaikhs. The majlis of the governor of Hofuf in Saudi Arabia has shifted from a predominance of tribal chiefs to merchants. In Kuwait, a parliament existed from 1962 to 1975 (when Palestinian agitation threatened its stability). In Bahrain, strikes and demonstrations since the 1950s gradually expanded the representation of Shiites and commoners in the top ranks of government; in 1972 and 1973 elections were held for a constituent assembly and subsequently a national assembly; the latter was dissolved in 1975 when the government failed in its attempt to pass a security law. Qatar in 1970 became the first of the emirates to have a written constitution, but the assembly was not instituted. All of these consultative forms have had extremely limited power and autonomy, yet their very existence in the hostile environment of rulers reluctant to delegate power serves as an indicator of shifts in social power.

A more sensitive index would be a careful analysis of the circles and clubs to which active members of society belong and which form a kind of shadow influence network. In Saudi Arabia, while three named opposition groups have existed since 1956, and a spectacular armed insurrection was attempted by seizing the grand mosque of Mecca last year on the first day of the new Islamic century, these have so far proved ineffective; more effective has been the constant pressure of notable and merchant families in the Hijaz (anti-Wahhabi puritanism, pro-liberalization) and the slowly growing cadre of educated professionals.

Of the countries bordering on the Gulf, before 1977 only Iraq had seen a social revolution in the class origin of its rulers: even in the 1920s the nationalists who exercised much influence often came from the middle or lower-middle classes, educated in Istanbul; since 1958 the leadership has been strongly middle class by both criteria of one's father's occupation and one's own education. Thirty-six percent of the 177 member top elite were educated abroad, 28 percent were educated at the Military Academy, and 22 percent at the Baghdad Law College. Yet Iraq has had difficulty undertaking the radical reforms called for in its Baathist ideology. Part of the problem again is control. Iraq is divided into three ethnic groups: 55 percent are Shiite Arabs, 24 percent are Sunni Arabs, and 20 percent are Kurds. The Sunni Arabs dominate the political arena, having controlled half the political posts since 1958 and 80 percent of the top posts. This dominance is a perpetuation of the favoritism shown by the Ottomans to their coreligionists in the last century. The regime is thus authoritarian, with ethnic competition complicating party alliances and the dislocations of modernization.

Finally there is the case of Oman and the Dhofar rebellion. Against a sultan opposed to any progress, the revolutionary movement attempted a wide range of development initiatives: two schools with 850 students by 1973, one-quarter of them female; the organization of agricultural cooperatives with modern agricultural techniques; a clinic manned by a Syrian doctor; local-level councils to mediate disputes; a mass-education campaign stressing socialism, the need for revolutionary struggle, equality of women; as well as fighting a guerrilla war. The leadership seems to have been university educated in Beirut, Egypt and Kuwait; others had foreign guerrilla training; much of the social support came from the many Dhofaris who could find work in the Gulf but not at home. This is not the place to review the story of how the rebellion was competitively supported by the Russians and the Chinese, then crushed with the support of Saudi Arabia, Jordan and Iran; but rather to point out a measure of political consciousness and a pool of emigrant labor (for example, 30,000 Omanis are listed in the Kuwait and Bahrain censuses) that can be called upon.

One thing that a survey of leftist oppositional groups in the region teaches us is the relative weakness of the middle classes, who provide the intelligentsia for these groups, as well as the weakness of the working-class organizations that are supposed to provide the rank and file. More detailed studies than have yet been attempted are required to illuminate the contradictions and dialectical adjustments between ideological positions, status, and social power. Lenczowski, for instance, commented in 1947 about the Iranian Tudeh, that, both in opposition and after seizing power in Azerbaijan, their demands were liberal not revolutionary: liberal labor legislation, legalization of unions, better peasant conditions, free education and health care, equality for minorities and women, judicial reform, constitutional government—but not nationalization of property nor collectivization. In Azerbaijan only absentee landlords were expropriated; there was no general land reform. The Shah attempted to coopt the most pressing demands of his critics: land reform, state farms, nationalization of forests and water resources, expansion of health care and education, equality for minorities and women. In Iraq, some of the contradictions are clearest: a ruling alliance of Baathists (and from time to time communists) is but a thin veneer over sharp ethnic group competition. The original Baath hope to use a generalized Islam as a rallying slogan for pan-Arabism (formulated by Michel Aflaq, a Greek Orthodox Christian) is rejected in Iraq as the Sunni Islam of the dominant politicians from the area around Takrit; similarly the communists are split into a pro-Moscow faction and a Shi'a, southern supported, pro-Peking faction.

It should be clear that the ideological drama of the Persian Gulf is not simply Western-trained technocrats attempting to steer a steady course between reactionary Islam and revolutionary Marxism. Reality is more complex. There is a legacy of at least four varieties of Islam associated with states in the history of the Gulf: Twelver Shiism with Iran, Wahhabism with Saudi Arabia, Sunnism with the Ottomans, and Ibadism with Oman. Still today the Gulf littoral is a checkerboard of confessional communities with complex networks of communication and identity. Islamic rhetoric is often conservative and opposed to "atheistic" modernism, but it also is a potent protest idiom against imperialism, often melding with the similar Marxist idiom. In Oman the rebels in PFLOAG were militantly atheistic, thereby alienating much potential support. In Iran modernist interpretations of Islam compete with more traditional ones. It is important to recognize that the uses to which the political elites, religious leaderships, and local populations put Islamic rhetorics are often in contradiction: indeed, differences in religious style are good indices of social cleavages in society. Foreigners attempting to engage these rhetorics need to be aware of their nuances and implications.

## Soviet Central Asia

A review of the history of Russian involvement in Central Asia leads to the question of whether the changes brought about there are structurally different, more effective, or more humane than those occurring in Iran or the Persian Gulf region. One major ideological issue is that the Soviet Union aggressively propagates a notion of social progress, a future-oriented vision of the historical process. Islam is one element in Central Asian anti-Russian nationalism, but it has yet to be demonstrated that Central Asians see Iran or Afghanistan as viable alternatives rather than simply backward country cousins.

A review of the political-economic effects of Russian advance into Central Asia since the nineteenth century suggests that they had much in common with the effects of the free world economy on other Middle Eastern countries. Both included the introduction of private property leading initially to the rich becoming landlords of former tribal lands; redistribution of agricultural land to peasants encountering problems with credit and indebtedness; inability of governments to settle nomads satisfactorily by force and the governments' rediscovery of nomadism as an efficient pastoral strategy; subordination of peripheral regions to capital centers first by unequal mercantile exchange rates (initially Tatar merchants backed by Russia, then Russian merchants), then by imposition of cash taxation, and expansion of industrial crops (cotton) at the expense of local food production; use of women's liberation as a means of destroying local autonomy and political alliance structures; and use of linguistic policies to reduce regional autonomy.

In the past decade Central Asia has been characterized by rapid demographic increase, the refusal of its inhabitants to migrate either to large cities or to labor-hungry Russia and Siberia (causing industry to be brought rather to them), and hints of increasing ethnic and cultural consciousness and competition with Russians for upper level jobs. In the decade 1959-69, while the overall Soviet growth rate was 16 percent, that of the Muslim population was 42 percent. In the following decade, 1969-79, the Muslim population grew from 35 to 43 million. While the Russian and Ukrainian populations are aging, half the Central Asian populations are under the age of fifteen. Increasingly the cohort of young men available to the army are rural non-Slavic recruits; eventually this may mean increasing numbers of non-Slavic officers or conflict over their exclusion, although for the time being few Central Asians voluntarily choose military careers.

Analysts have sensed such conflict already in the technocratic and party elite ("scientific workers" in Soviet jargon). In Uzbekistan, for instance, the most populous of the Central Asian republics, affirmative action to bring natives into the governing structure (korenizatsiia or nativization) has raised the percentage of native "scientific workers" from 14 percent in 1947 to 48 percent in 1975 (from 568 to 14,821 persons). As economic growth slows after a period of rapid expansion, competition is increasing, with natives in high positions preventing the upward mobility of Europeans and attempting to replace Russians with native Central Asians. There have also been some anti-Russian riots for the first time since the 1920s.

Bennigsen suggests that clan and tribal affiliations are still sufficiently psychologically important that they give local communist and governmental organizations "a curious and unexpected familial (mafia-type) character." This together with the underground Sufi brotherhoods and the reemergence of cultural pride asserted through rehabilitation of Arabic, Turkish, and Persian literature and philosophy provides an anti-Slavic nexus difficult for Russians or the Soviet secret police to infiltrate and control. The conflict of these ethnic identity processes with Soviet goals of cultural rapprochement (sblizeniye) and fusion (sliyaniye) is by no means unique to the Soviet Union, nor is the effort of the Russians to maintain hegemony at the expense of these same goals.

## CONCLUSIONS

The preceding surveys argue against basing a long-term foreign policy on either simple calculations about the survivability of current regimes and elites or on the contemporary impetus to Islamic fundamentalism given by the Iranian revolution. A secure and flexible foreign policy must be based on a sociological and anthropological understanding of the social changes these societies are undergoing and the adjustments that the politics will need to make to these changes. Iran presents a clear case where an ossified and rigid foreign policy was unable to cope with obvious social transformation; hence there was no ability to conceive of or plan for a post-Shah Iran. Although some variables such as that of foreign workers are very different, Iran presents a paradigmatic case— the sociologically most developed case—that we must plan for social changes. Soviet Central Asia presents similar problems (ethnicity, regional autonomy within a national structure, abridgment of individual rights in the service of progress, interface between traditional communal forms of organization and bureaucracy); if the USSR remains in Afghanistan, we will see Soviet solutions being applied there.

A sociological understanding is important for dealing with the century-old Islamic modernist set of movements. Islam—including Islamic modernism—is not a worked out political program; there are slogans, values, and key terms common to all Islamic movements. Egypt and Pakistan are the national arenas where there has been the most experimentation theoretically and institutionally with what an Islamic state, an Islamic economics, Islamic justice, the role of women and minorities in an Islamic milieu might be. But even in these countries it is tentative and programmatic. Analyses of the role of Islamic movements, be they in Iran, Pakistan, Egypt, or the Sudan, depend upon sociological context to make sense and to prepare for future contingencies.

Political institutions to foster the goals of enfranchisement, civil society, protection of individual and communal rights, and due process of law need discussion. There should be more analysis of the advantages and failures of Pakistan's experiments with basic democracies and parliamentary formulae; Turkey's experiments with constitutions and the problems of proportional representation and fragmented executive coalitions which result; and of course Iran's experiments with constitutionalism.

Finally the cultural analysis of Islamic discourse needs to recognize the parameters of debate within Islam, rather than naively looking for the single true Islamic position. For example, in Islamic economics, the debate revolves around the prohibition of *reba'* (usury): some legal experts insist this means all forms of interest, others only exorbitant interest (the distinction between just and unjust return on capital drawn by medieval Christians and Jews). There are various ways around interest, some traditional so-called "lawful deceits" or loans of goodness or other devices of equity banking where the risk of an enterprise is shared between supplier of capital and user of capital. At issue are philosophical principles of equity and justice. As in laissez-faire capitalism, the system can only work if the knowledge and volition of partners to any transaction is ensured, and so there are various rules of fair price, allowing return of a commodity if the price was unfair. But as in socialism, property ultimately belongs not to individuals but to God or the community, thus allowing for social intervention and guaranteeing of fair practices and communal interests. The individual has usufruct rights to property. Inequities that build up over time are subject to redistribution through the Islamic taxation system. There is nothing here that in principle is antagonistic to modern economic systems.

Similarly in the Iranian debate about the nature of an Islamic constitution, the debate revolves around the notions of *mashrutiyat mashrue*, from the Arabic root *shart* "condition": a constitution conditioned by the Quran. The Quran says (Sura Nesa 62): Oh ye who believe, obey God, obey the Prophet, and obey the *ulil amr* ("issuer of orders"). In Shiism the last are interpreted to be the Imams; but since the last went into occultation, leadership falls to those who are informed. Every Muslim ought to inform himself as best he can; with increasing literacy and sophistication, it will become increasingly difficult for the clergy to claim special expertise in matters where religious interpretation overlaps with practical affairs. Already since 1962 a group within the clergy as well as interested laymen have pointed out the incompetences of the traditional clergy, and have demanded specialized training for the ulema and the updating of interpretations. Ayatullah Shariatmadari has consistently supported democratic procedures during the revolution, and Ayatullah Khomeini more recently also seems to have come to value constitutionalism.

Insofar as we have a role to play in encouraging political developments in Iran and Central Asia, we should listen and respond in informed fashion, pointing out problems and potential solutions. Our ability to do this is increased by the availability of the electronic media, which we should not attempt to monopolize in a one-sided fashion—we might, for example, encourage Iranians and others to produce films about their situations that can be shown to us. More traditional devices of diplomacy, scholarly exchanges, educational exchanges, also need to be used. Monitoring of civil rights and due process needs to be encouraged, as do evaluations of development projects.

## SOURCES

Portions of this paper have been taken from the following:
Fischer, M. M. J. "Competing Ideologies and Social Structure in the Persian Gulf" in A. Cottrell, ed. *The Persian Gulf States* (Baltimore: Johns Hopkins University Press, 1980).

Fischer, M. M. J. "Introduction", to Elizabeth Bacon's *Central Asians under Russian Rule* (Ithaca: Cornell University Press, 1980).

Expansion of some of the themes of this paper may also be found in:

Fischer, M. M. J. "Persian Society: Transition and Strain" in H. Amirsadeghi & R. W. Ferrier, ed. *Twentieth Century Iran* (London: Heinemann, 1977).

Fischer, M. M. J. "Legal Postulates in Flux: Justice, Wit & Hierarchy in Iran" in D. Dwyer, ed. *The Politics of Law in the Middle East* (forthcoming).

Fischer, M. M. J. *Iran: From Religious Dispute to Revolution* (Cambridge: Harvard University Press, 1980).

Fischer, M. M. J. (with others). The Social Impact of Development on Ethnic Minorities: Iran, Afghanistan, the Sudan, Brazil. Cultural Survival.

Akhavi, Shahrough, *Religion and State in Contemporary Iran* (Albany: State University of New York Press, 1980).

Bennigsen, Alexandre, "The Nature of Ethnic Consciousness in Soviet Central Asia." Paper delivered at the Conference on Soviet Central Asia: Trends and Changes, International Communication Agency, Washington, D.C., 1978.

Gilsenan, Michael, *Saint and Sufi in Modern Egypt* (New York: Oxford University Press, 1973).

Holt, P. M., *The Mahdist State in the Sudan* (London: Oxford University Press, 1958).

Marr, P., "The Political Elite in Iraq" in G. Lenczowski, ed. *Political Elites in the Middle East* (Washington, D.C.: American Enterprise Institute, 1975).

Mitchell, R. P., *The Society of Muslim Brothers* (New York: Oxford University Press, 1969).

Richter, William L., "The Political Dynamics of Islamic Resurgence in Pakistan," *Asian Survey* 1979 (19:6).

Rugh, William, "Emergence of a New Middle Class in Saudi Arabia" *Middle East Journal* 27 (1): 7-20, 1973.

Warburg, Gabriel, *Islam, Nationalism, and Communism in a Traditional Society: The Case of Sudan* (London: F. Cass, 1978).

# Comments and Discussion

In presenting his paper *Fischer* added that the Soviets have been able to project an ideology built around the notion of social progress and future orientation. Surely we ought to be able to come up with an equivalent ideology that does all this *and* adds the notion of freedom. One can achieve progress with freedom without indiscriminately destroying religion or tradition, and without allowing the conservative or reactionary Muslims to set the agenda for how Islam is modernized, transformed, or utilized in the contemporary scene. Previous speakers had suggested that perhaps freedom should be defined somewhat differently within Islamic societies than in the West. Fischer would disagree. The definitions we have in the West are still appropriate. There are liberal wings of the Islamic movement supporting these definitions, and they need to be supported.

Fischer raised a problem of ideology for the intellectual classes of these countries. He finds the best statement of the problem in a book by Abdullah Laroui called *The Crisis Of the Arab Intellectual* (University of California, 1976), in which he states the position in very simple terms. He says that the Arabs had tried liberal democracy. Liberal democracy did not work. Laroui refers to the example of the parliament in Egypt. He thinks liberal democracy cannot restructure society. It cannot restructure the position of these economies within the world economy. It cannot restructure the subordinate legal status of smaller countries within the international legal order. (The latter is the argument the Iranians made: the United States because of its strong power has the ability to intervene against international law and no one says anything, so we need to take the hostages to make the point.) If democracy is not developed in these countries to accommodate change, then Laroui believes the intellectuals have two choices. One is to turn to revolutionary

Marxism-Leninism, develop a cadre, wait for a revolutionary opportunity, and try to seize control. The more backward the country, the more totalitarian the resulting regime will be. The other option is to attempt to utilize populist Islam as a means of mobilizing the masses against perceived injustices.

What can we do about all this? Probably not much in Iran—the horse has left the barn. But in the long term we can certainly pick up and support the progressive slogans of the revolution, things like constitutionalism and decentralization. We can talk about the different democratic experiments that have been tried (such as workers' committees), talk about regional autonomy within a national union, about due process of law (which was one of the key slogans of the first year of revolution).

As an aside Fischer thought it needed to be emphasized that all too often we project from what has gone on in the revolutionary courts since 1978 to a vision of an Islamic State. This is probably wrong. What is going on in the revolutionary courts probably has more to do with a revolutionary set of courts than it has to do with Islamic justice. There has been a series of very interesting struggles centered around the courts; even the clergy has objected to many executions and failures of due process. There have also been times when struggles between the revolutionary factions were less severe, and increasing attention was paid to due process procedures. There was initially very swift "justice"; now review procedures have been introduced. However, when conflict between factions increases, factions begin to use executions as a way of flexing their muscles. Just before the second round of elections to the parliament there was a series of highly symbolic executions—for example, seven Bahais and a family of Jewish hotel keepers were arrested and put on trial.

Fischer remarked that Gastil had distinguished between the theory of Islam and the legacy of the centuries, and that we have to deal with this legacy. Judaism and Christianity also have historical legacies that they have managed to transform. Islam is going through a similar process and perhaps we can help this along. We should be playing up the opinions of people like Teleqani, Shariatmadari, Shariati, and holding these up as a kind of mirror.

Finally, if Richter were right that most people in Pakistan would like some kind of transition to elections at this point, and Zia is the block to that, Fischer wondered if there were mechanisms whereby we could both support the integrity of Pakistan and at the same time encourage the country to move toward democracy.

On the question of Islamic history versus doctrine, *Gastil* said the point was precisely that what we think of as the Christian heritage now is actually based on a nineteenth century evolution of Christian thinking. It is not based on Jesus Christ or the Old Testament. These are not what informs our attitude toward Christianity and politics, but rather recent Christian history and Christian thinking. Similarly for Islamic countries, it is only partly relevant to repeat what the Quran or hadith had to say about these issues. We also need to know what the recent relation of Islam and politics has been, for this will play a major role in what happens. *Fischer* agrees, but points out we still have fundamentalist groups in our society that talk about Jesus Christ in a more traditional fashion, and we have learned how to provide a role for them without allowing them to take over.

*Griffith* commented that he would not call Shariati tolerant. He was rather radical. He was trying to assimilate some aspects of Marxism to an egalitarian, radical, Islam; Khomeini is far more traditionalist. In that sense, so far not only have the Tudeh, Fedayin, Mujahidin, and National Front been defeated, but the ideas of Shariati have been defeated, too. *Fischer* disagreed radically with that. *Griffith* agreed the ideas were certainly alive, but Khomeini was not in favor of them, and he rules. *Cottam* said Khomeini is radical.

*Gastil* asked whether we could say the distinction is between Islam as defined by the layman, and Islam as defined by the clergy. Isn't this the distinction of the Shariati group from Khomeini's? *Fischer* said that in a broad sense this is true, but with crossovers. Shariatmadari who before the revolution would certainly be put in the conservative camp has in the course of the revolution come out on the side of constitutional procedures at critical junctures.

In regard to the question of the relative importance of Islamic texts and history, *Ahmad* said there were of course different readings of both. One of the purposes of fundamentalism is to transcend history and go back to the original texts of Islam. They see Islamic history as the history of the orthodox caliphate. However, their view and perception of what happened then is highly idealized and romanticized. (This is, then, more theology than history.) Maulana Maudoodi's reading of the early caliphate and the distinction between the caliphate and monarchy is very well expressed in his book, *Caliphate and Monarchy*. His reading of the period is totally different from that of the orthodoxy. He reads much more democratic and liberal practices into it—electoral procedures, accountability of the caliph to the people, freedom of expression, protection of life, liberty and honor. The orthodox see the period as more authoritarian.

Ali Shariati is much more complex than Khomeini, who is very simple and straightforward. In Shariati French structuralism, existentialism, and Leninism are mixed together with a post-fundamentalist, basically eclectic Islam. But it is much more appealing to youth and to diverse ideological orientations within Islam.

*Cottam* thought the long-term, sociological trends Fischer discussed needed further examination. He argued correctly that we should do what we can to support trends toward the kind of world society that we would like to see. However, unless there is a decision-maker with extraordinary decisional latitude, it is naive to believe that foreign policy anywhere is going to address these questions. Even when you have someone with extraordinary decisional latitude (like Kissinger or Hitler), you still do not get an addressing of long-range trends.

Fischer has correctly played the role of the academic, a role in which we have failed in the past. We are the ones with the time and perspective to look at the long-range trends and to think of where foreign policy is going.

The failure to do the long-range analysis is the story of the last academic generation. The academic is culpable; our modernization literature is testimony to that. It is largely a literature based on immediate foreign-policy need. Cottam believed it was essentially ideological, and left out most of the points Fischer made. Trend analysis is very important for us to do. What we must do as well is relate it to a process of translation in a way that the practitioners would find not just pie-in-the-sky, as they see most of our stuff.

*Gastil* reported a personal experience on the problem of analyzing long-range policy. Four or five years ago he proposed to the Department of Defense a study of the long-range interests of Iran after the Shah. ''The Shah won't be there forever and we should analyze the interests of Iran without the Shah; to what extent were his interests the interests of Iran.'' They played with the proposal for a while but finally said it was just too dangerous. It would get back to the Shah, he would get very upset, and the research was not worth it. Of course, thinking about it now, Gastil said the study would never have imagined a government with the interests of Khomeini. So it would not have been all that helpful. *Fischer* said that was only if we assume that the Khomeini regime we have now will continue indefinitely.

*Gastil* added that one of the reasons academics with their long-range projections are not listened to is that projections are very hard to do well. *Fischer* thought one of the reasons we have the current outcome is because we did not do this sort of thing. He referred to the argument in his paper that as late as the summer of 1978 we might have helped mid-wife a different transition. Clearly, long before that we could have started talking about transition and perhaps aided transition to a middle class government. *Gastil* said that we make this assumption, but it may well have been that the Khomeini people were the best organized, and anything that was done, even earlier moves in the right direction, would not have succeeded.

*Cottam* recalled a similar study he did earlier in the 1970s for Hudson Institute. He had predicted a military alliance with the mullahs. He thought the generals would see the handwriting on the wall and desert the Shah. It is still a mystery to him that they did not.

*Henze* said he was troubled about the talk about Islamic states and Islamic forms of government. It was particularly troublesome because of our major concern, freedom. While Islam and freedom are not incompatible—in spite of the fact Islam means submission—the record of Islamic states in modern times is a very sorry one. No Islamic state has created a stable governmental system or done much to ensure freedom. The most successful transformation from Islamic to modern society was Turkey. It is far from complete but the fundamentals have been largely agreed on. Recent events in Turkey have underscored that. Their success was based on abandoning Islam; in Turkey Islam has no relation to the state beyond what Christianity has to the U.S. government. By drastic methods in the early Ataturk period the more extreme fringes of Islam (which were never as dominant in Turkey as they have been in Iran) were all but eliminated. All that survives of the Dervish orders and sects are cultural memories, residual survivals that are tolerated because they no longer threaten society.

This subject needs attention academically. If we take the North African states (Algeria, Tunisia, and Morocco), by and large they have been moderately successful because they have not tried to incorporate too much of Islam into the state structure. They do not make a strong claim to be Islamic states. Algeria, the most radical, makes the strongest claim. *Griffith* said Islam was rising there. It was a growth industry. *Henze* agreed. He added that unfortunately uncritical admiration of Islam has also become fashionable in our society—especially in government and academia. This obscures some of the unpleasant and even unpromising aspects of what we have seen over the last ten years. We tend to be too indulgent.

*Gastil* said that partially the "fad" was a realization of its growth. As Griffith said, Islam was a growth industry in many countries and could not be ignored.

Gastil added that as the author of a yearly Comparative Survey of Freedom he had noticed that Islamic countries, from the point of view of civil and political liberties, do not have a good record. By and large the black African countries have a somewhat better record than the Islamic, and from India east countries have a better record (several agree). However, he wondered whether this record should be related to the theology of Islam. Historically, close relationships between leaders and the clergy have been rare in Islam. Perhaps the problems of Islam and freedom are more related to the horrendous events of history than the belief system. Compared to much of the world Iranian history has a disastrous record century after century.

*Henze* thought it not much worse than that of North Africa and Ottoman Turkey. *Gastil* still thought the Ottomans gave Turkey more stability than Iran's rulers. *Fischer* said the point about Ataturk in Turkey was surely that there was a much longer modernizing period before Ataturk in the nineteenth century than Iran ever experienced.

*Henze* still thought the real genius of Ataturk was that he did not try to base the system on Islam. If he had, he would not have been so successful. *Fischer* agreed, but pointed out that this occurred in the 1930s. In the 1930s it was also possible for intellectuals in Iran and Egypt to stand up and say that Islam was what was keeping them backward. That is politically not possible today. We ought to analyze why this change occurred. More generally Fischer agreed with Henze. This is one reason why he opposed the balloon that Brezezinski floated at one point, that we organize a united front against the Soviet Union, a new crusade in which Christians and Muslims can come together. This would be disastrous from a civil rights point of view. We have to make distinctions within Islam between backward, authoritarian interpretations of it and more progressive ones, and support the latter.

*Henze* agreed. While we should not be needlessly provocative, we have been much too inclined not to criticize, much too inclined to let spokesmen for all kinds of Islamic societies claim all sorts of things that we would not tolerate for a moment from a Dutchman or a Mexican. *Khalilzad* wondered what he meant. *Henze* then referred to discussions of the great wisdom that supposedly lies in Islamic society. We are very indulgent of the backwardness of Saudi society and the hypocrisy within the upper levels of this society that may be one of the most contradictory in the world today.

*Fischer* said that the challenge the Saudis feared most was precisely the claim that the Saudi regime was not Islamic. It is what opposition is being organized around.

*Ahmad* disagreed with the condemnation of Islam. He thought it a very unscientific approach to isolate one single factor out of the many that determine the collective behavior of a society or group and put the blame of the entire behavior on that one factor. Islam is of course one of the important factors, but not the *only* factor that determines the behavior of past or present Islamic societies. There are structural factors, colonial legacies, and backwardness. The argument would hold only if we could show that the performance for human rights and freedom in those societies where Islam has not been dominant is relatively better.

He doubted it was possible. Latin American society where Islam is absent, or Soviet and Chinese societies are probably as bad as Muslim societies with respect to human rights. *Gastil* disagreed on Latin America.

*Gastil* suggested that the other great indulgence is nationalism. Self-determination is an important value in freedom. It makes sense to talk about Islamic nationalism itself as being a value for freedom. If Brezezinski says that we should support the idea that Muslim peoples should have the right to defend their way of life versus the Communists, this is not dissimilar from saying that the Afghans have a right to their own country no matter what the effect on other human rights. Do we really believe it is an unredeemable sin for the Soviet Union to come in and change Afghanistan even though from the point of view of many human rights issues, life under the Soviets—if it be like life in Soviet Central Asia—might be better for the people concerned than under the Afghans.

*Griffith* suggested we were culturally conditioned. Islam like other non-Western societies finds many aspects of the West—all except its technological modernization—disruptive and repulsive. Many people in our own society agree—ranging from the hippies to the moral majority. Why shouldn't this also be true abroad? Indeed, the ideas of tolerance and individual liberty are largely European and North American norms. We do not understand that our beliefs are a historical exception. Although we think of them as the wave of the future, there is no historical reason to assume this at all. We will be lucky if we maintain the freedoms we have. Still we should advocate freedom; we should advocate our beliefs. But as beliefs they have little or nothing to do with history—and certainly nothing to do with science. All one can say is that the great majority of countries over nearly all of history, and most countries even now, are neither tolerant, nor libertarian, nor individualistic, nor regard being these as anything but corrupting and self-indulgent. Griffith said that as an inveterate individualist, he was appalled by the fact that this was the situation, but that did not make him believe that it was going to change very fast. On the contrary, the nineteenth and early twentieth centuries—before the independence of much of the world—were the great, great exceptions. What we are now coming back to is a much more typical situation: a world with no more than islands of individualism, freedom and tolerance.

*Richter* said he would like to be a little indulgent of the Islamic point of view. One thing that can be said for Islam in Central Asia is that it is regarded by the people as more indigenous than what they are reacting against. Our unwillingness to be indulgent of their attitudes is an extension of what they are struggling against, and what they identify as imperialism. Richter did not believe that we have in the past, even in the recent past, been overly indulgent of Islam, or Islamic points of view. He thought we had a fair distance to go before even reaching the middle of the spectrum.

*Gastil* said to some extent Islam could itself be seen as an expression of popular democracy. In evaluating Griffith's point on the rarity of liberalism and democracy, we should always distinguish between the reactions of elite groups and the reactions of ordinary people. After examining evidence from many parts of the world, even poor parts such as India, he concluded that average people are very interested in their rights. While they may define them differently they want to express them, want to have a choice, and have a part in the process. They may not be willing to grant those rights to the man next door. Elite groups still find it necessary in almost all the world to talk about democracy, civil and political rights, but they have the more explicit interest in suppressing these rights. We should realize this contrast when we think about situations. It is not true that ordinary people in countries such as Argentina or South Korea are uninterested in freedom, or like to torture people. Gastil doubted average Argentinians liked torture; it is true they do not know how to organize to do anything about it.

*Harrison* agreed. Taking a Western conception of freedom and transposing it to the specific political institutions of these societies may be an outside imposition, but we are not doing that when we recognize ethnic identities and the broader problems of freedom for groups in the society. Gastil's introductory paper raised as a policy problem the value of assisting federalism in these countries as a way of approaching the question of freedom in them. This is a vexing policy dilemma. But to talk of the ethnic rights of minorities in these countries is not value laden in the sense that talking about issues of freedom in other respects is. But he did not know how to be effective. Maybe Richter's answer is the right one: in declaratory policy we should make it clear that when we are talking to Pakistan we are not just talking to Punjabis. We should identify and empathize with the other peoples in order to develop long-term bases of relationships so that we have the option of relating to any and all groups in different contingencies. The same should be done in Iran. The Soviets are able to talk in terms that make their psychological relationship with multiethnic peoples more broad-gauged than ours. If you are in a minority in any of these countries you can look at Soviet nationalities policy and feel it has something to do with you.

*Griffith* found an additional problem in all this from a policy point of view. He agreed that this country, given the tradition of the nonconformist conscience, will fail if it advocates purely *Realpolitik*, just as it will also fail if it is purely moralistic. Policy has to be a mixture of both. Therefore, one's attitude toward self-determination or human rights must be mixed. Human rights cannot be absolute for a government. If one is dealing with policy he must inevitably have both, with the mixture depending on the country, the time, our interests, and other factors. For a democracy like the United States, with a tradition of the nonconformist conscience, this balance is incredibly difficult to find and carry out.

*Nabawi* said that people might think this thought strange, but maybe the question of human rights in Islamic versus non-Islamic countries isn't the right question. Someone might even say, "Let's go back and look at the records of human rights and freedom in the countries that had very close ties with the United States compared to those that did not." That would be an interesting comparison—to compare what was happening in Iran under the Shah with what was going on in Afghanistan before the "communist" coup, to compare what was going on in Pakistan and South Korea with what was occurring in India and Japan, relative to human rights. This approach might suggest that Islamic versus non-Islamic may not be the only question involved in determining the probable extent of human rights in a country.

*Khalilzad* agreed that identifying long-range trends and seeing what one can do to encourage them is very important. He did not think we should discourage economic development just because this creates problems and instabilities. In the modernization process fragmentation takes place, and this leads to a variety of outcomes. In the case of Islam, there have been a number of responses as a result of modernization. These have variously led to domination by secular leftists, centrists, rightists, but certainly not always Islamic fundamentalists.

In the interaction of the region's intellectuals with the outside world there have been two or three main responses. Some look at Islamic history and say, "At one time we were a preeminent power and everybody looked up to us. What went wrong? Why are we so badly off? It must be that we have become bad Muslims. In those glorious days people were pure Muslims, so we should go back to it." Then there are those who say that something happened in history since those days. While the world changed, Islam, instead of marching forward in science and art, stopped progressing. So what we have to do is reinterpret Islam. Innately it is not anti-progress; it can be made consistent with the more scientific, contemporary ideas. This is the modernist response. The modernists accuse the fundamentalists of being terribly ignorant about Islam as well as society and what is going on in the world. Finally there are secularists of one kind or another. They see Islam as part of the problem. All three tendencies are present in every Islamic country. At one point one gains and the other loses. What factors encourage the growth of one rather than another? There is no one Islam or one Islamic response. We in the West can encourage one rather than another tendency, and alongside security issues, this is important. In a fundamental way this is itself a security issue.

*Gastil* returned to Harrison's point about relating to what he would call subnationalities. He would add other minorities, the religious for example—Ahmadiyya, Bahai, and so on. The problem is that majority peoples believe that outside concern for minorities is a way to weaken their nations. So interest in minorities harms rather than helps our reputation. Gastil thought it very important for the United States to develop a stance to this problem—not only in the Middle East but everywhere—that, without being destructive of our relationship to the states that exist, supports the rights of minorities. Some approaches to the problem in Pakistan have already been suggested. Perhaps Afghanistan also offers a chance, now that it is outside our sphere of responsibility for the moment, for the United States to develop a position on minorities that looks less destructive from the point of view of the Afghans involved than would otherwise be the case when there is an established state.

*Wriggins* noted that American and British statesmen have been wrestling with this problem for generations. We have not found a general answer. Some individuals, such as Gladstone, Disraeli, or Franklin Roosevelt, have had particular answers. No answers have proved very satisfactory because the state system imposes on statesmen the priority of dealing with governments in power. He thought we seldom had the luxury of dealing with minorities under regimes that take the view Gastil described—for outsiders to muck around supporting such groups means they want to weaken the state. This is particularly the attitude of governments in weak states.

In the discussion of the tendency of Islam to go in modernist or fundamentalist directions *Newell* noted that there have been hints that there is an obvious sociological dimension. There have been references to a Pakistani lower-middle class, and the same terms have been applied to the urban working class of south Teheran, where there seems to be a strong response to fundamentalist religious symbols. He did not know how broadly we could extend this relationship. In Afghanistan it is different because these classes do not exist in the same way. Still what might be called an elite tends toward modernism, usually because they can monopolize the baubles of it and have the prerequisites. Obviously "who has" has a lot to do with the view of Islam one ends up with. One of the aspects of our approach is whether we are for the status quo or not. Referring to Wriggins' point, Newell recalled there were times we were a revolutionary force in the world; then the status quo powers such as the Austro-Hungarian Empire felt threatened by our example.

*Wriggins* pointed out that we were never worried about a central balance then, and we are now. That is the dimension of our modern situation that inhibits us, although whether it should inhibit us in particular cases is an open question. The Carter administration downgraded the importance of the central balance to deal with other issues. The new administration is likely to again stress the central balance. In our discussion this issue has emerged as an underlying dimension of our problem that sets limits, although each participant sets the limits at different places.

*Richter* suggested there were a few examples where regional problems have been dealt with relatively successfully. He thought especially of India. India continues to have many problems, especially in the Northeast, but it has passed through what has been called its "most dangerous decades" without catastrophe. Sri Lanka might be another example. Although it has had difficulties it can be praised for its success. (*Wriggins* agrees.) One might ask how these states have held together. Bhutto in his final testament said among other things that India had been held together by the clashing of its democracy.

# Media Images:
# Soviet Practice and
# American Alternatives
# in Central Asia

Eden Naby

The war of words aimed at winning the hearts and minds of Muslim Central Asians, Soviet and non-Soviet, has been conducted in earnest for at least the period since the Russian Revolution. For most of this period, the war has been waged by one side only, the side which recognized early the long-term significance of the ideological battlefield as the indispensable companion, if not master, of the military in the overall war for power and conquest.

Long before the United States arrived half-heartedly in Iran and Pakistan and even more faint-heartedly in Afghanistan, the Soviet Union had found its socialist pro-Moscow allies among Indians and Iranians. Indigenous help has augmented the Soviet Union's wide array of resources for disseminating favorable opinion about itself, its policies, and its world goals. The American response to this sophisticated, new-world form of confrontation has been of late primarily bewilderment, puzzlement and defensiveness. This attitude is apparent when U.S. information services are contrasted with British efforts and perhaps even those of the West Germans,[1] who together with the Soviets and to a lesser extent the Chinese, provide the chief nonindigenous information sources for the people of Iran, Afghanistan, Pakistan, and Soviet Central Asia.

This paper will explore the relative position and broadcasting performance of United States information services to the countries mentioned and the contrasting efforts of the Soviet Union. It will also suggest some tentative means of working toward improving perceptions of American and democratic institutions.

The information and resulting analysis is based chiefly on my personal experience in these countries, particularly Soviet Central Asia and Afghanistan, and evaluations I have performed with regard to programming for these countries. This is obviously not a complete study, but my personal conclusions are offered now because as we see a decline of the United States image in the Middle East, and militarist proposals of archaic solutions to deal with complex issues, more people are turning to a scrutiny of the United States information services.[2]

## THE IDEOLOGICAL BATTLEFIELD

Fundamental to the functioning of any information service are the principles on which such services are founded. A chief difference between U.S. and other national services lies in the fact that the American government has treated its information services as poor relations, both in terms of the status it reserves for the services and the funds that are allocated for their operations. The value of the services is not appreciated widely by either the public or its elected representatives. As a result, not only are the services disjointed, with overlapping and frequently ill-staffed offices, especially in host countries, but the funding for these services is very poor. It often takes Herculean efforts by the United States International Communications Agency (ICA) and the Board for International Broadcasting (BIB) just to get budgets approved without "economizing" slashes.

The value of the ideological battlefield is not recognized. The reasons for this appear to involve at least three factors basic to our perception of ourselves and the third world. First, the largely Judeo-Christian, European origins of most immigrants to America have created an insularity with regard to alien cultures. Most Americans and public figures do not have means of bridging the gap between our own and the widely differing values of third world cultures such as Islam or tribally organized society. Therefore, until the last fifteen years even the most elementary efforts have not been made in our educational system, from first grade through undergraduate school, to understand, and more important, respect alien cultures. Similarly, representatives of these cultures themselves have inadequately conveyed their heritage abroad, especially in the United States. Most of those in a position to serve as bridges between cultures have suffered from severe cultural humiliation. Such a state was recognized in Iran during the 1930s in the writings of the social theorist, Ahmad Kasravi (d. 1946) who coined the term *Ūrūpāgarī* (European seeking). By the 1950s a more pejorative term had taken root; *gharbzadeh* (Western struck).

Alienated from their own heritage, these Western-oriented persons—often technocrats—have reinforced the perceptions in this country that no need exists to understand third world cultures because the people who count in those societies, from the Shah of Iran to a Pakistani engineering student, are eager to communicate all there is to know, and without our even bothering to learn a foreign language. The shock of recent events in Iran lies partially in the fact that politically powerful persons, such as Ayatollah Khomeini, appear to care little about American culture and will not even tell us so in a civilized manner; that is, in our own language. In sum, the need to translate (used in its widest sense) our message to the third world has received only passing attention because of our lack of appreciation for the depth of differences between cultures.

Second, the very words ideology and propaganda conjure up unpleasant notions of totalitarianism to many thoughtful persons. Therefore, even for those who recognize the need to transmit and translate between cultures, a fear of adopting an unsuitable methodology leads to a reluctance to deal with political ideas and ideals at all. To espouse actively democratic ideals might lead to undue curbing of freedom to express opposing political ideas. Such timidity leads to our spending more time on our messages abroad on sports than on Jeffersonian ideals, more time on the space program than on explaining the workings of democratic versus totalitarian systems.

Perhaps our trepidation comes from a lack of conviction that democracy works here, and can be made to work in all cultures. Such doubt has been frequently expressed of late with regard to our focus area by those who claim that the authoritarian regime of the Shah was the only system suited to the Iranian culture or by those who would assert that only totalitarian Russian communism can bring progress to the underdeveloped Afghans. Whatever the cause, a partial reason for the American lack of success in the ideological battlefield lies in our unwillingness to speak assertively for democracy.

The third and perhaps most telling reason for the lack of success of United States information services in this region must be sought in the elitist assumption that what the masses think and want is immaterial to the governing of a country. Given such an assumption, we speak only to elites, support only elites, and ignore not only the lower socioeconomic classes but also the elites that are out of power. Since we perceive no need to conduct any exchange with the disenfranchized and powerless, we see little need to expend funds on means of reaching them. Broadcast patterns in Afghanistan confirm the existence of such assumptions if other more blatant examples in our dealings with Iran have not. The United States (and Britain) has not broadcast to Afghanistan in either of its two official languages until September 1980 when, after much urging by Afghanists, Dari broadcasting was begun. It has been assumed that the Farsi broadcasts to Iran would be understood in Afghanistan. This certainly would be true if the audience were limited to high civil servants who are literate and bilingual. But it almost is not worth broadcasting in

foreign languages to an audience that is largely foreign educated and
often conversant in English. The mass of the Afghan population is
illiterate (and therefore would not comprehend literary Farsi) or uni-
lingually Pushtun speaking. Many of these persons are influential in their
own contexts and have access to transistor short-wave radios. They are
the ones who, in the present crisis, are waging what in many respects
amounts to an ideological war. They need to know what world opinion
says regarding the Soviet invasion of Afghanistan. But instead, their
source of information remains Kabul and the truly wonderous Pushtu
service from Moscow and Tashkent.

## SOVIET MEDIA PRACTICES IN THE REGION

Of all information services focused on non-Soviet Central Asia, the
most voluble and pervasive is that of the USSR. In terms of diversity of
broadcast languages, air time, and suitability of material to the audience
and the goals of the broadcasting country, the Soviet media network
operates well. Over the past several years, a greater amount of subtlety
than before has been introduced into the services and many more Soviet
Muslims have been integrated into the system.

Underlying Soviet success at reaching a mass audience have been
several factors, not the least of which are a positive approach and an
avoidance of political discussion directly in favor of social, economic
and cultural matters. What do we mean by a positive approach? Here are
some examples. Whereas the U.S. broadcasts to Tajiks may concentrate
on the ills of the Soviet system (sham elections, baseless arrests), the
Soviet broadcasts to Afghanistan will speak about the cultural
achievements of Muslims in the Soviet Union (for example, a speech in
Pushtu from Mufti Babakhanov of Tashkent), the hydroelectric development of Tajikistan, and the love of Pushtu literature in Soviet circles.[3]
American broadcasts (Radio Liberty) are intended to "inform Soviet
citizenry of events in their own country" and thereby raise the level of
dissatisfaction within the state while the Soviet broadcasts are intended
to mollify grievances against the Soviet presence in Afghanistan. Nevertheless, a more positive approach by the U.S. broadcaster would have
been to include in the program, for example, the pro-Muslim Afghan
statements of Iranian and other Muslim leaders. The irony, peevishness,
and a general negative tone that appear to be symptomatic of much U.S.
broadcasting make the news analysis portion of the fifteen to twenty
minute programs to this area as likely to offend as to arouse audiences.
Briefly put, the program content offers wholesale criticism rather than
alternative methods or theories.

The attention that Soviet broadcasting pays to socioeconomic and cultural issues is well calculated to stress material progress which is touted as more feasible for areas contiguous to Soviet Central Asia under the Russian socialist system than any other. Strongly emphasized in such media is the friendly and helpful role played by Russians who are portrayed as equal partners rather than superiors. Examples of such an approach can be traced back to the beginnings of the introduction of Russian communism to Muslim areas. Soviet Central Asian poetry and prose are peopled with Russians who work hand in hand with local Uzbeks and Tajiks to uplift Muslim society. Writers from Sadriddin Aini (1878-1953) to Askad Mukhtar (b. 1916) have included benevolent, Uzbek- and Tajik-speaking Russians in their cast of characters.[4]

Russian audiences applauding a Pushtu poet's recitation of his work, a real but certainly not widely experienced event, nevertheless presents a favorable image of the Soviet Union and those who run the system. It is far better than a traveling exhibition of photographs from outer space. Such exhibitions make little attempt to bridge the gap between cultures, particularly when inadequately captioned in Farsi for a Dari/Pushtu public. The effect of the exhibition is even more disappointing when it is learned that it is part of a touring exhibition that willy-nilly included Afghanistan. Such insensitivity, betraying lack of knowledge about Muslim Central Asian culture, occurs far too frequently.

Aside from a better understanding of indigenous values, reflected in the content of broadcasts and other information services, the widespread use of indigenous languages by Soviet personnel renders them far more effective with a stratum of society that is rarely touched by anything American. Soviet libraries and cultural centers in our focus area are manned by Soviet men and women who converse in host country languages. The Soviet cultural center in Tehran was run by a man who spoke good Persian. The woman in charge of the Soviet cultural center in Kabul in 1979 spoke Pushtu. These were not Soviet Central Asians but Slavs. In neither of the equivalent American centers were there any Americans who spoke Persian (let alone Pushtu in Kabul). Instead the U.S. information service relies on English-speaking natives, culled from the ranks of the upper classes (such as wives and daughters of high civil servants) who act as conduits for the Americans. This pattern of over-reliance on native informants (emigrés in broadcasting services) has reduced both the effectiveness and quality of American services.

The emphasis on language, understanding of the values and apprehensions of the audience, and most of all, aiming at an audience which is varied, with roots in rural or lower class levels, appear to serve the Soviets well. In recognition of the powerful role of the media and of broadcasting in particular, the Soviet Union boasts some of the most powerful transmitting stations in the world. The reception of its message in the Middle East is facilitated by proximity. Its credibility, a point raised often by Americans involved in the information service, compares well with the other primary source of available information—the state media in Middle Eastern countries. Given the lack of freedom of media in the Shah's Iran, there was no reason for Iranians to view Azeri, Turkmen, and Persian broadcasts from the Soviet Union as any more polemical or self-serving than Iranian ones. Therefore, among all but the most sophisticated, the professed Western emphasis on an impartial presentation of news and views made little sense.

This brings us to the British Broadcasting Corporation, the venerated BBC. Essentially the BBC aims for the same elite audience as Voice of America and Radio Liberty. The BBC has accumulated more experience in both broadcasting and Middle Eastern affairs, and boasts its own correspondents in critical areas.[5] British lack of direct political embroilment in the region as a matter of course confers upon the BBC a more impartial status. This is true also for Deutsche Welle (the West German radio service), but it is neither as widespread nor frequently heard as BBC. In the present transitional period in the region, the BBC continues to be well received although accusations of rumor-mongering have been launched against it as well, especially in connection with Afghanistan. The BBC will probably continue to retain its status as a reliable source of news because, unlike U.S. or Soviet services, the BBC refrains from a commentary on events; it presents capsulized news, based primarily on fresh, firsthand reports from its correspondents.

## AMERICAN MEDIA PRACTICES AND ALTERNATIVES

If the reasons for the poor quality of American media in Muslim Central Asia are lack of appreciation for the necessity to speak to other cultures, lack of a conviction in the efficacy of democracy, and focusing on elites instead of the people in general, then these long-term causes of mediocrity must be addressed first. However, this involves a re-education process among policy makers that cannot bring results overnight. The easier solution of emphasis on more nuclear and tactical weaponry will probably continue to be preferred to emphasis on alliance through persuasion. Yet in the meantime, other more secondary constraints upon American media abroad can be removed more easily.

The secondary constraints fall into the following broad categories: technical, staff, and content. Technical constraints consist of inadequate transmission stations and a lack of adequate and diverse language broadcasting. For example, the 1979 Annual Report of the Board for International Broadcasting identified Soviet Central Asia as an area to which broadcasts were made (in Kazakh, Kirghiz, Tajik, Uzbek and Turkmen) but where the Board could not ascertain whether programs were actually capable of being received due to weak transmission.[6] Information is not available as to whether budgetary allocations have been forthcoming to alleviate the problem. Incomplete target audience information, of course, handicaps program evaluation as well.

With regard to the adequacy of broadcasting languages, Radio Liberty appears to at least touch all important language bases within Soviet Central Asia. (Uyghur has been eliminated from the list of languages while Uzbek has been upgraded to receive more air time.) But the coverage of non-Soviet Central Asia, a role falling to the Voice of America (VOA) and therefore the ICA, appears to continue to be inadequate. The diversity of language groups with demands for cultural privileges is growing rapidly to include not only the ever-vociferous Kurds, but also the Azeris, the Baluch, and certainly the Pushtuns.

Motivated perhaps by the possible political role that Azeris might have seized in Iran during 1979, VOA has been recruiting Azeri speakers to staff its newly formed Azeri program. Otherwise, the other minority languages, such as Kurdish and Baluchi, wait in abeyance until there develops sufficient political motivation to commence broadcasting. Unfortunately Pushtu as well appears to be receiving little positive response as yet from the VOA staff.

For Pushtu, neither technical constraints nor the availability of staff appear to be the chief sources of the problem. The arguments against Pushtu broadcasting appear to stem from a need for funds and the fear that Pushtu broadcasts would offend Islamabad by exacerbating the transborder sensitivities that have long plagued Afghan-Pakistani relations. While this pattern of argument favors Pakistan (rather Punjabi sentiments), it ignores the critical issue of inadequate broadcasting to Afghanistan. Neither a Soviet satellite so that it could be "covered" by Radio Liberty, nor considered important enough, vis à vis its eastern and western neighbors, to warrant substantial United States commitment through the VOA, Afghanistan has been neglected. This pattern follows that of general United States relations with Afghanistan that called for bowing to real or imagined Pakistani pressure in every crisis involving Afghanistan.

Before arriving at a decision to continue to exclude Pushtu from its broadcasting schedule (and from its printed information service as well), the ICA must weigh the matter on the scales of the current situation, reassess the actual Pakistani objections, and review the legitimacy of such objections. Pakistani objections could be better met if the ICA could assure Pakistan of the aim of the broadcasts: to inform of world and regional events, to convey relevant information about the United States, its ideals and democratic practices. While efforts should be launched to allay Pakistani fears of Pushtu broadcasts, nonetheless, the vital need to institute such a language program at the earliest moment should not be missed by the U.S. At present resistance forces cannot continue their own radio transmission, mainly in Pushtu, commenced last year. Pakistani broadcasts are haphazard and unacceptable to Afghans who have for decades viewed Islamabad as the suppressor of Pushtun rights. Other Pushtu-language broadcasts originate from Kabul and Moscow/Tashkent. If and when Pushtu broadcasting is begun by VOA it would be advantageous if air-time was not taken from Persian/Dari but rather from English-language broadcasts to the region.

Personnel constraints on the quality of broadcasting form a serious obstacle to both VOA programs and those of the Board for International Broadcasting. The problem appears more pronounced in our area of focus than for Eastern Europe and Russia proper. Briefly, the information network relies heavily on emigrés to perform not only the actual broadcasts but to prepare the material as well. This employment of emigrés has resulted in both outdated and uneven programs. At times broadcasts appear to be aimed at other potential emigrés rather than the public at large.[7] Moreover, the emigré population from Soviet Central Asia, which arrived in the West during the 1940s, has aged to the point of inability to function well for physical as well as other reasons. Yet few replacements are available in view of the lack of training facilities (and scholarships) in the West. The new wave of emigrés from this Soviet region consists of Soviet Jews, mostly belonging to the category of Bokharan Jews. Unfortunately their cultural and political orientation renders them ill-suited to prepare broadcast material for Muslim populations.[8] Without proper American supervision, this source of new personnel would not fulfill the needs of the information services.

Solutions for the personnel problem appear to lie in the training and employment of American experts in Central Asian languages and civilizations. In addition, inducements to Americans to participate in the information service would have to be offered beyond what the emigrés have accepted. I refer not simply to financial inducements but also to such matters as location of broadcast preparation facilities and a system of sabbaticals to allow for opportunities to conduct long-term research.

The problem of content is certainly as crucial as any of the other problem areas outlined. Overseas broadcasts to our area of focus suffer from irrelevance ranging from wasteful litanies of the goings and comings of chiefs of state to articles taken directly from Soviet encyclopedias and journals.[9] Given proper evaluation procedures and the attraction of adequately trained personnel, together with a central news-feature service proposed by the Board for International Broadcasting, such content difficulties could be alleviated. Without adequate awareness of the problems on the part of the concerned public, however, the problems will continue for lack of attention and funds.

## CONCLUSIONS

The unsatisfactory nature of the American image abroad is chiefly of our own making, deriving from our unwillingness to recognize the need for image building in the third world. A lack of clarity with regard to whether Western democracy is actually transferable has hampered our information services from performing their tasks properly, as has a foreign policy which concentrates on communicating with elites only. Soviet awareness of the importance of image building, on the other hand, has led the USSR to concentrate great effort in this field of combat.

Once the United States becomes aware of the need for positive image building and sets out the principles upon which it will operate an effective information service, the chances of its being able to improve its image among Muslim Central Asians are good. Of course, despite what information services can accomplish among Muslims throughout the region, the American image will always be complicated by its role vis à vis Islam as perceived through the festering Arab-Israeli conflict. Because the Soviet Union too has damaged its image through invasion, suspected ethnic manipulation, and a long history of conquest and brutality in Muslim areas, the balance is not necessarily de facto in its favor, particularly among non-Arab Muslims. Therefore, concerted effort at image building, over the next few years could bear a rich harvest for the United States. There is a danger that the recent political and diplomatic defeats the U.S. has suffered in the region will cause the incoming administration to seek military solutions (that is, alliances on the post-World War II pattern) rather than commence a new chapter in its relations with the people inhabiting Central Asia.

## NOTES

1. United States overseas broadcasting services are under the auspices of two organizations with broad objectives: the Voice of America (an arm of USICA) has as its primary objective the disseminating of information about the United States, its culture and world view. VOA currently broadcasts in Farsi and Dari, Uzbek and Urdu as well as English. Radio Liberty operates as part of the Board for International Broadcasting under a mandate "to encourage a constructive dialogue with the peoples of Eastern Europe and the Soviet Union." RL broadcasts in all major Soviet Central Asian languages and in Azeri. BIB and USICA together control United States government media to the world, including the cultural offices in host countries run by USICA. Films and exhibitions, augmented by visiting lecturers drawn mainly from academia and the entertainment world form USICA activities. Publications on lectures in indigenous languages, or other activities conducted for non-English speakers, are virtually nonexistent in Central Asia.

Deutsche Welle and the BBC broadcast to both the Soviet and non-Soviet regions of Central Asia. U.S. language broadcasts offer more language diversity.

2. Relations between the Soviet and non-Soviet Middle East are the subject of a major project undertaken by David Nalle, former head of USICA.

3. Mufti Babakhanov frequently sends media messages to Afghanistan, Iran, and the Arab world as well as Africa. This Pushtu broadcast has been translated in FBIS- Soviet Union, August 1980.

4. See especially Aini's ODINA (reprinted in Aini's collected works, Stalinabad, Nashriyoti Davlatii Tojikiston, 1960) and Mukhtar's SISTERS (Moscow, n.d.)

5. This writer, when departing Kabul in February, 1979, was accused of passing "information to the BBC" because she spoke Persian and carried a foreign passport. Its inability to detect the source of the BBC correspondent's information was frustrating to Kabul because the BBC reports were lending authencity to rumors Kabul wished to squelch regarding resistance movements.

6. The Board for International Broadcasting, Fifth Annual Report, 1979, pp. 25-26.

7. The Board for International Broadcasting, Sixth Annual Report, 1980, pp. 18-19.

8. *Loc. cit.*, p. 20 (based on evaluation of the writer).

9. This appears to be the case in sample Azeri broadcasts from the summer of 1980 now under review. The paucity of broadcast material to Soviet Muslim areas reflects the dirth of facts known about the area and the scarcity of qualified analysts.

# Comments and Discussion

In summarizing her paper *Naby* noted that it stemmed from a long-standing interest, particularly because she was originally from the region. She had memories of a childhood in Azerbaijan during the 1945-46 crisis when her parents and neighbors would huddle around a radio and listen to BBC in English to see just what was going to be happening to them next. This was their only source of information. Later on in northern Afghanistan she had another experience with outside broadcasting that was quite different. She was listening to Tajik and Uzbek broadcasts that came in nearly twenty-four hours a day, very close by, very clearly, and in a very entertaining manner.

These two experiences introduced the issues she would like to focus on. They illustrate the importance of broadcasts in the lives of ordinary people, the general public. Her family was basically a village family. The anecdotes also illustrate the disparity in capacity between the USSR and the West. The Voice of America and BBC broadcast to elites more than the general public. Also, whatever the West broadcasts into the region generally has to be listened to on short wave, whereas what the Soviet Union broadcasts can be received on medium wave as well.

The anecdotes also focus on the Soviet Union's ability and willingness to make far more extensive use of transborder languages than Western countries. Finally, there was a basic difference between how audiences regarded Western and Soviet broadcasts. She and her family were listening to BBC because they trusted it to tell them what was the truth as it saw it, and they believed it was credible. On the other hand, Central Asians listen to Soviet broadcasts primarily for their entertainment value rather than for the message. This is not absolute, but, if one is to judge by the cassettes of music that are copies from Soviet radio broadcasts for Azerbaijan or Afghanistan and sold on the market, one can gain an idea of the entertainment value that the Soviets give to their broadcasts. Of course, the Soviets have an advantage because of proximity and their shared ethnic peoples.

Naby also brought out that through two decades we have had no Persian-language broadcasting. *Henze* confirmed that between 1958 and 1979 VOA had no Persian broadcasts. The President was surprised when he asked one morning in 1978 what we were saying to Iran in Persian and learned we were saying nothing. An interesting measure of the moribundness of the effort was that no one had suggested we have such a broadcast. *Naby* added that broadcasts began again in 1979.

*Henze* concluded that the performance of the United States in this field in the last two decades has been atrocious, but added that governments do not do much better than their people. There has been very little popular demand, and very little understanding in Congress. Obviously, the decision in 1958 to cut out Persian broadcasts was an absurd one. It was probably made in the context of cutting the budget and starting broadcasts to Africa. Henze said he was the first and the highest level officer in the United States government since C. E. Jackson served Dwight Eisenhower as a staff aid to be concerned with this problem. From the day he came back from Turkey to join Brezezinski in January 1977 it has been a major concern. Yet he has accomplished very little, for it is a problem most people aside from Brezezinski have ignored. He could spend six hours describing appalling shortcomings. What is frustrating is that no extraordinary technology is required; we do not have to invent anything new or devise unusual techniques. The technical problems were solved when Radio Free Europe went on full-scale operation in the 1950s. There is no magic formula for making the radios more effective, but a lot is known about how to do it. Radio Free Europe set the example, yet it was never followed through on, even for the Soviet Union, and never applied dynamically to the Voice of America (VOA).

VOA has always been looked on rather differently. Its job is to tell America's story to the world. Radio Free Europe and Radio Liberty were charged with providing the equivalent of "home services" to countries that do not have them. If a country does not have an opportunity to receive news freely from internal sources then we should fill that gap. In some periods VOA adopted a more vigorous policy; at other times it has bent over backwards to say as little provocatively as possible—to tell America's story benignly. Henze served six years with RFE in the 1950s, was a radio advisor to a couple of foreign governments, and is intimately familiar with what many broadcasting operations have done through the years. Yet since the 1950s broadcasting has not been the subject of a National Security Council formal meeting or of a major study within the government. There have been episodes of concern about particular areas.

There was a tendency in the earlier 1970s toward even greater retrenchment in the broadcasting effort, to draw back, to make minimal investment even in maintaining the physical plant, and to let operating levels decline. Later dollar budgets rose somewhat, but what a dollar would buy in 1970 requires four or five today. So in the early phase of the Carter administration the retreat actually continued. However, there was a gain in one small way. When the Carter administration came into office a technical group had a plan for building twenty-eight transmitters around the world—just a beginning on taking up the slack between our capability and the Russians'. They have always had more powerful transmitters. Brezezinski took the plan to the President in March 1977 and he signed it. Congress approved it, and most of the transmitters are in the process of coming into operation now. Unfortunately not yet those in Sri Lanka, which are most important for our region.

The broadcasts for the area we are talking about go out from Greece and Germany. That is as close as we can get—or on the other side, Thailand and the Philippines. We have nothing in between. We cannot push a country in the Middle East to take a transmitter or rent time. It may cause riots in Jordan or Saudi Arabia; even a country as friendly as Egypt does not want one. (*Wriggins* adds that we could not put it in Sri Lanka under Bandaranaike.)

*Henze* added that in the early days of the Carter administration there were not the obstacles that developed later in the Office of Management and Budget. When Bert Lance fell in September, 1977, he was succeeded by his deputy, a bookkeeper and a little-money man. Since then they had never been able to get anything through of any size, whether the President signed off on it or not. Last year, in December, there was a major meeting on Muslim broadcasting, and a plan for preliminary expansion of RL and VOA was approved, but not a penny has yet ever been allocated for it. By hook and by crook a little money has been found, and there has been some expansion.

The managements of the stations have done their best; they have been in the business for years and know what they want to do. They need the means. We have to hope that the incoming administration—and there is hope in some of their statements—has the vision and capacity to grab hold of this problem. Perhaps the country's descent to such a low level of effectiveness will shock people into wanting to do something about it. Our equipment has not caught up to today. It is nearly all vacuum tube. The basic plant of the stations shocks anyone from a minor American commercial station. They are museums. So we need agitation from everywhere, and if we are going to crack it in the Reagan administration, we will have to crack it early.

While Henze was very critical of the Carter administration, he saw the problem much deeper than that. It has a great deal to do with Congress. They want to squeeze, cut, and tighten the budget. The problem is more general than Afghanistan. Ethiopia after all fell into the disarray like Afghanistan several years ago, and we still are not broadcasting to Ethiopia in its national language—Amharic. We have had plans on the books for three years, but we have only gotten pennies here and there.

From his perspective Henze was glad we had anything going in Afghanistan at all. The broadcasts to Afghanistan were begun only because of an agitational article in the *Washington Post* last June that said the Voice of America claimed it was broadcasting to Afghanistan, but it was in the wrong language. This set up waves of concern and worrying, because the leadership of ICA (International Communications Agency) was very frightened of being accused of ineptitude. So it tried to be responsive. But ICA has never had the courage to have a real fight, get people in Congress to support them, overcome the opposition in OMB. They need someone with the skill the Pentagon has had over the years to get things through.

The problem of how you broadcast to Afghanistan is complicated. There are varying opinions. When they finally got the broadcasts underway to Afghanistan, ICA did a telephone survey of what language should be used first. There was a priority discussion and it was agreed that the first thing to be added would be broadcasting to Afghanistan. The experts surveyed concluded that Dari was the language to begin with. Now there appears to be a strong body of opinion that disagrees.

*Naby* suggested that those contacted had probably not included Americans who were trained in Pushtu. *Henze* said all these problems are difficult. Radio Liberty was wracked for years by the problem of whether it should have one Central Asian service or a separate service for each Central Asian language.

Henze said the highest priority now is expansion by hiring people and giving them the necessary support and research facilities. The next stage is to strengthen the broadcasting capability. We get through clearly to Poland. Without RFE (Radio Free Europe) the amount of freedom that exists in Poland would never have come close to existing. It takes only a modest amount of money.

Getting the locations is politically more difficult and can only be done against the background of having strengthened yourself in the world in general. Henze thought it important for a group like this to recognize we cannot hope to deal effectively with the Middle East unless we have a stronger position in the Middle East. We have to have someplace to broadcast from. Technically satellites may be possible in the 1990s, but not today.

*Richter* asked if we needed land to put transmitters on. *Henze* said boats did not work. Satellites won't until someone discovers how to store an enormous amount of power in a satellite. Satellites work now only if you have the technology on the ground to receive and retransmit broadcasts. Locations of transmitters are impossible to hide. That is why we know the "National Voice of Iran" comes from near Baku. *Wriggins* added that we considered Diego Garcia but it was a thousand miles further than other alternatives. Politically it would have been far better.

*Naby* wondered whether there was need for a basic attitudinal change that could underlie the increase in budget. How could such a change be created if our concentration was on military weaponry exclusive of other interests? How can it be done if the region is seen as no more than a pawn in an East-West game?

*Henze* suggested that any foreign policy thinking must be in several dimensions. He had argued on many occasions that the most important thing we can do for our national security interest is to communicate effectively. To many people this is a grotesque idea. The fact the United States has formidable means of communication with Eastern Europe, this has military significance. This would certainly be true in the Middle East. In earlier years we were in a more dynamic phase. Perhaps we can get back to it, for we have the basic prerequisites. When we had problems, for example, in Berlin, we strengthened an operation called RIAS (Radio in dem Amerikanischen Sektor), the basic American radio operation out of Berlin. It still exists today, but largely under German control. It is a distinguished operation, tailored to the specific needs of Berlin and East Germany. He did not see why we could not tailor a special radio for Afghanistan. The costs would be far less than sending in weaponry. *Wriggins* suggested we might put it in the defense budget. *Henze* agreed this would help.

*Gastil* asked if Tajik, Dari, and Persian were mutually intelligible? *Naby* said that they were on a written level by educated people, but on an oral, colloquial level we need separate broadcasts for Iran and Afghanistan. The broadcasts of Radio Liberty to Tajikistan use a different idiom than Dari because over the years there has been an introduction of Russian vocabulary, and other differences have been fostered.

*Nabawi* said that what the United States broadcasts as Dari would be the same as that broadcast from Kabul Radio, and what it broadcasts as Persian would be the same as that broadcast from Radio Tehran. If their difference is five percent, the difference of both from Tajik radio is probably twenty-five percent. It should be made clear that Kabul Radio broadcasts the language of the elite around Kabul, or "standard Dari," which is almost the same as "standard Persian." It does not broadcast local dialects or colloquial speech. (The use of a standard form of the language rather than either local dialects or colloquial speech is of course

the usual practice for news broadcasts the world over, including the
United States. Nabawi was glad there were Dari broadcasts now, but if
the VOA does not go on to broadcast in Pushtu, the other of
Afghanistans's two official languages, it will be a sensitive omission.
(*Naby* added that this is because of the internal politics.)

Communication is not only radio broadcasting. There is a large flow
of written literature from the Soviet Union to the countries of the area in
the native languages. Many institutions in the USSR study the peoples of
these countries. Students are native and Russian. Many Russians not
only know Pushtu, but in the school of Pushtu language in Leningrad the
teachers are Russians. Some Russians speak Pushtu dialects so fluently
that one can hardly tell them from natives. The West should recognize
the impact of this and reconsider its own policy in this respect, certainly
with respect to Pushtu programming from VOA.

*Gastil* asked if there was one Pushtu language that everyone would
understand. Several agreed there was, although there were dialects.

*Naby* noted that in 1968 the Soviet Ambassador's translator in Kabul
changed from a Dari speaker to a Pushtu speaker. This made it virtually
impossible for the Afghan bureaucracy to communicate with the Russian
Ambassador.

*Cottam* said that Naby's paper was controversial. He was in the
Teheran embassy in 1958. Although very junior, he may have played a
role in stopping the broadcasting. Selden Chapin, the Ambassador,
listened to Cottam on this issue, and Cottam had good reasons to urge
the Persian-language broadcasts be halted. His argument was based on
the situation at the time. They were both interested in broadening the
support of the Shah. (Cottam believed Chapin was the only one who
could have saved the Shah.) Chapin tried to push the Shah in the direction of broadening his support, and it was a period in which the Shah was
stable enough he could have. We had the image problem we still
have—we were considered his master and all-powerful. It is our image as
capitalist-Zionist-imperialist. But VOA had been one of the primary
targets of Joe McCarthy. Its response was to become ideological. Its
broadcasts were laissez faireist, while most of the people we wanted to attract were socialist; it constantly roared approval of the Shah, therefore
underlining the image Persian intellectuals already had of the Shah as an
American tool. Cottam believed that the only way we could combat that
image was to turn to a BBC format, so at least Iranians could see there
were American commentators that saw the situation in a detached way,
and we were not merely a set of Zionist imperialists. But since Cottam
had not thought this possible, he had argued that it was preferable to end
the broadcasts. Cottam ended his remarks by asking Naby what she now
would have us say to Saudi Arabia about democracy.

*Naby* thought that we should talk about democracy. This might lead to Saudi pressure, perhaps jamming, but if we do not try to present our case, we lose our credibility.

*Henze* agreed that the mistakes made in the fifties hurt the Voice. Since then it has been better protected, sometimes at the cost of being so bland it is hardly worth it. The question remains how you protect something like VOA.

*Wriggins* recalled that Naby had asked how we get more interest generated on behalf of understanding cultural diversities. He was working on the Hill in the fifties when *The Ugly American* came out. It had more impact on Congress than any other single publication on the importance of language training and learning about foreign languages and cultures. The Defense Education Act can be explained in part by that book and how it horrified so many Congressmen. They could not believe how little Americans knew of countries they were supposed to be dealing with. He wondered what would be an equally effective way today to dramatize the issue we are talking about.

*Henze* said he had spent a good deal of time on this in the last year. It was ironic that the Defense Education Act in its current form dates from 1958—which fits Wriggins' argument—and it is still on the books. A lot of university programs are funded through it. A rather thorough reexamination of the working of the Act has recently been done. As a result some changes are taking place through the Office of Education. It was discovered that over time the Act has largely worked to build up vested interests in university language and area study centers. These in turn lobby for the continuation of what they are doing. It is very hard to crack these interests to get something new going. Each university center has its senators and congressmen protecting it. This may lead to grotesque incongruities in the way money is divided under the Act. Henze had tried to turn this around on a number of key languages related to this area; the timetable is about three years.

Under the Act money can only be given to degree-granting institutions, and can only be granted in response to a request from an institution. The application has to be eighteen months before time of projected use, and the institution has to take the initiative.

*Gastil* summarized from the discussion the group's suggestions for broadcast content. There should be neutral news and information about the United States. Not much problem there. But the question of the stance we take toward the nationalities' movements and minorities in the area, and the stance we take toward Islam raise serious problems. One could think of a range of possibilities. Some criticism was made of taking a militant, pro-Islamic-fundamentalist point of view. This is probably not the way to go. But how we could say *anything* about Islam without doing more harm than good was hard for him to understand; still we should say something, particularly to support more modernist and liberal directions. We also need to address human rights questions, political rights and civil liberties. Maybe what we should do is emphasize what is going on in countries that we think are doing fairly well but are not identified with imperialism or Zionism. *Wriggins* added that we should not express American approval, but simply describe what others are doing. Our putting the stamp of approval can be deadening. *Gastil* concurred.

*Gastil* recalled that one of the points he hoped the conference would make is that whatever the policy question is—in this case it is information policy—it has to deal with the region as a whole. Broadcasting in Pushtu is a perfect example. We have got to be thinking of both Afghanistan and Pakistan. The Baluch are in several countries. Any Persian-language broadcast may well be understood throughout the area. The Azeri service should really be broadcasting to both sides of the border. It appeared to him that there should be a reorganization so that Soviet Muslim areas fell into a Middle Eastern or South Asian language area rather than being determined by the old (or new) Soviet border.

*Henze* concluded by requesting that anybody who is really interested in this should write his congressman, agitate about it. The state of our incapacity is disgraceful, given the modest amount of resources improvement requires.

# Summary and Conclusions*

The struggle for freedom in Muslim Central Asia is confused at the outset by conflicting definitions of freedom. To many freedom is and remains primarily national or ethnic self-determination, which politically often means independence. For Central Asians such "freedom" may be accompanied by the imposition of rigid schemes derived from Marxism or fundamentalist Islam that greatly restrict civil and political rights. To Americans, and we believe ultimately to most of the peoples involved, the freedoms that may be obtained under these conditions are not insubstantial but are tragically inadequate. Therefore, if we are to do more than exploit regional emotion, the United States must always support both independence for Central Asians and the strengthening of institutions that offer more adequate and general respect for individual and group rights.

From the American viewpoint the struggle in this region appears on three levels. On the first, the issue is the struggle between the United States and the Soviet Union. Our belief is that if we were to lose out in this struggle, ultimately freedom everywhere would be severely restricted. Therefore, to the extent we judge the struggle to be active and threatening, we will be willing to sacrifice most other foreign-policy considerations and interests in its pursuit. On the second level, we are concerned with preserving the independence and self-defense capabilities of all nations, including those of Central Asia. On the third level we are interested in supporting the freedoms of individuals

---

*This is the author's personal summarization of the conference proceedings and does not necessarily reflect the views of the other participants.

and groups, including ethnic minorities, within the countries of the area. Obviously these levels interact and conflict in every analyst's mind, yet the extent to which emphasis is placed on one or another is a key factor in the differentiation of positions. We cannot prove that one or another emphasis is correct, but it is possible to develop greater awareness of the degree to which our ability to resist the Soviet Union depends on our relations with other nations and peoples, and our ability to influence evolution toward freedom among these peoples depends on our ability to resist the Soviet Union.

The conference highlighted critical differences in analyses of the nature of the forces we face in the region. Some saw the recent regional evolution toward mass politics as fundamentally democratic; it had broken down the upper- and middle-class, and thereby often foreign, domination of politics. They saw American ability to influence future events in the region radically decreased in the face of the change to mass politics. In spite of the Soviet invasion of Afghanistan, they also saw the ability of the USSR to dominate the region actually receding, particularly if the United States did not give the Soviets explicit opportunities to intervene further. Others, including myself, saw less change. The United States never had had the power attributed to it, and it probably continued to have more than many believed. We see the USSR as little affected by the new mass politics. In this view Afghanistan's resistance is hardly an example of mass politics, and the USSR is deterred from further invasions of Iran and Pakistan more by the United States and world opinion than by fear of the difficulty of controlling the newly aroused peoples of the region. This interpretation obviously regards military power in more traditional terms, yet it does not doubt that the relations we have with the peoples of the area will be critical in the region's longer-term, political-military struggle.

The relation of the United States to Islamic revival on the one hand and to freedom on the other is an issue likely to bedevil our policy for many years. Islamic fundamentalism is seen by some as an authentic "revolt of the masses," and one extending at least symbolically into Soviet Central Asia. Others see the current revival as a short-lived deviation from the general secular trend affecting the whole region in the process of modernization. Those who see the fundamentalist trend as a basic change in regional direction believe that we must accept the limited freedoms offered by orthodox Islam as the price of true regional self-determination and of the mobilization of popular resistance to Russian advance. Those opposed to this view may be divided into two groups. One believes that the Islam of the future is and must be modernist, comparable perhaps to the liberal Christianity developed in the nineteenth century. The second regards Islam as a more serious barrier both to freedom and responsible government. They may regard the sharp break with the past that Ataturk forced on Turkish society as necessary. At the very least they regard it as incumbent upon Americans to support, wherever it is not counterproductive, liberalizing tendencies in Central Asian societies. In either event I do not see how in the name of cultural relativism Americans can fail to oppose repressions, such as those of the media, women, or minorities, that we regard as simply wrong.

The group heartily endorsed the need for more understanding by Americans of regional cultures. This means both more general understanding in our society as a whole and the finding and the training of area experts. The area language competence of American representatives and analysts in particular is minimal. However, we should not forget that the need is for critical "translators" between cultures rather than apologists for the region's cultures and political systems.

The decline of America's role in the region, accompanied by a decline in prospects for regional freedom, may be explained by a number of factors. The group generally felt that one of these was the inability of the United States to get across its message, and the message of the freedoms it stood for, in an effective manner. The imbalance in American and Soviet efforts in the field of international communication has always been far greater than any imbalance in military forces. Americans have not made the effort in this area because 1) they think propaganda disreputable, 2) they do not believe it works, and 3) they are no longer sure enough of the exportability of their system to make a serious effort to export it, particularly to the third world.

Communication is also hampered by the fact that we are not sure what our system is. Since the Soviet Union projects communism for propaganda purposes as an economic system, some Americans mistakenly think we must project capitalism as its counter. Obviously in this situation Americans not convinced of capitalism's particular value to others become tongue-tied.

Most conference participants were clear that Americans could do much more to promote and explain their most general ideas in the area of political and civil freedoms. Goodwill would also be attained by developing more reliable broadcasts informing the peoples of the area in their own languages of local and world events, with presentations couched in a cultural milieu attractive to them.

Our public communication policy must also improve its ability to complement standard diplomatic communication in a way that permits us to be effective on all three levels in our approach to the region. In particular the Soviet Union maintains correct and often friendly relations with area governments at the same time as it communicates a "nationalities" ideology that gives hope to the area's minority peoples (such as Baluch or Kurds) and a communist ideology that gives hope to opposition political parties. The United States, by contrast, feels it must do nothing to encourage nationalities or opposition parties as long as it has friendly intergovernmental relations. The result is that revolutionary forces of whatever stripe have often felt that only siding with the USSR is likely to advance their cause. This imbalance in communication needs to be addressed within the framework of a general expansion in the communication effort.

A start on this approach might be to present extended discusssions in American broadcasts and other media of federalism as it works in countries such as Switzerland, India, or Nigeria, and of the general American assumption that the rights of all minorities must be included in any democratic system. How this vision would be made to tie in with the minority problems of each country considered would of course be approached with care.

The proposition that any American policies or communications must be seen in area-wide terms was generally accepted. Some felt that instead of the United States developing an independent policy in regard to support for the Afghan resistance that an effort should be made to support the resistance through a grouping of more directly concerned Muslim states.

A particular reason to include Soviet Central Asia in the region of the conference's concern was that communication and awareness across the Soviet border among culturally related peoples has greatly increased since the invasion of Afghanistan. This offers dangers and opportunities to the United States, the Soviet Union, and the peoples of the region. Our ultimate goal must be to increase the ability of the region as a whole to stand on its own, and to develop a common consciousness of the possibility of a free society. We may be able to play a part in this long-term transition.

Most participants saw the key to Afghanistan in U.S.-Pakistan relations. Pakistan is the country most immediately threatened by events in Afghanistan, the country most able to help or crush the Afghan resistance, and the country most likely to come under severe Soviet pressure should the resistance receive substantial outside aid. Nevertheless, meeting the large-scale assistance demands of Pakistan raises serious objections. Its present government is repressive, both generally and of minority groups. In addition, to aid Pakistan substantially is to embitter relations between the United States and India, and to nudge India onto the Soviet side in regional conflicts. On the former question, it was hoped we could give aid while maintaining contacts with opposition groups, thereby making clear we were not supporting specifically the Zia regime. The group divided sharply, however, on the question of the degree our policy should adapt to Indian concerns. Some felt India's geopolitical position made its interests so dissimilar to ours that we could not take seriously its objections. Others felt that as the most important country in the area India could not be ignored, and that logically India should no longer have fears of an irretrievably weakened Pakistan. Their proposal was that the United States work for closer India-Pakistan relations, with United States support allocated by formula among the two. To me it seems clear on reflection that this latter must be a major aim of U.S. policy, at least in the longer term. As a relatively free polity India deserves special U.S. consideration in policy choices wherever possible.

As to Afghanistan itself, the group was strongly in favor of at least indirect U.S. support. The support should be such that it helps to raise the cost of the Soviet intervention while at the same time offering a plausible way out to the Soviets. Some believed this means supporting primarily those less fanatical and more liberal groups in the resistance that are most willing to seek a compromise solution. Others felt we should leave the complexion of the outcome up to the Afghans. My personal feeling is that we should at least make clear to all groups an outline of the Afghanistan we would like to emerge in terms of our values. How this translates into support for particular groups depends on the judgment of those Americans directly involved.

Ideas are the critical issue of the Central Asian struggle. We cannot allow Central Asians to continue to see the regional struggle as one between a communist system with an explicable, "scientific" vision of the future, and a capitalist system allied with the forces of reaction. We have a vision of the future, fundamentally a much more attractive vision than either communists or reactionaries. To make the vision of a free society a reality Central Asians will have to go through many of the struggles we have. But they will only take this path if we communicate it to them, and act as though we believe in it through both our words and our actions (actions, too, are communications).

Supporting freedom in Central Asia has a quixotic character. World history is not the history of freedom, and certainly Islamic history is no exception. Yet freedom is more generally enjoyed today than at any time in history. In spite of the Hellenic experience and other isolated examples, the civil and political freedoms enjoyed by most countries are very recently come by. Who would have predicted democracy for Germany, Japan, and Italy in 1940, or for Spain and Portugal in 1960? But their repressive traditions we set aside—and so, with difficulty, they may be everywhere.

Muslim Central Asia is not an area of freedom today. Yet there are sparks, and there is widespread knowledge of free society among the educated. If we winnow down what we are after, consistently support those with similar objectives, and open a dialogue with the people of the region as a whole, we can hope for renewed movement toward a more liberal and humane path. If we utilize our temporary eclipse of regional power on the ground—power that was always more imaginary than real—to get across our message, then our failures of the recent past can be turned into a better future for Central Asians and all of us.

# PART IV

# Country Summaries

# Introduction

The following country descriptions summarize the evidence that lies behind our ratings for each country. They first bring together for each country most of the tabular material of Part I. Then, political rights are considered in terms of the extent to which a country is ruled by a government elected by the majority at the national level, the division of power among levels of government, and the possible denial of self-determination to major subnationalities, if any. While decentralization and the denial of group rights are deemphasized in our rating system, these questions should not be ignored. The summaries also contain consideration of civil liberties, especially as these include freedom of the media and other forms of political expression, freedom from political imprisonment, torture, and other forms of government reprisal, and freedom from interference in nonpublic group or personal life. Equality of access to politically relevant expression is also considered. In some cases the summaries will touch on the relative degree of freedom from oppression outside of the government arena, for example, through slavery, labor bosses, capitalist exploitation, or private terrorism; this area of analysis is little developed at present.

At the beginning of each summary statement the country is characterized by the forms of its economy and polity. The meanings of the terms used in this classification may be found in Part I, "The Relation of Political-Economic Systems to Freedom," and its accompanying Table 6. The classification is highly simplified, but it serves our concern with the developmental forms and biases that affect political controls. The terms employed in Part I and Table 6 differ from those used in the following summaries only in that the capitalist-socialist term in the former discussion is divided into two classes in the summaries. *Mixed capitalist* systems, such as those in Israel, the Netherlands, or Sweden, provide social services on a large scale through governmental or other nonprofit institutions with the result that private control over property is sacrificed to egalitarian purposes. These nations still see capitalism as legitimate, but its legitimacy is accepted grudgingly by many in government. *Mixed socialist* states such as Iraq or Poland proclaim themselves to be socialist but in fact allow rather large portions of the economy to remain in the private domain. As in Table 6 the terms *inclusive* and *noninclusive* are used to distinguish between societies in which the economic activities of most people are organized in accordance with the dominant system and those dual societies in which they remain largely outside. The system should be assumed to be inclusive unless otherwise indicated.

Each state is categorized according to the political positions of the national or ethnic groups it contains. Since the modern political form is the "nation-state," it is not surprising that many states have a *relatively homogeneous population*. The overwhelming majority in these states belong to roughly the same ethnic group; people from this group naturally form the dominant group in the state. In relatively homogeneous states there is no large subnationality (this is, with more than one million people or twenty percent of the population) residing in a defined territory within the country: Austria, Costa Rica, Somalia, and West Germany are good examples. States in this category may be ethnically diverse (for example, Cuba or Colombia), but there are no sharp ethnic lines between major groups. These states should be distinguished from *ethnically complex states*, such as Guyana or Singapore, that have several ethnic groups, but no major group that has its historic homeland in a particular part of the country. Complex states may have large minorities that have suffered social, political, or economic discrimination in the recent past, but today governments in such states treat all peoples as equals as a matter of policy. In this regard complex states are distinguishable from *ethnic states with major nonterritorial subnationalities*, for the governments of such states have a deliberate policy of giving preference to the dominant ethnic group at the expense of other major groups. Examples are Burundi or China (Taiwan).

Another large category of states is labeled *ethnic states with (a) major territorial subnationalities (y)*. As in the homogeneous states there is a definite ruling people (or *Staatsvolk*) residing on its historic national territory within the state. But the state also incorporates other territories with other historic peoples that are now either without a state, or the state dominated by their people lies beyond the new border. As explained in *Freedom in the World 1978* (pp. 180-218), to be considered a subnationality a territorial minority must have enough cohesion and publicity that their right to nationhood is acknowledged in some quarters. Events have forged a quasi-unity among groups only recently quite distinct—as are Burma and the USSR; more marginally states such as Peru or Laos are also included. *Ethnic states with major potential territorial subnationalities* fall into a closely related category. In such states—for example, Ecuador or Bolivia—many individuals in the ethnic group have merged, with little overt hostility, with the dominant ethnic strain. The assimilation process has gone on for centuries. Yet in these countries the new consciousness that accompanies the diffusion of nationalist ideas through education may reverse the process of assimilation in the future, especially where the potential subnationality has preserved a more or less definable territorial base.

There are a few truly *multinational* states in which ethnic groups with territorial bases coexist in one state without a clearly definable ruling people or *Staatsvolk*. In such states the several "nations" each have autonomous political rights, although these do not in law generally include the right to secession. India and Nigeria are examples. One *trinational* and a few *binational* states complete the categories of those states in which several nations coexist.

The distinction between truly multinational states and ethnic states with territorial subnationalites may be made by comparing two major states that lie close to the margin between the categories—the ethnic Russian USSR and multinational India. In the USSR, Russian is in every way the dominant language. By contrast, in India Hindi speakers have not achieved dominance. English remains a unifying lingua franca, the languages of the several states have not been forced to change their script to accord with Hindi forms, and Hindi itself is not the distinctive language of a "ruling people"—it is a nationalized version of the popular language of a portion of the population of northern India. (The pre-British ruling class used a closely related language with Arabic, Persian, and Turkish infusions; it was generally written in Persian-Arabic script.) Unlike Russians in the non-Russian Soviet Republics, Hindi speakers from northern India do not have a special standing in their own eyes or those of other Indians. Calcutta, Bombay, and Madras are non-Hindi speaking cities, and their pride in their identities and cultures is an important aspect of Indian culture. By contrast, many Soviet Republics are dominated by Russian speakers, a situation developing even in Kiev, the largest non-Russian city.

Finally, *transethnic heterogeneous states*, primarily in Africa, are those in which independence found a large number of ethnically distinct peoples grouped more or less artificially within one political framework. The usual solution was for those taking over the reins of government to adopt the colonial approach of formally treating all local peoples as equal, but with the new objective of integrating all equally into a new national framework (and new national identity) as and when this would be possible. Rulers of states such as Senegal or Zaire often come from relatively small tribes, and it is in their interest to deemphasize tribalism. In some cases the tribes are so scattered and localistic that there is no short-term likelihood of secession resulting from tribalism. However, in other cases portions of the country have histories of separate nationhood making the transethnic solution hard to implement. In a few countries recent events have placed certain ethnic groups in opposition to one another or to ruling circles in such a way that the transethnic state remains only the *formal* principle of rule, replaced in practice by an ethnic hierarchy, as in Congo or Liberia (until 1980).

The descriptive paragraphs for political and civil rights are largely self-explanatory. Subnationalities are generally discussed under a sub-heading for political rights, although the subject has obvious civil liberties aspects. Discussion of the existence or nonexistence of political parties may be arbitrarily placed in one or the other section. These paragraphs only touch on a few relevant issues, especially in the civil liberties discussion. An issue may be omitted for lack of information, because it does not seem important for the country addressed, or because a particular condition can be inferred from the general statement of a pattern. It should be noted that we have tried to incorporate the distinction between a broad definition of political prisoners (including those detained for violent political crimes) and a narrow definition that includes those arrested only for nonviolent actions—often labeled "prisoners of conscience." At the end of each country summary we have included an overall comparative statement that places the country's ratings in relation to those of others. Countries chosen for comparison are often neighboring or similar ones, but juxtaposing very different countries is also necessary for tying together the system.

The following summaries take little account of the oppressions that occur within the social units of a society, such as family and religious groups, or that reflect variations in the nonpolitical aspects of culture. In particular, the reader will note few references in the following summaries to the relative freedom of women. This may be a serious gap in the Survey, but with limited resources we felt that it was better to omit this range of issues than to only tangentially include it. We suspect that including the freedom of women would not affect the ratings a great deal. Democracies today have almost universally opened political and civic participation to women on at least a formal basis of equality, while most nondemocratic societies that deny these equal rights to women also deny effective participation to most men. In such societies granting equal rights may have limited meaning. It is little gain for political and most civil rights when women are granted equal participation in a totalitarian society.

# AFGHANISTAN

**Economy:** noninclusive socialist
**Polity:** Communist one-party
**Population:** 15,900,000*

**Political Rights:** 7
**Civil Liberties:** 7
**Status of Freedom:** not free

An ethnic state with major territorial subnationalities

**Political Rights.** Afghanistan is now ruled by a communist party under the tutelage and direct control of the Soviet Union. The rule of this very small party (10,000 to 20,000) has no electoral or traditional legitimization. Soviet forces control the major cities but their control is contested by a variety of resistance movements throughout the country. *Subnationalities*: The largest minority is the Tajik (thirty percent), the dominant people of the cities and the western part of the country. Essentially lowland Persians, their language remains the lingua franca of the country, although it was government policy to require equal use of the language of the Pathan majority, especially in the bureaucracy. The Persian speaking Hazaras constitute five to ten percent of the population. Another ten percent belong to Uzbek and other Turkish groups in the north.

**Civil Liberties.** The press is government owned and under rigid censorship. Antigovernment organization or expression is forbidden. Conversation is guarded and travel is restricted. In a condition of civil war and foreign occupation, political imprisonment, torture, and execution are common, in addition to war deaths and massacres. The objectives of the state are totalitarian; their achievement is limited by the continuing struggle for control.

**Comparatively:** Afghanistan is as free as Vietnam, less free than Iran.

# ALBANIA

**Economy:** socialist
**Polity:** communist one-party
**Population:** 2,700,000

**Political Rights:** 7
**Civil Liberties:** 7
**Status of Freedom:** not free

A relatively homogeneous population

**Political Rights.** Albania has been a communist dictatorship under essentially one-man rule since 1944. While there are a number of elected bodies, including an assembly, the parallel government of the communist

*Population estimates for all countries are generally derived from the 1980 World Population Data Sheet of the Population Reference Bureau, Washington, D.C.

party (three percent of the people) is decisive at all levels; elections offer only one list of candidates. Candidates are officially designated by the Democratic Front, to which all Albanians are supposed to belong. In the 1970s several extensive purges within the party have apparently been designed to maintain the power of the top leaders.

**Civil Liberties.** Press, radio, and television are completely under government or party control, and communication with the outside world is minimal. Media are characterized by incessant propaganda, and open expression of opinion in private conversation is rare. Political imprisonment is common; torture is frequently reported. All religious institutions were abolished in 1967; religion is outlawed; priests are regularly imprisoned. Apparently there are no private organizations independent of government or party. Economic disparities are comparatively small: all people must work one month of each year in factories or on farms, and there are no private cars. Attempting to leave the state is a major crime. Private economic choice is minimal.

**Comparatively:** Albania is as free as Kampuchea, less free than Yugoslavia.

# ALGERIA

**Economy:** socialist                           **Political Rights:** 6
**Polity:** socialist one-party            **Civil Liberties:** 6
**Population:** 19,000,000                 **Status of Freedom:** not free
An ethnic state with a potential subnationality

**Political Rights.** Algeria has combined military dictatorship with one-party socialist rule. Elections at both local and national levels are managed by the party; they allow little opposition to the system, although individual representatives and specific policies may be criticized. Recent elections resulted in ninety-nine percent favorable votes. However, the pragmatic, puritanical, military rulers are probably supported by a fairly broad consensus. *Subnationalities*: About twenty percent of the people are Berbers: recent riots suggest a continual desire for enhanced self-determination.

**Civil Liberties.** The media are governmental means for active indoctrination; no opposition voice is allowed, and foreign publications are closely watched. Private conversation appears relatively open. Although not fully independent, the regular judiciary has established a rule of law in some areas. Prisoners of conscience are detained for short periods, but no long-term prisoners are now held. No appeal from the decisions of the special Revolutionary Courts for crimes against the state is allowed; there have been reports of torture. Land reform has transformed former French plantations into collectives. Although government goals are clearly socialist, many small farms and businesses remain.

Travel is generally free. Eighty percent of the people are illiterate; many are still very poor, but extremes of wealth have been reduced. Islam's continued strength provides a counterweight to governmental absolutism. There is religious freedom.

**Comparatively:** Algeria is as free as Tanzania, freer than Iraq, less free than Morocco.

# ANGOLA

**Economy:** noninclusive socialist    **Political Rights:** 7
**Polity:** socialist one-party    **Civil Liberties:** 7
**Population:** 6,700,000    **Status of Freedom:** not free
A transethnic heterogeneous state with major subnationalities

**Political Rights.** Angola is ruled by a very small communist-style socialist party in which military commanders may wield considerable power. The ruling party has relied heavily on Soviet equipment and Cuban troops to dominate the civil war and to stay in power. In 1980 an indirectly elected parliament was established. The country seems to be falling under increasing Soviet or Cuban control. *Subnationalities*: The party is not tribalist, but is opposed by groups relying on particular tribes or regions—especially in Cabinda, the northeast, and the south-central areas. The UNITA movement among the Ovimbundu people actively controls much of the south and east of the country.

**Civil Liberties.** There is no constitution; the nation remains in a state of war, with power arbitrarily exercised, particularly in the countryside. The media in controlled areas are government owned and do not deviate from its line. Political imprisonment and execution is common; repression of religious activity is reported. Travel is tightly restricted. Private medical care has been abolished, as has much private property—especially in the modern sectors. Strikes are prohibited and unions tightly controlled. Agricultural production is held down by peasant opposition to socialization and lack of markets.

**Comparatively:** Angola is as free as Vietnam, less free than Zambia.

# ARGENTINA

**Economy:** capitalist-statist    **Political Rights:** 6
**Polity:** military nonparty    **Civil Liberties:** 5
**Population:** 27,100,000    **Status of Freedom:** not free
A relatively homogeneous population

**Political Rights.** Ruled today by a military junta, Argentina oscillates between democracy and authoritarianism. The military's last intervention probably had initial popular support because of the high level of both right- and left-wing terrorism, and the corrupt and ineffective regime it replaced. The continued use of violence by the regime and its supporters to silence opposition has eroded this support. The regions are now under direct junta control. The government has only limited control over its security forces.

**Civil Liberties.** Private newspapers and both private and government broadcasting stations operate; to a limited degree they report unfavorable events and criticism by opponents of the government. Yet both self-censorship and newspaper closings are common. Censorship of media and private expression also occurs informally through the threat of terrorist attacks from radical leftist or rightist groups (with the latter apparently supported by, or associated with, elements of the military and police). The universities are closely controlled. While courts retain some independence, arbitrary arrest, torture, and execution have affected thousands and continue on a reduced scale. The church and trade unions play a strong opposition role, although there is frequent pressure on the unions. Human rights organizations are active. For non-Catholics religious freedom is curtailed.

**Comparatively:** Argentina is as free as Yugoslavia, freer than Cuba, less free than Chile.

# AUSTRALIA

**Economy:** capitalist                  **Political Rights:** 1
**Polity:** decentralized multiparty    **Civil Liberties:** 1
**Population:** 14,600,000              **Status of Freedom:** free
A relatively homogeneous population with small aboriginal groups

**Political Rights.** Australia is a federal parliamentary democracy with strong powers retained by its component states. With equal representation from each state, the Senate provides a counterbalance to the nationally representative House of Representatives. There have been recent changes in government, with the Labour Party gaining control in 1972 only to lose it again in 1975. The British appointed Governor General retains some power in constitutional deadlocks. Trade unions (separately and through the Labour Party) and foreign investors have great economic weight. The states have separate parliaments and premiers, but appointed governors. The relative power of rural peoples and aborigines has recently been strengthened, particularly through the establishment of the new Northern Territory.

**Civil Liberties.** All the newspapers and most radio and television stations are privately owned. The Australian Broadcasting Commission operates government radio and television stations on a basis similar to BBC. Although Australia lacks many formal guarantees of civil liberties, the degree of protection of these liberties in the common law is similar to that in Britain and Canada. Freedom of assembly is generally respected, although it varies by region. Freedom of choice in education, travel, occupation, property, and private association are perhaps as complete as anywhere in the world. Relatively low taxes enhance this freedom.

**Comparatively:** Australia is as free as the United Kingdom, freer than Italy.

# AUSTRIA

**Economy:** mixed capitalist
**Polity:** (centralized) multiparty
**Population:** 7,500,000
A relatively homogeneous population

**Political Rights:** 1
**Civil Liberties:** 1
**Status of Freedom:** free

**Political Rights.** Austria's parliamentary system has a directly elected lower house and an upper (and less powerful) house elected by the provincial assemblies. The president is directly elected, but the chancellor (representing the majority party in parliament) is the center of political power. The two major parties have alternated control since the 1950s but the government often seeks broad consensus. The referendum is used on rare occasions. Provincial legislatures and governors are elective. *Subnationalities*: Fifty thousand Slovenes in the southern part of the country have rights to their own schools.

**Civil Liberties.** The press in Austria is free and varied; radio and television are under a state-owned corporation that by law is supposed to be free of political control. Its geographical position and constitutionally defined neutral status places its media and government in a position analogous to Finland, but the Soviets have put less pressure on Austria to conform to Soviet wishes than on Finland. The rule of law is secure, and there are no political prisoners. Banks and heavy industry are largely nationalized.

**Comparatively:** Austria is as free as Belgium, freer than Greece.

# BAHAMAS

**Economy:** capitalist
**Polity:** centralized multiparty
**Population:** 200,000
A relatively homogeneous population

**Political Rights:** 1
**Civil Liberties:** 2
**Status of Freedom:** free

**Political Rights.** The Bahamas have a parliamentary system with a largely ceremonial British Governor General. The ruling party has a large majority, but there is an opposition in parliament. Most islands are administered by centrally appointed commissioners.

**Civil Liberties.** There are independent newspapers, but through re-stricting income and preventing hiring or keeping desired employees, the government has exerted pressure on the opposition press. Radio is government owned and is not completely free of government control. In other respects Bahamas' freedoms seem reasonably secure.

**Comparatively:** Bahamas is as free as Venezuela, freer than Malta, less free than Barbados.

# BAHRAIN

**Economy:** capitalist-statist  
**Polity:** traditional nonparty  
**Population:** 400,000  

**Political Rights:** 5  
**Civil Liberties:** 5  
**Status of Freedom:** partly free  

The citizenry is relatively homogeneous

**Political Rights.** Bahrain is a traditional shaikhdom with a modernized administration. Direct access to the ruler is encouraged. At present the legislature is dissolved, but powerful merchant and religious families place a check on royal power. There are local councils. *Subnationalities*: The primary ethnic problem has been the struggle between the Iranians who once ruled and the Arabs who now rule; in part this is reflected in the opposition of the ruling Sunni and majority Shiite Muslim sects.

**Civil Liberties.** The government and private press seldom criticize government policy. Radio and television are government owned. Al-though freedom of expression and assembly are cautiously expressed, a climate of fear does not exist. The legal and educational systems are a mixture of traditional Islamic and British. Short-term arrest is used to discourage dissent, and there are long-term political prisoners. In security cases involving violence fair and quick trials are delayed and torture occurs. Rights to travel, property, and religious choice are secured. There is a record of disturbances by workers groups, although union organization is restricted. Many free social services are provided. Citizen-ship is very hard to obtain; there is antipathy to foreign workers (but unlike neighboring shaikhdoms most people in the country are citizens).

**Comparatively:** Bahrain is as free as China (Taiwan), freer than Saudi Arabia, less free than India.

# BANGLADESH

**Economy:** noninclusive capitalist-statist  
**Polity:** centralized multiparty (military dominated)  
**Population:** 90,600,000  

**Political Rights:** 3  
**Civil Liberties:** 4  
**Status of Freedom:** partly free  

A relatively homogeneous population with Hindu and Bihari minorities

**Political Rights.** Bangladesh is ruled by a president and parliament. Recent parliamentary and presidential elections have shown a satisfactory degree of competition. The shadow of the violent military rule of the recent past still hangs over election processes and parliamentary independence. *Subnationalities*: Fighting with minor tribal groups along the border continues; the Bihari minority suffers discrimination.

**Civil Liberties.** The press is private, government, and party. The papers are not censored but there are still some controls. Radio and television are government controlled, but are not actively used for mobilization. The existence of a broad spectrum of political parties allows for the organization of dissent. Some political imprisonment continues to occur, but there are few prisoners of conscience. The courts can decide against the government. In spite of considerable communal antipathy, religious freedom exists. Travel is generally unrestricted. Although they do not have the right to strike, labor unions are active and strikes occur. Corruption remains a major problem.

**Comparatively:** Bangladesh is as free as Malaysia, freer than Burma, less free than India.

## BARBADOS

**Economy:** capitalist
**Polity:** centralized multiparty
**Population:** 300,000
A relatively homogeneous population

**Political Rights:** 1
**Civil Liberties:** 1
**Status of Freedom:** free

**Political Rights.** Barbados is governed by a parliamentary system, with a ceremonial British Governor General. Elections have been fair and well-administered. Power alternates between the two major parties. Local governments are also elected.

**Civil Liberties.** Newspapers are private and free of government control. There are both private and government radio stations, but the government-controlled radio station also controls the only television station on the BBC model. There is an independent judiciary, and general freedom from arbitrary government action. Travel, residence, and religion are free. Although both major parties rely on the support of labor, private property is fully accepted.

**Comparatively:** Barbados is as free as the United Kingdom, freer than Jamaica.

## BELGIUM

**Economy:** capitalist
**Polity:** decentralized multiparty
**Population:** 9,900,000
A binational state

**Political Rights:** 1
**Civil Liberties:** 1
**Status of Freedom:** free

**Political Rights.** Belgium is a constitutional monarchy with a bicameral parliament. Elections lead to coalition governments, generally of the center. Linguistic divisions have produced considerable instability. *Subnationalities*; The rise of nationalism among the two major peoples —Flemish and Walloon—has led to increasing transfer of control over cultural affairs to the communal groups. However, provincial governors are appointed by the national government.

**Civil Liberties.** Newspapers are free and uncensored. Radio and television are government owned, but the director of each station is solely responsible for programming. The full spectrum of private rights is respected, but voting is compulsory.

**Comparatively:** Belgium is as free as Switzerland, freer than France.

# BENIN

**Economy:** noninclusive socialist
**Polity:** socialist one-party (military dominated)
**Population:** 3,600,000
A transethnic heterogeneous state

**Political Rights:** 7
**Civil Liberties:** 6
**Status of Freedom:** not free

**Political Rights.** Benin is a military dictatorship buttressed by a one-party organization. Regional and tribal loyalties may be stronger than national. Elections are single-list, with no opposition. Local assemblies are closely controlled.

**Civil Liberties.** All media are rigidly censored; most are owned by the government. Opposition is not tolerated; criticism of the government often leads to a few days of reeducation in military camps. There are few long-term political prisoners, but the rule of law is very weak. Private schools have been closed. Jehovah's Witnesses are banned, independent labor unions forbidden. Permission to leave the country is closely controlled. Economically, the government's interventions have been in cash crops and internal trade, and industries have been nationalized; control over the largely subsistence and small entrepreneur economy remains incomplete.

**Comparatively:** Benin is as free as Burma, freer than Angola, less free than Senegal.

# BHUTAN

**Economy:** preindustrial
**Polity:** traditional nonparty
**Population:** 1,300,000
An ethnic state with a significant subnationality

**Political Rights:** 5
**Civil Liberties:** 5
**Status of Freedom:** partly free

**Political Rights.** Bhutan is a hereditary monarchy in which the king rules with the aid of a council and the indirectly elected National Assembly. There are no legal political parties and the Assembly does little more than approve government actions. Villages are traditionally ruled by their own headmen, but districts are directly ruled from the center. The Buddhist hierarchy is still very important in the affairs of the country. In foreign policy Bhutan's dependence upon India has been partially renounced; it is still dependent for defense. *Subnationalities*: The main political party operates outside the country, agitating in favor of the Nepalese minority (about 250,000) and a more open system.

**Civil Liberties.** The news media are government owned and operated, but outside media are freely available. There are few if any prisoners of conscience. The legal structure exhibits a mixture of traditional and British forms. There is religious freedom and freedom to travel. Traditional agriculture, crafts, and trade dominate the economy.

**Comparatively:** Bhutan is as free as Maldives, freer than Burma, less free than India.

# BOLIVIA

**Economy:** noninclusive capitalist-statist

**Polity:** military nonparty

**Population:** 5,300,000

**Political Rights:** 7

**Civil Liberties:** 5

**Status of Freedom:** not free

An ethnic state with major potential subnationalities

**Political Rights.** Bolivia is a military dictatorship. Provincial and local government is controlled from the center. Argentine participation in the 1980 coup that destroyed the developing democracy suggests a degree of outside control. *Subnationalities:* Over sixty percent of the people are Indians speaking Aymara or Quechua; these languages have been given official status alongside Spanish. The Indian peoples remain, however, more potential than active nationalities.

**Civil Liberties.** The press and most radio and television stations are private. Programming is, however, forced to strictly conform, and the press is under strong pressure. The military coup in July 1980 resulted in imposition of an "Argentine system," with disappearance, imprisonment, and torture affecting thousands. Even private criticism of the government is dangerous. Universities have been closed; labor unions disbanded. Although suffering from government violence the Church has retained a critical role. The people are overwhelmingly post-land-reform, subsistence agriculturists. The major mines are nationalized; the workers have a generous social welfare program, given the country's poverty.

**Comparatively:** Bolivia is as free as Cuba, freer than Guinea, less free than Brazil.

# BOTSWANA

**Economy:** noninclusive capitalist
**Polity:** decentralized multiparty
**Population:** 800,000
A relatively homogeneous population

**Political Rights:** 2
**Civil Liberties:** 3
**Status of Freedom:** free

**Political Rights.** The republican system of Botswana combines traditional and modern principles. The assembly is elected for a fixed term and appoints the president who rules. There is also an advisory House of Chiefs. Nine districts, led either by chiefs or elected leaders, have independent power of taxation, as well as traditional power over land and agriculture. Elections continue to be won overwhelmingly by the ruling party as they were even before independence, yet there are opposition members in parliament and local governments. There is economic and political pressure from both black African and white neighbors. *Subnationalities*: The country is divided among several major tribes belonging to the Batswana people, as well as minor peoples on the margins. The latter include a few hundred comparatively wealthy white farmers.

**Civil Liberties.** The radio and most newspapers are government owned; however, there is no censorship, and South African media present an available alternative. Rights of assembly, religion, and travel are respected; prisoners of conscience are not held. Unions are independent. Judicially, civil liberties appear to be guaranteed, although on the local scale the individual tribesman may have considerably less freedom.

**Comparatively:** Botswana is as free as Gambia, freer than Zambia, less free than Barbados.

# BRAZIL

**Economy:** capitalist-statist
**Polity:** decentralized multiparty
        (military dominated)
**Population:** 118,000,000
A complex but relatively homogeneous population with many small, territorial subnationalities

**Political Rights:** 4
**Civil Liberties:** 3
**Status of Freedom:** partly free

**Political Rights.** Brazil has been governed by a president, essentially elected by the military, and a popularly elected but weak assembly. Legislative elections in 1978 gave a majority to the opposition, although the opposition did not gain legislative majorities. Party organization is controlled, but party activity is increasingly competitive; only the communist party remains banned. Illiterates do not have the vote. There are independently organized elected governments at both state and local levels; governorships will soon also become elective. *Subnationalities:* The many small Indian groups of the interior are under both private and public pressure. Some still fight back in the face of loss of land, lives, and culture.

**Civil Liberties.** The media are private, except for a few broadcasting stations. The powerful press is now free of overt censorship; government control of most industry, and thus advertising and right-wing terrorism reduce freedom to criticize government. Radio and television practice limited self-censorship. There is a general right of assembly and organization, and few if any prisoners of conscience. Political exiles returned in 1979. Private violence against criminals and suspected communists may continue outside the law, and police brutality remains common. Opposition voices are regularly heard—including parliamentarians, journalists, and officials of the church. Union organization is powerful and strikes are widespread, though sometimes repressed. There is considerable large-scale government industry, but rights to property, religious freedom, travel, and education of one's choice are generally respected.

**Comparatively:** Brazil is as free as Mexico, freer than Uruguay, less free than Jamaica.

# BULGARIA

**Economy:** socialist  
**Polity:** communist one-party  
**Population:** 8,900,000  
A relatively homogeneous population

**Political Rights:** 7  
**Civil Liberties:** 7  
**Status of Freedom:** not free

**Political Rights.** Bulgaria is governed by its communist party, although the facade of a parallel government and two-party system is maintained. The same man has essentially ruled over the system since 1954 (his daughter is now perhaps the second most powerful political figure); elections at both national and local levels have little meaning.

Both economically and politically the country is subservient to the Soviet Union. *Subnationalities*: Muslim minorities of about one million are persecuted in several ways.

**Civil Liberties.** All media are controlled by the government or its party branches. Citizens have few if any rights against the state. There are hundreds or thousands of prisoners of conscience, many living under severe conditions. Psychiatric institutions are also used against prisoners of conscience. Brutality and torture are common. The detained may also be banished to villages, denied their occupations, or confined in psychiatric hospitals. Believers are subject to discrimination. The most common political crimes are illegally trying to leave the country, criticism of the government, and illegal contacts with foreigners.

**Comparatively:** Bulgaria is as free as Mongolia, less free than Hungary.

# BURMA

**Economy:** noninclusive mixed socialist
**Polity:** socialist one-party (military dominated)
**Population:** 34,400,000

**Political Rights:** 7
**Civil Liberties:** 6
**Status of Freedom:** not free

An ethnic state with major territorial subnationalities

**Political Rights.** Burma is a one-party socialist, military dictatorship. The government's dependence on the army makes its strengths and weaknesses more those of a military dictatorship than those of a communist regime. Elections are held at both national and local levels; the Party chooses the slate of candidates. *Subnationalities*: The government represents essentially the Burmese people that live in the heartland of the country. The Burmese are surrounded by millions of non-Burmese living in continuing disaffection or active revolt. Among the minorities in the periphery are the Karens, Shan, Kachins, Mon, and Chin.

**Civil Liberties.** All media are government owned, with alternative opinions expressed obliquely if at all; both domestic and foreign publications are censored. Organized dissent is forbidden; in part, this policy is explained by the almost continuous warfare the government has had to wage since independence against both rebellious subnationalities and two separate communist armies. This state of war has been augmented since the 1960s by the attempts of civilian politicians to regain power by armed force or antigovernment demonstration, as well as recent plots within the army itself. (Some opposition leaders have recently become reconciled to the regime.) Prisoners of conscience are common and torture is reported. The regular court structure has been replaced by "people's courts." Religion is free; union activity is not; both internal and external travel are very difficult. Although the eventual goal of the government is complete socialization, there are areas of private enterprise.

**Comparatively:** Burma is as free as Romania, freer than Kampuchea, less free than Thailand.

# BURUNDI

**Economy:** noninclusive mixed
**Polity:** socialist one-party (military dominated)
**Population:** 4,500,000

**Political Rights:** 7
**Civil Liberties:** 6
**Status of Freedom:** not free

An ethnic state with a majority, nonterritorial subnationality

**Political Rights.** Burundi is ruled by a self-appointed military president with the assistance of the Party Central Committee and Politburo. There is no elected assembly. *Subnationalities*: The rulers continue to be from the Tutsi ethnic group (fifteen percent) that has traditionally ruled; their dominance was reinforced by a massacre of Hutus (eighty-five percent) after an attempted revolt in the early 1970s.

**Civil Liberties.** The media are now all government controlled and closely censored. Lack of freedom of political speech or assembly is accompanied by political imprisonment and reports of brutality. Under current conditions there is little guarantee of individual rights, particularly for the Hutu majority. In recent years exclusion of the Hutu from public services, the party, and so forth, has declined. There are no independent unions. Traditional group and individual rights no doubt persist on the village level: Burundi is not a highly structured modern society. Travel is relatively unrestricted. Education is controlled, missionary activity closely regulated. Although officially socialist, private or traditional economic forms predominate.

**Comparatively:** Burundi is as free as Benin, freer than Somalia, less free then Kenya.

# CAMBODIA

## (See Kampuchea)

# CAMEROON

**Economy:** noninclusive capitalist
**Polity:** nationalist one-party
**Population:** 8,500,000

**Political Rights:** 6
**Civil Liberties:** 6
**Status of Freedom:** not free

A transethnic heterogeneous state with a major subnationality

**Political Rights.** Cameroon is a one-party state ruled by the same person since independence in 1960. The government has steadily centralized power. Referendums and other elections have little meaning; voters are given no alternatives and provide ninety-nine percent majorities. Provincial governors are appointed by the central government. An attempt has been made to incorporate all elements in a government of broad consensus. *Subnationalities*: The most significant opposition has come from those opposing centralization, particularly movements supported by the country's largest ethnic group, the Bamileke (twenty-six percent). Other ethnic groups are quite small.

**Civil Liberties.** The media are closely controlled and self-censorship common; works of critical authors are prohibited. Freedom of speech, assembly, and union organization are limited, while freedom of occupation, education, and property are respected. Prisoners of conscience are detained without trial and may be ill-treated. Allegations have been made of torture and village massacres. Internal travel and religious choice are relatively free; foreign travel may be difficult. Labor and business organizations are controlled. The government has supported land reform; although still relatively short on capital, private enterprise is encouraged wherever possible.

**Comparatively:** Cameroon is as free as Gabon, freer than Niger, less free than Ghana.

# CANADA

**Economy:** capitalist
**Polity:** decentralized multiparty
**Population:** 24,000,000
A binational state

**Political Rights:** 1
**Civil Liberties:** 1
**Status of Freedom:** free

**Political Rights.** Canada is a parliamentary democracy with alternation of rule between leading parties. The provinces have their own democratic institutions with a higher degree of autonomy than the American states. *Subnationalities*: In an attempt to prevent the breakup of Canada, the government had moved toward granting French linguistic equality; French has become the official language in Quebec. In addition, Quebec has been allowed to opt out of some national programs and maintains its own representatives abroad.

**Civil Liberties.** The media are free, although there is a government-related radio and television network. The full range of civil liberties is generally respected. In Quebec rights to choose education and language for many purposes have been infringed. There has been evidence of the invasion of privacy by Canadian security forces in recent years, much as in the United States. Many judicial and legal structures have been borrowed from the United Kingdom or the United States, with consequent advantages and disadvantages.

**Comparatively:** Canada is as free as the United States of America, freer than Italy.

# CAPE VERDE ISLANDS

**Economy:** noninclusive socialist
**Polity:** socialist one-party
**Population:** 315,000
A relatively homogeneous state

**Political Rights:** 6
**Civil Liberties:** 6
**Status of Freedom:** not free

**Political Rights.** The ruling, single party is small and tightly organized. Elections allow no choice but abstention and negative votes are allowed.

**Civil Liberties.** The media are government owned and closely controlled. Prisoners of conscience are frequently detained for short periods; rights to organize opposition, assembly, or political expression are not respected. The judiciary is weak. For its region Cape Verde's seventy-five percent literacy is very high. The Islands' plantation agriculture has been largely nationalized, but endemic unemployment continues to lead to emigration. Religion is relatively free, although under political pressure; labor unions are government controlled.

**Comparatively:** Cape Verde Islands is as free as Tanzania, freer than Ethiopia, less free than Ivory Coast.

# CENTRAL AFRICAN REPUBLIC

**Economy:** noninclusive capitalist
**Polity:** nonmilitary nonparty
**Population:** 2,200,000
A transethnic heterogeneous state

**Political Rights:** 7
**Civil Liberties:** 5
**Status of Freedom:** not free

**Political Rights.** In 1980 the Central African Republic was a dictatorship without representative institutions. (The system is evolving: presidential elections in early 1981 will raise the political rating.) Prefects are appointed by the central government in the French style. Heavily dependent on French economic and military aid, the recent change of government was due to direct French military intervention, and French forces are still present.

**Civil Liberties.** All media are government controlled, but there is some free expression and assembly. There are very few prisoners of conscience. Religious freedom is generally respected, as are other personal and economic freedoms. There is limited independent union activity and relatively uncontrolled movement.

**Comparatively:** Central African Republic is as free as Tanzania, freer than Togo, less free than Kenya.

# CHAD

**Economy:** noninclusive capitalist     **Political Rights:** 7
**Polity:** military decentralized     **Civil Liberties:** 6
**Population:** 4,500,000     **Status of Freedom:** not free
A collection of semi-autonomous ethnic groups

**Political Rights.** Chad has been torn apart by competing factional and ethnic armies. By the end of the year rule had been consolidated under groups supported by the Libyan army. *Subnationalities*: Ethnic struggle pits the southern Negroes (principally the Christian and animist Sara tribe) against a variety of northern Muslim groups (principally nomadic Arabs).

**Civil Liberties.** The media are controlled by the government, although journalists show some independence. In conditions of mixed anarchy and varying degrees of local and national control, rights have little meaning. Many have been killed or imprisoned without due process. Anarchy gives certain freedoms to local groups. Not an ideological state, traditional law is still influential.

**Comparatively:** Chad is apparently as free as Saudi Arabia, freer than Malawi, less free than Lebanon.

# CHILE

**Economy:** capitalist     **Political Rights:** 6
**Polity:** military nonparty     **Civil Liberties:** 5
**Population:** 11,300,000     **Status of Freedom:** partly free
A relatively homogeneous population

**Political Rights.** Chile is a military dictatorship. A 1980 plebiscite confirming government policy allowed an opposition vote of thirty percent. All power is concentrated at the center; there are no elective positions. An appointive Council of State is supposed to represent most sectors of society.

**Civil Liberties.** All media have both public and private outlets; newspapers are primarily private. The media, although censored and often threatened with closure, express a considerable range of opinion, occasionally including direct criticism of government policy. Limited party activity is tacitly allowed, and a human rights organization operates. Students, church leaders, and former political leaders regularly express dissent. While one can win against the government, the courts are under government pressure. After years of terror, disappearances, and other extralegal repressions appear to have ceased. However, prisoners of conscience are still commonly taken for short periods, and torture occurs. Unions are restricted but have some rights, including a limited right to strike. Rights to private property have been greatly strengthened both in the country and city, with government control of the economy now being limited to copper and petroleum. The right to travel, especially to leave Chile, is generally respected.

Comparatively: Chile is as free as Tunisia, freer than Czechoslovakia, less free than Peru.

# CHINA (Mainland)

Economy: socialist　　　　　　　　Political Rights: 6
Polity: communist one-party　　　Civil Liberties: 6
Population: 975,000,000　　　　　Status of Freedom: not free
An ethnic state with peripheral subnationalities

Political Rights. China is a one-party communist state under the collective leadership of the Politburo. A National Peoples Congress is indirectly elected within party guidelines, but does not function as a competitive parliament. National policy struggles are obscured by secrecy; choices are sharply limited. Recently there have been some more open local elections. Minor political parties have been revived, but it is not yet clear whether they will be allowed to function as a critical force. *Subnationalities*: There are several subordinated peripheral peoples such as the Tibetans, Uighurs, or Mongols. These are granted a very limited degree of separate cultural life. Amounting to not more than five percent of the population, non-Chinese ethnic groups have tended to be diluted and obscured by Chinese settlement or Sinification.

Civil Liberties. The mass media remain closely controlled. While the limited underground and wall poster literature of 1978-79 was suppressed, there are reports of a continuing and extensive underground literature. Non-political cultural freedom has, however, greatly expanded. The new constitution places an emphasis on legal procedures that has been lacking until recently. Although this may herald movement toward "socialist legality" on the Soviet model, court cases often appear to be decided in political terms. There are unknown thousands of political prisoners, including those in labor-reform camps; the government has forced millions to live indefinitely in undesirable areas. Although now less common, political executions are still reported. Millions of Chinese have been systematically discriminated against because of "bad class background," but such discrimination has recently been curtailed.

Compared to other communist states popular opinions and pressures play a considerable role. Recurrent poster campaigns, demonstrations, and evidence of private conversation show that pervasive factionalism allowed elements of freedom and consensus into the system; repression in 1979, including imprisonment, equally shows the government's determination to keep such campaigning from becoming a threat to the system or its current leaders. Rights to travel and emigration are limited, as are other economic and religious freedoms. Inequality derives from political position rather than wealth.

**Comparatively:** China (Mainland) is as free as Algeria, freer than Mongolia, and less free than China (Taiwan).

# CHINA (Taiwan)

**Economy:** capitalist-statist                     **Political Rights:** 5
**Polity:** centralized dominant-party       **Civil Liberties:** 5
**Population:** 17,800,000                         **Status of Freedom:** partly free
A quasi-ethnic state with a majority nonterritorial subnationality

**Political Rights.** Taiwan is ruled by a single party organized according to a communist model (although anticommunist ideologically). There is a parliament to which representatives from Taiwan are elected in fairly free elections; a few members oppose the regime but no effective opposition party is tolerated. Most parliamentarians are still persons elected in 1947 as representatives of districts in China where elections could not be held subsequently. Late 1980 elections allowed some opposition success. The indirect presidential election is *pro forma*, but the election of a Taiwanese as vice president in 1978 was significant. Important local and regional positions are elective, including those in the provincial assembly which are held by Taiwanese. *Subnationalities*: The people are eighty-six percent native Taiwanese (speaking two Chinese dialects), and an opposition movement to transfer control from the mainland immigrants to the Taiwanese has been repressed.

**Civil Liberties.** The media include government or party organs, but are mostly in private hands. Newspapers and magazines are subject to censorship or suspension, and practice self-censorship. In late 1979 a major confrontation led to the closing of publications and the imprisonment of major leaders of the opposition. Television is one-sided. Rights to assembly are limited, but were improved at least for the elections in 1980. There are several hundred political prisoners, but there has been only one recent political execution. Union activity is restricted; strikes are forbidden. Private rights to property, education, and religion are generally respected; there is no right to travel to the mainland.

**Comparatively:** China (Taiwan) is as free as Singapore, freer than South Korea, less free than Malaysia.

# COLOMBIA

**Economy:** capitalist                              **Political Rights:** 2
**Polity:** centralized multiparty             **Civil Liberties:** 3
**Population:** 26,700,000                         **Status of Freedom:** free
A relatively homogeneous population with scattered minorities

**Political Rights.** Colombia is a constitutional democracy. The president is directly elected, as are both houses of the legislature. Although campaigns are accompanied by both violence and apathy, there is little reason to believe they are fraudulent. Members of the two principal parties are included in the government and the list of departmental governors. Both of the leading parties have well-defined factions. There is one major third party; among the minor parties several are involved in revolutionary activity. The provinces are directly administered by the national government. The military is alleged to be only partly under government control.

**Civil Liberties.** The press is private, with some papers under party control, and quite free. Radio and television include both government and private stations. All media have been limited in their freedom to report subversive activity. Personal rights are generally respected; courts are relatively strong and independent. Riots and guerrilla activity have led to periodic states of siege in which these rights are limited. Assemblies are often banned for fear of riots. In these conditions the security forces have infringed violently personal rights, especially those of leftist unions, peasants, and Amerindians in rural areas. Although many persons are rounded up in antiguerrilla or antiterrorist campaigns, people are not given prison sentences simply for their nonviolent expression of political opinion. Torture occurs. Human rights organizations are active. The government encourages private enterprise where possible; union activity and strikes for economic goals are legal.

**Comparatively:** Colombia is as free as India, freer than Panama, less free than Venezuela.


# COMORO ISLANDS

**Economy:** noninclusive capitalist
**Polity:** decentralized nonparty
**Population:** 350,000
A relatively homogeneous population

**Political Rights:** 4
**Civil Liberties:** 5
**Status of Freedom:** partly free

**Political Rights.** The Comoran government came to power by armed attack in 1978. Subsequently, the voters approved a new constitution and president. The majority probably support the new system—the previous ruler had become very oppressive and the new president had been prime minister in the recent past. There were contested parliamentary elections in late 1978. The new constitution grants each island an elected governor and council. (The island of Mayotte is formally a part of the Comoros, but it has chosen to be a French dependency.)

**Civil Liberties.** Radio is government owned; there is no press. Some outside publications and meetings have been banned. There are prisoners of conscience, at least for short terms, and pressure is reported against opposition groups. There is a new emphasis on Islamic customs. Travel is free, and the economy largely in private hands. The poor population depends almost entirely on subsistence agriculture and emigration.

**Comparatively:** Comoro Islands appears to be as free as Kenya, freer than Seychelles, less free than Mauritius.

# CONGO

**Economy:** noninclusive mixed
**Polity:** socialist one-party (military dominated)
**Population:** 1,600,000
A formally transethnic heterogeneous state

**Political Rights:** 7
**Civil Liberties:** 6
**Status of Freedom:** not free

**Political Rights.** Congo is a military dictatorship with lethal factional infighting. One-party elections allow no opposition, but parliament can be critical. *Subnationalities*: Historically the country was established out of a maze of ethnic groups, without the domination of some by others. However, the army that now rules is said to come from tribes with not more than fifteen percent of the population.

**Civil Liberties.** The news media are heavily censored. Executions and imprisonment of political opponents have occurred, but there are now very few political prisoners. Only one union is allowed; it is not allowed to strike. Religious groups are limited but generally free. At the local and small entrepreneur level private property is generally respected; many larger industries have been nationalized. Literacy is remarkably high.

**Comparatively:** Congo is as free as Iraq, freer than Mozambique, less free than Cameroon.

# COSTA RICA

**Economy:** capitalist
**Polity:** centralized multiparty
**Population:** 2,200,000
A relatively homogeneous population

**Political Rights:** 1
**Civil Liberties:** 1
**Status of Freedom:** free

**Political Rights.** A parliamentary democracy, Costa Rica has a directly elected president and several important parties. No parties are prohibited. This structure is supplemented by an independent tribunal for the overseeing of elections. Elections are fair; rule alternates between parties. Provinces are under the direction of the central government.

**Civil Liberties.** The media are notably free, private, and varied; they serve a society ninety percent literate. The courts are fair, and private rights, such as those to movement, occupation, education, religion, and union organization, are respected.

**Comparatively:** Costa Rica is as free as Ireland, freer than Colombia.

# CUBA

**Economy:** socialist
**Polity:** communist one-party
**Population:** 10,000,000
A complex but relatively homogeneous population

**Political Rights:** 6
**Civil Liberties:** 6
**Status of Freedom:** not free

**Political Rights.** Cuba is a one-party communist state on the Soviet model. Real power lies, however, more in the person of Fidel Castro and in the Russian leaders upon whom he depends than is the case in other noncontiguous states adopting this model. Popular election at the municipal level has recently been introduced. Provincial and national assemblies are elected by municipalities but can be recalled by popular vote. The whole system is largely a show: Political opponents are excluded from nomination by law, many others are simply disqualified by party fiat; no debate is allowed on major issues; once elected the assemblies do not oppose party decisions.

**Civil Liberties.** The media are state controlled and publish only as the state directs. Thousands of political prisoners have been released recently, mostly into exile. Torture has been reported only in the past, but hundreds who have refused to recant continue to be held in difficult conditions, and new arrests are frequent. There are hundreds of thousands of others who are formally discriminated against as opponents of the system. There appears to be some freedom to criticize informally, but writing against the system, even privately, may be punished severely. There are reports of psychiatric institutions also being used to incarcerate. Freedom to choose work, education, or residence is greatly restricted; new laws force people to work harder. It is generally illegal to leave Cuba, but some have been forced to leave. The practice of religion is discouraged by the government.

**Comparatively:** Cuba is as free as Tanzania, freer than Czechoslovakia, less free than Mexico.

# CYPRUS

**Economy:** capitalist
**Polity:** decentralized multiparty
**Population:** 650,000
A binational state (no central government)

**Political Rights:** 3
**Civil Liberties:** 3
**Status of Freedom:** partly free

**Political Rights.** At present Cyprus is one state only in theory. Both the Greek and the Turkish sectors are parliamentary democracies, although the Turkish sector is in effect a protectorate of Turkey. Elections have seemed reasonably fair in both sectors, but in the violent atmosphere pressure has been applied to all nonconforming groups or individuals. Greek Cypriots in the North are denied voting rights. *Nationalities*: Greeks and Turks now live almost exclusively in their own sectors. Eighty percent of the population is Greek, sixty percent of the land is in the Greek sector.

**Civil Liberties.** The newspapers are free and varied in both sectors, with the constraints mentioned above. Radio and television are under the respective governments or semigovernmental bodies. The usual rights of free peoples are respected in each sector, including occupation, labor organization, and religion, although somewhat more circumscribed in the Turkish sector. Because of communal strife and invasion, property has often been taken from members of one group by force (or abandoned from fear of force) and given to the other. Under these conditions rights to choose one's sector of residence or to travel between sectors are greatly restricted.

**Comparatively:** Cyprus is as free as Mauritius, freer than Lebanon, less free than Turkey.

# CZECHOSLOVAKIA

**Economy:** socialist
**Polity:** communist one-party
**Population:** 15,400,000
A binational state

**Political Rights:** 7
**Civil Liberties:** 6
**Status of Freedom:** not free

**Political Rights.** Czechoslovakia is a Soviet-style, one-party communist state, reinforced by the presence of Soviet troops. Elections are noncompetitive and there is essentially no legislative debate. *Subnationalities*: The division of the state into separate Czech and Slovak socialist republics has only slight meaning since the Czechoslovak Communist Party continues to run the country (under the guidance of the Soviet Communist Party). Although less numerous and poorer than the Czech people, the Slovaks are probably granted their rightful share of power within this framework.

**Civil Liberties.** Media are government or party owned and rigidly censored. However, some private and literary expression occurs that is relatively free. Freedom of assembly, organization, and even association are denied. Rights to travel, occupation, and private property are restricted. Heavy pressures are placed on religious activities, especially through holding ministerial incomes at a very low level and curtailing religious education. There are a number of prisoners of conscience; exclusion of individuals from their chosen occupation and short detentions are more common sanctions. The beating of political suspects is common, and psychiatric detention is employed. Successful defense in political cases is possible, but lawyers may be arrested for overzealous defense. Travel to the West and emigration are restricted. Independent trade unions and strikes are forbidden. Human rights groups are persecuted.

**Comparatively:** Czechoslovakia is as free as Romania, freer than Bulgaria, less free than Poland.

# DENMARK

**Economy:** mixed capitalist
**Polity:** centralized multiparty
**Population:** 5,100,000
A relatively homogeneous population

**Political Rights:** 1
**Civil Liberties:** 1
**Status of Freedom:** free

**Political Rights.** Denmark is a constitutional monarchy with a unicameral parliament. Elections are fair. Since a wide variety of parties achieve success, resulting governments are based on coalitions. Districts have governors appointed from the center and elected councils; local officials are under local control.

**Civil Liberties.** The press is free (and more conservative politically than the electorate). Radio and television are government owned but relatively free. All other rights are guaranteed, although the very high tax level constitutes more than usual constraint on private property in a capitalist state. Religion is free but state supported.

**Comparatively:** Denmark is as free as Norway, freer than Finland.

# DJIBOUTI

**Economy:** capitalist
**Polity:** centralized one-party
**Population:** 300,000*

**Political Rights:** 3
**Civil Liberties:** 4
**Status of Freedom:** partly free

Independence led initially to a Somali majority ruling over a territorial Afar minority

**Political Rights.** Djibouti is a parliamentary democracy under French protection. In the elections of 1977, only one list of parliamentary candidates was presented, a list dominated by the majority of Somali people. Resulting governments have included representatives of all former political parties and ethnic groups and appear to be broadly representative.

---

*Population estimates vary widely.

**Civil Liberties.** Law is based on French codes and modified overseas French practice. The media are mostly government owned and apparently apolitical. There is no direct censorship. In an atmosphere of violence there are prisoners of conscience and torture. Labor has the right to strike in a free market economy.

**Comparatively:** Djibouti appears to be as free as Malaysia, freer than Somalia, less free than Israel.

# DOMINICA

Economy: capitalist                 **Political Rights:** 2
**Polity:** centralized multiparty     **Civil Liberties:** 2
**Population:** 100,000             **Status of Freedom:** free
A relatively homogeneous population with a minority enclave

**Political Rights.** Dominica is a parliamentary democracy with competing political parties. An opposition party came to power in highly competitive 1980 elections. The rights of the native Caribs are said not to be fully respected.

**Civil Liberties.** Press is private and the radio public. The press is generally free and critical, and radio presents alternative views. Rights of assembly and organization are guaranteed. There is a rule of law with no remaining cases of political imprisonment. A special law on the Rastaferians is discriminatory. Otherwise, personal freedoms of travel, residence, union rights of workers, and property rights are secured.

**Comparatively:** Dominica is as free as Nauru, freer than Guyana, less free than Barbados.

# DOMINICAN REPUBLIC

Economy: capitalist                 **Political Rights:** 2
**Polity:** centralized multiparty     **Civil Liberties:** 3
**Population:** 5,400,000           **Status of Freedom:** free
A complex but relatively homogeneous population

**Political Rights.** The Dominican Republic is a presidential democracy on the American model. Fairly contested elections in 1978 were won by the opposition. The ensuing regime has greatly reduced military influence. Provinces are under national control, municipalities under local.

**Civil Liberties.** The media are generally privately owned, free, and diverse; pressure on broadcasting is alleged. Public expression is generally free; the spokesmen of a wide range of parties openly express their opinions. The communist party was recently legalized, but far left groups still find holding public meetings difficult. In the recent past guerrilla activity has led to government violence in which rights have not been respected. Although the government has shown itself quick to detain persons suspected of plotting against it, there are no prisoners of conscience. The courts appear relatively independent and human rights groups are active. Labor unions operate under constraint. Travel overseas is sometimes restricted.

**Comparatively:** Dominican Republic is as free as Colombia, freer than Panama, less free than Barbados.

# ECUADOR

**Economy:** noninclusive capitalist
**Polity:** centralized multiparty
**Population:** 8,000,000

**Political Rights:** 2
**Civil Liberties:** 2
**Status of Freedom:** free

An ethnic state with a potential subnationality

**Political Rights.** Ecuador is governed by an elected president and parliament. Elections in 1978-79 establishing the system were essentially free and widely contested. There were, however, some restrictions on party activity and nominations. There are elected local and provincial councils. *Subnationalities*: Perhaps forty percent of the population is Indian and many of these speak Quechua. However, this population does not at present form a conscious subnationality in a distinctive homeland.

**Civil Liberties.** Newspapers are under private or party control and quite outspoken; there is no censorship. Radio and television are mostly under private control. There are few, if any, prisoners of conscience, but persons are detained for criticizing government officials. Human rights organizations are active. The Court system is not strongly independent, and imprisonment for belief may recur. Unions are powerful and independent, but government repression may occur. Personal freedoms to travel, residence, education, and religion are secured. Although there are state firms, particularly in major industries, Ecuador is essentially a capitalist and traditional state.

**Comparatively:** Ecuador is as free as Portugal, freer than Colombia, less free than Costa Rica.

# EGYPT

**Economy:** mixed socialist
**Polity:** centralized dominant-party
**Population:** 42,100,000

**Political Rights:** 5
**Civil Liberties:** 5
**Status of Freedom:** partly free

A relatively homogeneous population with a communal religious minority

**Political Rights.** Egypt is a controlled democracy. Within limits political parties may organize: communist and religious extremist parties are forbidden. Referendums receive unlikely ninety-eight and ninety-nine percent approvals. The ruling party won ninety percent of parliamentary seats in the 1979 election, but other parties achieved representation. *Subnationalities*: Several million Coptic Christians live a distinct communal life.

**Civil Liberties.** The Egyptian press is mostly government owned. Radio and television are under governmental control. All media are governmental means for active indoctrination, but opposition journals are allowed to appear sporadically; a fairly broad range of literary publications has recently developed. There is limited freedom of assembly. Severe riot laws have led to large-scale imprisonment, but the independence of the courts has been strengthened recently. Many prisoners of conscience have been arrested in the last few years; but few are held for long periods. Women's rights have improved. In both agriculture and industry considerable diversity and choice exists within a social democratic framework. Unions have developed some independence from the government, but there is no right to strike. Travel and other private rights are generally free.

**Comparatively:** Egypt is as free as Indonesia, freer than Saudi Arabia, less free than Mexico.

# EL SALVADOR

**Economy:** capitalist (transitional)  **Political Rights:** 5
**Polity:** military nonparty  **Civil Liberties:** 5
**Population:** 4,800,000  **Status of Freedom:** partly free
A relatively homogeneous population

**Political Rights.** El Salvador is ruled by an appointed civilian president with the backing of the officer corps. He was previously an elected political leader. In the country a bloody struggle between rightist and leftist organizations and the government continues.

**Civil Liberties.** Newspapers and radio are largely in private hands. The media are under strong pressures from all sides. There have been opposition papers throughout the recent turmoil, and a spectrum of opinion is available in the media. The rule of law is weak; assassination common. Guerrilla war reduces the security of all. The judiciary is ineffective in political cases. Human rights organizations have been very active. The Church remains a force. Although still a heavily agricultural country, rural people are to a large extent involved in the wage and market economy.

**Comparatively:** El Salvador appeared to be as free as Iran, freer than Haiti, less free than Panama.

# EQUATORIAL GUINEA

**Economy:** noninclusive capitalist-
    statist
**Polity:** military nonparty
**Population:** 400,000

**Political Rights:** 7
**Civil Liberties:** 6
**Status of Freedom:** not free

An ethnic state with a territorial minority

**Political Rights.** Equatorial Guinea is a military dictatorship. The coup that replaced the former dictator was popular, but the population as a whole played and plays little part.

**Civil Liberties.** All media are government owned. The rule of law is tenuous; there are political prisoners, but perhaps none of conscience. Religious freedom was reestablished in 1979 and private property is recognized. Labor unions do not exist.

**Comparatively:** Equatorial Guinea appears to be as free as Congo, freer than Somalia, less free than Tanzania.

# ETHIOPIA

**Economy:** noninclusive socialist
**Polity:** military nonparty
**Population:** 32,600,000

**Political Rights:** 7
**Civil Liberties:** 7
**Status of Freedom:** not free

An ethnic state with major territorial subnationalities

**Political Rights.** Ethiopia is ruled by a military committee that has successively slaughtered the leaders of the *ancien régime* and many of its own leaders. A spectrum of mass organizations has been established on the model of a one-party socialist state. Popular control in the villages may be significant. *Subnationalities:* The heartland of Ethiopia is occupied by the traditionally dominant Amhara and acculturated portions of the diffuse Galla people. In the late nineteenth century Ethiopian rulers united what had been warring fragments of a former empire in this heartland, and proceeded to incorporate some entirely new areas. At this time the Somali of the south came under Ethiopian rule; Eritrea was incorporated as the result of a UN decision in 1952. Today Ethiopia is crosscut by linguistic and religious divisions: most important is separatism due to historic allegiances to ancient provinces (especially Tigre), to different experiences (Eritrea), and to the population of a foreign nation (Somalia).

**Civil Liberties.** Individual rights as we know them are unprotected under conditions of despotism and anarchy. Political imprisonment, forced confession, execution, disappearance, and torture are common. There are no rights to assembly. Many thousands have been killed aside from those dying in civil war. Education is totally controlled.

What independence there was under the Ethiopian monarchy has been largely lost, but the land reform benefited many. Choice of residence and workplace is often made by the government. Religious groups have been persecuted, but there is general religious freedom. Travel outside the country is strictly controlled; hostages or guarantors are often required before exit. The words and actions of the regime indicate little respect for private rights in property or worker rights to independent organization.

**Comparatively:** Ethiopia is as free as Kampuchea, less free than Sudan.

# FIJI

**Economy:** noninclusive capitalist
**Polity:** centralized multiparty
**Population:** 600,000
A binational state

**Political Rights:** 2
**Civil Liberties:** 2
**Status of Freedom:** free

**Political Rights.** Fiji has a complex political structure designed to protect the interests of both the original Fiji people and the Indian people, who now form a slight majority. The Lower House is directly elected on the basis of both communal and national rolls. The Upper House is indirectly elected by a variety of electors (including the council of chiefs, the prime minister, and the opposition leader). Local government is organized both by the central government and by a Fijian administration headed by the council of chiefs. In 1977 the opposition won its first election, but was unable to hold together a majority that could rule. This inability led to its decisive defeat in a subsequent election later in the year.

**Civil Liberties.** The press is free and private (but government positions must sometimes be published); government radio is under a separate and independent commission. There are slight limits on freedom to assemble. The full protection of the rule of law is supplemented by an ombudsman to investigate complaints against the government. Right to property is limited by special rights of inalienability that are granted to the Fijians and cover most of the country. Strong unions have full rights. Religion, travel, and other personal rights are secured. The nation may be about evenly divided between a subsistence economy, based on agriculture and fishing, and a modern market economy.

**Comparatively:** Fiji is as free as Papua New Guinea, freer than Tonga, less free than New Zealand.

# FINLAND

**Economy:** mixed capitalist
**Polity:** centralized multiparty
**Population:** 4,800,000

**Political Rights:** 2
**Civil Liberties:** 2
**Status of Freedom:** free

An ethnic state with a small territorial subnationality

**Political Rights.** Finland has a parliamentary system with a strong, directly elected president. Since there are a large number of relatively strong parties, government is almost always by coalition. Elections have resulted in shifts in coalition membership. Soviet pressure has influenced the maintenance of the current president in office for over twenty years; by treaty foreign policy cannot be anti-Soviet. The provinces have centrally appointed governors. *Subnationalities*: The rural Swedish minority (seven percent) has its own political party and strong cultural ties to Sweden. The Swedish-speaking Åland Islands have local autonomy and other special rights.

**Civil Liberties.** The press is private. Most of the radio service is government controlled, but there is an important commercial television station. Discussion in the media is controlled by a political consensus that criticism of the Soviet Union should be highly circumspect. Those who cross the line are often admonished by the government to practice self-censorship. There is a complete rule of law, and private rights are secured.

**Comparatively:** Finland is as free as Portugal, freer than Spain, less free than Sweden.

# FRANCE

**Economy:** capitalist
**Polity:** centralized multiparty
**Population:** 53,600,000

**Political Rights:** 1
**Civil Liberties:** 2
**Status of Freedom:** free

An ethnic state with major territorial subnationalities

**Political Rights.** France is a parliamentary democracy. However, the directly elected president is more powerful than the premier and assembly. There is also a constitutional council that oversees elections and passes on the constitutionality of assembly or executive actions on the model of the United States Supreme Court. The multiparty system ensures that governments are generally coalitions. *Subnationalities*: Territorial subnationalities continue to have few rights as ethnic units and have little power under a rigidly centralized provincial administration. The recent election of a Paris mayor for the first time in a century and hesitant steps toward regionalization has slightly improved the situation. At present the Alsatian minority seems well satisfied, but there is a demand for greater autonomy among many Bretons, Corsicans, and Basques.

**Civil Liberties.** The French press is free, although often party-related. Criticism of the President and top officials may be muted by government threats and court actions. The news agency is private; radio and television are divided among a variety of theoretically independent companies under indirect government control. In spite of recent changes there is still an authoritarian attitude in government-citizen relations, publications may be banned at the behest of foreign governments, and arrest without explanation still occurs, particularly of members of sub-nationalities. Police brutality is commonly alleged. Information and organization in regard to conscientious objection is restricted. France is, of course, under the rule of law, and rights to occupation, residence, religion, and property are secured.Both through extensive social programs and the creation of state enterprises France is quite far from a pure capitalist form.

**Comparatively:** France is as free as Germany (West), freer than Spain, less free than the United Kingdom.

## GABON

Economy: noninclusive capitalist       **Political Rights:** 6
**Polity:** nationalist one-party        **Civil Liberties:** 6
**Population:** 600,000                   **Status of Freedom:** not free
A transethnic heterogeneous state

**Political Rights.** Gabon is a moderate dictatorship operating in the guise of a one-party state, with noncompetitive elections characteristic of this form. Candidates must be party approved. Major cities have elected local governments; provinces are administered from the center.

**Civil Liberties.** All media are government controlled, and no legitimate opposition voices are raised. Some critical items appear in local or available foreign media. There is no right of political assembly, and there are few if any prisoners of conscience. Only one labor union is sanctioned. The authoritarian government generally does not care to interfere in private lives, and respects religious freedom, private property, and the right to travel.

**Comparatively:** Gabon is as free as Jordan, freer than Angola, less free than Ghana.

## GAMBIA

Economy: noninclusive capitalist       **Political Rights:** 2
**Polity:** centralized multiparty       **Civil Liberties:** 3
**Population:** 600,000                   **Status of Freedom:** free
A transethnic heterogeneous state

**Political Rights.** There appears to be a fully functioning parliamentary democracy, although the same party and leader have been in power since independence in 1965, and electoral margins are very high. There is no evidence of serious irregularities. There is local, mostly traditional, autonomy, but not regional self-rule. (The maintenance of the system may be partly explained by the small size of the government and the lack of an army.) Senegalese troops helped preserve order in 1980.

**Civil Liberties.** The private and public newspapers and radio stations provide generally free media. Two small parties have been banned for alleged terrorism. An independent judiciary maintains the rule of law. Labor unions operate, but within limits. The agricultural economy is largely dependent on peanuts, but remains traditionally organized. The illiteracy rate is very high.

**Comparatively:** Gambia is as free as Botswana, freer than Senegal, less free than Barbados.

# GERMANY, EAST

**Economy:** socialist
**Polity:** communist one-party
**Population:** 16,700,000
A relatively homogeneous population

**Political Rights:** 7
**Civil Liberties:** 7
**Status of Freedom:** not free

**Political Rights.** East Germany is in practice a one-party communist dictatorship. No electoral competition is allowed that involves policy questions; all citizens are compelled to vote for a government-selected list of candidates. In addition, the presence of Soviet troops and direction from the Communist Party of the Soviet Union significantly reduces the sovereignty (or group freedom) of the East Germans.

**Civil Liberties.** Media are government owned and controlled. Dissidents are repressed by imprisonment and exclusion; the publication or importation of materials with opposing views is forbidden. One may be arrested for private conversation. Among the thousands of prisoners of conscience, the most common offense is trying to leave the country illegally (or in some cases even seeking permission to leave), or propaganda against the state. Prisoners of conscience may be severely beaten or otherwise harmed. Political reeducation may be a condition of release. The average person is not allowed freedom of occupation or residence. Once defined as an enemy of the state, a person may be barred from his occupation and his children denied higher education. Particularly revealing has been the use of the "buying out scheme" by which West Germany has been able intermittently to obtain the release of prisoners in the East through cash payments and delivering goods such as bananas and coffee. There is considerable religious freedom, with the

Catholic and Protestant hierarchies possessing some independence. Freedom exists within the family, although there is no right to privacy or the inviolability of the home, mail, or telephone.

**Comparatively:** Germany (East) is as free as Bulgaria, less free than Poland.

# GERMANY, WEST

**Economy:** capitalist                    **Political Rights:** 1
**Polity:** decentralized multiparty        **Civil Liberties:** 2
**Population:** 61,100,000                  **Status of Freedom:** free
A relatively homogeneous population

**Political Rights.** West Germany is a parliamentary democracy with an indirectly elected and largely ceremonial president. Both major parties have ruled since the war. The weak Senate is elected by the assemblies of the constituent states and loyally defends states' rights. Successive national governments have been based on changing party balances in the powerful lower house. The states have their own elected assemblies; they control education, internal security, and culture.

**Civil Liberties.** The papers are independent and free, with little governmental interference by European standards. Radio and television are organized in public corporations under direction of the state governments. Generally the rule of law has been carefully observed, and the full spectrum of private freedoms is available. In recent years jobs have been denied to some individuals with radical leftist connections; terrorist activities have led to tighter security regulations, invasions of privacy, and less acceptance of nonconformity. Arrests have been made for handling or producing inflammatory literature, for neo-Nazi propaganda or organization, or for calling in question the courts or electoral system. Government participation in the economy is largely regulatory; in addition, complex social programs and worker participation in management have limited certain private freedoms while possibly expanding others.

**Comparatively:** West Germany is as free as France, freer than Spain, less free than the United States of America.

# GHANA

**Economy:** capitalist-statist            **Political Rights:** 2
**Polity:** centralized multiparty          **Civil Liberties:** 3
**Population:** 11,700,000                  **Status of Freedom:** free
A transethnic heterogeneous state with subnationalities

**Political Rights.** Since Fall 1979 Ghana has been ruled by a parliament and president representing competitive parties. On the local level traditional sources of power are still significant. There are elected district and local councils. *Subnationalities:* The country is composed of a variety of peoples, with those in the south most self-conscious. The latter are the descendants of a number of traditional kingdoms, of which the Ashanti was the most important. A north-south, Muslim-Christian opposition exists but is weakly developed, because of the economic and numerical weakness and the incomplete hold of Islam in the north. In the south and center of the country a sense of Akan identity is developing among the Ashanti, Fanti, and others; since they include forty-five percent of the people, this amounts to strengthening the ethnic core of the nation. The leaders of the one million Ewe in the southeast (a people divided between Ghana and Togo) have on occasion asked for separation or enhanced self-determination.

**Civil Liberties.** The critical press is both government and private; there is a degree of autonomy to the government-owned radio and television systems and criticism is now freely offered. Private opinion is freely expressed on most matters, and freedom of assembly is honored. There are few if any prisoners of conscience, but military intervention led to political executions in 1979. Private businesses and independent organizations such as churches and labor unions thrive. There has been a great deal of government control in some areas—especially in cocoa production, on which the economy depends, and in modern capital-intensive industry. Like Senegal, Ghana has a relatively highly developed industry and its agriculture is dependent on world markets. Religion and travel are generally free.

**Comparatively:** Ghana is as free as Spain, freer than Senegal, less free than Venezuela.

# GREECE

**Economy:** capitalist
**Polity:** centralized multiparty
**Population:** 9,600,000
A relatively homogeneous state

**Political Rights:** 1
**Civil Liberties:** 2
**Status of Freedom:** free

**Political Rights.** Greece is a parliamentary democracy with a theoretically strong, but indirectly elected, president. The stabilization of free institutions is proceeding rapidly: recent elections have been competitive and open to the full spectrum of parties. Provincial administration is centrally controlled; there is local self-government.

**Civil Liberties.** Newspapers are private and the judiciary is independent. There are no known prisoners of conscience. Because of the recent revolutionary situation all views are not freely expressed (a situation similar to that in post-fascist Portugal). One can be imprisoned for insulting the authorities or religion. Private rights are respected. Union activity is free.

**Comparatively:** Greece is as free as France, freer than Finland, less free than Netherlands.

# GRENADA

**Economy:** mixed socialist
**Polity:** centralized dominant-party
**Population:** 100,000
A relatively homogeneous population

**Political Rights:** 6
**Civil Liberties:** 5
**Status of Freedom:** not free

**Political Rights.** In 1979 a major opposition party came to power by force. The change was initially popular, but the new leaders have increasingly monopolized power and have now postponed elections indefinitely. Opposition parties were not active in 1980.

**Civil Liberties.** The news media are government controlled. Opposition assembles have regularly been broken up. Many opposition political leaders have been detained indefinitely on vague charges. All expression is controlled by an atmosphere of fear. Unions and private business are under government pressure.

**Comparatively:** Grenada is as free as Argentina, freer than Haiti, less free than Panama.

# GUATEMALA

**Economy:** noninclusive capitalist
**Polity:** centralized multiparty
    (military dominated)
**Population:** 7,000,000
An ethnic state with a major potential territorial subnationality

**Political Rights:** 6
**Civil Liberties:** 6
**Status of freedom:** not free

**Political Rights.** Guatemala is formally a constitutional democracy on the American model. The 1974 presidential election results were apparently altered in favor of the ruling coalition's candidate; in 1978 there were counting irregularities, but congressional seats went to a variety of parties. Most opposition parties are now heavily repressed. The provinces are centrally administered. Military and other security forces maintain decisive extra-constitutional power at all levels: those politicians who oppose them generally retire, go into exile, or are killed. The vice-president resigned in 1980 in protest. *Subnationalities:* Various groups of Mayan and other Indians make up half the population; they do not yet have a subnationalist sense of unity, but are very involved in guerrilla activity.

**Civil Liberties.** The press and a large portion of radio and television are privately controlled. The press is generally free, but pervasive self-censorship is common because of the ever-present threat of torture and murder. In the cities, at least, some legal opposition political activity remains. Murder of university faculty and students is meant to intimidate. The struggle against rural guerrillas has led to frequent attacks on recalcitrant peasants or Indians by security forces. The judiciary is under both leftist and governmental pressure in political or subversive cases and has become relatively ineffective in this area. Illegal armed groups often associated with the government, are responsible for thousands of deaths, including important opposition leaders. Unions are intimidated, land rights are not secure, but other private rights seem fairly well respected.

**Comparatively:** Guatemala is as free as Cuba, freer than Ethiopia, less free than Mexico.

# GUINEA

**Economy:** preindustrial socialist
**Polity:** socialist one-party
**Population:** 5,000,000
A transethnic heterogeneous state

**Political Rights:** 7
**Civil Liberties:** 7
**Status of Freedom:** not free

**Political Rights.** Guinea is a one-party socialist dictatorship. Elections for president and parliament are uncontested. Provincial and local governments are highly centralized.

**Civil Liberties.** All media are government or party owned and censorship is rigid. Ideological purity is demanded in all areas except religion. There are prisoners of conscience; torture has been common and execution frequent. Hundreds or thousands may have died in detention. Everyone must participate in guided political activity. Few private rights, such as those to organize unions, develop property, or choose one's education are recognized. Private lawyers are not permitted. Movement within the country or over the border seems relatively easy. There is no legal sanctity of the home.

**Comparatively:** Guinea is as free as Ethiopia, less free than Zambia.

# GUINEA-BISSAU

**Economy:** noninclusive socialist
**Polity:** socialist one-party
**Population:** 600,000
A transethnic heterogeneous state

**Politcal Rights:** 6
**Civil Liberties:** 6
**Status of Freedom:** not free

**Politcal Rights.** Guinea-Bissau is administered by one party; all other parties are illegal. A 1980 coup dissolved the previous formally representative institutions. Local economic control under party guidance is emphasized.

**Civil Liberties.** The media are government controlled, and criticism of the system is forbidden. There are prisoners of conscience. Political executions are alleged to have been common. Union activity is government directed. All land has been nationalized—there is some private property. Travel and religion are relatively free.

**Comparatively:** Guinea-Bissau is as free as Tanzania, freer than Guinea, less free than Senegal.

# GUYANA

**Economy:** mixed socialist
**Polity:** centralized multiparty
**Population:** 900,000
An ethnically complex state

**Political Rights:** 5
**Civil Liberties:** 4
**Status of Freedom:** partly free

**Political Rights.** Guyana is a parliamentary democracy. However, in recent elections the government has been responsibly charged with irregularities that resulted in its victory. The 1980 parliamentary elections were criticized by both foreign and local observers for lack of adequate controls. Opposition parties are denied equal access to the media, and their supporters are discriminated against in employment. Administration is generally centralized but there are some elected local officials.

**Civil Liberties.** Radio is now government owned. Several opposition newspapers have been nationalized; the last opposition daily was forced to a weekly schedule in 1979. However, a variety of foreign news media are still available. There is a right of assembly, but harassment occurs. There is an operating human rights organization. All private schools have been nationalized recently, and the government has interfered with university appointments. It is possible to win against the government in court; there are no prisoners of conscience. Art and music are under considerable government control. Unions are under increasing pressure. Private property (as distinct from personal property) is no longer considered legitimate.

**Comparatively:** Guyana is as free as Kenya, freer than Nicaragua, less free than Colombia.

# HAITI

**Economy:** noninclusive capitalist
**Polity:** dominant party
**Population:** 5,800,000
A relatively homogeneous population

**Politcal Rights:** 7
**Civil Liberties:** 6
**Status of Freedom:** not free

**Political Rights.** Haiti is a dictatorship with an ephemeral ruling party. Elections in 1979 were the first to allow an opposition candidate to be elected, but this candidacy was a notable exception. Small parties have been organized, but effectively neutralized.

**Civil Liberties.** The media are both private and public. Censorship is legal for all media, including films and theatre; attempts at independence in journalism were severely repressed in 1980. Rights of assembly and organization are restricted. A government-sponsored militia has suppressed opposition; political murders, imprisonment without trial, exile, and torture have characterized the system intermittently. An acceptable rule of law has been in abeyance during a prolonged "state of siege." Many people attempt to flee the country illegally every year. Union activity is restricted. Corruption seriously infringes rights to political equality.

**Comparatively:** Haiti is as free as Benin, freer than Guinea, less free than Panama.

# HONDURAS

**Economy:** noninclusive capitalist
**Polity:** centralized multiparty
    (military dominated)
**Population:** 3,800,000
A relatively homogeneous population

**Political Rights:** 4
**Civil Liberties:** 3
**Status of Freedom:** partly free

**Political Rights.** The government is jointly composed of military representatives and representatives of leading civilian parties. Although some parties were excluded, the 1980 constituent assembly election was relatively fair. Full restoration of multiparty government is expected in 1981. Provincial government is centrally administered.

**Civil Liberties.** The media are largely private and free of prior censorship. In spite of some pressure there is general freedom. Militant peasant organizations and political parties continue to function outside government control. In 1980 partisan political demonstrations were again allowed. The struggle of peasants for land often leads to violence, but the government seems to actively seek peaceful resolutions. Most private rights are respected—insofar as government power reaches. Labor unions have suffered oppression, but are relatively strong, especially in plantation areas. There is freedom of religion and movement.

**Comparatively:** Honduras is as free as Malaysia, freer than El Salvador, less free than Peru.

# HUNGARY

**Economy:** socialist
**Polity:** communist one-party
**Population:** 10,800,000
A relatively homogeneous population

**Political Rights:** 6
**Civil Liberties:** 5
**Status of Freedom:** not free

**Politcal Rights.** Hungary is ruled as a one-party communist dictatorship. Although there is an elective national assembly as well as local assemblies, all candidates must be approved by the party, and the decisions of the politburo are decisive. Within this framework recent elections have allowed little or no choice among candidates. The group rights of the Hungarian people are diminished by the government's official acceptance of the right of the Soviet government to interfere in the domestic affairs of Hungary by force.

**Civil Liberties.** Media are under government or party control. Basic criticism of top leaders, communism, human rights performance, or the Soviet presence is inadmissable, but some criticism is allowed, especially through papers, plays, books, and the importation of foreign publications or listening to foreign broadcasts. Prisoners of conscience are detained regularly, though usually for short periods. Control over religious affairs is more relaxed than in most communist states. Although private rights are not guaranteed, in practice there is considerable private property, and permission to travel into and out of the country is easier to obtain than in most of Eastern Europe. The border with Austria is essentially open. Unions are party directed and have no right to strike.

**Comparatively:** Hungary is as free as Yugoslavia, freer than Czechoslovakia, less free than Egypt.

# ICELAND

**Economy:** capitalist
**Polity:** centralized multiparty
**Population:** 228,000
A relatively homogeneous population

**Political Rights:** 1
**Civil Liberties:** 1
**Status of Freedom:** free

**Political Rights.** Iceland is governed by a parliamentary democracy. Recent years have seen important shifts in voter sentiment, resulting successively in right- and left-wing coalitions. Although a small country Iceland has pursued a highly independent foreign policy. Provinces are ruled by central government appointees.

**Civil Liberties.** The press is private or party and free of censorship. Radio and television are state owned, but supervised by a public board representing major parties and interests. There are no political prisoners and the judiciary is independent. Private rights are respected; few are poor or illiterate.

**Comparatively:** Iceland is as free as Norway, freer than Portugal.

# INDIA

**Economy:** noninclusive capitalist-
  statist
**Polity:** decentralized multiparty
**Population:** 676,200,000
A multinational and complex state

**Political Rights:** 2
**Civil Liberties:** 3
**Status of Freedom:** free

**Political Rights.** India is a parliamentary democracy in which the opposition has had an opportunity to rule. The strong powers retained by its component states have been compromised in recent years by the central government's frequent imposition of direct rule. Calling immediate state elections where the opposition continues to rule after a national change of government is a recent practice compromising the federal system.

*Subnationalities.* India contains a diverse collection of mostly territorially distinct peoples united by historical experience and the predominance of Hinduism. India's dominant peoples are those of the north central area who speak as a first language either the official language, Hindi (Hindustani), or a very closely related dialect of Sanskrit origin. The other major subnational peoples of India may be divided into several groups: (1) peoples with separate states that are linguistically and historically only marginally distinct from the dominant Hindi speakers (for example, the Marathi, Gujerati, or Oriya); (2) peoples with separate states that are of Sanskrit background linguistically, but have a relatively strong sense of separate identity (for example, Bengalis or Kashmiris); (3) peoples with separate states that are linguistically and to some extent racially quite distinct (for example, Telegu or Malayalam); and (4) peoples that do not have states of their own and are often survivors of India's pre-Aryan peoples (for example, Santali, Bhuti-Lapcha, or Mizo). With the exception of the last group, the Indian federal system accords a fair amount of democratic rights to all peoples. Several peoples from groups (2), (3), and (4) have shown through legal (especially votes) and illegal means a strong desire by a significant part of the population for independence or greater autonomy (notably Kashmiris, Nagas, and Mizos). This accounting leaves out many *nonterritorial* religious and caste minorities, although, here again, the system has granted relatively broad rights to such groups to reasonable self-determination.

**Civil Liberties.** The Indian press is strong and independent. The fact that radio and television are not independent in this largely illiterate country is disquieting. There have been illegal arrests, questionable killings, and reports of torture by the police which in some cases have been out of control. The judiciary is generally responsive, fair, and independent.

The problem of extreme trial delay has recently been addressed. There are few, if any, prisoners of conscience, but there are hundreds imprisoned for political violence, and demonstrations may lead to fatalities and large-scale jailings. Due to the decentralized political structure there is a great deal of regional variation in the operation of security laws. Kashmir has especially repressive security policies in relation to the press and political detention; Sikkim is treated as an Indian colony, and the same might be said for other border areas. Indians enjoy freedom to travel, to worship as they please, and to organize for mutual benefit, especially in unions. Lack of education, extreme poverty, and surviving traditional controls certainly reduce the meaning of such liberties for large numbers of Indians.

**Comparatively:** India is as free as Spain, freer than Malaysia, less free than Japan.

# INDONESIA

**Economy:** noninclusive capitalist-statist

**Polity:** centralized dominant-party (military dominated)

**Population:** 144,300,000

**Political Rights:** 5

**Civil Liberties:** 5

**Status of Freedom:** partly free

A transethnic heterogeneous state with active and potential subnationalities

**Political Rights.** Indonesia is a controlled parliamentary democracy under military direction. Recent parliamentary elections showed the ability of the rather tame opposition parties to gain ground at the expense of the governing party, but the government's majority is still overwhelming. The number and character of opposition parties is carefully controlled, parties must refrain from criticizing one another, candidates of both government and opposition require government approval, and opposition activities in rural areas are restricted. In any event parliament does not have a great deal of power. Provincial governors are indirectly elected from centrally approved lists. Local assemblies are elected.

*Subnationalities.* Indonesia includes a variety of ethnic groups and is divided by crosscutting island identities. Although the island of Java is numerically dominant, the national language is not Javanese, and most groups or islands do not appear to have strong subnational identifications. Both civilian and military elites generally attempt to maintain religious, ethnic, and regional balance. Groups demanding independence exist in Sulawesi, the Moluccas, Timor, West Irian, and northern Sumatra, and continue to mount revolts against the government.

**Civil Liberties.** Most newspapers are private. All are subject to fairly close government supervision; criticism of the system is muted by periodic suppressions. Radio and television are government controlled. Freedom of assembly is restricted, but citizens are not compelled to attend meetings. There continue to be prisoners of conscience, but most are now detained only for short periods. Thousands of released prisoners remain in a second-class status, especially in regard to residence and employment. In this area the army rather than the civilian judiciary is dominant. Torture has been infrequent recently; the army has been responsible for many thousands of unnecessary deaths in its suppression of revolt in, or in conquest of, East Timor. Union activity is closely regulated, but labor organization is widespread and strikes occur. Movement, especially to the cities, is restricted; other private rights are generally respected. The Indonesian bureaucracy has an unenviable reputation for arbitrariness and corruption, practices that reduce the effective expression of human rights. There are many active human rights organizations.

**Comparatively:** Indonesia is as free as Nicaragua, freer than Burma, less free than Bangladesh.

# IRAN

**Economy:** noninclusive capitalist-statist  
**Polity:** quasi-dominant party  
**Population:** 38,500,000  

**Political Rights:** 5  
**Civil Liberties:** 5  
**Status of Freedom:** partly free  

An ethnic state with major territorial subnationalities

**Political Rights.** Iran is a competitive democracy, though the direction of the nonelective theocratic leadership greatly limits the alternatives. The 1980 elections of president and legislature were partly free: those elected had limited powers. *Subnationalities:* Among the most important non-Persian peoples are the Kurds, the Azerbaijani Turks, the Baluch, and a variety of other (primarily Turkish) tribes. Many of these have striven for independence in the recent past when the opportunity arose. The Kurds are in active revolt.

**Civil Liberties.** Newspapers are private or party, but have been repeatedly suppressed or otherwise controlled during the year. Other media are largely government owned and are propaganda organs. The right of assembly has been sporadically denied to those who do not approve of the new system. There are many prisoners of conscience and executions (though now at a reduced level). Anarchy has led to vigilante groups competing with the official security system, and many private rights have become highly insecure. This is especially so for Bahais and other religious minorities.

**Comparatively:** Iran is as free as Egypt, freer than Iraq, less free than Bangladesh.

# IRAQ

**Economy:** noninclusive socialist     **Political Rights:** 6
**Polity:** socialist one-party     **Civil Liberties:** 7
    (military dominated)     **Status of Freedom:** not free
**Population:** 13,200,000
An ethnic state with a major territorial subnationality

**Political Rights.** Iraq is essentially a one-party state under military leadership. A 1980 parliamentary election allowed some choice of individuals, but all candidates were carefully selected and no policy choices were allowed. Parliament appears to have little, if any, power. Provinces are governed from the center. *Subnationalities:* The Kurds have been repeatedly denied self-determination, most recently through reoccupation of their lands and an attempt to disperse them about the country.

**Civil Liberties.** Newspapers are largely public or party and are closely controlled by the government; both foreign and domestic books and movies are censored. Radio and television are government monopolies. The strident media are emphasized as governmental means for active indoctrination. Political imprisonment, brutality, and torture are common, and execution frequent. The families of suspects are often imprisoned. Rights are largely de facto or those deriving from traditional religious law. Religious freedom and freedom to organize for any purpose is very limited. Education is intended to serve the party's purposes. Iraq has a dual economy, with a large preindustrial sector. The government has taken over much of the modern petroleum-based economy and, through land reform leading to collectives and state farms, has limited private economic choice.

**Comparatively:** Iraq is as free as Libya, freer than Somalia, less free than Iran.

# IRELAND

**Economy:** capitalist     **Political Rights:** 1
**Polity:** centralized multiparty     **Civil Liberties:** 1
**Population:** 3,300,000     **Status of Freedom:** free
A relatively homogeneous population

**Political Rights.** Ireland is a parliamentary democracy which successfully shifts national power among parties. The bicameral legislature has an appointive upper house with powers only of delay. Local government is not powerful, but is elective rather than appointive. The referendum is also used for national decisions.

**Civil Liberties.** The press is free and private, and radio and television are under an autonomous corporation. Strong censorship has always been exercised over both publishers and the press, but since this is of social rather than political content, it lies within that sphere of control permitted a majority in a free democracy. The rule of law is firmly established and private rights are guaranteed.

**Comparatively:** Ireland is as free as Canada, freer than France.

# ISRAEL

**Economy:** mixed capitalist  
**Polity:** centralized multiparty  
**Population:** 3,900,000  
**Political Rights:** 2  
**Civil Liberties:** 2  
**Status of Freedom:** free  
An ethnic state with microterritorial subnationalities

**Political Rights.** Israel is governed under a parliamentary system. Recent elections have resulted in major shifts of power among the many political parties. Provinces are ruled from the center, although there are important local elective offices in the cities. *Subnationalities:* National elections do not involve the Arabs in the occupied territories; Arabs in Israel proper participate in Israeli elections as a minority. Arabs both in Israel and the occupied territories must live in their homeland under the cultural and political domination of twentieth-century immigrants.

**Civil Liberties.** Newspapers are private or party, and free of censorship except for restrictions relating to the always precarious national security. Radio and television are government owned. In general the rule of law is observed, although Arabs in Israel are not accorded the full rights of citizens, and the Orthodox Jewish faith holds a special position in the country's religious, customary, and legal life. Detentions, house arrest, and brutality have been reported against Arabs opposing Israel's Palestine policy. Because of the war, the socialist-cooperative ideology of its founders, and dependence on outside support, the role of private enterprise in the economy has been less than in most of Euro-America. Arabs are, in effect, not allowed to buy land from Jews, and Arab land has been expropriated for Jewish settlement. Freedom House's rating of Israel is based on its judgment of the situation in Israel proper and not that in the occupied territories.

**Comparatively:** Israel is as free as Portugal, freer than Lebanon, less free than France.

# ITALY

**Economy:** capitalist  
**Polity:** centralized multiparty  
**Population:** 57,200,000  

**Political Rights:** 1  
**Civil Liberties:** 2  
**Status of Freedom:** free  

A relatively homogeneous population with small territorial subnationalities

**Political Rights.** Italy is a bicameral parliamentary democracy. Elections are generally free. Since the 1940s governments have been dominated by the Christian Democrats, with coalitions shifting between dependence on minor parties of the left or right. The fascist party is banned. Referendums are used to supplement parliamentary rule. Opposition parties gain local political power, but regional and local power are generally quite limited. Regional institutions are developing.

**Civil Liberties.** Italian newspapers are free and cover a broad spectrum. Radio and television are both public and private and provide unusually diverse programming. Laws against defamation of the government and foreign and ecclesiastical officials exert a slight limiting effect on the media. Freedom of speech is inhibited in some areas and for many individuals by the violence of both right- and left-wing extremist groups. Since the bureaucracy does not promptly respond to citizen desires, it represents, as in many countries, an additional impediment to the full expression of the rule of law. Detention may last for years without trial. Since major industries are managed by the government, and the government has undertaken major reallocations of land, Italy is only marginally a capitalist state.

**Comparatively:** Italy is as free as Greece, freer than Morocco, less free than the Netherlands.

# IVORY COAST

**Economy:** noninclusive capitalist  
**Polity:** nationalist one-party  
**Population:** 8,000,000  

**Political Rights:** 5  
**Civil Liberties:** 5  
**Status of Freedom:** partly free  

A transethnic heterogeneous state

**Political Rights.** Ivory Coast is ruled by a one-party, capitalist dictatorship. Assembly elections have recently allowed choice of individuals, but not policies. Organized in the 1940s, the ruling party incorporates a variety of interests and forces. Provinces are ruled directly from the center. Contested mayoralty elections occur.

**Civil Liberties.** Although the legal press is mostly party or government controlled, it presents a limited spectrum of opinion. Foreign publications are widely available. While opposition is discouraged, there is no ideological conformity. Radio and television are government controlled. Short-term imprisonment and other pressures are used to control opposition. Travel and religion are generally free. There is a limited right to strike and organize unions. Economically the country depends on small private farms; in the modern sector private enterprise is encouraged.

**Comparatively:** Ivory Coast is as free as Egypt, freer than Guinea, less free than Senegal.

# JAMAICA

**Economy:** mixed capitalist
**Polity:** centralized multiparty
**Population:** 2,200,000
A relatively homogeneous population

**Political Rights:** 2
**Civil Liberties:** 3
**Status of Freedom:** free

**Political Rights.** Jamaica is a parliamentary democracy in which power changes from one party to another. However, political life has become increasingly violent; the last election was accompanied by murders, a state of siege, bans on political rallies, and government supervision of publicity. Regardless of who is to blame, and both sides may be, this degrades the meaning of political rights. Regional or local administrations have little independent power, although there are elected parish councils.

**Civil Liberties.** In spite of nationalization of several of the news media, critical media are widely available to the public. Freedom of assembly and organization are generally respected. The judiciary and much of the bureaucracy retain independence. Although some foreign companies have been nationalized, the economy remains largely in private hands.

**Comparatively:** Jamaica is as free as Colombia, freer than Panama, less free than Dominica.

# JAPAN

**Economy:** capitalist
**Polity:** centralized multiparty
**Population:** 116,800,000
A relatively homogeneous population

**Political Rights:** 1
**Civil Liberties:** 1
**Status of Freedom:** free

**Political Rights.** Japan is a bicameral, constitutional monarchy with a relatively weak upper house. The conservative-to-centrist Liberal Democratic Party ruled with solid majorities from independence in the early 1950s until the mid-1970s. Although the Liberal Democrats have lost considerable support in recent elections, through coalitions with independents they have maintained control at the national level, and have recently showed increased strength at the local level. Concentrated business interests have played a strong role in maintaining Liberal Party hegemony through the use of their money, influence, and prestige. In addition, a weighting of representation in favor of rural areas tends to maintain the Liberal Party position. Opposition parties are fragmented. They have local control in some areas, but the power of local and regional assemblies and officials is limited. Since electoral and parliamentary procedures are democratic, we assume that Japan's system would freely allow a transfer of national power to an opposition group should the majority desire it. Democracy within the Liberal Party is increasing.

**Civil Liberties.** News media are generally private and free, although many radio and television stations are served by a public broadcasting corporation. Television is excellent and quite free. Courts of law are not as important in Japanese society as in Europe and America; both the courts and police appear to be relatively fair. Travel and change of residence are unrestricted. The public expressions and actions of many people are more restricted than in most modern democracies by traditional controls. Japanese style collectivism leads to strong social pressures, especially psychological pressures, in many spheres (unions, corporations, or religious-political groups, such as Soka Gakkai). Human rights organizations are very active.

**Comparatively:** Japan is as free as Australia, freer than France.

# JORDAN

**Economy:** capitalist
**Polity:** traditional nonparty
**Population:** 3,200,000
A relatively homogeneous population

**Political Rights:** 6
**Civil Liberties:** 6
**Status of Freedom:** not free

**Political Rights.** Jordan is an absolute monarchy in the guise of a constitutional monarchy. There are no parties; parliament provides no check on the king's broad powers, since it has not met since 1967. In 1978 an appointive National Consultative Council was established. Provinces are ruled from the center and elected local governments have limited autonomy. The king and his ministers are regularly petitioned by citizens.

**Civil Liberties.** Papers are private but self-censored and occasionally suspended. Television and radio are government controlled. Free private conversation and mild public criticism are allowed. Under continuing emergency laws normal legal guarantees for political suspects are suspended, and organized opposition is not permitted. There are prisoners of conscience and instances of torture. Labor has a limited right to organize and strike. Private rights such as those to property, travel, or religion appear to be respected.

**Comparatively:** Jordan is as free as Saudi Arabia, freer than South Yemen, less free than Egypt.

# KAMPUCHEA (Cambodia)

**Economy:** socialist
**Polity:** communist one-party states
**Population:** 6,000,000
A relatively homogeneous population

**Political Rights:** 7
**Civil Liberties:** 7
**Status of Freedom:** not free

**Political Rights.** Kampuchea is divided between the remnants of the Pol Pot tyranny and the only slightly less tyrannical, imposed Vietnamese regime. The people have little part in either regime.

**Civil Liberties.** The media continue to be completely controlled in both areas; outside publications are rigorously controlled. Political execution has been a common function of government. Reeducation for war captives is again practiced by the new government. There is no rule of law; private freedoms are not guaranteed. Kampucheans continue to be one of the world's most tyrannized peoples. At least temporarily much of economic life has been decollectivized.

**Comparatively:** Kampuchea is as free as Ethiopia, less free than Thailand.

# KENYA

**Economy:** noninclusive capitalist
**Polity:** nationalist one-party
**Population:** 15,900,000
A formally transethnic heterogeneous state with active and potential subnationalities

**Political Rights:** 5
**Civil Liberties:** 4
**Status of Freedom:** partly free

**Political Rights.** Kenya is a one-party capitalist state with Kikuyu domination, at least until recently. Only the ruling party competes in elections. Election results often express popular dissatisfaction, but candidates avoid discussion of basic policy or the president. Selection of top party and national leaders is by consensus or acclamation. The administration is centralized, but elements of tribal and communal government continue at the periphery. *Subnationalities*: Comprising twenty percent of the population, the Kikuyu are the largest tribal group. In a very heterogeneous society, the Luo are the second most important subnationality.

**Civil Liberties.** The press is private. It is not censored but under government pressure to avoid criticism. Radio and television are under government control. Rights of assembly, organization, and demonstration are limited. The courts have considerable independence. There are few if any prisoners of conscience. Unions are active but strikes generally illegal; private rights are generally respected. Land is gradually coming under private rather than tribal control.

**Comparatively:** Kenya is as free as Guyana, freer than Tanzania, less free than Mauritius.

# KIRIBATI

**Economy:** noninclusive capitalist-statist
**Polity:** decentralized nonparty
**Population:** 57,000

**Political Rights:** 2
**Civil Liberties:** 2
**Status of Freedom:** free

A relatively homogeneous population with a territorial subnationality

**Political Rights.** Both the legislature and chief minister are elected in a fully competitive system. Local government is significant.

**Civil Liberties.** Public expression appears to be free and the rule of law guaranteed. The modern economy is dominated by government-controlled phosphate mining and investments.

**Comparatively:** Kiribati is as free as Fiji, freer than Western Samoa, less free than Australia.

# KOREA, NORTH

**Economy:** socialist
**Polity:** communist one-party
**Population:** 17,900,000

**Political Rights:** 7
**Civil Liberties:** 7
**Status of Freedom:** not free

A relatively homogeneous state

**Political Rights.** North Korea is a hard-line communist dictatorship in which the organs and assemblies of government are merely a facade for party rule. National elections allow no choice. The politburo is under one-man rule; the dictator's son is the dictator's officially annointed successor. Military officers are very strong in top positions.

**Civil Liberties.** The media are all government controlled, with glorification of the leader a major responsibility. External publications are rigidly excluded and those who listen to foreign broadcasts severely punished. No individual thoughts are advanced publicly or privately. Individual rights are minimal. Opponents are even kidnapped overseas.

Rights to travel internally and externally are perhaps the most restrictive in the world. Tourism is unknown—even to communist countries. Social classes are politically defined in a rigidly controlled society. There are large numbers of prisoners of conscience; torture is reportedly common.

**Comparatively:** North Korea is as free as Albania, less free than South Korea.

# KOREA, SOUTH

**Economy:** capitalist
**Polity:** military nonparty
**Population:** 38,200,000
A relatively homogeneous state

**Political Rights:** 5
**Civil Liberties:** 6
**Status of Freedom:** partly free

**Political Rights.** In 1980 the country was ruled for the bulk of the year by the military under a strong nonparliamentary institution, and parties were closed down. A 1980 constitutional referendum suggested considerable popular backing for the military. (A slight improvement occurred in early 1981 in connection with a presidential election.)

**Civil Liberties.** Although most newspapers are private, as well as many radio stations and one television station, they have been reorganized by government fiat. Nearly all freedom to express differing opinion had withered by the end of the year. Because of government pressure, self-censorship is the rule. Special laws against criticizing the constitution, the government, or its policies have resulted in many prisoners of conscience and the use of torture. The resulting climate of fear in activist circles has been sharpened by extralegal harassment of those who were not imprisoned, and the inability of the courts to effectively protect the rights of political suspects or prisoners. Outside this arena private rights have been generally respected. Rapid, capitalistic economic growth has been combined with a relatively egalitarian income distribution. Human rights organizations are active, but were under heavy pressure during 1980.

**Comparatively:** South Korea is as free as Chile, freer than China (Mainland), less free than Thailand.

# KUWAIT

**Economy:** mixed capitalist-
       statist
**Polity:** traditional nonparty
**Population:** 1,300,000
The citizenry is relatively homogeneous

**Political Rights:** 6
**Civil Liberties:** 4
**Status of Freedom:** partly free

**Political Rights.** Kuwait in 1980 was a traditional monarchy preparing for a new experiment in constitutional monarchy. (A parliamentary election with a limited franchise was held in early 1981.) The recent monarchical succession was uneventful, and citizens have access to the monarch. More than half the population are immigrants; their political, economic, and social rights are much inferior to those of natives.

**Civil Liberties.** Although the private press presents diverse opinions and ideological viewpoints, papers are subject to suspension for "spreading dissension." Radio and television are government controlled. Freedom of assembly is curtailed. Public critics may be detained, expelled, or have their passports confiscated. Private discussion is open and few, if any, political prisoners are held. Private freedoms are respected, and independent unions operate. There is a wide variety of enabling government activity in fields such as education, housing, and medicine that is not based on reducing choice through taxation.

**Comparatively:** Kuwait is as free as Egypt, freer than Saudi Arabia, less free than Lebanon.

# LAOS

**Economy:** noninclusive socialist   **Political Rights:** 7
**Polity:** communist one-party       **Civil Liberties:** 7
**Population:** 3,700,000             **Status of Freedom:** not free
An ethnic state with active or potential subnationalities

**Political Rights.** Laos has established a traditional communist party dictatorship in which the party is superior to the external government at all levels. The government is subservient to the desires of the Vietnamese communist party, upon which the present leaders must depend. There is continued resistance in rural areas, where many groups have been violently suppressed. *Subnationalities*: Pressure on the Hmong (Meo) hill people has caused the majority of them to flee the country.

**Civil Liberties.** The media are all government controlled. There are many political prisoners; large numbers remain in reeducation camps. There are few accepted private rights, but there has been some relaxation of opposition to traditional ways recently. Travel within and exit from the country is highly restricted.

**Comparatively:** Laos is as free as Vietnam, less free than China (Mainland).

# LEBANON

**Economy:** capitalist                **Political Rights:** 4
**Polity:** decentralized multiparty    **Civil Liberties:** 4
**Population:** 3,200,000               **Status of Freedom:** partly free
A complex, multinational, microterritorial state

**Political Rights.** In theory Lebanon is a parliamentary democracy with a strong but indirectly elected president. In spite of the calamities of the last few years the constitutional system still functions to varying degrees in much of the country. The parliament is elected, although the last general election was in 1972. Palestinians, local militias, and Syrian forces reduce its sovereignty. *Subnationalities*: Leading administrative and parliamentary officials are allocated among the several religious or communal groups by complicated formulas. These groups have for years pursued semi-autonomous lives within the state, although their territories are often intermixed.

**Civil Liberties.** Renowned for its independence, the press still offers a highly diverse selection to an attentive audience. Most censorship is now self-imposed, reflecting the views of locally dominant military forces. Radio is government and party; television is part government and now officially uncensored. Widespread killing in recent years has inhibited the nationwide expression of most freedoms and tightened communal controls on individuals. In many areas the courts cannot function effectively, but within its power the government secures most private rights. In 1980 the area under law appeared to have increased significantly. Few if any prisoners of conscience are detained by the government. There is an active human rights organization.

**Comparatively:** Lebanon is as free as Panama, freer than Syria, less free than Cyprus.

# LESOTHO

**Economy:** noninclusive capitalist
**Polity:** partially centralized
    dominant party
**Population:** 1,300,000

**Political Rights:** 5
**Civil Liberties:** 5
**Status of Freedom:** partly free

A relatively homogeneous population

**Political Rights.** Lesotho is a constitutional monarchy essentially under the one-man rule of the leader of the ruling political party who suspended the constitution to avoid being defeated in 1970. Opposition parties as well as the king have been repressed. Yet major elements of the traditional system (chiefs) remain, and members of other parties have been introduced into the government. There is some local government. Although there are frequent expressions of national independence, Lesotho remains under considerable South African economic and political pressure. Lesotho is populated almost exclusively by Basotho people, and the land has never been alienated. A large percentage of the male citizenry works in South Africa.

**Civil Liberties.** The media are government and church controlled, and criticism is allowed. Opposition political activity or assembly is repressed. The judiciary seems to preserve considerable independence vis-à-vis the government. Limited union activity is permitted. Internal travel is un-restricted, as are most private rights, but political opponents may be denied foreign travel.

**Comparatively:** Lesotho is as free as Indonesia, freer than South Africa, less free than Botswana.

# LIBERIA

**Economy:** noninclusive capitalist
**Polity:** military nonparty
**Population:** 1,900,000
A formally transethnic heterogeneous state

**Political Rights:** 6
**Civil Liberties:** 6
**Status of Freedom:** not free

**Political Rights.** Libya is a military dictatorship apparently effectively by noncommissioned officers after a bloody coup. Although initially welcomed by many, the new system remained unjustified by any legit-imization.

**Civil Liberties.** The press is private, but now exercises careful self-censorship. Radio and television are partially government controlled. The coup resulted in executions, imprisonment, and a general collapse of legal protections, but the situation has since been normalized. Travel and other private rights are generally respected. Only blacks can become citizens. Union organization is partly free; there is no right to strike.

**Comparatively:** Liberia is as free as Gabon, freer than Togo, less free than Ghana.

# LIBYA

**Economy:** capitalist-statist
**Polity:** socialist quasi-one-party
    (military dominated)
**Population:** 3,000,000
A relatively homogeneous state

**Political Rights:** 6
**Civil Liberties:** 7
**Status of Freedom:** not free

**Political Rights.** Libya is a militaryt dictatorship apparently effectively under the control of one person. Although officially there is no party, the effort to mobilize and organize the entire population for state pur-poses follows the socialist one-party model. The place of a legislature is taken by the direct democracy of large congresses. Whatever the form, no opposition is allowed on the larger questions of society. Institutional self-management has been widely introduced in schools, hospitals, and factories. Sometimes the system works well enough to provide a meaningful degree of decentralized self-determination.

**Civil Liberties.** The media are government controlled means for active indoctrination. Private conversation is very circumspect on political issues. There are many political prisoners; the use of military and people's courts for political cases suggests little respect for the rule of law, yet acquittals in political cases occur. Torture and mistreatment are frequent; executions for crimes of conscience occur—even in foreign countries. Oil and oil-related industry are the major government enterprises. Although ideologically socialist, even some of the press remains in private hands. Socialization tends to be announced at the top and imposed rather anarchically and sporadically at the bottom. Respect for Islam provides some check on arbitrary government.

**Comparatively:** Libya is as free as Benin, freer than Afghanistan, less free than Tunisia.

# LUXEMBOURG

**Economy:** capitalist
**Polity:** centralized multiparty
**Population:** 368,000
A relatively homogeneous state

**Political Rights:** 1
**Civil Liberties:** 1
**Status of Freedom:** free

**Political Rights.** Luxembourg is a constitutional monarchy on the Belgian model, in which the monarchy is somewhat more powerful than in the United Kingdom or Scandinavia. The legislature is bicameral with the appointive upper house having only a delaying function. Recent votes have resulted in important shifts in the nature of the dominant coalition.

**Civil Liberties.** The media are private and free. The rule of law is thoroughly accepted in both public and private realms.

**Comparatively:** Luxembourg is as free as Iceland, freer than France.

# MADAGASCAR

**Economy:** noninclusive mixed
    socialist
**Polity:** nationalist one-party
    (military dominated)
**Population:** 8,700,000
A transethnic heterogeneous state

**Political Rights:** 6
**Civil Liberties:** 6
**Status of Freedom:** not free

**Political Rights.** Madagascar is a military dictatorship with a very weak legislature. Elections are restricted to candidates selected by parties grouped in a "national front," a government sponsored coalition; parliament appears to play a very small part in government. Anarchical conditions call into question the extent to which the people are willing to grant the regime legitimacy. Emphasis has been put on developing the autonomy of local Malagasy governmental institutions, but the restriction of local elections to approved front candidates belies this emphasis.

**Civil Liberties.** There is a private press, but papers are carefully censored and may be suspended. Broadcasting is government controlled. Movie theatres have been nationalized. The government replaced the national news agency with one which will "disregard information likely to be harmful to the government's socialist development policies." There is no right of assembly; one must be careful of public speech. There are few long-term prisoners of conscience but short-term political detentions are common. The rule of law is weak. Labor unions are not strong, but religion is free and most private rights respected. Public security is very weak. Overseas travel is restricted. While still encouraging private investment, most businesses and large farms are nationalized.

**Comparatively:** Madagascar is as free as Tanzania, freer than Mozambique, less free than Egypt.


# MALAWI

**Economy:** noninclusive capitalist     **Political Rights:** 6
**Polity:** nationalist one-party         **Civil Liberties:** 7
**Population:** 6,100,000             **Status of Freedom:** not free
A transethnic heterogeneous state

**Political Rights.** Malawi is a one-man dictatorship with party and parliamentary forms. A 1978 election allowed some choice among individuals for the first time. Administration is centralized, although the paramount chiefs retain power locally through control over land.

**Civil Liberties.** The press is private or religious but under strict government control, as is the government-owned radio service. Private criticism of the administration remains dangerous. Foreign publications are carefully screened. The country has been notable for the persecution of political opponents. In recent years there have been fewer prisoners of conscience. Asians suffer discrimination. Corruption and economic inequality are characteristic. Traditional courts offer some protection against arbitrary rule, as do the comparatively limited interests of the government. Foreign travel and union activity are closely controlled.

**Comparatively:** Malawi is as free as South Yemen, freer than Somalia, less free than Zambia.

# MALAYSIA

**Economy:** capitalist
**Polity:** decentralized dominant
    party
**Population:** 14,000,000

**Political Rights:** 3
**Civil Liberties:** 4
**Status of Freedom:** partly free

An ethnic state with major nonterritorial subnationalities

**Political Rights.** Malaysia is a parliamentary democracy with a weak, indirectly elected and appointed senate and a powerful lower house. The relatively powerless head of state is an elective monarch, rotating among the traditional monarchs of the constituent states. A multinational front has dominated electoral and parliamentary politics. By such devices as imprisonment or the banning of demonstrations the opposition is not given an equal opportunity to compete in elections. The states of Malaysia have their own rulers, parliaments, and institutions, but it is doubtful if any state has the power to leave the federation. *Subnationalities:* Political, economic, linguistic, and educational policies have favored the Malays (forty-four percent) over the Chinese (thirty-six percent), Indians (ten percent), and others. Malays dominate the army. Traditionally the Chinese had been the wealthier and better educated people. Although there are Chinese in the ruling front, they are not allowed to question the policy of communal preference.

**Civil Liberties.** The press is private and highly varied. However, nothing that might influence communal relations can be printed, and editors are constrained by the need to renew their publishing licenses annually. Foreign journalists are closely controlled. Radio is mostly government owned, television entirely so. Universities have been put under government pressure and foreign professors encouraged to leave. There have been several reports of the development of an atmosphere of fear in both academic and opposition political circles, as well as widespread discrimination against non-Malays. In 1978 an attempt to establish a private university for Chinese language students was blocked. Perhaps 1000 political suspects are detained at any one time, generally on suspicion of communist activity. Some are clearly prisoners of conscience; several have held responsible political positions. Confessions are often extracted. Nevertheless, significant criticism appears in the media, and in parliament campaigns are mounted against government decisions. Unions are partly free and have the right to strike. Economic activity is free, except for government favoritism to the Malays.

**Comparatively:** Malaysia is as free as Mexico, freer than Indonesia, less free than Sri Lanka.


# MALDIVES

**Economy:** noninclusive capitalist
**Polity:** traditional nonparty
**Population:** 151,000
A relatively homogeneous population

**Political Rights:** 5
**Civil Liberties:** 5
**Status of Freedom:** partly free

**Political Rights.** The Maldives have a parliamentary government in which a president (elected by parliament and confirmed by the people) is the real ruler. Regional leaders are presidentially appointed. Both economic and political power are concentrated in the hands of a very small, wealthy elite. Islam places a check on absolutism.

**Civil Liberties.** Newspapers present some diversity of views but are under pressure to conform; the radio station is owned by the government. Foreign publications are received; political discussion is limited. There are few if any long-term political prisoners. Law is traditional Islamic law; most of the people rely on a traditional subsistence economy; the small elite has developed commercial fishing and tourism.

**Comparatively:** Maldives is as free as Qatar, freer than Seychelles, less free than Mauritius.


# MALI

**Economy:** noninclusive mixed
   socialist
**Polity:** nationalist one-party
   (military dominated)
**Population:** 6,600,000
A transethnic heterogeneous state

**Political Rights:** 7
**Civil Liberties:** 6
**Status of Freedom:** not free

**Political Rights.** Mali is a military dictatorship with a recently constructed political party to lend support. The regime appears to function without broad popular consensus. National elections allow no choice, though there is some at the local level. *Subnationalities:* Although the government is ostensibly above ethnic rivalries, repression of the northern peoples has been reported.

**Civil Liberties.** The media are all government controlled. Antigovernment demonstrations are forbidden. Private conversation is relatively free. Political imprisonment and torture are frequent. Reeducation centers are brutal. Student protests are controlled by conscription. Religion is free; unions are controlled; travelers must submit to frequent police checks. Private economic rights in the modern sector are minimal, but collectivization has recently been deemphasized for subsistence agriculturists, the majority of the people.

**Comparatively:** Mali is as free as Benin, freer than Somalia, less free than Liberia.

# MALTA

**Economy:** mixed capitalist-statist
**Polity:** centralized multiparty
**Population:** 338,000
A relatively homogeneous population

**Political Rights:** 2
**Civil Liberties:** 3
**Status of Freedom:** free

**Political Rights.** Malta is a parliamentary democracy in which power has shifted between the major parties. The most recent election, maintaining the governing party in its position, was marked by violence. The government also altered the composition of a constitutional court in the middle of a case concerning alleged coercion of voters in a particular district.

**Civil Liberties.** The press is free, but foreign and domestic journalists are under government pressure. Broadcasting is under a licensed body; Italian media are also available. Although the rule of law is generally accepted, the government is suspected of fomenting gang violence against its opponents. The government has concentrated a great deal of the economy in its hands, and social equalization programs have been emphasized. The governing party and major union have been amalgamated.

**Comparatively:** Malta is as free as Sri Lanka, freer than Turkey, less free than the United Kingdom.

# MAURITANIA

**Economy:** noninclusive capitalist-
    statist
**Polity:** military nonparty
**Population:** 1,600,000
An ethnic state with a major territorial subnationality

**Political Rights:** 7
**Civil Liberties:** 6
**Status of Freedom:** not free

**Political Rights.** Mauritania has been ruled by a succession of military leaders without formal popular or traditional legitimation. *Subnationalities:* There is a subnational movement, concerned particularly with linguistic questions in the non-Arab, southern part of the country.

**Civil Liberties.** The media are government owned and censored, but foreign publications and broadcasts are freely available. There are few if any long-term prisoners of conscience. Conversation is free; no ideology is imposed, but assembly is restricted and demonstrations repressed. Travel may be restricted for political reasons. Union activity is government controlled. There is religious freedom. The government controls much of industry and mining, as well as wholesale trade, but there have been recent moves to reduce government involvement. Only in 1980 did the government make a strong move to abolish slavery.

**Comparatively:** Mauritania is as free as Romania, freer than South Yemen, less free than Morocco.

# MAURITIUS

**Economy:** capitalist
**Polity:** centralized multiparty
**Population:** 900,000
An ethnically complex state

**Political Rights:** 3
**Civil Liberties:** 3
**Status of Freedom:** partly free

**Political Rights.** Mauritius is a parliamentary democracy. The last election showed an important gain for the opposition, but the government managed to retain power through coalition (and amidst controversy). A variety of different racial and religious communities are active in politics, although they are not territorially based. There are a number of semi-autonomous local governing bodies. Municipal elections have been postponed recently for allegedly partisan reasons.

**Civil Liberties.** The press is private or party and without censorship. Broadcasting is under a single corporation, presumably private in form. Freedom of assembly is restricted: opposition members of parliament have been imprisoned for illegal demonstration. The labor union movement is quite strong, as are a variety of communal organizations. Strikes are frequent. There is religious and economic freedom; taxes can be quite high.

**Comparatively:** Mauritius is as free as Cyprus, freer than Bangladesh, less free than India.

# MEXICO

**Economy:** capitalist-statist
**Polity:** decentralized dominant
        party
**Population:** 68,200,000
An ethnic state with potential subnationalities

**Political Rights:** 3
**Civil Liberties:** 4
**Status of Freedom:** partly free

**Political Rights.** Mexico is ruled by a governmental system formally modeled on that of the United States; in practice the president is much stronger and the legislative and judicial branches much weaker. The states have independent governors and legislatures. The ruling party has had a near monopoly of power on all levels since the 1920s. In the last presidential election the party candidate received ninety-four percent of the vote. Political competition has been largely confined to factional struggles within the ruling party. However, in 1979 new parties participated, and the new election law gave twenty-five percent of the seats to minor parties by proportional representation; the resulting congress showed unusual independence. Voting and campaign irregularities have been common, particularly on the local level. The clergy are not allowed to participate in the political process. *Subnationalities*: There is a large Mayan area in Yucatan that has formerly been restive; there are also other smaller Indian areas.

**Civil Liberties.** The media are mostly private. Although they have operated under a variety of direct and indirect government controls (including take-overs), newspapers are generally free of censorship. Literature and the arts are free. The judicial system is not strong. However, decisions can go against the government; it is possible to win a judicial decision that a law is unconstitutional in a particular application. Religion is free. Widespread bribery and lack of control over the behavior of security forces greatly limits operative freedom, especially in rural areas. Disappearances occur, detention is prolonged, torture and brutality have been common. Private economic rights are respected; government ownership predominates in major industries. Nearly all labor unions are associated with the ruling party. Critical human rights organizations exist.

**Comparatively:** Mexico is as free as Malaysia, freer than Nicaragua, less free than Colombia.

# MONGOLIA

**Economy:** socialist      **Political Rights:** 7
**Polity:** communist one-party      **Civil Liberties:** 7
**Population:** 1,700,000      **Status of Freedom:** not free
A relatively homogeneous population

**Political Rights.** A one-party communist dictatorship, for many years Mongolia has been firmly under the control of one man. Power is organized at all levels through the party apparatus. Those who oppose the government cannot run for office. In the 1977 parliamentary elections, 99.9 percent of eligible voters participated; only two persons failed to properly vote for the single list of candidates. Mongolia has a subordinate relationship to the Soviet Union, which it depends on for defense against Chinese claims. It must use the USSR as an outlet for nearly all of its trade, and its finances are under close Soviet supervision.

**Civil Liberties.** All media are government controlled, and apparently quite effectively. Religion is greatly restricted, Lamaism having been nearly wiped out. Freedom of travel, residence, and other civil liberties are denied.

**Comparatively:** Mongolia is as free as Bulgaria, less free than the USSR.

# MOROCCO

**Economy:** noninclusive capitalist       **Political Rights:** 4
**Polity:** centralized multiparty          **Civil Liberties:** 4
**Population:** 21,000,000                    **Status of Freedom:** partly free
An ethnic state with active and potential subnationalities

**Political Rights.** Morocco is a constitutional monarchy in which the king has retained major executive powers. Recent elections at both local and national levels were fair and well contested in most localities. Most parties participated (including the communist); independents (largely supporters of the king) were the major winners. Opposition leaders were included in the subsequent government. The results of 1980 referendums were more questionable. The autonomy of local and regional elected governments is limited. *Subnationalities*: Although people in the newly acquired land of the Western Sahara participate in the electoral process, it has an important resistance movement. In the rest of the country the large Berber minority is a potential subnationality.

**Civil Liberties.** Newspapers are private or party, and quite diverse. Recently there has been no formal censorship; there are other pressures, including the confiscation of particular issues. Monarchical power must not be criticized. Both public and private broadcasting stations are under government control. In the past the use of torture has been quite common and may continue; the rule of law has also been weakened by the frequent use of prolonged detention without trial. There are many political prisoners; some are prisoners of conscience. Private organizational activity is vigorous and includes student, party, and human rights groups. There are strong independent labor unions; religious and other private rights are respected.

**Comparatively:** Morocco is as free as Senegal, freer than Algeria, less free than Spain.

# MOZAMBIQUE

**Economy:** noninclusive socialist
**Polity:** socialist one-party
**Population:** 10,300,000
A transethnic heterogeneous state

**Political Rights:** 7
**Civil Liberties:** 7
**Status of Freedom:** not free

**Political Rights.** Mozambique is a one-party communist dictatorship in which all power resides in the party leadership. The Liberation Front has now officially been converted into a "vanguard party." All candidates are selected by the ruling party at all levels, but there is some popular control of selection at local levels. Regional administration is controlled from the center.

**Civil Liberties.** All media are rigidly controlled; no public criticism is allowed. Rights of assembly and foreign travel do not exist. There are no private lawyers. Secret police are powerful; thousands are in reeducation camps, and executions occur. Police brutality is common. Unions are prohibited. Heavy pressure has been put on all religions, especially Jehovah's Witnesses. Villagers are being forced into communes, leading to revolts in some areas. However, the socialization of private entrepreneurs has been partially reversed. The emigration of citizens is restricted.

**Comparatively:** Mozambique is as free as Angola, less free than Tanzania.


# NAURU

**Economy:** capitalist-statist
**Polity:** traditional nonparty
**Population:** 9,100
An ethnically complex state

**Political Rights:** 2
**Civil Liberties:** 2
**Status of Freedom:** free

**Political Rights.** Nauru is a parliamentary democracy in which governments change by elective and parliamentary means. Realignments have led to considerable political instability. The country is under Australian influence.

**Civil Liberties.** The media are free of censorship but little developed. The island's major industry is controlled by the government, but otherwise private economic rights are respected.

**Comparatively:** Nauru is as free as Fiji, freer than the Maldives, less free than New Zealand.

# NEPAL

**Economy:** noninclusive capitalist    **Political Rights:** 3
**Polity:** traditional nonparty    **Civil Liberties:** 4
**Population:** 14,000,000    **Status of Freedom:** partly free
An ethnic state with active and potential subnationalities

**Political Rights.** Nepal is a constitutional monarchy in which the king is dominant. The national parliament has been elected indirectly through a series of tiers of government in which the lower levels are directly elected. The government's movement generally selects those elected; some members of the opposition have been included in the government. However, the system is now transitional. A referendum held in 1980 rejected a move toward party government, but a new constitution promises considerable opening of the system, with direct parliamentary election. The referendum was conducted in relative freedom. *Subnationalities:* There are a variety of different peoples, with only fifty percent of the people speaking Nepali as their first language. Hinduism is a unifying force for the vast majority. The historically powerful ruling castes continue to dominate.

**Civil Liberties.** Principal newspapers are public; private journals carry criticism of the government but not the king. Some offending publications were suspended in 1980. Radio is government owned. Private contacts are relatively open. Political arrests, banishment from the capital, and exile have occurred, but political campaigning for a variety of different alternatives has recently been quite open. Parties are again banned, but human rights organizations function. Unions exist only informally. The judiciary is not independent. Religious proselytizing and conversion is prohibited, and the emigration of those with valuable skills or education is restricted. The population is nearly all engaged in traditional occupations; illiteracy levels are very high.

**Comparatively:** Nepal is as free as Thailand, freer than Bhutan, less free than Mauritius.

# NETHERLANDS

**Economy:** mixed capitalist    **Political Rights:** 1
**Polity:** centralized multiparty    **Civil Liberties:** 1
**Population:** 14,100,000    **Status of Freedom:** free
A relatively homogeneous population

**Political Rights.** Netherlands is a constitutional monarchy in which nearly all the power is vested in a directly elected legislature. The results of elections have periodically transferred power to coalitions of the left and right. There is some diffusion of political power below this level, but not a great deal. The monarch retains more power than in the United

Kingdom both through the activity of appointing governments in frequently stalemated situations, and through the advisory Council of State.

**Civil Liberties.** The press is free and private. Radio and television are provided by private associations under state regulation. The courts are independent, and the full spectrum of private rights guaranteed. The burden of exceptionally heavy taxes limits economic choice.

**Comparatively:** The Netherlands is as free as Belgium, freer than Portugal.

## NEW ZEALAND

**Economy:** capitalist                     **Political Rights:** 1
**Polity:** centralized multiparty          **Civil Liberties:** 1
**Population:** 3,200,000                    **Status of Freedom:** free
A relatively homogeneous state with a native subnationality

**Political Rights.** New Zealand is a parliamentary democracy in which power alternates between the two major parties. There is elected local government, but it is not independently powerful. *Subnationalities*: About eight percent of the population are Maori, the original inhabitants.

**Civil Liberties.** The press is private and free. Television and most radio stations are owned by the government. The rule of law and private rights are thoroughly respected. Since taxes (a direct restriction on choice) are not exceptionally high, and industry is not government owned, we label New Zealand capitalist. Others, emphasizing the government's highly developed social programs and penchant for controlling prices, wages, and credit, might place New Zealand further toward the socialist end of the economic spectrum.

**Comparatively:** New Zealand is as free as the United States, freer than France.

## NICARAGUA

**Economy:** capitalist-socialist            **Political Rights:** 5
**Polity:** quasi-nonparty                   **Civil Liberties:** 5
**Population:** 2,600,000                     **Status of Freedom:** partly free
A relatively homogeneous population

**Political Rights.** Government is in the hands of the Sandinista political-military movement and a governing junta installed by them. Although not elected, the new government initially had widespread popular backing. In late 1980 the remaining non-Sandinistas left the Council of State.

**Civil Liberties.** The journals and radio stations are private and diverse; private television is not allowed. There is pressure on dissident or radical journalists. A radio station and a paper have been closed. However, papers and private persons still vocally oppose the new system. No organizations representing previous Somoza movements are allowed to exist. Political activity by parties outside the Sandinista movement is closely restricted. Torture, widespread killing, and brutality occur, especially in rural areas. Disappearances are commonly recorded. The independence of the judiciary is not well developed, but the government does not always win in the courts. Unions are under pressure to join a new government-sponsored federation. A private human rights organization is active.

**Comparatively:** Nicaragua is as free as the Phillippines, freer than Cuba, less free than Honduras.

# NIGER

**Economy:** noninclusive capitalist
**Polity:** military nonparty
**Population:** 5,500,000
A transethnic heterogeneous state

**Political Rights:** 7
**Civil Liberties:** 6
**Status of Freedom:** not free

**Political Rights.** Niger is a military dictatorship with no elected assembly or legal parties. All districts are administered from the center.

**Civil Liberties.** Niger's very limited media are government owned and operated. Dissent is seldom tolerated, although ideological conformity is not demanded. Foreign publications are not censored. A military court has taken the place of a suspended Supreme Court, and a few political prisoners are held. Labor union and religious organization are relatively independent but nonpolitical. Foreign travel is relatively open; outside of politics the government does not regulate individual behavior.

**Comparatively:** Niger is as free as Mali, freer than North Korea, less free than Liberia.

# NIGERIA

**Economy:** noninclusive capitalist-
statist
**Polity:** decentralized multiparty
**Population:** 80,000,000*
A multinational state

**Political Rights:** 2
**Civil Liberties:** 3
**Status of Freedom:** free

**Political Rights.** A multiparty democracy with an elected president and elected provincial governments was reestablished in 1979. Only five strong parties have been authorized, but these seem to include the full

---

*There are widely varying estimates.

spectrum of known leaders. *Subnationalities:* Nigeria is made up of a number of powerful subnational groupings. Speaking mainly Hausa, the people of the north are Muslim. The highly urbanized southwest is dominated by the Yoruba; and the east by the Ibo. Within each of these areas and along their borders there are other peoples, some of which are conscious of their identity and number more than one million persons. Strong loyalties to traditional political units—lineages or kingdoms—throughout the country further complicate the regional picture. With nineteen states, and independent institutions below this level, the present rulers seem dedicated to taking into account the demands of this complexity in the new federal structure.

**Civil Liberties.** Traditionally, Nigeria's media have been some of the freest in Africa. Television and radio are now wholly federal or state owned, as are all but two of the major papers, in part as the result of a Nigerianization program. However, in spite of occasional suppressions, the media have considerable editorial independence. Political organization, assembly, and publication are now freely permitted. The universities, secondary schools, and the trade unions have been brought under close government control or reorganization in the last few years. Apparently the judiciary remains strong and independent, including, in Muslim areas, *sharia* courts. No prisoners of conscience are held; citizens can win in court against the government. However, police are often brutal, and military riot control has led to many deaths. There is freedom of religion and travel, but rights of married women are quite restricted. The country is in the process of moving from a subsistence to industrial economy—largely on the basis of government-controlled oil and oil-related industry. Government intervention elsewhere in agriculture (cooperatives and plantations) and industry has been considerable. Since private business and industry are also encouraged, this is still far from a program of massive redistribution. General corruption in political and economic life has frequently diminished the rule of law. Freedom is respected in most other areas of life.

**Comparatively:** Nigeria is as free as India, freer than Kenya, less free than Portugal.

# NORWAY

**Economy:** mixed capitalist  
**Polity:** centralized multiparty  
**Population:** 144,300,000  

**Political Rights:** 1  
**Civil Liberties:** 1  
**Status of Freedom:** free  

A relatively homogeneous population with a small Lapp minority

**Political Rights.** Norway is a centralized, constitutional monarchy. Labor remains the strongest party, but other parties have formed several governments since the mid-1960s. There is relatively little separation of powers. Regional governments have appointed governors, and cities and towns their own elected officials.

**Civil Liberties.** Newspapers are privately or party owned; radio and television are state monopolies. This is a pluralistic state with independent power in the churches and labor unions. Relatively strong family structures have also been preserved. Norway is capitalistic, yet the extremely high tax burden, perhaps the highest in the noncommunist world, the government's control over the new oil resource, and general reliance on centralized planning reduce the freedom of economic activity.

**Comparatively:** Norway is as free as the United Kingdom, freer than West Germany.

# OMAN

**Economy:** noninclusive capitalist-statist
**Polity:** centralized nonparty
**Population:** 900,000

**Political Rights:** 6
**Civil Liberties:** 6
**Status of Freedom:** not free

An ethnic state with a territorial subnationality

**Political Rights.** Oman is an absolute monarchy with no political parties or elected assemblies. Regional rule is by centrally appointed governors, but the remaining tribal structure at the local and regional level gives a measure of local autonomy. The government is under British influence because of their long record of aid and advice. *Subnationalities*: Quite different from other Omani, the people of Dhofar constitute a small subnationality in periodic revolt.

**Civil Liberties.** The media are very limited and government controlled. Foreign publications are censored regularly. Except in private, criticism is not generally allowed. Although the preservation of traditional institutions provides a check on arbitrary action, the right to a fair trial is not guaranteed. Freedom of assembly and freedom of public religious expression are curtailed. There are no independent unions. There is freedom of travel; private property is respected.

**Comparatively:** Oman is as free as Saudi Arabia, freer than South Yemen, less free than the United Arab Emirates.

# PAKISTAN

**Economy:** noninclusive capitalist-statist
**Polity:** military nonparty
**Population:** 86,500,000
A multinational state

**Political Rights:** 7
**Civil Liberties:** 5
**Status of Freedom:** not free

**Political Rights.** Pakistan is under centralized military dictatorship. The political parties, religious leaders, provincial leaders, and judiciary (and bar association) continue to be factors in the situation but consensus has progressively withered. The former prime minister was executed following a political trial; political parties were officially disbanded and promised elections put off indefinitely. Local elections of limited significance were held. *Subnationalities*: Millions of Pathans, Baluch, and Sindis have been represented since the origin of Pakistan as desiring greater regional autonomy or independence. Provincial organization has sporadically offered a measure of self-determination.

**Civil Liberties.** Newspapers are censored; the frequent detention of journalists and closing of papers lead to strict self-censorship. Radio and television are government controlled. For crime punishments are often severe; torture is alleged, and executions have been common. Thousands of members of the opposition have been imprisoned or flogged in the violent political climate. The officially dissolved parties retain considerable de facto organization. There is a human rights society. Rights of assembly are limited, as are those of travel for some political persons. Courts preserve some independence. Union activity has been banned. Emphasis on Islamic conservatism curtails private rights, especially freedom of religion: religious minorities suffer discrimination. Private property is respected, although some basic industries have been nationalized.

**Comparatively:** Pakistan is as free as Algeria, freer than the USSR, less free than Iran.

# PANAMA

**Economy:** capitalist-statist
**Polity:** quasi-dominant party
    (military dominated)
**Population:** 1,900,000
A relatively homogeneous population

**Political Rights:** 4
**Civil Liberties:** 4
**Status of Freedom:** partly free

**Political Rights.** Officially Panama is governed by a president elected for a six-year term by the assembly. Assembly members are elected from very unequal districts, and assembly powers are very limited. The assembly elects in turn a smaller council with greater powers. In 1980 popular elections were also held for some council seats. Although a major party abstained, some opposition candidates were elected. The National Guard retains major political power. The provinces are administered by presidential appointees.

**Civil Liberties.** There are opposition papers, and critical opposition positions are widely reported in all news media. Still, too much criticism can lead to government sanctions, such as expulsion from journalism. Political arrests are now uncommon. Political parties maintain their opposition role, and rights to organization and assembly are generally respected. The judiciary is not independent; the rule of law is very weak in both political and nonpolitical areas. The government owns major concerns; private property is generally respected; labor unions are under some restrictions. There is freedom of religion, although foreign priests are not allowed. Travel is generally free.

**Comparatively:** Panama is as free as Morocco, freer than Uruguay, less free than Colombia.

# PAPUA NEW GUINEA

**Economy:** noninclusive capitalist
**Polity:** decentralized multiparty
**Population:** 3,000,000

**Political Rights:** 2
**Civil Liberties:** 2
**Status of Freedom:** free

A transethnic heterogeneous state with subnationalities

**Political Rights.** Papua New Guinea is an independent parliamentary democracy, although it remains partially dependent on Australia economically, technically, and militarily. Elections appear fair and seats are divided among two major and several minor parties—party allegiances are still fluid. Because of its dispersed and tribal nature, local government is in some ways quite decentralized. Elected provincial governments with extensive powers have been established. *Subnationalities*: Development of provincial government is meant to contain strong secessionist movements in the North Solomons, Papua, and elsewhere.

**Civil Liberties.** The press is not highly developed but apparently free. Radio is government controlled but presents critical views; Australian stations are also received. There are no political prisoners. Rights to travel, organize, demonstrate, and practice religion are legally secured. The legal system adapted from Australia is operational, but a large proportion of the population lives in a preindustrial world with traditional controls, including violence, that limit freedom of speech, travel, occupation, and other private rights.

**Comparatively:** Papua New Guinea is as free as Portugal, freer than Malaysia, less free than Australia.

# PARAGUAY

**Economy:** noninclusive capitalist-
     statist
**Polity:** centralized dominant-party
     (military dominated)
**Population:** 3,300,000

**Political Rights:** 5
**Civil Liberties:** 5
**Status of Freedom:** partly free

A relatively homogeneous state with small Indian groups

**Political Rights.** Paraguay has been ruled as a modified dictatorship since 1954. In addition to an elected president there is a parliament that includes members of opposition parties. Elections are regularly held, but they have limited meaning: the ruling party receives eighty to ninety percent of the vote, a result guaranteed by direct and indirect pressures on the media, massive government pressure on voters, especially in the countryside, and interference with opposition party organization. The most important regional and local officials are appointed by the president. *Subnationalities*: The population represents a mixture of Indian (Guarani) and Spanish peoples; ninety percent continue to speak Guarani as well as Spanish. Several small tribes of primitive forest peoples are under heavy pressure from both the government and the public.

**Civil Liberties.** There is a private press, and a combination of private, government, and church radio and television. In spite of censorship and periodic suppression of publications, dissenting opinion is expressed, especially by the church hierarchy and opposition newspapers. Opposition political organization continues, as do human rights organizations. Torture, imprisonment, and execution of political opponents, particularly peasants, have been and to a limited extent still are an important part of a sociopolitical situation that includes general corruption and anarchy. There are now few if any long-term prisoners of conscience, but the rule of law is very weak. Union organization is restricted. Political opponents may be refused passports. Beyond the subsistence sector, private economic rights are restricted by government intervention and control. Perhaps a majority of peasants now own land, partly as a result of government policy.

**Comparatively:** Paraguay is as free as Nicaragua, freer than Cuba, less free than Brazil.

# PERU

**Economy:** noninclusive mixed capitalist
**Polity:** centralized multiparty
**Population:** 17,600,000

**Political Rights:** 2
**Civil Liberties:** 3
**Status of Freedom:** free

An ethnic state with a major potential territorial subnationality

**Political Rights.** Peru is now ruled by an elected multiparty system. At election time the media were largely government controlled, but access was given to all groups. Provincial administration is not independent, but local elections are now significant. *Subnationalities*: Several million people speak Quechua in the highlands, and it has become an official language. There are other important Indian groups.

**Civil Liberties.** The media have been largely returned to private control under the new government. Censorship has been abolished. Essentially all positions are freely expressed, but there is still the shadow of the military and the recent past. There are now no political prisoners. Travel is not restrained. Rights to religion, travel, and occupation are generally respected. Labor is independent of government; private property has regained governmental acceptance.

**Comparatively:** Peru is as free as Colombia, freer than Brazil, less free than Costa Rica.

# PHILIPPINES

**Economy:** noninclusive capitalist        **Political Rights:** 5
**Polity:** dominant party                        **Civil Liberties:** 5
**Population:** 47,700,000                       **Status of Freedom:** partly free
A transethnic heterogeneous state with active and potential subnationalities

**Political Rights.** The Philippines is ruled as a plebiscitory family dictatorship with the aid of a docile assembly. The present ruler was elected in a fair election, but more recent referendums affirming his rule, his constitutional changes, and martial law have not been conducted with open competition, free discussion, or acceptable voting procedures. Previously legitimate political parties exist, but they have no part to play in current political life. Assembly elections in 1978 were held with severely restricted opposition activity and were boycotted by the major parties. The results were subject to questionable tabulations. Local elections in 1980 were similarly disabled. There is some decentralization of power to local assemblies, but provincial and local officials are centrally appointed. *Subnationalities*: The Philippines includes a variety of different peoples of which the Tagalog speaking are the most important (although a minority). A portion of the Muslim (Moro) subnationality is in active revolt along the front of Christian-Muslim opposition. There are several major potential subnationalities that may request autonomy in the near future on the basis of both territorial and linguistic identity.

**Civil Liberties.** Newspapers and broadcasting are largely private but under indirect government control. Only minor opposition papers exist; diverse foreign publications are widely available. Access to radio and television for the opposition are restricted. Rights of assembly are restricted to pre-election periods—and even then quite incomplete. The courts have retained some independence although it has been much reduced. Hundreds of prisoners of conscience are held; torture is used but is sporadically condemned by the top levels of government—torturers have been punished. Unions have only limited independence, but strikes are permitted. Military actions against insurgents have led to many unnecessary arrests, killings, and destruction. The Church still maintains its independence. The private economy is marginally capitalist, but there has been rapid growth in government intervention, favoritism, and direct ownership of industries.

**Comparatively:** The Philippines is as free as Singapore, freer than Vietnam, less free than Malaysia.

# POLAND

**Economy:** mixed socialist
**Polity:** communist one-party
**Population:** 35,500,000
A relatively homogeneous population

**Political Rights:** 6
**Civil Liberties:** 4
**Status of Freedom:** partly free

**Political Rights.** Poland is effectively a one-party communist dictatorship, with noncompetitive, one-list elections. However, in recent years a few nonparty persons have gained election to the assembly and recent sessions have evidenced more than pro forma debate. There are elected councils at provincial levels. Although the party apparatus operating from the top down is the formal locus of power, the Catholic Church, academics, peasants, and newly organized independent workers unions have countervailing powers. The Soviet Union's right of interference and continual pressure diminishes Poland's independence.

**Civil Liberties.** The Polish newspapers are both private and government, and broadcasting is government owned. There is a small independent press that occasionally differs with the government. Censorship has been pervasive; yet there are legal anti-Marxist publications with limited circulations. In 1980 all media became noticeably more open and diverse. There are prisoners of conscience, no formal right of assembly, nor concept of an independent judiciary. This situation also improved in 1980. Short imprisonment, beating, and harassment have been the most common means of restricting opposition. Illegal attempts to leave Poland frequently lead to arrest, but travel is now permitted for most citizens. Important but limited rights to organize independently and strike have recently been granted. Demonstrations have become common and nongovernmental organizations developed. Most agriculture and considerable commerce remain in private hands.

**Comparatively:** Poland is as free as Philippines, freer than Hungary, less free than Mexico.

# PORTUGAL

**Economy:** mixed capitalist                    **Political Rights:** 2
**Polity:** centralized multiparty               **Civil Liberties:** 2
**Population:** 9,900,000                         **Status of Freedom:** free
A relatively homogeneous population

**Political Rights.** At present Portugal is a parliamentary democracy with the military command playing a relatively strong role through the presidency and the Council of the Revolution. There is vigorous party competition over most of the spectrum (except the far right), and fair elections. Elections are competitive and power is shared by several groups. Provincial government is centrally directed.

**Civil Liberties.** The most important papers and journals are private or party owned, and are now quite free. Radio and television are government owned except for one Catholic station. The government has restored the rule of law. There are few prisoners of conscience, yet one can be imprisoned for insult to the government or military. Long periods of detention without trial occur in isolated instances. Imprisonment for "fascist" organization or discussion was promulgated in 1978. The Catholic Church, unions, peasant organizations, and military services remain alternative institutions of power. Although there is a large nationalized sector, capitalism is the accepted form for much of the economy.

**Comparatively:** Portugal is as free as Finland, freer than Jamaica, less free than France.

# QATAR

**Economy:** capitalist-statist                  **Political Rights:** 5
**Polity:** traditional nonparty                 **Civil Liberties:** 5
**Population:** 250,000                           **Status of Freedom:** partly free
A relatively homogeneous citizenry

**Political Rights.** Quatar is a traditional monarchy. The majority of the residents are recently arrived foreigners; of the native population perhaps one-fourth are members of the ruling family. There is an appointed advisory council. The role of consensus is suggested by the fact that extravagence and lack of attention to affairs of state recently led the ruling family to replace the monarch.

**Civil Liberties.** The media are public and private, and passively loyalist. Discussion is fairly open; foreign publications are controlled. Political parties are forbidden. This is a traditional state still responsive to Islamic and tribal laws that moderate the absolutism of government. The family government controls the nation's wealth through control over oil, but there is also independently powerful merchant and religious classes. There are no organized unions. The rights of women and religious minorities are quite limited.

**Comparatively:** Qatar is as free as the United Arab Emirates, freer than Saudi Arabia, less free than Lebanon.

# RHODESIA

### (See Zimbabwe)

# ROMANIA

**Economy:** socialist
**Polity:** communist one-party
**Population:** 22,300,000
An ethnic state with territorial subnationalities

**Political Rights:** 7
**Civil Liberties:** 6
**Status of Freedom:** not free

**Political Rights.** Romania is a now-traditional communist state. Assemblies at national and regional levels are subservient to the party hierarchy. Although the party is very large, all decisions are made by a small elite and especially the dictator. Elections involve only candidates chosen by the party; for some assembly positions the party may propose several candidates. Soviet influence is relatively slight. *Subnationalities*: The Magyar and German minorities are teritorially based. If offered self-determination one Magyar area would surely opt for rejoining neighboring Hungary; many of the Germans evidently wish to migrate to Germany, and this movement has been developing. In Romania the cultural rights of both groups are narrowly limited.

**Civil Liberties.** The media include only government or party organs; self-censorship committees replace centralized censorship. Private discussion may be relatively candid. Dissenters are frequently imprisoned. Forced confessions, false charges, and psychiatric incarceration are characteristic. Treatment may be brutal; physical threats are common. Many arrests have been made for attempting to leave the country or importing foreign literature (especially Bibles and material in minority languages). Contacts with foreigners must be reported if not given prior approval. Religious and other personal freedoms are quite restricted. Outside travel and emigration are not considered rights, and are very difficult. Private museums have been closed. Independent labor and management rights are essentially nonexistent. Attempts to form a trade union in 1979 were crushed.

**Comparatively:** Romania is as free as the USSR, freer than Bulgaria, less free than Hungary.

# RWANDA

**Economy:** noninclusive mixed  
**Polity:** nationalist one-party  
   (military dominated)  
**Population:** 5,100,000

**Political Rights:** 6  
**Civil Liberties:** 6  
**Status of Freedom:** not free

An ethnic state with a minority nonterritorial subnationality

**Political Rights.** Rwanda is a military dictatorship with an auxiliary party organization. Elections are not free and candidates are pre-selected. There is no legislature and districts are administered by the central government. However, everyone belongs to the party and party elections and deliberations have some competitive and critical aspects. There are elected local councils. *Subnationalities*: The former ruling people, the Tutsi, have been persecuted and heavily discriminated against, but the situation has improved.

**Civil Liberties.** The weak press is church or governmental; radio is government owned. Only the mildest criticism is voiced. Political prisoners are held, and beating of prisoners and suspects may be common. The courts have some independence. Considerable religious freedom exists. Travel is restricted both within the country and across its borders. Labor unions are very weak. There are no great extremes of wealth. The government is socialist in intent, but missionary cooperatives dominate trade, and private business is active in the small nonsubsistence sector. Traditional ways of life rather than government orders regulate the lives of most.

**Comparatively:** Rwanda is as free as Gabon, freer than Burundi, less free than Zambia.

# ST. LUCIA

**Economy:** mixed capitalist  
**Polity:** centralized multiparty  
**Population:** 115,000  
A relatively homogeneous state

**Political Rights:** 2  
**Civil Liberties:** 2  
**Status of Freedom:** free

**Political Rights.** This is a functioning parliamentary democracy in which the incumbent party was replaced through election in 1979. The government has at times been paralyzed by factional struggles.

**Civil Liberties.** The media are largely private and uncensored. Organization and assembly are free, but harassment and violence accompany their expression. Personal rights are secured.

**Comparatively:** St. Lucia is as free as Portugal, freer than Jamaica, less free than Barbados.

# ST. VINCENT AND THE GRENADINES

**Economy:** mixed capitalist
**Polity:** centralized multiparty
**Population:** 123,000
A relatively homogeneous state

**Political Rights:** 2
**Civil Liberties:** 2
**Status of Freedom:** free

**Political Rights.** St. Vincent is an operating multiparty state. In a 1979 election the ruling party was returned to office, winning 11 of 13 seats with fifty-three percent of the vote.

**Civil Liberties.** Weekly papers present a wide variety of uncensored opinion. The election period suggested access by all groups to the public through assemblies, demonstrations, and the media. Radio was accused of progovernment policies. There is a rule of law.

**Comparatively:** St. Vincent is as free as Portugal, freer than Colombia, less free than Barbados.

# SAO TOME AND PRINCIPE

**Economy:** socialist
**Polity:** socialist one-party
**Population:** 85,000
A relatively homogeneous population

**Political Rights:** 6
**Civil Liberties:** 6
**Status of Freedom:** not free

**Political Rights.** Sao Tome and Principe are governed under strong-man leadership by the revolutionary party that led the country to independence. The degree of implementation of the post-independence constitutional system remains unclear. Popular dissatisfaction and factional struggles appear serious. Angolan troops have been used to maintain the regime.

**Civil Liberties.** The media are government controlled; opposition voices are not heard; there is no effective right of political assembly. The largely plantation agriculture has been socialized, as has most of the economy. Labor unions are not independent. The rule of law does not extend to political questions, but there are few known political prisoners. There is little evidence of brutality or torture.

**Comparatively:** Sao Tome and Principe appear to be as free as Guinea-Bissau, freer than Guinea, less free than Senegal.

# SAUDI ARABIA

**Economy:** capitalist-statist
**Polity:** traditional nonparty
**Population:** 8,200,000
A relatively homogeneous population

**Political Rights:** 6
**Civil Liberties:** 6
**Status of Freedom:** not free

**Political Rights.** Saudi Arabia is a traditional family monarchy ruling without representative assemblies. Political parties are prohibited. The right of petition is guaranteed. Regional government is by appointive officers; there are some local elective assemblies.

**Civil Liberties.** The press is both private and governmental; strict self-censorship is expected. Radio and television are mostly government owned, although ARAMCO also has stations. Private conversation is relatively free; there is no right of political assembly or political organization. Islamic law limits arbitrary government, but the rule of law is not fully institutionalized. There are political prisoners and torture is reported; there may be prisoners of conscience. Citizens have no freedom of religion—all must be Muslims. Strikes and unions are forbidden. Private rights in areas such as occupation or residence are generally respected, but marriage to a non-Muslim or non-Saudi is closely controlled. Women may not marry non-Muslims, and suffer other special disabilities, particularly in the right to travel. The economy is overwhelmingly dominated by petroleum or petroleum-related industry that is directly or indirectly under government control.

**Comparatively:** Saudi Arabia is as free as Algeria, freer than Iraq, less free than Iran.


# SENEGAL

**Economy:** mixed capitalist
**Polity:** centralized dominant-party
**Population:** 5,700,000
A transethnic heterogeneous state

**Political Rights:** 4
**Civil Liberties:** 4
**Status of Freedom:** partly free

**Political Rights.** After several years under a relatively benevolent one-party system, limited multiparty activity is allowed; the number and nature of political parties remains under arbitrary control. (This is to be liberalized.) In parliamentary elections eighteen of one hundred seats were obtained by an opposition party. Decentralization is restricted to the local level where contested elections occur. *Subnationalities.* Ethnically eighty percent are Muslims; the Wolof people represent thirty-six percent of the population, including most of the elite, the urban population, and the more prosperous farmers. However, regional loyalties, both within and outside of this linguistic grouping, seem to be at least as important as communal groupings in defining potential subnationalities. In addition, rapid assimilation of rural migrants in the cities to Wolof culture has reduced the tendency toward ethnic cleavage.

**Civil Liberties.** The press is predominantly public, and government regulations restrict the independence of private publications. Opposition papers and journals appear. Both papers and parties are brought before the courts for going too far in their opposition, yet the government sometimes loses in the courts. Unions have gained increasing independence. Religion, travel, occupation, and other private rights are respected. Although much of the land remains tribally owned, government-organized cooperatives, a strong internal private market, and dependence on external markets have transformed the preindustrial society.

**Comparatively:** Senegal is as free as Panama, freer than Ivory Coast, less free than Gambia.

# SEYCHELLES

**Economy:** mixed capitalist
**Polity:** socialist one-party
**Population:** 65,000
A relatively homogeneous population

**Political Rights:** 6
**Civil Liberties:** 6
**Status of Freedom:** not free

**Political Rights.** Seychelles is a one-party state allowing personal competition for parliament but not president. The former ruling party is said to have "simply disappeared." Tanzanian troops continue to help maintain the government in power. There is no local government.

**Civil Liberties.** There is no independent opinion press, and radio is largely governmental. No opposition in publication or even conversation is legal. Individuals have little judicial protection. There is no right of political assembly and the security services have broad powers of arrest. Opposition party activities are banned; people have frequently been arrested on political charges. Labor and government are interconnected. Private rights, including private property, are generally respected, despite the extensive government services of a largely urban, if impoverished, welfare state.

**Comparatively:** Seychelles is as free as Tanzania, freer than Somalia, less free than Maldives.

# SIERRA LEONE

**Economy:** noninclusive capitalist
**Polity:** socialist one-party
**Population:** 3,500,000
A formally transethnic heterogeneous state

**Political Rights:** 5
**Civil Liberties:** 5
**Status of Freedom:** partly free

**Political Rights.** After progressively excluding opposition candidates from power by violence, arrest, parliamentary exclusion, or electoral malpractice, in 1978 Sierra Leone's rulers used a possibly fraudulent referendum to establish a one-party state. The new cabinet included, however, members of the former opposition. There is little independent local government.

**Civil Liberties.** The press is private and governmental. Radio is government controlled. Both are now closely controlled, but there is considerable freedom of private speech. The courts do not appear to be very powerful or independent. Special emergency powers have given the government untrammeled powers of detention, censorship, restriction of assembly, and search for the last few years. There may now be no prisoners of conscience. Identity cards have recently been required of all citizens. Labor unions are relatively independent and travel is freely permitted. The largely subsistence economy has an essentially capitalist modern sector. Corruption is pervasive.

**Comparatively:** Sierra Leone is as free as Nicaragua, freer than Gabon, less free than Senegal.

# SINGAPORE

**Economy:** mixed capitalist-statist          **Political Rights:** 5
**Polity:** centralized dominant-party        **Civil Liberties:** 5
**Population:** 2,400,000                     **Status of Freedom:** partly free
An ethnically complex state

**Political Rights.** Singapore is a parliamentary democracy in which the ruling party has won all of the legislative seats in recent elections. Reasonable grounds exist for believing that economic and other pressures against all opposition groups (exerted in part through control of the media) make elections very unfair. Opposition leaders have been sentenced for such crimes as defaming the prime minister during the campaign. This may exclude them from future contests. The opposition still obtains thirty percent of the votes. There is no local government.

**Civil Liberties.** The press is nominally free, but owners of shares with policy-making power must be officially approved—in some cases the government owns the shares. Broadcasting is largely a government monopoly. By closing papers and imprisoning editors and reporters, the press is kept under close control. University faculties are also under considerable pressure to conform. Most opposition is treated as a communist threat and, therefore, treasonable. Prisoners of conscience are held; in internal security cases the protection of the law is weak—the prosecution's main task appears to be obtaining forced confessions of communist activity. Torture is alleged. Trade union freedom is inhibited by the close association of government and union. Private rights of religion, occupation, or property are generally observed, although a large and increasing percentage of manufacturing and service companies are government owned.

**Comparatively:** Singapore is as free as Sierra Leone, freer than Vietnam, less free than Malaysia.

# SOLOMON ISLANDS

**Economy:** preindustrial capitalist
**Polity:** decentralized multiparty
**Population:** 200,00
A relatively homogeneous state with subnational strains

**Political Rights:** 2
**Civil Liberties:** 2
**Status of Freedom:** free

**Political Rights.** The Solomon Islands are a parliamentary democracy under the British monarch. Elections are intensely contested. There is some decentralization of power at the local level; further decentralization at the provincial level is planned.

**Civil Liberties.** Radio is government controlled; the press is both government and private. There is no censorship. The rule of law is maintained in the British manner alongside traditional ideas of justice. Published incitement to inter-island conflict has led to banishment for several persons. The government is heavily involved in major businesses. Trade unions have full rights.

**Comparatively:** The Solomon Islands are as free as Tuvalu, freer than Mauritius, less free than New Zealand.

# SOMALIA

**Economy:** noninclusive mixed
  socialist
**Polity:** socialist one-party
  (military dominated)
**Population:** 37,800,000
A relatively homogeneous state

**Political Rights:** 7
**Civil Liberties:** 7
**Status of Freedom:** not free

**Political Rights.** The Somali Republic is under one-man military rule combining glorification of the ruler with one-party socialist legitimization. 1979 elections with 99 percent approval allowed no choice. Even an assembly elected on this basis was suspended in 1980. Ethnically the state is homogeneous, although until the military coup in 1969 the six main clan groupings and their subdivisions were the major means of organizing loyalty and power. While politics is still understood in lineage terms, in its centralizing drive the government has tried to eliminate both tribal and religious power.

**Civil Liberties.** The media are under strict government control, private conversation is controlled, and those who do not follow the government are considered to be against it. There are many political prisoners, including prisoners of conscience. There have been jailings for strikes and executions of rebels. Travel is restricted. Beyond the dominant subsistence economy, some individual freedoms have been curtailed by establishing state farms, state industries, and welfare programs. However, a definite private sector of the economy has also been defined.

**Comparatively:** Somalia is as free as Ethiopia, less free than Kenya.

# SOUTH AFRICA

**Economy:** capitalist-statist           **Political Rights:** 5
**Polity:** centralized multiparty        **Civil Liberties:** 6
**Population:** 25,000,000*                **Status of Freedom:** partly free
An ethnic state with major territorial and nonterritorial subnationalities

**Political Rights.** South Africa is a parliamentary democracy in which over eighty percent of the people are excluded from participation in the national political process because of race. For the white population elections appear fair and open. There is, in addition, a limited scope for the nonwhites to influence affairs within their own communities. *Subnationalities*: In the several Bantustans that have not yet separated from the country, black leaders have some power and support from their people. Most black political parties are banned, but operating political parties among Indians and people of mixed blood work for the interests of their respective peoples. Regionally, government within the white community includes both central government officials and elected councils.

**Civil Liberties.** The white South African press is private and quite outspoken, although pressures have been increasing, especially on reporters. Freedom for the nonwhite press is restricted. Broadcasting is under government control. The courts are independent, but do not effectively control security forces. There are political prisoners and torture —especially for black activists, who live in an atmosphere of terror. Private rights are generally respected for whites. Rights to labor organization have improved for blacks recently. Legal separation of the races remains, but has relaxed in some respects. Rights to choice of residence and occupation remain very restricted for nonwhites. Hundreds of thousands are arrested or forcibly moved every year as a result of discriminatory laws. Human rights organizations are quite active in both white and black communities.

**Comparatively:** South Africa is as free as Chile, freer than Tanzania, less free than Morocco.

---

*More when Transkei and the new dependencies, the other independent "Bantustans," are included.

# SPAIN

**Economy:** capitalist
**Polity:** centralized multiparty
**Population:** 37,800,000
An ethnic state with major subnationalities

**Political Rights:** 2
**Civil Liberties:** 3
**Status of Freedom:** free

**Political Rights.** Spain has recently established a constitutional monarchy in the European manner. The current parliament has been fairly elected from a wide range of parties. Municipalities are often controlled by the opposition. Regional and local government is changing the previous centralized character of the state. *Subnationalities*: The Basque and Catalan territorial subnationalities have had their rights greatly expanded in the last few years, and regional power is being extended to the other parts of the country.

**Civil Liberties.** The press is private and is now largely free. The television network and some radio stations are government owned. Radio is no longer a state monopoly and television is controlled by an all-party committee. There are few prisoners of conscience; imprisonment still threatens those who insult the security services, the courts, or the state. Short detention periods are often used with little legal redress. Police brutality and torture still occur. However, criticism of the government and suspected human rights violations are quite freely expressed publicly and privately. Private freedoms are respected. Continued terrorism and reaction to terrorism affect some areas. Union organization is quite free and independent.

**Comparatively:** Spain is as free as Colombia, freer than Egypt, less free than France.

# SRI LANKA

**Economy:** capitalist-statist
**Polity:** centralized multiparty
**Population:** 14,800,000
An ethnic state with a major subnationality

**Political Rights:** 2
**Civil Rights:** 3
**Status of Freedom:** free

**Political Rights.** Sri Lanka is a parliamentary democracy in which power has alternated between the major parties. The constitution was changed in 1977-78 to a presidential system along French lines. Regional government is centrally controlled, but local government is by elected councils. A number of individuals have been barred from government for breach of trust. *Subnationalities*: Receiving a large vote in the most recent election, the Tamil minority constitutes an important secessionist tendency. Repression or private violence against the Tamils occurs; the present government is inclined to meet Tamil demands up to but not including that for independence or equal linguistic standing.

**Civil Liberties.** The press has been strong, both private and governmental. However, even the private papers feel under government pressure. Broadcasting is under government control and presents a relatively narrow range of views. Limited censorship has been applied to prevent violence at particular places and times. The rule of law has been threatened by communal violence. Courts remain independent of the government; an important human rights movement supports their independence. A few prisoners of conscience have been arrested, at least for advocating Tamil independence; and torture or brutality is alleged. There is freedom of assembly but not demonstration. Private rights to movement, residence, religion, and occupation are respected. Strikes in public services are restricted, but unions are well developed. There has been extensive land reform; the State has nationalized a number of enterprises in this largely plantation economy. The system has done an excellent job in providing for basic nutrition, health, and educational standards within a democratic framework.

**Comparatively:** Sri Lanka is as free as India, freer than Malaysia, less free than the United Kingdom.

# SUDAN

**Economy:** noninclusive mixed
**Polity:** nationalist one-party
    (military dominated)
**Population:** 18,700,000

**Political Rights:** 5
**Civil Liberties:** 5
**Status of Freedom:** partly free

An ethnic state with a major but highly diverse subnationality

**Political Rights.** Sudan is a military dictatorship with a supportive single party and legislature. There has been a general reconciliation of the government and its noncommunist opposition. Legislative elections allow the participation and frequent victory of individuals from de facto opposition groups. Several cabinet and party central committee members are also from these groups. There is considerable power "in the streets" and there has been a continuing devolution of power to the regions. *Subnationalities*: The Southern (Negro) region has been given a separate assembly; its former guerrillas form a part of the Southern army.

**Civil Liberties.** The press is weak and nationalized. Radio and television are government controlled. The media have been used for active indoctrination, but the messages in the last few years have necessarily been mixed. Limited criticism is allowed, especially in private. The university campus maintains a tradition of independence, but the courts are not strong. There are many prisoners of conscience, reports of torture, and detention without trial. Religion is relatively free. Unions are government organized but nevertheless lead illegal strikes. Sudan is socialist theoretically, but in business and agriculture the private sector has recently been supported by denationalizations.

**Comparatively:** Sudan is as free as Egypt, freer than Ethiopia, less free than Kenya.

# SURINAME

**Economy:** capitalist
**Polity:** military nonparty
**Population:** 450,000
An ethnically complex state

**Political Rights:** 7
**Civil Liberties:** 5
**Status of Freedom:** not free

**Political Rights.** Suriname is ruled by a president and military council without legitimization by elections or other means. The head of state is a civilian, but he has no independent political backing.

**Civil Liberties.** The press is under strong pressure. Political organization or assembly is forbidden. Political prisoners are held. Courts and unions retain some independence. Houses are searched at will.

**Comparatively:** Suriname is as free as Liberia, freer than Haiti, less free than El Salvador.

# SWAZILAND

**Economy:** noninclusive capitalist
**Polity:** traditional nonparty
**Population:** 600,000
A relatively homogeneous population

**Political Rights:** 5
**Civil Liberties:** 5
**Status of Freedom:** partly free

**Political Rights.** Swaziland is ruled directly by the king with the aid of of his royal advisors. The majority of the people probably support the king who is both a religious and political figure and has been king since 1900. Indirect elections for the advisory legislature are held. Local councils invite popular participation. South African political and economic influence is extensive.

**Civil Liberties.** Private media exist alongside governmental; little criticism is allowed; South African and other foreign media present available alternatives. Opposition leaders have been repeatedly detained, and partisan activity is forbidden. Parliamentary and council criticism occurs, but public assemblies are restricted, unions limited, emigration difficult. Religious, economic, and other private rights are maintained. The traditional way of life is continued, especially on the local level.

Several thousand whites in the country and in neighboring Transvaal own the most productive land and business.

**Comparatively:** Swaziland is as free as Lesotho, freer than South Africa, less free than Botswana.

# SWEDEN

**Economy:** mixed capitalist
**Polity:** centralized multiparty
**Population:** 8,300,000
A relatively homogeneous population

**Political Rights:** 1
**Civil Liberties:** 1
**Status of Freedom:** free

**Political Rights.** Sweden is a parliamentary democracy in which no party monopolizes power. Referendums are held. Although there are some representative institutions at regional and local levels, the system is relatively centralized. The tendency of modern bureaucracies to regard issues as technical rather than political has progressed further in Sweden than elsewhere.

**Civil Liberties.** The press is private or party; broadcasting is by state-licensed monopolies. Although free of censorship, the media are accused of presenting a rather narrow range of views. There is the rule of law. The defense of those accused by the government may not be as spirited as elsewhere, but, on the other hand, the ombudsman office gives special means of redress against administrative arbitrariness. Most private rights are respected; but state interference in family life is unusually strong. The national church has a special position. In many areas, such as housing, individual choice is restricted more than in other capitalist states—as it is of course by the very high tax load. Unions are a powerful part of the system.

**Comparatively:** Sweden is as free as Denmark, freer than West Germany.

# SWITZERLAND

**Economy:** capitalist
**Polity:** decentralized multiparty
**Population:** 6,300,000
A trinational state

**Political Rights:** 1
**Civil Liberties:** 1
**Status of Freedom:** free

**Political Rights.** Switzerland is a parliamentary democracy in which all major parties are given a role in government determined by the size of the vote for each party. Parties that increase their vote above a certain level are invited to join the government, although such changes in party strength rarely occur. The lack of a decisive shift in power from one party to another in the last fifty years is the major limitation on the democratic effectiveness of the Swiss system. However, its dependence on the grand coalition style of government is a partial substitute, and the Swiss grant political rights in other ways that compensate for the lack of a transfer of power. Many issues are decided by the citizenry through national referendums or popular initiatives. After referendums in keeping with the Swiss attitude, even the losing side is given part of what it wants if its vote is sufficiently large. *Subnationalities*: The three major linguistic groups have separate areas under their partial control. Their regional and local elected governments have autonomous rights and determine directly much of the country's business. National governments try to balance the representatives of the primary linguistic and religious groups; this is accomplished in another way by the upper house that directly represents the cantons (regions) on an equal basis.

**Civil Rights.** The high quality press is private and independent. Broadcasting is government operated, although with the considerable independence of comparable West European systems. The rule of law is strongly upheld; as in Germany it is against the law to question the intentions of judges. Private rights are thoroughly respected.

**Comparatively:** Switzerland is as free as the United States, freer than Italy.

# SYRIA

**Economy:** mixed socialist  
**Polity:** centralized dominant-party  
    (military dominated)  
**Population:** 8,600,000  
A relatively homogeneous population

**Political Rights:** 5  
**Civil Liberties:** 7  
**Status of Freedom:** not free

**Political Rights.** Syria is a military dictatorship assisted by an elected parliament. The election of the military president is largely pro forma, but in recent assembly elections a few opposition candidates defeated candidates of the National Front, organized under the leadership of the governing party. The ruling Front includes several ideologically distinct parties, and cabinets have included representatives of a variety of such parties. Some authenticity to the election procedure is suggested by the fact that due to apathy and a boycott by dissident party factions in 1977 elections, the government had such great difficulty achieving the constitutionally required voter participation that it was forced to extend the voting period. Because of its position in the army the Alawite minority (ten percent) has a very unequal share of national power. Provinces have little separate power, but local elections are contested.

**Civil Liberties.** The media are in the hands of government or party. Broadcasting services are government owned. Although the media are used as governmental means for active indoctrination, a limited number of legalized political parties have articulated a narrow range of viewpoints. Because of threats to the regime, 1980 saw an intensification of government repression. Thousands may have been arrested and beaten while hundreds were killed. Syria's human rights organization was forced into inactivity; the executive councils of Syria's professional organizations were dissolved and many arrested. The courts are neither strongly independent nor effective in political cases where long-term detention with trial occurs. Political prisoners are often arrested following violence, but there are prisoners of conscience. Torture has frequently been employed in interrogation. Private rights, such as those of religion, occupation, or residence are generally respected; foreign travel and emigration are closely controlled for certain groups. Syria's economy is a mixture of governmental and private enterprise; labor is not independent of the party.

**Comparatively:** Syria is as free as Algeria, freer than Libya, less free than Kuwait.

# TANZANIA

**Economy:** noninclusive socialist
**Polity:** socialist one-party
**Population:** 18,600,000

**Political Rights:** 6
**Civil Liberties:** 6
**Status of Freedom:** not free

A transethnic heterogeneous nation in union with Zanzibar

**Political Rights.** Tanzania is a union of the paternalistic socialist mainland with the radical socialist Zanzibar. Although the governments are still not unified except in name, the single parties of each state have joined to form one all-Tanzanian party. Elections offer choice between individuals, but no issues are to be discussed in campaigns; all decisions come down from above, including the choice of candidates. *Subnationalities*: Ethnically, the country is divided into a large number of peoples (none larger than thirteen percent); most are not yet at the subnational level. The use of English and Swahili as national languages enhances national unity. Since the two subnations (Zanzibar and Tanganyika) are in a voluntary union at present, there is no question of dominance of one over the other.

**Civil Liberties.** Civil liberties are essentially subordinated to the goals of the socialist leadership. No contradiction of official policy is allowed to appear in the government-owned media, or in educational institutions; private and limited criticism of implementation appears. The people learn only of those events the government wishes them to know. There is no right of assembly or organization. Millions of people have been forced into communal villages; people from the cities have been abruptly transported to the countryside. Thousands have been detained for political crimes, and torture has ocurred. There are now few prisoners of conscience. Lack of respect for the independence of the judiciary and individual rights is especially apparent in Zanzibar. Union activity is government controlled. Neither labor nor capital have legally recognized rights—strikes are illegal. Most business and trade and much of agriculture are nationalized. Religion is free, at least on the mainland; overseas travel is restricted.

**Comparatively:** Tanzania is as free as Algeria, freer than Malawi, less free than Zambia.

# THAILAND

**Economy:** noninclusive capitalist
**Polity:** centralized multiparty
    (military dominated)
**Population:** 47,300,000

**Political Rights:** 3
**Civil Liberties:** 4
**Status of Freedom:** partly free

An ethnic state with a major territorial subnationality

**Political Rights.** Under the controlled parliamentary system the prime minister was successfully replaced by constitutional means in 1980. Major parties participate in the government. Repeated military interventions in recent years limit the freedom of civilian politicians. Government is highly centralized. *Subnationalities*: There is a Muslim Malay community in the far south, and small ethnic enclaves in the north.

**Civil Liberties.** The press is private, but periodic suppressions and warnings lead to self-censorship. Broadcasting is government or military controlled. Some books are banned as subversive. There are few long-term prisoners of conscience, but many are periodically detained for communist activity. In rural areas arrest may be on vague charges and treatment brutal. Human rights organizations are active. Labor activity is relatively free, but strikes are illegal. Private rights to property, choice of religion, or residence are secure; foreign travel or emigration is not restricted. However, corruption limits the expression of all rights. Government enterprise is quite important in the basically capitalist modern economy.

**Comparatively:** Thailand is as free as Bangladesh, freer than Pakistan, less free than Sri Lanka.

# TOGO

**Economy:** noninclusive mixed
**Polity:** nationalist one-party
    (military dominated)
**Population:** 2,500,000

**Political Rights:** 7
**Civil Liberties:** 6
**Status of Freedom:** not free

A transethnic heterogeneous state

**Political Rights.** Togo is a military dictatorship ruled in the name of a one-party state. In this spirit there is a deliberate denial of the rights of separate branches of government, including a separate judiciary, or even of private groups. National elections allow little or no choice. Below the national level only the cities have a semblance of self-government. *Subnationalities*: The southern Ewe are culturally dominant and the largest group (twenty percent), but militant northerners now rule.

**Civil Liberties.** No criticism of the government is allowed in the media, and foreign publications may be confiscated. There is little guarantee of a rule of law: people have been imprisoned and beaten on many occasions for offenses such as the distribution of leaflets or failure to wear a party badge. There are long-term prisoners of conscience. Religious freedom is limited. There is occasional restriction of foreign travel. Union organization is closely regulated. In this largely subsistence economy the government is heavily involved in trade, production, and the provision of services. All wage earners must contribute heavily to the ruling party.

**Comparatively:** Togo is as free as Haiti, freer than Ethiopia, less free than Sierra Leone.

# TONGA

**Economy:** noninclusive capitalist
**Polity:** traditional nonparty
**Population:** 94,000
A relatively homogeneous population

**Political Rights:** 5
**Civil Liberties:** 3
**Status of Freedom:** partly free

**Political Rights.** Tonga is a constitutional monarchy in which the king and nobles retain power. Only a minority of the members of the legislative assembly are elected directly by the people; but the veto power of the assembly can be effectively expressed. Regional administration is centralized.

**Civil Liberties.** The main paper is a government weekly and radio is under government control. There is a rule of law, but the king's decision is still a very important part of the system. Private rights within the traditional Tonga context seem guaranteed.

**Comparatively:** Tonga is as free as Morocco, freer than Seychelles, less free than Western Samoa.

# TRANSKEI

**Economy:** noninclusive capitalist
**Polity:** centralized dominant-party
**Population:** 2,400,000
A relatively homogeneous population

**Political Rights:** 5
**Civil Liberties:** 6
**Status of Freedom:** partly free

**Political Rights.** In form Transkei is a multiparty parliamentary democracy; in fact it is under the strong-man rule of a paramount chief supported by his party's majority. The meaning of recent elections was largely nullified by governmental interference, including the jailing of opposition leaders. Chiefs remain very important in the system, but beyond that there is little decentralization of power. South Africa has a great deal of de facto power over the state, particularly because of the large number of nationals that work in South Africa. However, Transkei is more independent than the Soviet satellites; it has had continuing disputes with South Africa.

**Civil Liberties.** The press is private, but under strong government pressure. Broadcasting is government controlled. Many members of the opposition have been imprisoned; new retroactive laws render it illegal to criticize Transkei or its rulers. Freedom of organization is very limited, although an opposition party still exists. Private rights are respected within the limits of South African and Transkei custom. Capitalist and traditional economic rights are diminished by the necessity of a large portion of the labor force to work in South Africa.

**Comparatively:** Transkei is as free as Tunisia, freer than Mozambique, less free than Swaziland.

## TRINIDAD AND TOBAGO

**Economy:** capitalist-statist
**Polity:** decentralized multiparty
**Population:** 1,200,000
An ethnically complex state

**Political Rights:** 2
**Civil Liberties:** 2
**Status of Freedom:** free

**Political Rights.** Trinidad and Tobago is a parliamentary democracy in which one party has managed to retain power since 1956. A new opposition party has recently gained almost thirty percent of the assembly seats. There is local government. A regional government has recently been developed in Tobago.

**Civil Liberties.** The private or party press is generally free of restriction; broadcasting is under both government and private control. Opposition is regularly voiced. There is the full spectrum of private rights, although violence and communal feeling reduce the effectiveness of such rights for many. Major sections of the economy are government owned. Human rights organizations are active.

**Comparatively:** Trinidad and Tobago is as free as Dominica, freer than Guyana, less free than Bahamas.

## TUNISIA

**Economy:** mixed capitalist
**Polity:** socialist one-party
**Population:** 6,500,000
A relatively homogeneous population

**Political Rights:** 6
**Civil Liberties:** 5
**Status of Freedom:** partly free

**Political Rights.** Tunisia is a one-party dictatorship that preserves alongside one-man leadership the trappings of parliamentary democracy. Elections to the assembly are contested primarily within the one-party framework. In 1979 elections the opposition publicly called for abstention. Regional and local government are dependent on central direction.

**Civil Liberties.** The private, party, or government media are controlled. Although frequently banned or fined, opposition papers have been published since 1978. Private conversation is relatively free, but there is no right of assembly. Organizational activity is generally free, including that of the Tunisian Human Rights League. The courts demonstrate only a limited independence, but it is possible to win against the government. Unions have been relatively independent; however, a general strike called in early 1978 lead to riots and subsequent large-scale imprisonment; in 1980 the unions were slowly regaining their position. By the end of the year there were few remaining prisoners of conscience and some exiles had returned. The unemployed young are drafted for government work. Overseas travel is occasionally blocked. Most private rights seem to be respected, including economic rights since doctrinaire socialism was abandoned.

**Comparatively:** Tunisia is as free as Zambia, freer than Algeria, less free than Egypt.

# TURKEY

**Economy:** capitalist-statist
**Polity:** military nonparty
**Population:** 45,500,000
An ethnic state with a major territorial subnationality

**Political Rights:** 5
**Civil Liberties:** 5
**Status of Freedom:** partly free

**Political Rights.** In 1980 Turkey came under at least temporary military rule. The change was widely welcomed because of the severe internal security and financial situations and political crisis. *Subnationalities*: Several million Kurds are denied self-determination: it is even illegal to teach or publish in Kurdish.

**Civil Liberties.** The press is private; the government controls the broadcasting system directly or indirectly. Suspensions and arrests by the new government have produced general self-censorship. There are now many prisoners of conscience under martial law. Torture has been common, but the military government has made arrests of some of the accused. Private rights are generally respected in other areas such as religion. Nearly fifty percent of the people are subsistence agriculturists. State enterprises make up more than one-half of Turkey's industry.

**Comparatively:** Turkey is as free as Philippines, freer than Iraq, less free than Spain.

# TUVALU

**Economy:** noninclusive capitalist
**Polity:** traditional nonparty
**Population:** 9,000
A relatively homogeneous state

**Political Rights:** 2
**Civil Liberties:** 2
**Status of Freedom:** free

**Political Rights.** Tuvalu is a parliamentary democracy under the British monarch. Each island is represented; seats are contested individually. An opposition bloc has been formed in the assembly.

**Civil Liberties.** Media are little developed. The rule of law is maintained in the British manner, alongside traditional ideals of justice.

**Comparatively:** Tuvalu is as free as Kiribati, freer than Tonga, less free than New Zealand.

# UGANDA

**Economy:** noninclusive, mixed
    capitalist
**Polity:** multiparty (military
    dominated)
**Population:** 13,700,000
A transethnic heterogeneous state with major subnationalities

**Political Rights:** 4
**Civil Liberties:** 4
**Status of Freedom:** partly free

**Political Rights.** Uganda is ruled by an elected government with the aid of the Tanzanian army. The 1980 election was not entirely free or fair, but parties opposed to the ruling group received a substantial number of seats. *Subnationalities*: The population is divided among a wide variety of peoples, some of which are subnationalities based on kingdoms that preceded the present state. The most important of these is Buganda, a kingdom with special rights within the state, that was suppressed in 1967. Sixteen percent of the people are Ganda.

**Civil Liberties.** The government and private media showed extensive freedom in late 1980. Political violence and an incomplete rule of law inhibited all expression to some extent. Assembly and travel are similarly restricted within the country. Arbitrary arrests were frequent at times during the year; politicians were arbitrarily killed by the government or murdered by unknown assailants. Torture occurred as Tanzanian troops roamed the country. Religious freedom has been reestablished.

**Comparatively:** Uganda is as free as Senegal, freer than Kenya, and less free than Zimbabwe.

# UNION OF
# SOVIET SOCIALIST REPUBLICS

**Economy:** socialist                   **Political Rights:** 6
**Polity:** communist one-party          **Civil Liberties:** 7
**Population:** 266,000,000              **Status of Freedom:** not free

A complex ethnic state with major territorial subnationalities

**Political Rights.** The Soviet Union is ruled by parallel party and governmental systems: the party system is dominant. Elections are held for both systems, but in neither is it possible for the rank and file to determine policy. Candidacy and voting are closely controlled and the resulting assemblies do not seriously question the policies developed by party leaders (varying by time or issue from one individual to twenty-five). The Soviet Union is in theory elaborately divided into subnational units, but in fact the all-embracing party structure renders local power minimal.

*Subnationalities.* Russians account for half the Soviet population. The rest belong to a variety of subnational groupings ranging down in size from the forty million Ukrainians. Most groups are territorial, with a developed sense of subnational identity. The political rights of all of these to self-determination, either within the USSR or through secession, is effectively denied. In many cases Russians or other non-native peoples have been settled in a subnational territory in such numbers as to make the native people a minority in their own land (for example, Kazakhstan). Expression of opinion in favor of increased self-determination is repressed at least as much as anticommunist opinion. Most of these peoples have had independence movements or movements for enhanced self-determination in the years since the founding of the USSR. Several movements have been quite strong since World War II (for example, in the Ukraine or Lithuania); the blockage of communication by the Soviet government makes it very difficult to estimate either the overt or latent support such movements might have. In 1978 popular movements in Georgia and Armenia led to the retention of the official status of local languages in the Republics of the Caucasus.

**Civil Liberties.** The media are totally owned by the government or party and are, in addition, regularly censored. Elite publications occasionally present variations from the official line, but significant deviations are found only in underground publications. Recent cases of arrests and exile have forced nearly all criticism underground. Crimes against the state, including insanity (demonstrated by perverse willingness to oppose the state), are broadly defined; as a result political prisoners are present in large numbers both in jails and insane asylums. Nearly all imprisonment and mistreatment of prisoners in the Soviet Union are now carried out in accordance with Soviet security laws—even though these laws conflict with other Soviet laws written to accord with international standards. Since the Bolshevik Revolution there has never been an acquittal in a political trial. Insofar as private rights, such as those to religion, education, or choice of occupation, exist, they are de facto rights that may be denied at any time. Travel within and outside of the USSR is highly controlled; many areas of the country are still off-limits to foreigners—especially those used as areal prisons for dissidents. Nearly all private entrepreneurial activity is outside the law; there are rights to nonproductive personal property. Other rights such as those to organize an independent labor union are strictly denied. Literacy is high, few starve, and private oppression is no more.

**Comparatively:** The USSR is as free as Malawi, freer than East Germany, less free than Hungary.

## UNITED ARAB EMIRATES

**Economy:** capitalist-statist
**Polity:** decentralized nonparty
**Population:** 800,000
A relatively homogeneous citizenry

**Political Rights:** 5
**Civil Liberties:** 5
**Status of Freedom:** partly free

**Political Rights.** The UAE is a confederation of seven shaikhdoms in which the larger are given the greater power both in the assembly and the administrative hierarchy. There is a great deal of consultation in the traditional pattern. Below the confederation level there are no electoral procedures or parties. Each shaikhdom is relatively autonomous in its internal affairs. The majority of the people are recent immigrants and noncitizens.

**Civil Liberties.** The press is private or governmental. There is self-censorship, but some opposition is expressed. Broadcasting is under UAE control. There are no political assemblies or labor unions, but there are also few, if any, prisoners of conscience. The courts dispense a combination of British, tribal, and Islamic law. Private rights are generally respected; there is freedom of travel and some religious freedom. Many persons may still accept the feudal privileges and restraints of their tribal position. The rights of the alien majority are less secure: "troublemakers" are deported. Private economic activity exists alongside the dominance of government petroleum and petroleum-related activities.

**Comparatively:** United Arab Emirates are as free as Kuwait, freer than North Yemen, less free than Tonga.

# UNITED KINGDOM

**Economy:** mixed capitalist          **Political Rights:** 1
**Polity:** centralized multiparty     **Civil Liberties:** 1
**Population:** 55,800,000             **Status of Freedom:** free
An ethnic state with major subnationalities

**Political Rights.** The United Kingdom is a parliamentary democracy
with a symbolic monarch. Fair elections are open to all parties, including
those advocating secession. There are elected local and regional governments, but to date these are primarily concerned with administering national laws. The devolution of more substantial powers is currently under
discussion and development. *Subnationalities*: Scots, Welsh, Ulster
Scots, and Ulster Irish are significant and highly self-conscious territorial
minorities. In 1978 parliament approved home rule for Scotland and
Wales, but the Welsh and (more ambiguously) the Scots voters rejected
this opportunity in 1979. Northern Ireland's home rule is in abeyance
because of an ethnic impasse. Ulster Scots and Irish live in intermixed
territories in Northern Ireland. Both want more self-determination—the
majority Ulster Scots as an autonomous part of the United Kingdom, the
minority Ulster Irish as an area within Ireland.

**Civil Liberties.** The press is private and powerful; broadcasting has
statutory independence although it is indirectly under government control. British media are comparatively restrained because of strict libel
and national security laws, and a tradition of accepting government suggestions for the handling of sensitive news. In Northern Ireland a severe
security situation has led to the curtailment of private rights, to imprisonment, and on occasion to torture and brutality. However, these
conditions have been relatively limited, have been thoroughly in-
vestigated by the government, and improved as a result. Elsewhere the
rule of law is entrenched, and private rights generally respected. In certain areas, such as medicine, housing, inheritance, and general
disposability of income, socialist government policies have limited choice
for some while expanding the access of others.

**Comparatively:** The United Kingdom is as free as the United States,
freer than West Germany.

# UNITED STATES OF AMERICA

**Economy:** capitalist                **Political Rights:** 1
**Polity:** decentralized multiparty   **Civil Liberties:** 1
**Population:** 222,500,000            **Status of Freedom:** free
An ethnically complex state with minor territorial subnationalities

**Political Rights.** The United States is a constitutional democracy with
three strong but separate centers of power: president, congress, and
judiciary. Elections are fair and competitive. Parties are remarkably

weak: in some areas they are little more than temporary means of organizing primary elections. States, and to a lesser extent cities, have powers in their own rights; they often successfully oppose the desires of national administrations. Each state has equal representation in the upper house, which in the USA is the more powerful half of parliament.

*Subnationalities.* There are many significant ethnic groups, but the only clearly territorial subnationalities are the native peoples. The largest Indian tribes, the Navaho and Sioux, number 100,000 or more each. About 150,000 Hawaiians still reside on their native islands, intermingled with a much larger white and oriental population. Spanish-speaking Americans number in the millions; except for a few thousand residing in an area of northern New Mexico, they are mostly twentieth-century immigrants living among English-speaking Americans, particularly in the large cities. Black Americans make up over one-tenth of the U.S. population; residing primarily in large cities, they have no major territorial base. Black and Spanish-speaking Americans are of special concern because of their relative poverty; their ethnic status is quite comparable to that of many other groups in America, including Chinese, Japanese, Filipinos, Italians, or Jews.

**Civil Liberties.** The press is private and free; both private and public radio and television are government regulated. There are virtually no government controls on the content of the printed media (except in nonpolitical areas such as pornography) and few on broadcasting. There are no prisoners of conscience or sanctioned uses of torture; some regional miscarriages of justice and police brutality have political and social overtones. Widespread use of surveillance techniques and clandestine interference with radical groups or groups thought to be radical have occurred; as a reduction of liberties the threat has remained largely potential; in recent years these security excesses have been greatly attenuated if not eliminated. Wherever and whenever publicity penetrates, the rule of law is generally secure, even against the most powerful. The government often loses in the courts. Private rights in most spheres are respected. Although a relatively capitalistic country, the combination of tax loads with the decisive government role in agriculture, energy, defense, and other industries restricts individual choice as it increases majority power.

**Comparatively:** The United States is as free as Australia, freer than Italy.

# UPPER VOLTA

**Economy:** noninclusive mixed
    capitalist
**Polity:** military nonparty
**Population:** 6,900,000
A transethnic heterogeneous state

**Political Rights:** 6
**Civil Liberties:** 5
**Status of Freedom:** partly free

**Political Rights.** Upper Volta is under command of a military committee as the result of a coup in late 1980.

**Civil Liberties.** Media are both government and private; criticism has appeared regularly in both. As a result of the coup there are a number of prisoners of conscience, and freedom of assembly or of political organization is denied. The rule of law seems fairly well established and within traditional limits private rights are respected. Trade unions are important. Travel is unrestricted. Essentially the economy remains dependent on subsistence agriculture, with the government playing the role of regulator and promoter of development. The situation was unclear as of January 1981.

**Comparatively:** Upper Volta is as free as Tunisia, freer than Liberia, less free than Sierra Leone.

# URUGUAY

**Economy:** mixed capitalist          **Political Rights:** 5
**Polity:** military nonparty          **Civil Liberties:** 5
**Population:** 2,900,000              **Status of Freedom:** partly free
A relatively homogeneous population

**Political Rights.** Uruguay is a military dictatorship supplemented by an appointed civilian head of state and appointed advisory council. The leading parties are inactive but still exist legally. The state is highly centralized. In 1980 the constitution submitted to the people was rejected—apparently a reasonably fair vote.

**Civil Liberties.** The press is private, and broadcasting private and public. Both are under censorship and threats of confiscation or closure, as are book and journal outlets. No criticism of the military is permitted. The right of assembly has been very restricted. However, in late 1980 censorship and assembly regulations were greatly relaxed for the referendum. The independence of the judiciary and the civil service has been drastically curtailed. In 1980 there remained nearly 1,000 prisoners of conscience. Torture has been routinely used until recently; convictions have been generally based on written confessions. Many parties have been banned, but there is still considerable room for political discussion of alternatives beyond the limits of the present system. All organizations, including unions, are under close government supervision. There is no inviolability of the home. Private rights are generally respected. The tax load of an overbuilt bureaucracy and emphasis on private and government monopolies have also restricted choice in this now impoverished welfare state.

**Comparatively:** Uruguay is as free as Indonesia, freer than Argentina, less free than Brazil.

# VANUATU

**Economy:** capitalist-statist
**Polity:** decentralized multiparty
**Population:** 100,000
**Political Rights:** 2
**Civil Liberties:** 3
**Status of Freedom:** free

A relatively homogeneous society with geographical subnationalities

**Political Rights.** Vanuatu has a parliamentary system with an indirectly elected president. Elections have been freely contested by multiple parties. Opposition exists between islands and between the French and English educated. The constitution provides for decentralized powers.

**Civil Liberties.** Media are limited but generally free. The full spectrum of civil freedoms have been observed, but in the aftermath of the suppression of secessionist (largely French supported) movements at independence, many political arrests, trials, and mistreatment generated a less than free atmosphere.

**Comparatively:** Vanuatu is as free as India, freer than Maldives, less free than Fiji.

# VENEZUELA

**Economy:** capitalist-statist
**Polity:** centralized multiparty
**Population:** 13,900,000
**Political Rights:** 1
**Civil Liberties:** 2
**Status of Freedom:** free

A relatively homogeneous population

**Political Rights.** Venezuela is a parliamentary democracy in which power has alternated between major parties in recent years. Campaigns and voting appear fair. The opposition presidential victory in 1978 provided a good example of the power of the average voter. Regional and local assemblies are relatively powerful, but governors are centrally appointed. Each state has equal representation in the upper house.

**Civil Liberties.** The press is private and free; most broadcasting is also in private hands. Censorship occurs only in emergencies, but television scripts on certain subjects must be approved in advance, and there are recurrent attempts at government control. The rule of law is generally secured, but in the face of guerrilla actions the security services have on occasion arbitrarily imprisoned persons, used torture, and threatened to prosecute for antimilitary statements. A paper may be confiscated for slandering the president. Many persons have been detained for long periods without trial; on rare occasions members of parliament have been arrested. However, there is little evidence that those detained have been prisoners of conscience, and the government has taken steps to prevent torture. The court can rule against the government and charges are brought against the security forces. Most private rights are respected; government involvement in the petroleum industry has given it a predominant economic role. Human rights organizations are very active.

**Comparatively:** Venezuela is as free as France, freer than Colombia, less free than Costa Rica.

# VIETNAM

**Economy:** socialist
**Polity:** communist one-party
**Population:** 53,300,000
An ethnic state with subnationalities

**Political Rights:** 7
**Civil Liberties:** 7
**Status of Freedom:** not free

**Political Rights.** Vietnam is a traditional communist dictatorship with the forms of parliamentary democracy. Actual power is in the hands of the communist party; this is in turn dominated by a small group at the top. Officially there is a ruling national front as in several other communist states, but the noncommunist parties are essentially meaningless. Administration is highly centralized, with provincial boundaries arbitrarily determined by the central government. The flow of refugees and other evidence suggest that the present regime is very unpopular, especially in the South which is treated as an occupied country. *Subnationalities*: Continued fighting has been reported in the Montagnard areas in the South. Combined with new resettlement schemes non-Vietnamese peoples are under pressure in both North and South Vietnam. Many Chinese have been driven out of the country.

**Civil Liberties.** The media are under direct government, party, or army control; only the approved line is presented. While the people do not suffer the fears and illegalities of anarchy, they have essentially no rights against the interests of the state. Arbitrary arrest is frequent. Severe repression of the Buddhist opposition has led to many immolations—pressure on the Hoa Hao and Catholics is comparable. In spite of superficial appearances religious freedom is generally denied. Perhaps one-half million persons have been put through reeducation camps, hundreds of thousands have been forced to move into new areas, or to change occupations; hundreds of thousands remain political prisoners or in internal exile. Former anticommunist and other groups are regularly discriminated against in employment, health care, and travel. There are no independent labor union rights, rights to travel, choice of education; many have been forced into collectives.

**Comparatively:** Vietnam is as free as Korea (North), less free than China (Mainland).

# WESTERN SAMOA

**Economy:** noninclusive capitalist  
**Polity:** traditional nonparty  
**Population:** 160,000  
A relatively homogeneous population

**Political Rights:** 4  
**Civil Liberties:** 3  
**Status of Freedom:** partly free

**Political Rights.** Western Samoa is a constitutional monarchy in which the assembly is elected by 9,500 "family heads." There have been important shifts of power within the assembly as the result of elections, although there are no political parties. Village government has preserved traditional forms and considerable autonomy; it is also based on rule by "family heads."

**Civil Liberties.** The press is private and government; radio is government owned; television is received only from outside. Government media have limited independence. There is general freedom of expression, organization, and assembly. The rule of law and private rights are respected within the limits set by the traditional system.

**Comparatively:** Western Samoa is as free as Bangladesh, freer than Indonesia, less free than Nauru.

# YEMEN, NORTH

**Economy:** noninclusive capitalist  
**Polity:** military nonparty  
**Population:** 5,600,000  
A complex but relatively homogeneous population

**Political Rights:** 6  
**Civil Liberties:** 5  
**Status of Freedom:** not free

**Political Rights.** North Yemen is under collective military dictatorship supplemented by an appointive People's Assembly. Leaders are frequently assassinated. The tribal and religious structures still retain considerable authority, and the government must rely on a wide variety of different groups in an essentially nonideological consensual regime. Some local elective institutions have recently been developed. Political parties are forbidden. The country is divided between city and country, a variety of tribes, and two major religious groupings.

**Civil Liberties.** The weak media are largely government owned; the papers have occasional criticisms—the broadcast media have more. Foreign publications are routinely censored. Yet proponents of both royalist and far left persuasions are openly accepted in a society with few known prisoners of conscience. There is no right of assembly. Politically active opponents may be encouraged to go into exile. The traditional Islamic courts give some protection; many private rights are respected. There is no right to strike or to engage in religious proselytizing. Unions are nonexistent and there is little evidence of professional associations. Economically the government has concentrated on improving the infrastructure of Yemen's still overwhelmingly traditional economy.

**Comparatively:** North Yemen is as free as Argentina, freer than South Yemen, less free than Iran.

## YEMEN, SOUTH

**Economy:** noninclusive socialist
**Polity:** socialist one-party
**Population:** 1,900,000
A relatively homogeneous population

**Political Rights:** 6
**Civil Liberties:** 7
**Status of Freedom:** not free

**Political Rights.** South Yemen considers itself a communist country governed according to the communist one-party model. It is doubtful that the party retains the tight party discipline of its exemplars; it is government by coup and violence. Parliamentary elections in 1978 followed the one-party model; they allowed some choice among individuals. Soviet influence in internal and external affairs is powerful.

**Civil Liberties.** The media are government owned and controlled, and employed actively as a means of indoctrination. Even conversation with foreigners is highly restricted. In the political and security areas the rule of law hardly applies. Thousands of political prisoners, torture, and hundreds of "disappearances" have instilled a pervasive fear in those who would speak up. Death sentences against protesting farmers have been handed down by people's courts. Independent private rights are few, although some traditional law and institutions remain. Industry and commerce have been nationalized.

**Comparatively:** South Yemen is as free as Malawi, freer than Somalia, less free than Oman.

## YUGOSLAVIA

**Economy:** mixed socialist
**Polity:** communist one-party
**Population:** 22,400,000
A multinational state

**Political Rights:** 6
**Civil Liberties:** 5
**Status of Freedom:** not free

**Political Rights.** Yugoslavia is governed on the model of the USSR, but with the addition of unique elements. These include: the greater role given the governments of the constituent republics; and the greater power given the assemblies of the self-managed communities and industrial enterprises. The Federal Assembly is elected indirectly by those successful in lower level elections. In any event, the country is directed by a small elite of the communist party; evidence suggests that in spite of some earlier liberalizing tendencies to allow the more democratic formal structure to work, Yugoslavia is now no more democratic than Hungary. No opposition member is elected to state or national position, nor is there public opposition in the assemblies to government policy on the national or regional level.

*Subnationalities.* The several peoples of Yugoslavia live largely in their historical homelands. The population consists of forty percent Serbs, twenty-two percent Croats, eight percent Slovenes, eight percent Bosnian Muslims, six percent Macedonians, six percent Albanians, two percent Montenegrins, and many others. The Croats have an especially active independence movement.

**Civil Liberties.** The media in Yugoslavia are controlled directly or indirectly by the government, although there is ostensible worker control. There is no right of assembly. Hundreds have been imprisoned for ideas expressed verbally or in print that deviated from the official line (primarily through subnationalist enthusiasm, anticommunism, or communist deviationism). Dissidents are even pursued overseas. Torture and brutality occur; psychiatric hospitals are also used to confine prisoners of conscience. As long as the issue is not political, however, the courts have some independence; there is a realm of de facto individual freedom that includes the right to seek employment outside the country. Travel outside Yugoslavia is often denied to dissidents, and religious proselytizing is forbidden. Labor is not independent but has rights through the working of the "self-management" system. Although the economy is socialist or communalist in most respects, agriculture in this most agricultural of European countries remains overwhelmingly private.

**Comparatively:** Yugoslavia is as free as Hungary, freer than Romania, less free than Morocco.

# ZAIRE

**Economy:** noninclusive capitalist-statist  
**Polity:** nationalist one-party (military dominated)  
**Population:** 29,300,000  

**Political Rights:** 6  
**Civil Liberties:** 6  
**Status of Freedom:** not free  

A transethnic heterogeneous state with subnationalities

**Political Rights.** Zaire is under one-man military rule, with the ruling party essentially an extension of the ruler's personality. Elections in 1977 at both local and parliamentary levels were restricted to one party, but allowed for extensive choice among individuals. The majority of the party's ruling council was also elected in this manner. A subsequent presidential election offered no choice. Regions are deliberately organized to avoid ethnic identity: regional officers all are appointed from the center, generally from outside of the area, as are officers of the ruling party.

*Subnationalities.* There are such a variety of tribes or linguistic groups in Zaire that no one group has as much as twenty percent of the population. The fact that French remains the dominant language reflects the degree of this dispersion. Until recently most of the Zaire people have seen themselves only in local terms without broader ethnic identification. The revolts and wars of the early 1960s saw continually shifting patterns of affiliation, with the European provincial but not ethnic realities of Katanga and South Kasai being most important. The most self-conscious ethnic groups are the Kongo people living in the west (and Congo and Angola) and the Luba in the center of the country. In both cases ethnicity goes back to important ancient kingdoms. There is continuing disaffection among the Lunda and other ethnic groups.

**Civil Liberties.** Private newspaper ownership remains. There is some freedom to criticize, but censorship is pervasive. There is no right of assembly, and union organization is controlled. Government has been arbitrary and capricious. The judiciary is not independent; political arrest is common, as are execution and torture. Individual names as well as clothing style have had to be changed by government decree. All ethnic organizations are forbidden. Arrested conspirators have been forbidden their own lawyers. Major churches retain some autonomy, but independent churches have been proscribed. When founded on government power, the extravagance and business dealings of those in high places reduces economic freedom. Nationalization of land has often been a prelude to private development by powerful bureaucrats. Pervasive corruption and anarchy reduce human rights. There is also considerable government enterprise.

**Comparatively:** Zaire is as free as Gabon, freer than Benin, less free than Zambia.


# ZAMBIA

**Economy:** preindustrial mixed          **Political Rights:** 5
**Polity:** socialist one-party            **Civil Liberties:** 6
**Population:** 5,800,000                  **Status of Freedom:** partly free
A transethnic heterogeneous state

**Political Rights.** Zambia is ruled as a one-party dictatorship, although there have been elements of freedom within that party. Party organs are constitutionally more important than governmental. Although elections have had some competitive meaning within this framework, recently the government has repressed opposition movements within the party. Expression of dissent is possible through abstention. A 1978 presidential election allowed no choice and little opposition campaigning; it allowed negative votes.

**Civil Liberties.** All media are government controlled. A considerable variety of opinion is expressed, but it is a crime to critize the president, the parliament, or the ideology. Foreign publications are censored. There is a rule of law and the courts have some independence: cases have been won against the government. Political opponents have been detained, and occasionally tortured, yet most people talk without fear. Traditional life continues. The government does not fully accept private rights in property or religion; important parts of the economy, especially copper mining, have been nationalized. Both union and business organization are under government pressure.

**Comparatively:** Zambia is as free as Chile, freer than Angola, less free than Morocco.

# ZIMBABWE

**Economy:** noninclusive
    capitalist-statist
**Polity:** centralized multiparty
**Population:** 7,400,000

**Political Rights:** 3
**Civil Liberties:** 4
**Status of Freedom:** partly free

An ethnically complex state with a territorial subnationality

**Political Rights.** Zimbabwe is a parliamentary democracy. The ruling party came to power in 1980 through elections marked by considerable coercion of the electorate. The whites retain special political rights. All military forces are still not controlled.

*Subnationalities.* The formerly dominant white, Indian, and colored populations (five percent) are largely urban. The emerging dominant people are the majority Shona-speaking groups (seventy-four percent). The Ndebele (eighteen percent) are territorially distinct and politically self-conscious.

**Civil Liberties.** The press is private.* It is under pressure to conform; it now offers a narrow spectrum of opinion. The broadcast media are more active organs of government propaganda. There is a generally fair application of the rule of law, with freedom of residence and occupation.

---

*In early 1981 the principle newspapers were nationalized.

Racial discrimination is officially outlawed, especially in residence, occupation, and conscription. Much of the country may live in apprehension of the ruling parties and their former guerrilla forces. The economy is mixed capitalist, socialist, and statist.

**Comparatively:** Zimbabwe is as free as Bangladesh, freer than South Africa, less free than Botswana.

# Index

Adhikari, G., 146
Afghanistan: broadcasting to, 302, 304; conflict with Pakistan, 235-36; Islam, role of, in guerrilla war in, 88; language and ideology, 291-92, 293, 296; Soviet invasion of, 241-46, 250, 251-52, 260; Soviet invasion, Baluch response to, 150, 151-52, 156-57, 164; Soviet problem, 49; summary of, 319; United Nations Resolution Reaffirming Demand for Soviet Withdrawal from, 41; U.S. aid to, 244-45, 253-55; U.S.-Pakistan relations and, 310-11; U.S. support of, 93, 311; turmoil in, 229, 231-34. *See also* Central Asia, turmoil in
—, freedom in, prospects for, 167-91; anti-government armed struggle, 181-82; democratic Afghans, as possible leaders, 184; food, problem of, 185; guerrilla groups, 184-85, 188; hierarchies, tribal, 182-83; Islam, role of, 179-80; Marxism and, 170-71, 172; pacification and Parcham government controlling, as most likely outcome of Soviet invasion, 168-72; Pakistan, role of, 185; resistance succeeds—Soviet withdrawal, as possible outcome of invasion, 173-75; Soviet intentions, 190-91; Soviet invasion and, 167-68; "Tajik" ethnic group, 186-87; U.S. contributions, 175-77, 189-90, 191; Wakhan Corridor, 187-88; war, continued, without decision, as possible outcome of Soviet invasion, 172-73; warfare conditions, 182

Aflaq, Michel, 270
Aftab Ahmad Khan, 132
Agha Shahi, 131, 132
agriculture, Iranian Revolution and, 265
Ahmad, Eqbal, 253
Ahmad, Ghaffur, 165
Ahmad, Mumtaz, 81
Aini, Sadriddin, 293
Albania, summary of, 319-20
Algeria: subnationalities, 49-50; summary of, 320-21
Allen, George, 260
Allworth, Edward, 81
Amanullah, King, 232
Amin, Idi, 50
Amin, Hafizullah, 159, 160, 169, 184, 225
Amnesty International, 11; on Pakistan military courts, 116
Angola: subnationalities in, 50; summary of, 321
Argentina: economics and freedom in, 8; oppression in, 10; summary of, 321-22
Aron, Raymond, 35
Ataturk, 281, 282, 309
Australia: subnationalities in, 48; summary of, 322-23
Austria, summary of, 323
authoritarianism, 8-10
Ayub Khan (General), 118-19, 122, 123, 128, 130, 133, 135

Babakhanov, Mufti, 212, 292
Bahamas, summary of, 323-24
Bahrain, summary of, 324. *See also* Persian Gulf

New Hebrides. *See* Vanuatu
News Media Control by Country (table), 60-63
new world information and communication order (NWICO), 70, 71-72
New Zealand: subnationalities in, 48; summary of, 381
Niazi, Kausar, 117
Nicaragua: freedom in, 29; summary of, 381-82
Niger, summary of, 382
Nigeria: subnationalities in, 50; summary of, 382-83
Nixon doctrine, 225, 252
Nizamani, Kadir Bux, 148, 149
Nizam-i-Mustafa (Order of the Prophet) (Pakistan), 119, 121
non-aligned movement, Soviet Union and, 40
nonmilitary nonparty systems, 39
North Atlantic Treaty Organization (NATO), Central Asian turmoil and, 239, 252
Norway, summary of, 383-84
Nove, Alec, 197
Nyerere, Julius, 7

oil: Iranian Revolution and, 264, 266; as source of turmoil in Central Asia, 228, 259
Oman: summary of, 384. *See also* Persian Gulf
one-party systems, freedom and, 5, 35, 39
"Operation Fairplay" (Pakistan), 115, 119
Oveissi, General Gholam Ali, 103, 106, 107

Pahlavi, Shah Muhammad Reza, 5, 9, 92, 95, 98, 99, 100, 136, 158, 225, 226, 227, 228, 229, 235, 237, 250, 252, 262, 263, 264, 270, 281, 285, 291, 304
Pakistan: Afghanistan and, 185, 235-36; authoritarianism in, 85; Baluch nationalism and, 143-45, 164-65; Communist Party, 149; conflict with India, 235-36, 259-60; language and American influence in, 295-96; nationalism in, 84; subnationalities in, 49; summary of, 384-85; turmoil in, 229-30, 231; U.S. policy toward, 241-45, 252-53, 254, 259; U.S. relations with, as key to

Afghanistan problem, 310-11. *See also* Central Asia, turmoil in
—, freedom in, prospects for, 29, 111-37; basic-democracy type of polity, transition to, 118-19; bureaucracy and, 131-32; communism and, 134-35; encouraging, 123-25; ethnic freedom, 127, 129-30; history of oppression, 111-12; Islam, as religion, 112-14, 132-33, 134; Islam, as type of polity, transition to, 119-21, 127-28, 129, 134, 135-36; mass protest, 122; military coup, another, 121-22, 131, 133; parliamentary democracy, restoration of, 117-18; Soviet threat, 127; status quo, persistence of, 122-23, 130-31, 133; U.S. policy and, 136-37; under Zia-ul-Haq, 114-16, 128-29
Pakistan National Alliance (PNA), 115, 117, 119, 128, 133, 231
Pakistan People's Party (PPP), 115, 117, 124
Panama: advance of freedom in, 27; summary of, 385-86
Papua New Guinea, summary of, 386
Paraguay, summary of, 386-87
Parcham Party in Afghanistan, 169, 181, 182
peoples: of Central Asia, 193-95; major, with self-determination (table), 44-45; Peoples Democratic Party of Afghanistan, 171, 180
Peoples Party of Pakistan, 230, 231
Persian Gulf, civil society, evolution of modern in, 267-71; constitutional change, 268-71; labor organization, 267-68. *See also* Central Asia; Islam; Muslim
Peru: advance of freedom in, 27; summary of, 387-88
Philippines: subnationalities in, 48; summary of, 388-89
Plato, 114
Poland: advance of freedom in, 52; summary of, 389
political-economic systems, relation to freedom, 29, 35, 38-39; capitalist/socialist distinction, 35, 38; Euro-American type society, 35; multiparty systems and, 29, 35; party systems, 39; Sino-Soviet type society, 35; third world